ISBN: 9781313016629

Published by:
HardPress Publishing
8345 NW 66TH ST #2561
MIAMI FL 33166-2626

Email: info@hardpress.net
Web: http://www.hardpress.net

MISCELLANEOUS PAPERS

Yours most truly

H. Hertz

MISCELLANEOUS PAPERS

BY

HEINRICH HERTZ

LATE PROFESSOR OF PHYSICS IN THE UNIVERSITY OF BONN

WITH AN INTRODUCTION

BY

PROF. PHILIPP LENARD

AUTHORISED ENGLISH TRANSLATION

BY

D. E. JONES, B.Sc.

LATELY PROFESSOR OF PHYSICS IN THE UNIVERSITY COLLEGE OF WALES, ABERYSTWYTH

AND

G. A. SCHOTT, B.A., B.Sc.

DEMONSTRATOR AND ASSISTANT LECTURER IN THE UNIVERSITY COLLEGE OF WALES, ABERYSTWYTH

London

MACMILLAN AND CO., Ltd.

NEW YORK: MACMILLAN & CO.

1896

EDITOR'S PREFACE

THE present volume consists mainly of the earlier investigations which Heinrich Hertz carried out before his great electrical researches. Hitherto they have been difficult of access, being scattered amongst various journals, and some (*e.g.* his inaugural dissertation) could scarcely be obtained at all. Of later date are the last experimental investigation, the Heidelberg lecture (published by the firm of Emil Strauss in Bonn, by whose kind permission it is included in the present volume), and the closing paper, which is a further proof of the gratitude and admiration which Hertz cherished towards his great master, who has now followed him.

The papers are for the most part arranged in the order of their publication. By the kindness of Senator Dr. Gustav Hertz I have been able to include in the Introduction extracts from Hertz's letters to his parents, which give us an insight into the course of his scientific development, and the way in which he was led to attack the problems herein discussed.

P. LENARD.

February 1895.

TRANSLATORS' NOTE

HERTZ's Miscellaneous Papers form the first volume of his collected works, as edited by Dr. Philipp Lenard. The second volume is a reprint of his Researches on the Propagation of Electric Action (already published in English under the title of *Electric Waves*). The third volume consists of his *Principles of Mechanics,* of which an English translation is now in the press.

Professor Lenard has shown a warm interest in the translation, and we desire to express our hearty thanks to him for his kind assistance.

The portrait which forms the frontispiece to this volume has been specially engraved for it from a photograph by R. Krewaldt of Bonn.

D. E. J.

G. A. S.

March 1896.

CONTENTS

CONTENTS

INTRODUCTION

In October 1877, at the age of twenty, Heinrich Hertz went to Munich in order to carry on his engineering studies. He had chosen this as his profession, and had already made some progress in it; for in addition to completing the usual year of practical work he had thoroughly grounded himself in the preliminary mathematical and scientific studies. He had now to apply himself to engineering work proper, to the technical details of his profession. At this point he began to doubt whether his natural inclinations lay in the direction of this work—whether he would find engineering as satisfactory as the studies which led up to it. The study of natural science had been a delight to him: now he feared lest his life-work should prove a burden. He stood at the parting of the ways. In the following letter he consults his parents in the matter.

MUNICH, *1st November* 1877.

MY DEAR PARENTS — No doubt you will wonder why this letter follows so quickly after my previous one. I had no intention of writing so soon again, but this time it is about an important matter which will not brook any long delay.

I really feel ashamed to say it, but I must: now at the last moment I want to change all my plans and return to the study of natural science. I feel that the time has come for me to decide either to devote myself to this entirely or else to say good-bye to it; for if I give up too much time to science in the future it will end in neglecting my professional studies and becoming a second-rate engineer. Only recently, in arranging my plan of studies, have I clearly seen this—so clearly that I can no longer feel any doubt about it; and my first impulse was to renounce all un-

INTRODUCTION

IN October 1877, at the age of twenty, Heinrich Hertz went to Munich in order to carry on his engineering studies. He had chosen this as his profession, and had already made some progress in it; for in addition to completing the usual year of practical work he had thoroughly grounded himself in the preliminary mathematical and scientific studies. He had now to apply himself to engineering work proper, to the technical details of his profession. At this point he began to doubt whether his natural inclinations lay in the direction of this work—whether he would find engineering as satisfactory as the studies which led up to it. The study of natural science had been a delight to him: now he feared lest his life-work should prove a burden. He stood at the parting of the ways. In the following letter he consults his parents in the matter.

MUNICH, 1st *November* 1877.

MY DEAR PARENTS — No doubt you will wonder why this letter follows so quickly after my previous one. I had no intention of writing so soon again, but this time it is about an important matter which will not brook any long delay.

I really feel ashamed to say it, but I must: now at the last moment I want to change all my plans and return to the study of natural science. I feel that the time has come for me to decide either to devote myself to this entirely or else to say good-bye to it; for if I give up too much time to science in the future it will end in neglecting my professional studies and becoming a second-rate engineer. Only recently, in arranging my plan of studies, have I clearly seen this—so clearly that I can no longer feel any doubt about it; and my first impulse was to renounce all unnecessary dealings with mathematics and natural science. But then, all at once, I saw clearly that I could not bring myself to do this; that these had been my real occupation up to now, and were still my chief joy. All else seemed hollow and unsatisfying. This conviction came upon me quite suddenly, and I felt inclined to sit down and write to you at once. Although I have restrained myself for a day or two, so as to consider the matter thoroughly, I can come to no other result. I cannot understand why all this was not clear to me before; for I came here filled with the idea of working at mathematics and natural science, whereas I had never given a thought to the essentials of my professional training — surveying, building construction, builders' materials, and such like. I have not forgotten what I often used to say to myself, that I would rather be a great scientific investigator than a great engineer, but would rather be a second-rate engineer than a second-rate investigator. But now when I am in doubt, I think how true is Schiller's saying, " *Und setzet Ihr nicht das Leben ein, nie wird Euch das Leben gewonnen sein,*" and that excessive caution would be folly. Nor do I conceal from myself that by becoming an engineer I would be more certain of earning my own livelihood, and I regret that in adopting the other course I shall probably have to rely upon you, my dear father, all the longer for support. But against all this there is the feeling that I could devote myself wholly and enthusiastically to natural science, and that this pursuit would satisfy me; whereas I now see that engineering science would not satisfy me, and would always leave me hankering after something else. I hope that I am not deceiving myself in this, for it would be a great and woful piece of self-deception. But of this I feel positive, that if the decision is in favour of natural science, I shall never look back with regret towards engineering science, whereas if I become an engineer I shall always be longing for the other; and I cannot bear the idea of being only able to work at natural science for the purpose of passing an examination. When I think of it, it seems to me that I used to be much more frequently encouraged to go on with natural science than to become an engineer. I may be better grounded in mathematics than many, but I doubt whether this would be much of an advantage in engineering; so much more seems to depend, at any rate in the first ten years of practice, upon business capacity, experience, and knowledge of data and formulæ, which do not happen to interest me. This and much else I have carefully considered (and shall continue to think it over until I receive your reply), but when all is said and done, even admitting that there are many sound practical reasons in favour of becoming an engineer, I still feel that this would involve a sense of failure and disloyalty to myself, to which I would not willingly submit if it could be avoided. And so I ask you, dear father, for your decision rather than for your advice; for it isn't advice that I need, and there is scarcely time for it now. If you will allow me to study natural science I shall take it as a great kindness on your part, and whatever diligence and love can do in the matter that they shall do. I believe this will be your decision, for you have never put a stone in my path, and I think you have often looked with pleasure on my scientific studies. But if you consider it best for me to continue in the path on which I have started (which I now doubt), I will carry out your wish, and do so fully and freely; for by this time I am sick of doubt and delay, and if I remain in the state I have been in lately I shall never make a start. . . . So I hope to have an early answer, and until it comes I shall continue to think the matter over. Meanwhile I send my love to you all, and remain your affectionate son, HEINRICH.

Matters were decided as he had hoped, and, full of joy at being able to carry out his wishes, Hertz now proceeded to arrange his plan of studies. He remained altogether a year at Munich. He devoted the winter-semester of 1877-78 in all seclusion to the study of mathematics and mechanics, using for the most part original treatises such as those of Laplace and Lagrange. Most of the following summer-semester he spent at practical work in the physical laboratory. By attending the elementary courses in practical physics at the University (under v. Jolly) and at the same time in the Technical Institute (under v. Bezold), he was able to supplement what he had already learned by means of his own home-made apparatus.

Thus prepared he proceeded in October 1878 to Berlin, eager to become a pupil of v. Helmholtz and Kirchhoff. When he had arrived there, in looking at the notices on the black notice-board of the University his eye fell on an intimation of a prize offered by the Philosophical Faculty for the solution of a problem in physics. It referred to the question of electric inertia. To him it did not seem so hopelessly difficult as it might have appeared to many of his contemporaries, and he decided to have a try at it.

This brings us to the beginning of his first independent research (the first paper in the present volume). We cannot read without astonishment the letters in which this student of twenty-one reports to his parents the starting of an in-

b

vestigation which might well be taken for the work of an experienced investigator.

BERLIN, 31st October 1878.

I have been attending lectures—Kirchhoff's—since Monday : another course only begins on Wednesday next. Besides this I have also started practical work ; one of the prize problems for this year falls more or less in my line, and I am going to work at it. This was not what I intended at first, for a course of lectures on mineralogy, which I wished to attend, clashed with it ; but I have now decided to let these stand over until the next semester. I have already discussed the matter with Professor Helmholtz, who was good enough to put me on the track of some of the literature.

A week later we find him already at his experiments.

6th November 1878.

Since yesterday I have been working in the laboratory. The prize problem runs as follows : If electricity moves with inertia in bodies, then this must, under certain circumstances, manifest itself in the magnitude of the extra-current (*i.e.* of the secondary current which is produced when an electric current starts or stops). Experiments on the magnitude of the extra-current have to be made such that a conclusion can be drawn from them as to inertia of the electricity in motion. The work has to be finished by 4th May ; it was given out as early as 3rd August, and I am sorry that I did not know of it before. I ought, however, to say that at present I am only trying to work out the problem, and I may not succeed in solving it satisfactorily : so I would not readily have spoken of it as a prize research, indeed I would not have mentioned it at all, if it were not necessary by way of explanation. Anyhow I find it very pleasant to be able to attack such an investigation. So yesterday I informed Professor Helmholtz that I had considered the matter and would like to start work. He then took me to the demonstrators and very kindly remained some twenty minutes longer, talking with me about it, as to how I had better begin and what instruments I should require. So yesterday and to-day I have begun to make my arrangements. I have a room all to myself as large as our morning room,[1] but nearly twice as high. I can come and go as I like, and you will easily see that I have room enough. Everything else is capitally arranged. . . . Nothing could be more convenient, and I can only hope now that my work will come up to its environment. Of

---

[1] A large room in his parents' house.

avoided. And so I ask you, dear father, for your decision rather than for your advice; for it isn't advice that I need, and there is scarcely time for it now. If you will allow me to study natural science I shall take it as a great kindness on your part, and whatever diligence and love can do in the matter that they shall do. I believe this will be your decision, for you have never put a stone in my path, and I think you have often looked with pleasure on my scientific studies. But if you consider it best for me to continue in the path on which I have started (which I now doubt), I will carry out your wish, and do so fully and freely; for by this time I am sick of doubt and delay, and if I remain in the state I have been in lately I shall never make a start. . . . So I hope to have an early answer, and until it comes I shall continue to think the matter over. Meanwhile I send my love to you all, and remain your affectionate son, HEINRICH.

Matters were decided as he had hoped, and, full of joy at being able to carry out his wishes, Hertz now proceeded to arrange his plan of studies. He remained altogether a year at Munich. He devoted the winter-semester of 1877-78 in all seclusion to the study of mathematics and mechanics, using for the most part original treatises such as those of Laplace and Lagrange. Most of the following summer-semester he spent at practical work in the physical laboratory. By attending the elementary courses in practical physics at the University (under v. Jolly) and at the same time in the Technical Institute (under v. Bezold), he was able to supplement what he had already learned by means of his own home-made apparatus.

Thus prepared he proceeded in October 1878 to Berlin, eager to become a pupil of v. Helmholtz and Kirchhoff. When he had arrived there, in looking at the notices on the black notice-board of the University his eye fell on an intimation of a prize offered by the Philosophical Faculty for the solution of a problem in physics. It referred to the question of electric inertia. To him it did not seem so hopelessly difficult as it might have appeared to many of his contemporaries, and he decided to have a try at it.

This brings us to the beginning of his first independent research (the first paper in the present volume). We cannot read without astonishment the letters in which this student of twenty-one reports to his parents the starting of an in-

b

whereas only about half a year ago I scarcely knew any more about it than what still remained in my memory since the time when I was with Dr. Lange.[1] I hope my work won't suffer from this. At present it looks promising. I have already surmounted the difficulties which Helmholtz pointed out to me at the start as being the principal ones; and in a fortnight, if all goes well, I shall be ready with a scanty kind of solution, and shall still have time left to work it up properly.

He asks his parents to send on a tangent galvanometer which he had made during the last holidays at home, without having any suspicion that it would so soon be used in this way.[2]

A week later, in writing to report progress, he is not so cheerful. "When one difficulty is overcome, a bigger one turns up in its place." These were the difficulties mentioned in pp. 5-6. The Christmas holidays were now at hand, and while at home in Hamburg he made the commutator shown on Fig. 1, p. 13, respecting which he later on reports.

12th January 1879.

The apparatus which I made works very well, even better than I had expected; so that within the last three days I have been able to make all my measurements over again, and more accurately than before.

Within three months after he had first turned his attention to this investigation he is able to report the conclusion of the first part of it.

21st January 1879.

It has delighted me greatly to find that my observations are in accordance with the theory, and all the more because the agreement is better than I had expected. At first my calculations gave a value which was much greater than the observed value. Then I happened to notice that it was just twice as great. After a long search amongst the calculations I came upon a 2 which had been forgotten, and then both agreed better than I could have expected. I have now set about making more accurate observa-

---

[1] The Head-Master of the *Bürgerschule*, which he attended up to his sixteenth year.
[2] This is the galvanometer referred to on p. 12 (3)—a simple wooden disc turned upon the lathe and wound with copper wire, with a hole in the centre for the magnet. It is still in good order.

tions; the first attempt has turned out badly, as generally happens, but I hope in due course to pull things into shape. The apparatus which I have made at home really works well, so well that I wouldn't exchange it for one made out of gold and ivory in the best workshop. (Mother might like to hear this, and if I find that it pleases her I will try it again.)

Ten days later the experiments with rectilinear wires were completed.

31st January 1879.

I have now quite finished my research, much more quickly than I had expected. This is chiefly because the more accurate set of experiments have led to a very satisfactory, although negative, result: *i.e.* I find that, to the greatest degree of accuracy I can obtain, the theory is confirmed. I should much have preferred some positive result; but as there is nothing of the kind here I must be satisfied. My experiments agree as well as I could wish with the current theory, and I do not think that I can push matters any further with the means now at my disposal. So I have finished the experiments, and hope the Commission will be satisfied; as far as I can see, any further experiments would only lead to the same result. I shall begin writing my paper in a few days; just at present I don't feel in the humour for it.

The paper was written during a period of military service at Freiburg.

In these successive reports on his work we nowhere find signs of his having encountered difficulties in developing the theory of it; and this is all the more surprising because at this time he could scarcely have made any general survey of what was already known. But it is clear that even at this early stage he was able to find his own way through regions yet unknown to him, and to do this without first searching anxiously for the foot-prints of other explorers. Thus just about this time he writes as follows :—

9th February 1879.

Kirchhoff has now come to magnetism in his lectures, and a great part of what he tells us coincides with what I had worked out for myself at home last autumn. Now it is by no means pleasant to hear that all this has long since been well known; still it makes the lecture all the more interesting. I hope my knowledge will soon grow more extensive, so that I may know what has already been done, instead of having to take the trouble of finding it out again for myself. But it is some satisfaction to find gradually that things which are new to me make their appearance less frequently ; at any rate that is my experience in the special department at which I have worked.

His research gained the prize.

4th August 1879.

Happily I have not only obtained the prize, but the decision of the Faculty has been expressed in terms of such commendation that I feel twice as proud of it. . . . I had gone with Dr. K. and L. [to hear the public announcement of the decision] without having said anything, but fully determined not to show any disappointment if the result was unfavourable.

11th August 1879.

I have chosen the medal, in accordance with your wish, for the prize. It is a beautiful gold medal, quite a large one, but by a piece of incredible stupidity it has no inscription whatever on it, nothing even to show that it is a University prize.

This prize research was Hertz's first investigation, and it is to this he refers in the Introduction to his *Electric Waves*, as being engaged upon it when von Helmholtz invited him to attack the problem[1] propounded for the prize of the Berlin Academy. For reasons now known to us, he gave up the idea of working at the problem. He preferred to apply himself to other work, which was perhaps of a more modest nature, but promised to yield some tangible result.

So he turned his attention to the theoretical investigation "On Induction in Rotating Spheres" (II. in this volume). This extensive investigation was made in an astonishingly short time. The first sketch of it, which still exists, is dated from time to time in Hertz's handwriting, and one sees with surprise what rapid progress he made from day to day. He had made preliminary studies at home during the autumn vacation of 1896, and the results of these are partly contained

[1] This latter seems to be the problem in electromagnetics to which von Helmholtz refers in his Preface to Hertz's *Principles of Mechanics* as having been proposed by himself in the belief that it was one in which his pupil would feel an interest.

in the paper "On the Distribution of Electricity over the Surface of Moving Conductors " (III. in this volume), which was first published two years later. In November 1879 he began to work at induction, and no later than the following January this investigation was submitted as an inaugural dissertation for the degree of doctor to the Philosophical Faculty. We hear of this rapid progress in the letters to his parents :—

27th November 1879. ⎪

I secured a place in the laboratory and started working there at the beginning of term, but do not feel much drawn in that direction just now. I am busy with a theoretical investigation which gives me great pleasure, so I work at this in my rooms instead of going to the laboratory : indeed I wish that I had made no arrangements for practical work. The investigation which I now have in hand is closely connected with what I did at home. Unless I discover (which would be very disagreeable) that this particular problem has already been solved by some one else, it will become my dissertation for the doctorate.

13th December 1879.

There is little news to send about myself. I have been working away, with scarcely time to look about me, at the research which I have undertaken. It is getting on as well and as pleasantly as I could wish.

17th January 1880.

As soon as I got here [from Hamburg, after the Christmas holidays] I settled down to my research, and by the end of the week had it ready : I had to keep working hard at it, for it became much more extensive than I had expected.

In its extent this second research differs from all of Hertz's other publications; he had clearly decided to follow the usual custom with respect to inaugural dissertations. Although long, it will be found to repay the most careful study. The decision of the Berlin Philosophical Faculty (drawn up by Helmholtz) was *Acuminis et doctrinæ specimen laudabile*. Together with a brilliant examination it gained for him the title of doctor, with the award *magna cum laude*, which is but rarely given in the University of Berlin.

In the following summer of 1880 Hertz was again engaged

upon an experimental investigation on the formation of residual charge in insulators. He did not seem well satisfied with the result; at any rate he did not consider it worth writing out. It was only by v. Helmholtz's special request that he was subsequently induced to give an account of this research at a meeting of the Physical Society of Berlin on 27th May 1881. It did not appear in Wiedemann's *Annalen* (XIV. in this volume) until three years later, after the quantitative data had been recovered by a repetition of the experiments made for this purpose at Hertz's suggestion.

Soon afterwards, in October 1880, Hertz became assistant to v. Helmholtz. He now revelled in the enjoyment of the resources of the Berlin Institute. He was soon engaged, in addition to the duties of his office, upon many problems both experimental and theoretical; and expresses his regret at not being able to use all the resources at his disposal, and to solve all the problems at once. At this time he sowed the seeds which during his three years' term as assistant developed one after the other into the investigations which appear as IV.-XVI. in this volume.

He was first attracted by a theoretical investigation "On the Contact of Elastic Solids" (V.) During the frequent discussions on Newton's rings in the Physical Society of Berlin it had occurred to Hertz that although much was known in detail as to the optical phenomena which takes place between the two glasses, very little was known as to the changes of form which they undergo at their point of contact when pressed together. So he tried to solve the problem and succeeded. Most of the investigation was carried out during the vacation of Christmas 1880. Its publication, at first in the form of a lecture to the Physical Society (on 21st January 1881), was at once greeted with much interest. A new light had been thrown upon the phenomena of contact and pressure, and it was recognised that this had an important and direct bearing upon the conduct of all delicate measurements. For example, determinations of a base-line for the great European measurement of a degree were just then being calculated out at Berlin. The steel measuring-rods used in these determinations were lightly pressed against each other with a glass sphere interposed between them. This elastic contact

necessarily introduced an element of uncertainty depending
upon the pressure exerted: a method of ascertaining its
magnitude with certainty was wanting. Now the question
could be answered definitely and at once. In technical circles
equal interest was exhibited, and this induced Hertz to extend
the investigation further and to allow it to be published not
only in Borchardt's *Journal* (V. in this volume) but also in a
technical journal, with a supplement on Hardness (VI.)
About this he writes to his parents as follows :—

9th May 1882.

I have been writing a great deal lately ; for I have rewritten
the investigation once more for a technical journal in compliance
with suggestions which reached me from various directions. . . .
I have also added a chapter on the hardness of bodies, and hope to
lecture on this to the Physical Society on Friday. I have had
some fun out of this too. For hardness is a property of bodies of
which scientific men have as clear, *i.e.* as vague, a conception as
the man in the street. Now as I went on working it became quite
clear to me what hardness really was. But I felt that it was
not in itself a property of sufficient importance to make it
worth while writing specially about it ; nor was such a subject,
which would necessarily have to be treated at some length, quite
suitable for a purely mathematical journal. In a technical
journal, however, I thought I might well write something about
the matter. So I went to look round the library of the *Gewerbe-
akademie*, and see what was known about hardness. And I found
that there really was a book written on it in 1867 by a Frenchman.
It contained a full account of earlier attempts to define hardness
clearly, and to measure it in a rational way, and of many experiments made by the writer himself with the same object, interspersed
with assurances as to the importance of the subject. Altogether
it must have involved a considerable amount of work, which was
labour lost—so I think, and he partly admits it—because there
was no right understanding at the bottom of it, and the measurements were made without knowing what had to be measured. So
I concluded that now I might with a quiet conscience make my
paper a few pages longer ; and since this I have naturally had
much more pleasure than before in writing it out.

Whilst these problems on elasticity were engaging his
attention Hertz was also busy with the researches on evaporation (VIII. and IX. in this volume) and the second investigation on the Kinetic Energy of Electricity in Motion (IV.)

Both of these had been commenced in the summer of 1881. In order to push on the three-fold task to his satisfaction he devoted to it the greater part of the autumn vacation. Thus the investigation on electric inertia was soon finished; on the other hand the evaporation problems took up much more time without giving much satisfaction.

15th October 1881.

I am now devoting myself entirely to the research on evaporation, which I began thinking of in the spring, and of which I have now some hope.

10th March 1882.

The present research is going on anything but satisfactorily. Fresh experiments have shown me that much, if not all, of my labour has been misapplied; that sources of error were present which could scarcely have been foreseen, so that the beautiful positive result which I thought I had obtained turns out to be nothing but a negative one. At first I was quite upset, but have plucked up courage again; I feel as fit as ever now, only I do regret the valuable time which cannot be recovered.

13th June 1882.

I am writing out my paper on evaporation, *i.e.* as much of the work as turns out to be correct; I am far from being pleased with it, and feel rather glad that I am not obliged to work it out completely, as originally intended.

In the midst of this period of strenuous exertion comes the slight refreshing episode of the invention of the hygrometer (VII. in this volume). In sending a charming description of this little instrument, " so simple that there is scarcely anything in it," Hertz explains to his parents how the air in a dwelling-room should be kept moist in winter. There can be no harm in reproducing the explanation here.

2nd February 1882.

I may here give a little calculation which will show father how the air in the morning-room should be kept moist. On an average the atmosphere contains half as much water-vapour as is required to saturate it; in other words, the average relative humidity is 50 per cent. Assume then that this proportion is suitable for men, that it is the happy—or healthy—mean. In a cubic metre of air there should then be definite quantities of water, which are different for different temperatures—2·45 gm. at 0° C., 4·70 gm. at 10° C., and 8·70 gm. at 20° C., for these amounts would give the air a relative humidity of 50 per cent. Now let us assume that the temperature is 0° out of doors, and 20° in the (heated) room. Then in the room there would be (since the air comes ultimately from the outside) only 2·45 gm. of water in each cubic metre of air. In order to get the correct proportion there should be 8·70 gm. of water. Hence the air is relatively very dry and needs $6\frac{1}{4}$ gm. more of water per cubic metre. Since the room is about 7 metres long, 7 metres broad, and 4 metres high, it contains $7 \times 7 \times 4$ cubic metres, and the additional amount of water required in the room is $7 \times 7 \times 4 \times 6\frac{1}{4}$ gm., or nearly $1\frac{1}{4}$ litres. Thus if the room were hermetically closed, $1\frac{1}{4}$ litres of water would have to be sprinkled about in order to secure the proper degree of humidity. Now the room is not hermetically closed. Let us assume that all the air in it is completely changed in n hours; then every n hours $1\frac{1}{4}$ litres of water would have to be sprinkled about or evaporated into it. I think we may assume that through window-apertures, opening of doors, etc., the air is completely changed every two or three hours; hence from $\frac{5}{8}$ to $\frac{5}{12}$ of a litre of water, or a big glassful, would have to be evaporated per hour. All this would roughly hold good whenever rooms are artificially heated, and the external temperature is below 10° C. If you were to set up a hygrometer and compare the humidity when water is sprinkled and when it is not, you could from this find within what time the air in the room is completely changed. . . . This has become quite a long lecture, and the postage of the letter will ruin me; but what wouldn't a man do to keep his dear parents and brothers and sister from complete desiccation?

As soon as the research on evaporation was finished Hertz turned his attention to another subject, in which he had always felt great interest—that of the electric discharge in gases. He had only been engaged a month upon this when he succeeded in discovering a phenomenon accompanying the spark-discharge which had hitherto remained unnoticed (see XII. in this volume). But he was too keen to allow this to detain him long: he at once made plans for constructing a large secondary battery, which seemed to him to be the most suitable means for obtaining information of more importance. His letters tell us how he attacked the subject.

29th June 1882.

I am busy from morn to night with optical phenomena in rarefied gases, in the so-called Geissler tubes—only the tubes I mean are very different from the ones you see displayed in public exhibitions. For once I feel an inclination to take up a somewhat more experimental subject and to put the exact measurements aside for a while. The subject I have in mind is involved in much obscurity, and little has been done at it; its investigation would probably be of great theoretical interest. So I should like to find in it material for a fresh research; meanwhile I keep rushing about without any fixed plan, finding out what is already known about it, repeating experiments and setting up others as they occur to me; all of which is very enjoyable, inasmuch as the phenomena are in general exceedingly beautiful and varied. But it involves a lot of glass-blowing; my impatience will not allow me to order from the glass-blower to-day a tube which would not be ready until several days later, so I prefer to restrict myself to what can be achieved by my own slight skill in the art. In point of expense this is an advantage. But in a day one can only prepare a single tube, or perhaps two, and make observations with these under varied conditions, so that naturally it is laborious work. At present, as already stated, I am simply roaming about in the hope that one or other of the hundred remarkable phenomena which are exhibited will throw some light upon the path.

31st July 1882.

I have made some preliminary attempts in the way of building up a battery of 1000 cells. This will cost some money and a good deal of trouble; but I believe it will prove a very efficient means of pushing on the investigation, and will amply repay its cost.

After devoting the first half of the ensuing autumn vacation to recreation, he begins the construction of the battery.

6th September 1882.

I am now back again, after having had a good rest, and as there is nothing to disturb me here I have at once started fitting up the battery. So I am working away just like a mechanic. Every turn and twist has to be repeated a thousand times; so that for hours I do nothing but bore one hole and then another, bend one strip of lead after the other, and then again spend hours in varnishing them one by one. I have already got 250 cells finished and the remaining 750 are to be made forthwith; I expect to have the lot ready in a week. I don't like to interrupt the work, and that is why I haven't written to you before. For a while I feel quite fond of this monotonous mechanical occupation.

20th September 1882.

The battery has practically been ready since the middle of last week; since last Sunday night it has begun to spit fire and light up electric tubes. To-day for the first time I have made experiments with it—ones which I couldn't have carried out without it.

7th October 1882.

I have got the battery to work satisfactorily, and a week ago succeeded in solving, to the best of my belief, the first problem which I had propounded to myself (a problem solved, when it really is solved, is a good deal!). But even this first stage was only attained with much trouble, for the battery turned sick, and its sickness has proved to be a very dangerous one.

By preventive measures the battery was kept going for yet a little while, and later on he reports, " Battery doing well." How the battery finally came to grief is explained in the account of the investigation (XIII.) By its aid he was able, in six weeks of vigorous exertion, to bring to a successful issue most of the experiments which he had planned out. The investigation was first published in April 1883 at Kiel, in connection with Hertz's induction to the position of *Privat-docent* there. It brought him recognition from one who rarely bestowed such tokens, and whose opinion he valued most highly. Hertz treasured as precious mementoes two letters from Helmholtz. One of these notified his appointment as assistant at Berlin; the other is the following :—

BERLIN, *29th July* 1883.

GEEHRTER HERR DOKTOR!—I have read with the greatest interest your investigation on the cathode discharge, and cannot refrain from writing to say Bravo! The subject seems to me to be one of very wide importance. For some time I have been thinking whether the cathode rays may not be a mode of propagation of a sudden impact upon the Maxwellian electromagnetic ether, in which the surface of the electrode forms the first wave-surface. For, as far as I can see, such a wave should be propagated just as these rays are. In this case deviation of the rays through a magnetisation of the medium would also be possible. Longitudinal waves could be more easily conceived; and these could exist if the constant k in my electromagnetic researches were not zero. But transversal waves could also be produced. You seem to have similar thoughts in your own mind. However that may be, I should like you to feel free to make any use of what I have mentioned above, for I have no time at present to work at the subject. These ideas suggest themselves so readily in reading your investigation that they must soon occur to you if they have not already done so. . . .—With kindest regards, yours,

H. HELMHOLTZ.

While still busily engaged in completing this investigation on the discharge Hertz began to reflect upon another problem which seems to have been suggested to him by sheets of ice floating upon water during the winter.

BERLIN, 24*th February* 1883.

My researches are going on all right. From the date of my last letter until to-day I have been wholly absorbed in a problem which I cannot keep out of my head, viz. the equilibrium of a floating sheet of ice upon which a man stands. Naturally the sheet of ice will become somewhat bent, thus [follows a small sketch of the bent sheet], but what form will it take, what will be the exact amount of the depression, etc. ? One arrives at quite paradoxical results. In the first place a depression will certainly be produced underneath the man; but at a certain distance there will be a circular elevation of the ice; after this there follows another depression, and so on, somewhat in this way [another sketch]. As a matter of fact the elevations and depressions decrease so rapidly that they can never be perceived : but to the intellectual eye an endless series of them is visible. Even more paradoxical is the following result. Under certain circumstances a disc heavier than water, and which would therefore sink when laid upon water, can be made to float by putting a weight on it; and as soon as the weight is taken away it sinks. The explanation is that when the weight is put on, the disc takes the form of a boat, and thus supports both the weight and itself. If the load is gradually removed the disc becomes flatter and flatter; and finally there comes an instant when the boat becomes too shallow and so sinks with what is left of the load. This is the theoretical result, and the way I explain it to myself, but meanwhile there may be errors in the calculation. Such a subject has a peculiar effect upon me. For a whole week I have been struggling to have done with it, because it is not of great importance, and I have other things to do, e.g. I ought to be writing out the research which is to serve for my induction at Kiel, which is all ready in my mind but not a stroke of it on paper. Still it seems impossible to finish it off properly ; there always remains some contradiction or improbability, and so long as anything of that sort is left I can scarcely take my mind away from it. Then the formulæ which I have deduced for the accurate solution are so complicated that it takes a lot of time and trouble to make out clearly their meaning. But if I take up a book or try to do anything else my thoughts continually hark back to it. Shouldn't things happen in this way or that? Isn't there still some contradiction here? All this is a perfect plague when one doesn't attach much importance to the result.

Soon afterwards Hertz had to remove to Kiel. This removal, his induction, and his lectures there took up much of his time, so that his investigation on floating plates was not published until a year later. Its place was taken by the investigation on the fundamental equations of electromagnetics (XVII.) At this time he kept a day-book, from which it appears that in May 1884 he was alternately working at his lectures, at electromagnetics, and at microscopic observations taken up by way of change. On six successive days there are brief but expressive entries—"Hard at Maxwellian electromagnetics in the evening," "Nothing but electromagnetics"; and then follows on the next day, the 19th of May—"Hit upon the solution of the electromagnetic problem this morning." This will remind the reader of v. Helmholtz's remark that the solution of difficult problems came to him soonest, and then often unexpectedly, when a period of vigorous battling with the difficulties had been followed by one of complete rest.

In close connection with this subject, and immediately following it in order of time, came the paper "On the Dimensions of Magnetic Pole" (XVIII. in this volume). Directly after this came the meteorological paper "On the Adiabatic Changes of Moist Air" (XIX.) A diagram illustrating the latter is reproduced at the end of this volume from the original; the drawing of this, as a recreation after other work, seems to have given Hertz great pleasure.

We may complete our account of Hertz's scientific work during his two years at Kiel by adding that at this time he repeatedly, although unsuccessfully, attacked certain hydrodynamic problems, and that his thoughts already turned frequently towards that field in which he was afterwards to reap such a rich harvest. Nearly five years before he had carried out his investigation " On Electric Radiation " we find in his day-book the notable remark—" 27*th January* 1884. Thought about electromagnetic rays," and again, " Reflected on the electromagnetic theory of light." He was always full of schemes for investigations, and never liked to be without some experimental work. So he did his best to fit up in his house a small laboratory with home-made apparatus, thus transporting himself back to the times when chemists worked with the modest spirit-lamp. But before his experiments were concluded or any of his schemes carried out he was called to Karlsruhe, and his removal thither relieved him from much unprofitable exertion caused by the lack of proper experimental facilities.

This brings us to the end of the series of papers around which we have grouped the events of the author's life. After this follow the great electrical investigations which now form the second volume of his collected works. At this point we have introduced the lecture which Hertz gave at Heidelberg on these discoveries, and which will still be fresh in the remembrance of many who heard it.

After this follows the last experimental investigation which Hertz made. Whilst his colleagues, and in Bonn his pupils as well, were eagerly pushing forward into the country which he had opened up, he returned to the study of electric discharges in gases, which had interested him before. Again he was rewarded by an immediate and unexpected discovery. Early in the summer-semester of 1891 he found that cathode rays could pass through metals. The investigation was soon interrupted, but was published early in the ensuing year; from now on the subject-matter of his last work, the Principles of Mechanics, wholly absorbed his attention.

I

EXPERIMENTS TO DETERMINE AN UPPER LIMIT TO THE KINETIC ENERGY OF AN ELECTRIC CURRENT.

(Wiedemann's Annalen, 10, pp. 414-448, 1880.)

ACCORDING to the laws of induction the current i in a linear circuit, in which a variable electromotive force A acts, is given by its initial value together with the differential equation

$$ir = A - P\frac{di}{dt},$$

where r is the resistance and P the inductance of the circuit.[1] Multiplying by idt we get the equation

$$A idt = i^2 rdt + \tfrac{1}{2}d(Pi^2),$$

which shows that the law expressed by the above equation is in agreement with the principle of the conservation of energy on the assumption that the work done by the battery on the one hand, and the heat developed in the circuit and the increase of potential energy on the other hand, are the only amounts of energy to be considered. This supposition is not true, and hence the above equations cannot lay claim to complete accuracy, in case the electricity in motion possesses inertia, the effect of which is not quite negligible. In this case we must add to the right-hand side of the second equation

---

[1] [The notation has been altered in accordance with English custom and the necessary changes in the equations made. The original has 2P.—TR.]

a term corresponding to the increase in the kinetic energy of the current. This is proportional to the square of the current and may therefore be put equal to $\frac{1}{2}mi^2$, where m is a constant depending on the form and size of the circuit. We thus get in place of the above the following corrected equations

$$A i dt = i^2 r dt + \tfrac{1}{2}d(P i^2) + \tfrac{1}{2}d(m i^2),$$

$$i r = A - P\frac{di}{dt} - m\frac{di}{dt},$$

$$= A - (P + m)\frac{di}{dt}.$$

Analogous conclusions apply to the case of a system of circuits in which electromotive forces A_1, A_2 . . . act. When the correction for inertia is introduced, the well-known differential equations which determine the currents take the form

$$i_1 r_1 = A_1 - (P_{11} + m_1)\frac{di_1}{dt} - P_{12}\frac{di_2}{dt} - \quad - P_{1n}\frac{di_n}{dt},$$

$$i_2 r_2 = A_2 - P_{12}\frac{di_1}{dt} - (P_{22} + m_2)\frac{di_2}{dt} - \ldots - P_{2n}\frac{di_n}{dt},$$

$$\vdots$$

$$i_n r_n = A_n - P_{1n}\frac{di_1}{dt} - \qquad \cdot - (P_{nn} + m_n)\frac{di_n}{dt}.$$

Thus the only alteration which the mass of the electricity has produced in these equations consists in an increase of the self-inductance, and it is at once obvious

1. That the electromotive force of the extra-currents is independent of the induction-currents simultaneously generated in other conductors, and of the mass of the electricity moving in them.

2. That the complete time-integrals of the induction-currents are not affected by the mass of the electricity moved, whether in the inducing or induced conductors.

3. That, on the other hand, the integral flow of the extra-currents becomes greater than that calculated from inductive actions alone.[1]

[1] With reference to these simple deductions the philosophical faculty of the Frederick-William University at Berlin in 1879 propounded to the students th

The amount of this increase depends on the quantities m, whose meaning we will now consider more closely, basing our investigation on Weber's view of electric currents. The presence of the terms involving m is, however, independent of the correctness of this view and of the existence of electric fluids at all; every explanation of the current as a state of motion of inert matter must equally introduce these terms, and only the interpretation of the quantities m will be different.

Suppose unit volume of the conductor to contain λ units of positive electricity, and let the mass of each unit be ρ milligrammes. Let the length of the conductor be l, and its cross-section, supposed uniform, q. Then unit length of the conductor contains $q\lambda$ electrostatic units, and the total positive electricity in motion in the conductor has the mass $\rho q\lambda l$ mgm. If the current (in electromagnetic measure) be i, the number of electrostatic units which cross any section in unit time is equal to $155,370 \times 10^6 i$, and is also equal to the velocity v multiplied by $q\lambda$. Thus

$$v = \frac{155,370 \times 10^6}{q\lambda} i,$$

and the kinetic energy of the positive electricity contained in the conductor is

$$\tfrac{1}{2} l\rho q\lambda \left\{ \frac{155,370 \times 10^6}{\lambda} \right\} \frac{2i^2}{q^2}$$

$$= \tfrac{1}{2}\frac{li^2}{q} \cdot \rho \frac{155,370^2 \times 10^{12}}{\lambda} = \tfrac{1}{2}\mu \frac{li^2}{q}.$$

The quantity $\tfrac{1}{2}li^2/q$ can be expressed in finite measure. The quantity $\rho .155,370^2 \times 10/^{12}\lambda$, which has been denoted by μ, is a constant depending only on the material of the conductor; for different conductors it is inversely as the density of the electricity in them. Its dimensions are those of a surface; in milligramme-millimetres it gives the kinetic energy of the two

problem "to make experiments on the magnitude of extra-currents which shall at least lead to a determination of an upper limit to the mass moved." It was pointed out that for such experiments extra-currents flowing in opposite directions through the wires of a double spiral would be especially suitable. The present thesis is essentially the same as that which gained the prize.

electricities, *i.e.* the total kinetic energy of the current in a cubic millimetre of a conductor in which the current has unit magnetic density.

The object of the following experiments is to determine the quantity μ, or at any rate an upper limit to it.

METHOD OF EXPERIMENTING.

Since we have put the kinetic energy of the total electricity equal to $mi^2/2$, and also equal to $(l\mu/q)i^2$, it follows that $\mu = qm/2l$. In order to determine m it would have sufficed to measure the integral flow of the extra-current in a conductor of known resistance r and self-inductance P; m would at once follow from the equation $J = (i/r)(P + m)$. But extra-currents can only be measured in branched systems of conductors, and this would necessitate the measuring of a large number of resistances. Hence it is preferable to generate extra-currents in the same circuit by two different inductions, when we obtain two equations for the quantities r and m. If the current in the unbranched circuit is to that current by which the extra-current is measured as $a : 1$, and if J is the total flow measured, then the equations in question are

$$\frac{arJ}{i} = P + m , \qquad \frac{arJ'}{i'} = P' + m,$$

whence

$$m = \frac{P\frac{J'}{i'} - P'\frac{J}{i}}{\frac{J}{i} - \frac{J'}{i'}}.$$

It is well to choose one inductance P' so large that the influence of mass is negligible in comparison, but the other P as small as possible. The equations then take the simpler form

$$\frac{arJ}{i} = P + m, \qquad \frac{arJ'}{i'} = P'$$

$$m = \frac{i'\mathrm{J}}{i\mathrm{J}'}\mathrm{P}' - \mathrm{P}, \text{ or if } i' = i,$$

$$m = \mathrm{P}\left(\frac{\mathrm{J}\,\mathrm{P}'}{\mathrm{J}'\mathrm{P}} - 1\right).$$

The experiments were carried out according to this principle. The system of conductors through which the currents flowed consisted in the earlier experiments of spirals wound with double wires, in the later ones of two wires stretched out in parallel straight lines side by side. These systems of wires could without change of resistance be coupled in such a way that the currents in the two branches flowed in the same or in opposite directions. The inductances following from the two methods of coupling were calculated and the integral flows of the corresponding extra-currents were determined by experiment. If these flows were proportional to the calculated inductances, no effect of mass would be demonstrated; if a deviation from proportionality were observed, the kinetic energy of the currents would follow by the above formulæ.

The extra-currents were always measured by means of a Wheatstone's bridge, one branch of which contained the system of wires giving the currents, while the other branches were chosen to have as little inductance as possible. The bridge was adjusted so that a steady current flowing through it produced no permanent deflection of the galvanometer needle; but when the direction of the current outside the bridge was reversed, then two equal and equally directed extra-currents traversed the galvanometer, and their integral flow was measured by the kick of the needle. As soon as the needle returned from its kick the reversing could be repeated, and in this manner the method of multiplication could be applied.

The chief difficulty in these measurements was to be met in the smallness of the observed extra-currents, and on this account the method described was impracticable in its simplest form. It is true that by merely increasing the strength of the inducing current the extra-currents could be made as strong as desired, but the difficulties in exactly adjusting the bridge increased very much more quickly than the intensities

thus obtained. With the greatest strength, which still permitted permanently of such an adjustment, a single extra-
current from the two branches, when traversed in opposite
directions, only moved the galvanometer needle through a
fraction of a scale division, whilst the mere approach of the
hand to one of the mercury cups, or the radiation of a distant
gas flame falling on the spirals, sufficed to produce a deflection
of more than 100 scale divisions. Hence I attempted to
make use of very strong currents by allowing them to pass
for a very short time only through the bridge, which was
adjusted by using a weak current. But the electromotive
forces generated momentarily in the bridge by the heating
.effects of the current were found to be of the same order of
magnitude as the extra-currents to be observed, so that it
was impossible to get results of any value. These experiments only showed that at any rate there was no considerable deviation from the laws of the dynamical theory of
induction.

On this account, in order to obtain measurable deflections
with weaker currents, I passed a considerable number of extra-
currents through the galvanometer at each passage of the
needle through its position of rest. For this purpose the
current was at the right moment rapidly reversed twenty
times in succession outside the bridge, and at the same time
the galvanometer was commutated between every two successive
reversals of the current. In order to avoid any considerable
damping, after the bridge had been once adjusted the galvanometer circuit remained open generally, and was only put in
circuit with the rest of the combination during the time
needed to generate the extra-currents.

The operations described were carried out by means of a
special commutator and occupied about two seconds, an interval of time which was sufficiently long to allow of all the
extra-currents being fully developed, and which also proved to
be sufficiently small in comparison with the time of swing of
the needle.

This method possessed several advantages. In the first
place accurately measurable effects could be produced even
with very weak, and therefore also very constant, inducing
currents. In all of the following experiments the external

circuit consisted of one Daniell cell and a ballast resistance of from 3 to 80 Siemens units. Further, if the resistances of the bridge are not exactly adjusted, and if in consequence a fraction of the inducing current also passes through the galvanometer, this fraction will yet be continually reversed in the galvanometer; so that, if the want of balance be only small, the error due to it almost entirely vanishes.

Again, since the connection of the galvanometer with the remaining wires of the combination is constantly changing its direction those electromotive forces which exist in the bridge or are generated by the current, and which are not reversed when the current is reversed, are without influence on the needle. It is a circumstance of great value, that for the greater part of a swing the galvanometer is withdrawn from all disturbing influences.

In consequence of these favourable conditions the observations agreed together very satisfactorily when we consider the smallness of the quantities to be measured: the deviation of the results obtained from their mean was in general less than $\frac{1}{30}$ of the whole. Here also the proceeding was repeated each time the needle passed through its position of rest. But the multiplication could not be carried so far as to obtain a constant deflection; for to the constant small damping of the needle due to air-resistance was added the damping which was produced whenever the galvanometer was put in circuit with the bridge, and which lasted only for a very short time. The time during which connection was made was not always exactly the same, and thus the damping produced could not be exactly determined. As, however, its effect became very marked with large swings, the method was limited to smaller deflections, and generally only from 7 to 9 elongations were measured. The method which was used to deduce the most probable value of the extra-current from the complete arcs of vibration thus obtained will now be explained.

Let T be the period of vibration of the galvanometer needle, λ the logarithmic decrement constantly present, $q = \epsilon^{-\lambda}$ the ratio of any swing to the preceding one, and let, for shortness,

$$\frac{T}{\sqrt{\pi^2 + \lambda^2}} \epsilon^{-\frac{\lambda}{\pi} \tan^{-1} \frac{\pi}{\lambda}} = \kappa \,.$$

Further, let a_1, a_2, a_3 be successive elongations right and left of the position of rest, $a_1 = a_1 + a_2$, $a_2 = a_2 + a_3$, etc., the complete arcs of vibration, and k_1, k_2, . . . the increments of velocity in the position of rest, which measure the inductive effects. Then, if for the present any special damping during the impact be neglected

$$a_2 = \kappa k_1 + q a_1,$$
$$a_3 = \kappa k_2 + q a_2 = \kappa k_2 + \kappa q k_1 + q^2 a_1;$$

hence we get

$$a_1 = \kappa k_1 + a_1(1 + q),$$
$$a_2 = \kappa k_2 + \kappa k_1(1 + q) + a_1 q(1 + q).$$

If we multiply the first equation by q and subtract it from the second, we find

$$a_2 - a_1 q = \kappa(k_1 + k_2),$$

and similarly

$$a_3 - a_2 q = \kappa(k_2 + k_3),$$
$$\vdots$$
$$a_n - a_{n-1} q = \kappa(k_{n-1} + k_n).$$

Hence we find the mean value of the impacts k_1, k_2, . . . which should all be equal if the apparatus worked quite exactly

$$\kappa k = \frac{a_2 + a_3 + \cdots + a_n - q(a_1 + a_2 + \cdots + a_{n-1})}{2(n-1)},$$

or, if we denote the sum of all the complete arcs of vibration by Σ,

$$\kappa k = \frac{(\Sigma - a_1) - q(\Sigma - a_n)}{2(n-1)}.$$

The application of this formula is very easy and is always advisable when the separate impacts are not regular enough to produce a constant limiting value of the arcs of swing, or when for other reasons only a limited number of elongations has been observed.

If in addition to the constantly occurring damping a further damping occur during the instant of closing of the circuit, this latter may be regarded as an impact in a direction opposed to the motion which is proportional to the duration of the closing of the circuit and to the velocity of the needle. If the former be τ, the latter v, and the logarithmic decrement during closing λ', the magnitude of such an impact is

$$- 4\frac{\lambda'}{T}\tau v .$$

If a_1, a_2 be the preceding and succeeding elongations the needle reaches its position of rest with a velocity $a_1 q/\kappa$ and leaves it with a velocity a_2/κ. As the increase of velocity is nearly uniform, we must put for v the mean value $(a_1 q + a_2)/2\kappa$, and thus the magnitude of the impact is

$$- 2\frac{\lambda'\tau}{T\kappa}(a_1 q + a_2) = - \frac{c}{\kappa}(a_1 q + a_2).$$

By adding this increase of velocity to that caused by the impact due to induction we obtain the equations

$$a_2 = k_1\kappa + a_1 q - c(a_2 + a_1 q),$$
$$a_3 = k_2\kappa + a_2 q - c(a_3 + a_2 q), \text{ etc.,}$$

or

$$(1 + c)a_2 = \kappa k_1 + (1 - c)a_1 q,$$
$$(1 + c)a_3 = \kappa k_2 + (1 - c)a_2 q, \text{ etc. ;}$$

and by a similar calculation to that above

$$(1 + c)a_2 - (1 - c)q a_1 = \kappa(k_1 + k_2),$$
$$(1 + c)a_3 - (1 - c)q a_2 = \kappa(k_2 + k_3),$$
$$\cdot \quad \cdot \quad \cdot \quad \cdot$$
$$(1 + c)a_n - (1 - c)q a_{n-1} = \kappa(k_{n-1} + k_n).$$

If instead of the quantities k_1, k_2, . . we write their theoretical value k, we get after a simple transformation the equations

$$a_2 - q a_1 + c(a_2 + q a_1) = 2k c\kappa,$$
$$a_3 - q a_2 + c(a_3 + q a_2) = 2k c\kappa,$$
$$\vdots$$
$$a_n - q a_{n-1} + c(a_n + q a_{n-1}) = 2k c\kappa ;$$

and from these the most probable values of the unknown quantities k, etc. must be calculated by the method of least squares.

The very complicated calculation was, however, not carried through for all the observations, but from a number of them the value of c was calculated, and the mean of the closely-agreeing values obtained was assumed to be true for the remaining observations. When c is known we get, more simply

$$\kappa k = \frac{(\Sigma - a_1) - q(\Sigma - a_n) + c\{(\Sigma - a_1) + q(\Sigma - a_n)\}}{2(n-1)}.$$

Since the term involving c only occurs as a correction, it is not necessary to know c with absolute accuracy. By taking the mean between two successive impacts, namely

$$k_m \kappa = \frac{a_m - q a_{m-1} + c(a_m + q a_{m-1})}{2}.$$

we can get some notion as to how far the individual values differ from their mean.

As in what follows only the final results will be given, I shall give here one series of multiplied deflections with the individual impacts completely calculated, so that it may be seen how far the observations agree amongst themselves.

EXTRA-CURRENTS FROM RECTILINEAR WIRES (WIRES TRAVERSED IN THE SAME DIRECTION).

STRENGTH OF THE INDUCING CURRENT: 75·7.

$$q = 0·9830, \qquad c = 0·016.$$

Readings reduced to arc.	Arcs of Vibration. a_n	$a_n - q a_{n-1}$	$a_n + q a_{n-1}$	Magnitude of Individual Impacts in Scale Divisions. $k\kappa = \frac{a_n - q a_{n-1} + c(a_n + q a_{n-1})}{2}$
517·2	30·7	—	—	—
547·9	72·0	41·8	102·3	21·7
475·9	111·3	40·5	182·5	21·7
587·2	149·4	40·0	258·8	22·1
437·8	186·5	39·6	338·4	22·4
624·3	222·3	39·0	405·6	22·7
402·0	254·7	36·2	473·2	21·9
656·7	285·5	35·1	535·9	21·8
371·2				

The mean value of $k\kappa = 22.05$; the greatest difference amounts to less than $\frac{1}{30}$ of the whole. As in each impact 40 extra-currents were combined, the deflection produced by a single one was only 0.551 scale division. The remaining series of multiplied deflections showed about the same degree of agreement when the individual impacts were calculated.

DESCRIPTION OF THE APPARATUS.

Before proceeding to discuss the individual experiments I shall describe those arrangements which were common to all the experiments.

1. If we desire the strength of the extra-current to be a maximum in the galvanometer for a given strength of the inducing current and given values of the inductances, we must choose the resistance of the galvanometer as small as possible, and the resistances of the other branches all equal. This arrangement has another special advantage. For different paths are open to the currents at make and break, since the former can also discharge through the external circuit whilst the latter cannot. In order to reduce all the experiments to similar conditions a correction has in general to be made which depends on the resistance of the external circuit. This correction vanishes when the resistances of the four branches are the same. In fact, if r be this resistance, r_g the resistance of the galvanometer, and r_x that of the battery, we get for the current in the galvanometer, when an electromotive force E acts in one of the branches, the value $E/2(r + r_g)$, which is independent of r_x

Hence, when the four branches were made equal, the results obtained with different batteries could be directly compared.

2. The passive resistances of the bridge had to be so chosen that the part of the extra-current due to them was as small as possible. In this respect columns of large diameter of unpolarisable liquids would have been most suitable, since the inductance of such columns is very small. But it was impossible with the great delicacy of the bridge to obtain

them of sufficient constancy. Hence I employed wires of German-silver, which were passed through glass tubes and surrounded by distilled water, so as to guard against changes of temperature. These were so arranged that those belonging to different branches and traversed in opposite directions lay side by side. The values of the inductances still remaining were small and could be allowed for with sufficient accuracy in the calculation. Since the German-silver wires were very thin there was a danger that they might, when the current was reversed, be subjected to small but sudden changes of temperature. Such changes would, at the instant when the current was started, have disturbed the balance of the bridge, and so would have produced an increase or decrease of the extra-current very difficult to estimate. Therefore, in a last series of experiments I employed rods of Bunsen gas-carbon, 5 mm. in diameter, such as are used for electric lighting.

3. The strength of the inducing current was measured outside the bridge; the tangent galvanometer used consisted of a single copper ring 213·2 mm. in diameter, at the centre of which a needle about 25 mm. long was suspended by a single silk fibre. In order to damp its vibrations as quickly as possible it was placed in a vessel of distilled water. The readings were taken by telescope and scale; the distance of the latter from the needle was 1295 mm., and one scale-division corresponded to a current of 0·01218 in absolute electro-magnetic units. The measurements were always made by observing a deflection to the right, then one to the left, and then again one to the right. The result is correct to $\frac{1}{100}$ of its value.

The extra-current was measured by a Meyerstein galvan-ometer of very low resistance, such as is used for measurements with the earth-inductor. The pair of needles was suspended astatically by twelve fibres of cocoon silk; the time of swing was 27·66 seconds. The galvanometer was set up on an isolated stone pillar, 2905 mm. from the scale and telescope, and about the same distance from the bridge, and was connected with the latter by thick parallel copper wires.

4. The commutator, at each passage of the needle through its position of rest, had to perform the following operations quickly one after the other :—

Connection of the galvanometer to the bridge.

Reversal of the current.

Reversal of the galvanometer.

. . . (Repeated twenty times.) . . .

Reversal of the current.

Throwing the galvanometer out of circuit.

Its arrangement is shown in Fig. 1. A circular disc revolving about a vertical axis has attached to its edge radially

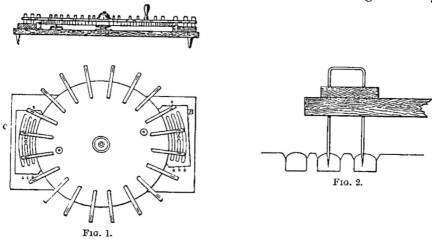

Fig. 1.

twenty amalgamated copper hooks of the form shown in Fig. 2, which just dip into the mercury contained in the vessels *B* and *C*. They are alternately nearer to and farther from the axis, so that the inside ends of the farther ones and the outside ends of the nearer ones lie on the same circle about the axis. They reverse the current in passing over the vessel *B*, and the galvanometer in passing over *C*. The

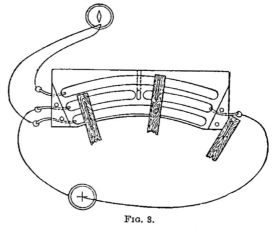

Fig. 3.

arrangement of the vessels of mercury and the method of reversal are shown in Fig. 3. The vessel *B* is not exactly opposite to *C*, but is displaced relatively to it through half the distance between successive hooks, so that a reversal of the galvanometer occurs between every two reversals of the current. While the needle is completing its swing after the induction impact, the hooks are symmetrically situated with respect to the vessel C, so that one hook is above the space between the two halves of the middle mercury cup, and the neighbouring ones are right and left at the sides of the cups; the connection of the galvanometer with the bridge is then broken. As soon as the needle reaches its position of rest the disc is turned by hand and after a whole turn is stopped by a simple catch, so that then the commutator performs the above operations.

It may be mentioned that generally the wires of the bridge, wherever possible, were soldered directly to each other; binding-screws and mercury-cups were only used where connections had to be broken and remade repeatedly.

EXPERIMENTS WITH DOUBLE-WOUND SPIRALS.

I now come to the individual experiments, and first to those with double-wound spirals. I had at my disposal two spirals, exactly similar and very carefully wound, whose length was 73·9 mm. and whose external and internal diameters were respectively 83·6 and 67·3 mm. They consisted of eight layers, each with sixty-eight turns. The total length of wire was found by comparison of its resistance with that of the outer layer to be 130,032 mm. The diameter of the wire was 0·93 mm., the total resistance about 3·1 Siemens units. As the spirals were exactly alike, they were used together and put in the diagonally opposite arms of the bridge. The extra-currents produced by them were then added together in the bridge.

According to the above explanations the inductive effects of two inductances P and P′ were to be observed whilst the resistance of the circuit remained unchanged. The inductance P was that of the spiral when the current in its two branches flowed in opposite directions. To obtain a second inductance P′ a branch of one spiral was thrown out of circuit and replaced by an equal ballast resistance, the magnitude of which could be very exactly adjusted in the bridge.

When a current was passed through the branch thus detached, and reversed in a suitable manner, the current induced by this branch in the other could be measured. The quantity P′ was then the mutual inductance of the one branch on the other. Of course the extra-current might also have been used with the current flowing the same way through both branches of the spirals, but this was too large compared with that obtained from the spirals with their branches traversed oppositely to be accurately observable under like conditions.

We have first to calculate the numerical values of P and P′. P may be determined with a sufficient accuracy from the geometrical relations of the spirals and the calculation will be performed immediately; but P′ can in this way be found only by means of simplifying assumptions, which introduce a considerable error. Hence I preferred to determine it directly by experiment by comparing it with the known inductance of straight wires.

Determination of P.—The following assumptions are made as regards the arrangement of the wires and are very nearly correct :—

1. In one and the same layer wires traversed positively and negatively alternate with each other : the distances between their central axes are equal to each other and to the mean distance, which is got by dividing the length of the spiral by the number of turns. 2. Two neighbouring layers are laterally displaced relatively to each other through half the distance between two centres. These assumptions completely determine the geometrical position of the wires; but whether the extreme wires near the ends of the spiral are all traversed in the like direction or in opposite directions alternately, it was impossible to decide in the case of the inner layers. For this reason and because of the unavoidable irregularities an accurate calculation of the inductance is not possible; we can only determine limits between which it must lie and we shall see that these limits may be drawn rather closely. In calculating the inductance of one layer we may without appreciable error cut it open, develop it on a

plane and consider it as part of an infinitely long system of straight wires, whose thickness is the same as that of the layer. For the position of any element is unchanged relatively to its neighbours, and the action of distant portions on each other is zero.

We shall first determine the self-inductance Π of a single layer. Let the length of the wires be S, their radius R, the distance of two neighbouring ones q, their number n.[1] Further, let a_0 be the self-inductance of a single wire, a_m the mutual inductance of two wires distant mq; then we have

$$a_0 = 2S\left(\log \frac{2S}{R} - \tfrac{3}{4}\right), \quad a_m = 2S\left(\log \frac{2S}{mq} - 1\right).$$

By counting we find

$$\Pi = 2na_0 - 2(2n-1)a_1 + 2(2n-2)a_2 - \ldots - 2a_{2n-1},$$

and introducing the values of the a's

$$\Pi = 4Sn\left\{\tfrac{1}{4} + \log\frac{q}{R} + \frac{1}{n}\log\frac{1^{2n-1}\cdot 3^{2n-3}\ldots(2n-3)^3\cdot(2n-1)}{2^{2n-2}\cdot 4^{2n-4}\ldots(2n-2)^2}\right\}.$$

Hence the quotient Π/S here has a perfectly determinate value, which may be called the self-inductance per unit length. The logarithm involved in the above expression cannot well be directly calculated for large values of n; for such values we must use an approximation. For this purpose we split up the expression into

$$n\log\frac{1^2 3^2 5^2\ldots(2n-3)^2(2n-1)}{2^2 4^2\ldots(2n-2)^2}$$

$$+\log\frac{2^2}{1\cdot 3}\cdot\frac{4^4}{3^2 5^2}\cdot\frac{6^6}{5^3 7^3}\cdots\frac{(2n-2)^{2n-2}}{(2n-3)^{n-1}(2n-1)^{n-1}}$$

the two parts of which will be evaluated separately. The first may be written

$$= n\sum_{1}^{n-1}\log\frac{(2m-1)(2m+1)}{(2m)^2} = n\sum_{1}^{n-1}\log\left(1 - \frac{1}{4m^2}\right).$$

[1] [n is really the number of double wires, positive and negative counting as one.—TR.]

Since $\dfrac{1}{4m^2}<1$ for all the values concerned, we may expand $\log(1-1/4m^2)$, and thus obtain for the first part

$$-n\left\{\tfrac{1}{4}\sum_{1}^{n-1}\frac{1}{m^2}+\tfrac{1}{32}\sum_{1}^{n-1}\frac{1}{m^4}+\ldots\right\},$$

or, when we develop the sums by well-known formulæ,

$$=-n\left\{\text{const.}-\frac{1}{4(n-1)}+\frac{1}{8(n-1)^2}-\frac{1}{24(n-1)^3}\right.$$
$$\left.+\ldots-\frac{1}{96(n-1)^3}+\ldots\right\}.$$

The constant is clearly $-\log(2/\pi)$, for when n becomes infinitely great the whole expression converges to $n\log(2/\pi)$. If we develop the remaining terms in descending powers of n and collect together like powers, we finally find the first part to be

$$\log\left(\frac{2}{\pi}\right)^n+\tfrac{1}{4}+\frac{1}{8n}+\frac{5}{96n^2}+\ldots.$$

An analogous calculation may be performed for the second part, which is

$$=\sum_{1}^{n-1}\log\frac{2m^{2m}}{(2m-1)^m(2m+1)^m}=\sum_{1}^{n-1}\log\left(1-\frac{1}{4m^2}\right)^{-m}$$

$$=\tfrac{1}{4}\sum_{1}^{n-1}\frac{1}{m}+\tfrac{1}{32}\sum_{1}^{n-1}\frac{1}{m^3}+\tfrac{1}{192}\sum_{1}^{n-1}\frac{1}{m^5}+\ldots$$

and hence, by a calculation similar to the above,

$$=\tfrac{1}{4}\left\{0\cdot577216+\log(n-1)+\frac{1}{2(n-1)}-\frac{1}{12(n-1)^2}+\ldots\right\}$$

$$+\tfrac{1}{32}\left\{\sum_{1}^{\infty}\frac{1}{m^3}+\ldots\right.\qquad\qquad -\frac{1}{2(n-1)^2}+\ldots\left.\right\}$$

$$+\tfrac{1}{192}\left\{\sum_{1}^{\infty}\frac{1}{m^5}+\ldots\right\}$$

$$+\tfrac{1}{1024}\left\{\sum_{1}^{\infty}\frac{1}{m^7}+\ldots\right\}$$

$$+\ldots$$

If here we calculate the constant term directly and expand the remaining terms in descending powers of n, we find the second part to be

$$0{\cdot}18848 + \tfrac{1}{4} \log n - \frac{1}{8n} - \frac{7}{192n^2} - \ldots$$

The sum of both parts gives the required term

$$= 0{\cdot}43848 + \log \sqrt[4]{n}\left(\frac{2}{\pi}\right)^n + \frac{3}{192n^2} - \cdots$$

$$= \log\left\{1{\cdot}5503 \sqrt[4]{n}\left(\frac{2}{\pi}\right)^n\right\} + \frac{3}{192n^2} - \cdots$$

$$= n \log\left\{\sqrt[4n]{5{\cdot}7773n}\cdot\frac{2}{\pi}\right\} + \frac{3}{192n^2} - \cdots,$$

and hence to a considerable degree of approximation the self-inductance of a single layer becomes

$$\Pi = 4Sn\left\{\tfrac{1}{4} + \log\frac{2q\sqrt[4n]{5{\cdot}7773n}}{R\pi}\right\}.$$

For large values of n the root involved in this expression rapidly converges to unity, so that for such values of n we may write more simply

$$\Pi = 4Sn\left\{\tfrac{1}{4} + \log\frac{2q}{R\pi}\right\}.$$

We get this approximation at once by calculating the induction of the whole arrangement on one of the middle wires, and assuming it true for all the wires. We may use this simpler method in calculating the mutual inductance of two different layers.

Let ϵ be the perpendicular distance between two layers, and suppose that in them the individual pairs of wires are so placed that the wires traversed in the same direction are opposite, with their axes in one plane perpendicular to the two layers. Then the mutual inductance of one layer and a median wire of the second layer is

$$2S\left\{\begin{array}{l}\log 2S - \log \epsilon \qquad\qquad -1 \\ -2\log 2S + 2\log\sqrt{\epsilon^2+q^2}\ +2 \\ +2\log 2S - 2\log\sqrt{\epsilon^2+4q^2}-2 \\ \qquad\qquad\qquad . \qquad\qquad . \\ -\log 2S + \log\sqrt{\epsilon^2+(2n+1)^2q^2}+1\end{array}\right\},$$

$$= -2S\log\frac{\epsilon(\epsilon^2+2^2q^2)(\epsilon^2+4^2q^2)\ldots(\epsilon^2+(2n)^2q^2)}{(\epsilon^2+q^2)(\epsilon^2+3^2q^2)\ldots\sqrt{\epsilon^2+(2n+1)^2q^2}},$$

$$= 2S\log\frac{1^2+\left(\dfrac{\epsilon}{q}\right)^2}{\dfrac{\epsilon}{q}}\cdot\frac{3^2+\left(\dfrac{\epsilon}{q}\right)^2}{2^2+\left(\dfrac{\epsilon}{q}\right)^2}\ldots\frac{\sqrt{(2n+1)^2+\left(\dfrac{\epsilon}{q}\right)^2}}{\epsilon^2+(2n)^2q^2}.$$

We get an approximate value in finite form of the expression behind the logarithm sign by dividing the equation

$$\cos\frac{z}{2} = \left(1-\frac{z^2}{1^2\pi^2}\right)^2\left(1-\frac{z^2}{3^2\pi^2}\right)^2\left(1-\frac{z^2}{5^2\pi^2}\right)^2\ldots$$

by this second equation,

$$\sin z = z\left(1-\frac{z^2}{1^2\pi^2}\right)\left(1-\frac{z^2}{2^2\pi^2}\right)\ldots$$

by putting $v\sqrt{-1}$ for z on both sides and dividing the result by $\sqrt{-1}$; thus we get the equation

$$\frac{1+e^{-v}}{1-e^{-v}} = \text{limit}\left\{\frac{1^2+\left(\dfrac{v}{\pi}\right)^2}{\dfrac{v}{\pi}}\cdot\frac{3^2+\left(\dfrac{v}{\pi}\right)^2}{2^2+\left(\dfrac{v}{\pi}\right)^2}\ldots\frac{\sqrt{(2n+1)^2+\left(\dfrac{v}{\pi}\right)^2}}{2n^2+\left(\dfrac{v}{\pi}\right)^2}\right\}$$

and thus the above inductance becomes approximately for a large value of n

$$= 2S\log\frac{1+e^{-\frac{\epsilon\pi}{q}}}{1-e^{-\frac{\epsilon\pi}{q}}},$$

or, if we neglect terms of the order $e^{-3\pi\epsilon/q}$,

$$4Se^{-\frac{\epsilon\pi}{q}}.$$

Multiplying this expression by $2n$, we find the mutual inductance of the two layers to be

$$+ 8Sne^{-\frac{\epsilon\pi}{q}} .$$

If now one of them be displaced laterally through a distance q the inductance obviously becomes

$$- 8Sne^{-\frac{\epsilon\pi}{q}} .$$

For all intermediate positions the inductance has a value
between these two extremes.   Hence, if we neglect altogether
the effect of the different layers on each other, the error for
each pair of layers to be considered is less than $8Sne^{-\epsilon\pi/q}$.
But any two contiguous layers may be altogether left out of
account, for the induction between them is in fact zero to a
high degree of approximation.   By substituting values of q, ϵ,
R, such as occur in ordinary cases, we easily convince ourselves
that the error considered amounts to less than the $\frac{1}{140}$ part
of the self-inductance of the layer.   In so far as we neglect
it we get the self-inductance of the whole spiral by adding the
self-inductances of the individual layers.   Hence, if l denote
the whole length of wire contained in the spiral, we have
finally

$$P = 2l \left\{ \tfrac{1}{4} + \log \frac{2q\sqrt[4n]{5\cdot7773n}}{R\pi} \right\} .$$

For the spirals used in our case

$$l = 130032 \text{ mm.,} \quad n = 34, \quad R = 0\cdot465 \text{ mm.,}$$

$$q = 1\cdot087 \text{ mm.,} \quad P = 178,500 \text{ mm.}$$

A calculation of the error possibly committed on the above
principle gave it as less than 1200 mm.

Determination of P'.—The mutual inductance P' of the
two branches of the spiral, as has been already remarked, was
determined by comparison with the inductance of straight
wires.   The arrangement of the experiment is shown in Fig. 4.
A and *B* are rectilinear systems of wires of the dimensions
marked on the figure, and were stretched out on the floor of

the laboratory. In A (the secondary circuit) the galvanometer and one branch of the spiral C were introduced; in B the battery, the tangent galvanometer, and the commutator.

The induction of the circuit B on A was first determined. As this was very small, the above described method of experimenting and calculating was used, in which the circuit A was as a rule broken. As the action of the rectilinear system B on the spiral C was not zero, the latter was inserted in the circuit in both of the two possible ways. The values of the inductive kick

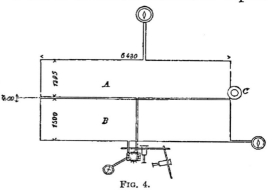

Fig. 4.

were observed for different strengths of the primary current; after reduction to the same strength (100 scale divisions of the tangent galvanometer) they were found to be—

1. For the first position of the spiral:

In scale divisions of the galvanometer,

$$0\cdot3997, \ 0\cdot3955, \ 0\cdot3791, \ 0\cdot4006. \quad \text{Mean} = 0\cdot3939;$$

2. For the second position:

$$0\cdot3034, \ 0\cdot3102. \quad \text{Mean} = 0\cdot3068.$$

The mean of the two values, namely $0\cdot3502$, gives the induction of the circuit B on A. The corresponding logarithmic decrement was that of the needle swinging freely, namely

$$\lambda = 0\cdot0172.$$

In order to compare the kick with experiments made with a different damping we must multiply it by

$$\frac{\sqrt{\pi^2 + \lambda^2}}{T} e^{\frac{\lambda}{\pi} \tan^{-1}\frac{\pi}{\lambda}},$$

which gives the value

$$\frac{1\cdot1097}{T}.$$

The remaining detached branch of the spiral C was now

put in the circuit *B*, so that the actions of the spiral and of the rectilinear circuit aided each other, and the action of the one branch on the other was observed by simply reversing the current *B* each time the needle passed through its position of rest. After reduction to the strength 100 the inductive kick was found to be

$$164\cdot3, \; 164\cdot7. \quad \text{Mean} = 164\cdot5 \; \text{scale divisions.}$$

The corresponding decrement was $\lambda = 0\cdot6362$, and the reduction to an unresisted needle gives the value of the kick

$$\frac{696\cdot0}{T}$$

We may here and in what follows neglect the effect of damping in altering the period. Hence the mutual inductance of the branches of the spiral is to that of the rectilinear circuits in the ratio of

$$696\cdot0 - 1\cdot1 : 1\cdot1097 = 694\cdot9 : 1\cdot1097.$$

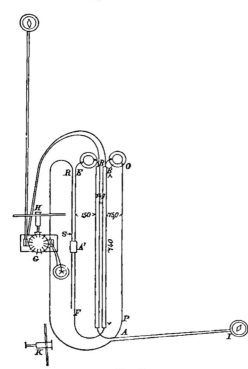

FIG. 5.

The latter inductance was easily calculated from the geometrical relations of the wires, and was found to be 60428 mm., whence it follows that the mutual inductance of the branches of the spiral = 37,840,000 mm.

I had already found for the same quantity the value

38,680,000 mm.

by a different but more uncertain method. The two values agree sufficiently well, but we shall only use the first one.

Execution of the Experiments.—The arrangement of the bridge used for measuring the extra-currents is shown in greater detail in Fig. 5. The current enters at A and A'; the galvanometer is connected at B and B'. The bridge is adjusted by moving the connection A' of the battery with the thick copper wire EF. The spirals are inserted in the diagonally opposite branches $A'B$ and AB', the passive German-silver resistances are placed in the other two branches and lie close together side by side, with the currents flowing through them in opposite directions. The wires from the battery and those to the galvanometer pass through the commutator G, which is placed so that the observer can set it in motion while observing with the telescope H. In every one of its revolutions 20 double extra-currents from each of the two spirals, in all 80 simple extra-currents, pass through the galvanometer. The tangent galvanometer is at I and is read by the telescope K.

The value of the extra-current was first determined when the branches of the spirals were traversed in opposite directions. The following values were obtained :—

Strength of Primary Current in Scale Divisions.	Strength of Secondary Current in Scale Divisions.
48·8	0·1790
50·0	0·1738
123·2	0·4621
122·2	0·4417

By reduction to strength 100 we get the values

0·3664, 0·3476, 0·3750, 0·3600.   Mean = 0·3622.

The logarithmic decrement of the needle for these experiments was $\lambda = 0.0172$. If we therefore multiply the above kick by the factor $3.168/T$, we get the reduced value

$$\frac{1.1476}{T}.$$

In accordance with previous explanations, one of the branches of one spiral was next thrown out of circuit; the bridge was readjusted, and the inductive action of the detached branch on the other was observed. When in the former a current 100 ceased to flow, the kick observed in the galvanometer was

61·50, 61·66.   Mean = 61·58 scale divisions.

The logarithmic decrement in this experiment was $\lambda = 0\cdot4396$, and the corresponding factor $3\cdot876/\mathrm{T}$: hence the reduced kick was

$$\frac{238\cdot67}{\mathrm{T}}.$$

Thus for the resistances of the bridge and the arrangement of circuits used this kick corresponded to the mutual inductance

$$\mathrm{P}' = 37,840,000.$$

When the branches of the spirals were traversed in opposite directions, the corresponding electromotive force of the extra-current was for each of the spirals

$$\mathrm{P} = 178,500.$$

But we have to correct for the induction of the rest of the bridge as follows :—

1. The self-inductance of each of the German-silver wires (diameter $= 0\cdot246$ mm.) is $12,790$; twice this must be subtracted, so that the correction is $-25,580$.

2. This action is in part compensated by the action of the neighbouring German-silver wire. Their mutual inductance is 5348; this value is to be taken twice, so the correction is $+10,696$.

3. The self-inductance of the wire OP is $+9028$.

4. The mutual inductance of the wire OP and the nearer German-silver wire is $+2789$.

5. The same for the further one is -1230.

6. The mutual inductance of RS and EA$'$, taken twice because of the double strength in RS, gives $+5254$. The sum of all these corrections only amounts to $+957$, of which one half goes to the account of each spiral, namely $+478$ mm.

Hence, finally, the inductive electromotive force is measured by $178,978$, which is almost exactly that due to the spirals alone. The error in this value, due to neglecting portions of the induction of the spirals, according to what precedes, at most amounts to 2400 mm. The error due to neglecting portions of the bridge will presumably be of the same order.

According to theory, the extra current from the spirals with branches traversed oppositely should have the value

$$\frac{238\cdot67}{T}\cdot\frac{178,978}{37,840,000}=\frac{1\cdot1351}{T}.$$

The value actually observed was $1\cdot1476/T$. The difference between the two amounts to little more than $1/100$ of the total value, while the errors of experiment and of calculation at most may amount to $1/30$. Hence, though the great agreement between the calculated and observed values is merely fortuitous, yet the experiment shows that at most $1/20$ to $1/30$ of the very small extra-current from doubly wound spirals can owe its existence to a possible mass of the moving electricity; and the formula given above does in fact represent the induction of such a spiral to a high degree of accuracy.

I took it to be unnecessary to make further experiments with spirals; for even if the observations could be carried to a higher degree of accuracy, still it was impossible to calculate exactly the values of the inductances which entered into the experiments.

First Series of Experiments with Rectilinear Wires.

With a view to getting conditions of experiment more favourable in this respect, I attempted to measure the strength of the extra-current obtained from rectilinear double wires traversed in opposite directions, and to compare its value with theory.

For these experiments the bridge was arranged as follows. Three or four resistances, as before all equal, were made of thin German-silver wires. Two of these were formed exactly alike, so that the extra-currents from them neutralised each other. The third consisted of a wire folded back on itself, whose self-inductance was small and could be easily calculated; it was found to be $p = 13\cdot194$ mm. In opposition to this acted the fourth resistance of the bridge, the system of wires under observation. This was stretched out on the floor of the laboratory and connected by vertical wires with the experimental tables. In form it was a rectangle 7229 mm. long by 946 mm. wide. Its sides were formed of two parallel wires close together, each of which formed one branch of the system. A commutator enabled the currents to flow through them in the same or in opposite directions. The wire used was hard copper wire, its diameter was determined at several places by microscope and micrometer screw, and, with small deviations, was found in the mean = 0·4104 mm. To keep the distance between the two branches everywhere exactly the same, the wires were passed over wooden supports with nicks cut in them and fitting exactly. These supports were prepared by the aid of two brass stencil plates. The distance between the wires was measured on these latter by microscope and micrometer screw and thus found to be in the mean 2·628 mm. from centre to centre. The wires were covered throughout their length with a layer of cotton wool, so as to guard them from rapid temperature changes due to air-currents.

The inductance of the whole arrangement, which consisted partly of parallel, partly of perpendicular wires, could be easily calculated with accuracy by the formulæ already given. It was found that—

1. When the current flowed the same way through both branches

$$P' = 972,400 \text{ mm.};$$

2. When the currents flowed in opposite directions

$$P = 193,160 \text{ mm.}$$

Hence we find the ratio of the strengths of the extra-currents to be expected in the two cases

$$\frac{P' - p}{P - p} = 5·330.$$

In this calculation only the action of the commutator, of the movable arrangement used to adjust the bridge, and of the external circuit on the parts of the bridge has been neglected. These actions have only a very small effect, and the error caused by them certainly vanishes in comparison with the error due to the observations themselves.

The observations and calculations performed in the manner already explained gave the following results :—

1. BRANCHES TRAVERSED IN LIKE DIRECTIONS.

Primary Current in Scale Divisions of tangent Galvanometer.	Simple Extra-Current in Scale Divisions of Galvanometer.	Primary Current in Scale Divisions of tangent Galvanometer.	Simple Extra-Current in Scale Divisions of Galvanometer.
152·7	1·121	78·9	0·561
75·7	0·551	78·4	0·548
93·6	0·673	74·2	0·549
116·4	0·831	145·2	1·065
67·6	0·478	...	...

By reduction to a current of 100 scale divisions we get the values ·743, ·728, ·720, ·714, ·707, ·711, ·701, ·737, ·733. Mean = ·7213, with a mean error of 0·0137 or 1/50 of the whole value.

2. BRANCHES TRAVERSED OPPOSITELY.

Primary Current.	Extra-Current.	Primary Current.	Extra-Current.
152·7	0·2088	150·5	0·2025
152·7	0·2051	116·1	0·1443
140·1	0·1872	228·9	0·3992
139·0	0·1817	...	...

By reduction to a current 100 we get the values 0·1367, 0·1344, 0·1337, 0·1307, 0·1345, 0·1243, 0·1382.

The large deviation of the sixth observation from the others is evidently due to some special error, and it will be rejected. The others give the mean value 0·1348, with a mean error of 0·0028 or about 1/50 of the whole value. The ratio of the two extra-currents observed,

$$\frac{\cdot 7213}{\cdot 1348} = 5 \cdot 352,$$

differs from the calculated ratio 5·330 only by 1/250. The difference certainly is less than the unavoidable errors of observation.

It is to be remarked that in the above results all observations without exception have been included.

Second Series of Experiments with Rectilinear Wires.

A second series of observations with rectilinear wires was made, which differed from the preceding one only in that the German-silver resistance A′B was replaced by a resistance of Bunsen gas carbon, and in that a thicker copper wire was chosen for the circuit giving the current. This change was intended to remove a danger to be apprehended in the preceding experiment, viz. that the small changes of temperature attending the reversal itself might produce an apparent alteration in the strength of the extra-current, and so might hide any deviation of it from the induction law. In order to render these and similar disturbances observable, the experiments were made with as many different values as possible of the primary current. The deviations of the integral flow of the extra-currents from proportionality to the strength of the primary necessarily had their origin in such disturbances.

The diameter of the wire used was 0·6482 mm.; the distance between the two branches was 3·441 mm. The inductances were calculated exactly as above, and were found to be

$$P' = 920{,}956 \text{ mm.}, \quad P = 185{,}282 \text{ mm.}$$

The self-inductance of the opposing carbon resistance was

$$P = 2997 \text{ mm.},$$

and hence the calculated ratio of the extra-currents was

$$\frac{P' - p}{P - p} = 5 \cdot 0367$$

The experiments gave the following results :—

No.	Primary Current.	Extra-Current.		Reduced to Strength 100.	
		Branches Opposed.	Branches Like.	Branches Opposed.	Branches Like.
1	11·3	0·0275	0·1225	0·2434	1·084
2	17·2	0·0492	0·1940	0·2860	1·127
3	18·8	0·0478	0·2082	0·2542	1·107
4	20·9	0·0582	0·2430	0·2784	1·162
5	24·1	0·0628	0·2775	0·2606	1·152
6	27·7	0·0700	0·3235	0·2527	1·167
7	33·3	0·0857	0·3792	0·2537	1·138
8	37·2	0·0957	0·4015	0·2572	1·080
9	47·7	0·1057	0·5243	0·2216	1·099
10	57·8	0·1330	...	0·2301	...
11	66·2	0·1478	0·7357	0·2234	1·112
12	72·7	0·1555	...	0·2139	...
13	88·7	0·2135	...	0·2135	...
14	108·6	0·2432	...	0·2240	...
15	128·7	0·2945	1·1425	0·2158	1·051
16	141·3	0·3005	1·1825	0·2128	1·049
17	172·6	0·3872	...	0·2276	...
18	192·1	0·4105	...	0·2138	...

We get the mean value of the extra-current from branches traversed in like directions and with strength 100 to be 1·111, with a mean error of 0·038. From this and the calculated value of the ratio we get for the extra-current from branches oppositely traversed the value 0·2203. If we compare this with the observed values we see that the observed values for very weak currents are very much larger; and the mean of all the observations, viz. 0·2379, differs considerably from the calculated value. At the same time we easily see that this difference in no wise justifies us in drawing any inference as to mass; for it only occurs in the case of those observations which were already uncertain because of the smallness of the effects, and which agree only badly amongst themselves. If we use only the better part of the experiments from No. 8 onwards we get for the extra-current from oppositely traversed branches the mean value 0·2197, with a mean error 0·0060, and for the ratio of the two extra-currents the value 5·054, a value which differs from 5·037, the calculated one, by a quantity much less than the unavoidable errors of experiment. The deviation of the values observed for smaller strengths may easily and in various ways be reduced to thermal, magnetic, or diamagnetic causes, whose effect does not increase in proportion to the current, but quickly reaches a maximum.

RECAPITULATION OF RESULTS AND INFERENCES.

We shall shortly recapitulate the results in order to deduce from the experiments an upper limit to the quantity μ, the meaning of which was explained in the introduction.

We start from the formulæ

$$m = \mathrm{P}\left(\frac{\mathrm{J\,P'}}{\mathrm{J'P}} - 1\right), \qquad \mu = \frac{qm}{2l}.$$

The quantities occurring here in the various experiments had the following values :—

1. In the experiments with spirals we had

$$l = 130,032, \qquad \mathrm{P'} = 37,840,000,$$
$$q = 0\text{·}6793, \qquad \mathrm{J} = 1\text{·}1467,$$
$$\mathrm{P} = 178,500, \qquad \mathrm{J'} = 238\text{·}67.$$

The probable error of the various values cannot be stated exactly, as the corresponding measurements and the sources of error present were so various. Nevertheless it is certain that in none of the measurements was an error committed greater than 1/20 of the whole ; and the errors of the calculation, by which P was determined, cannot, according to what was said above, reach this amount. Hence, if we assume that the quantity JP'/J'P, which is compounded from the results, is in error by 1/20 of its value, in such a way as to hide any effect of mass perhaps present, we shall obtain a limit which is most unlikely to be exceeded, namely,

$$m < 178,500\left(\frac{\mathrm{J\,P'}}{\mathrm{J'P}} \cdot \tfrac{21}{20} - 1\right),^{1}$$

$$m < 13,356, \qquad \mu < 0\text{·}0348 \ \mathrm{mm}^2.$$

2. We obtain a smaller limit from the first series of experiments with rectilinear wires. Here we had

---

[1] [The fraction $\frac{\mathrm{P'}}{\mathrm{P}}$ is in the original replaced by $\frac{\mathrm{P'}}{2\mathrm{P}}$ since P' denotes a mutual inductance, and P there stands for a " potential on itself," which Hertz defines as half a self-inductance.—TR.]

$$l = 35{,}892, \quad P = 179{,}960, \quad J' = 0{\cdot}7213,$$

$$q = 0{\cdot}1323, \quad \frac{P'}{P} = 5{\cdot}330, \quad J = 0{\cdot}1348.$$

The calculated inductions may be regarded as exact, as their error can hardly amount to $1/100$. The probable errors for the quantities J and J′ may be deduced from the experiments, and are found to be

for J′ $= 0{\cdot}0092$,   for J $= 0{\cdot}0019$.

If we here assume that both strengths are measured wrongly to the full extent of the probable error, and both in the unfavourable sense, that is J too small, J′ too large, we get

$$m < 179{\cdot}960 \left(5{\cdot}330 \cdot \frac{0{\cdot}1367}{0{\cdot}7121} - 1\right),$$

$$m < 4190, \quad \mu < 0{\cdot}0077 \text{ mm}^2.$$

3. In the second series of experiments with rectilinear wires we had

$$l = 35{,}892, \quad P = 185{,}240, \quad J' = 1{\cdot}111,$$

$$q = 0{\cdot}3300, \quad \frac{P'}{P} = 5{\cdot}0367, \quad J = 0{\cdot}2196.$$

In determining J only experiments from No. 8 onwards have been used. The probable errors resulting from the experiments are

for J′ $0{\cdot}026$,   for J $= 0{\cdot}0040$.

The same assumption as above gives here

$$m < 185{,}240 \left(5{\cdot}0367 \cdot \frac{0{\cdot}2236}{1{\cdot}085} - 1\right),$$

$$m < 7042, \quad \mu < 0{\cdot}0323 \text{ mm}^2.$$

The limit here is not so close as in the preceding experiments, chiefly because there q, the cross-section of the wire, was less, and thus the conditions were more favourable for rendering prominent the effect of mass.

Hence, using the first series of experiments with rectilinear wires as being the best, we obtain this result :—

The kinetic energy of the electric flow in one cubic millimetre of a copper wire, which is traversed by a current of
density equal to 1 electromagnetic unit, amounts to less than

$$0 \cdot 008 \text{ milligramme-millimetre.}$$

As the kinetic energy is half the product of the mass by
the square of the velocity, the mass of the positive electricity
in 1 cubic millimetre

$$< \frac{0 \cdot 008 \text{ mg}}{v^2},$$

e.g. if $v = 1 \dfrac{\text{mm}}{\text{sec}}, \quad 10 \dfrac{\text{mm}}{\text{sec}}, \ldots$ the mass of positive electricity
$< 0 \cdot 008$ mg., $< \cdot 00008$ mg., etc.

But we must bear in mind the possibility of the kinetic
energy of the current exceeding the limit here marked out,
without the observations necessarily being erroneous on that
account.   For if the conductivity of the metals is in the ratio
of the densities of the electricity in them, then the electromotive forces arising from inertia will be equal in two wires
of equal resistance, whatever be the material, length, and cross-
section of the wires.   In this case the extra-currents from
the four branches of the bridge, in so far as they were due to
mass, would also be equal, and would thus neutralise each
other.   It is only on the assumption that the above proportionality does not exist, but that the density of electricity is
approximately the same in different conductors, that it is
allowable to neglect, as we have done, the effect of the mass
moved in the short branches of German-silver and of gas-
carbon.

Vice versa, if by some other method we succeeded in proving that the kinetic energy of the electric current exceeds the
limit stated, the above experiments would show that the
densities of electricity in the materials used are in the ratio
of their conductivities.

A decision as to the possibility mentioned could theoretically be obtained by dynamometric experiments, or by
observing the values at different times of induction and extra-
currents; but in practice all the arrangements of experiment

I have been able to find out only offer a hope of success if the inert mass exceeds the limit here determined many thousand times.

In conclusion, excluding the assumption last discussed, I shall introduce the limit found for the quantity μ into the calculations which have been developed by Helmholtz in vol. lxxii. of Borchardt's *Journal*.[1] It is there shown, on certain definite assumptions there stated, including the truth of Weber's law, that in a conducting sphere of radius R certain types of currents, of given order a, become unstable when in our notation [2]

$$ R < a\sqrt{\frac{\mu\pi}{2}} . $$

From this and from the limit found for μ, viz. $\mu = 0\cdot008$ mm., it follows that on the assumptions made, the first, the fundamental, type-current would become unstable in a sphere of $0\cdot11$ mm. radius, and that in a sphere of 1 cm. radius the first 90 component currents, almost the whole current, might increase indefinitely.

EXTRA-CURRENTS IN IRON WIRES.

If the wire conveying the current be capable of being magnetically polarised, this circumstance will lead to an increase of the self-induction like that due to any existing inert mass of electricity; hence the magnitude of the capacity for polarisation may be determined by the method we have employed in attempting to discover the existence of electric inertia.

I have made several experiments with iron wires, partly to convince myself of the applicability of the method for this purpose, partly to obtain an estimate as to how far magnetic properties in other metals might give rise to disturbances. In these the resistance of the bridge under examination consisted of a soft iron wire $0\cdot66$ mm. in diameter and $14,070$ mm. in total length. This, like the copper wire previously used,

---

[1] H. Helmholtz, *Wiss. Abhandl.* vol. i. p. 589.
[2] Our quantity μ is expressed by $\mu/2A^2$ in the notation there used.

consisted of two branches which could be connected up in two
different ways. The wire was again rectangular in form, so
that the self-inductance could be exactly calculated for both
arrangements. From the extra-currents obtained with these
two self-inductances it should be possible to calculate the
increase of self-induction due to magnetisation ; in practice
this was found to be inadvisable, for the effect of magnetisation was not small but very large compared with the purely
inductive effect. Hence the iron wire was replaced by a
branch of one of the above-mentioned spirals with the necessary ballast resistance, and the extra-current produced by
this known inductance was compared with that from the iron
wire.

The observations were made by the method above described :
their details are of no interest, but they supply the data from
which the magnetic forces acting in the iron wire and the
polarisations attained may be determined in absolute measure.
The results are given in the small table which follows. The
first column gives in absolute measure the values of the
magnetising force K at the surface of the cylindrical wire
(whence it diminishes towards the axis in proportion to the
distance from the axis). The second column gives the values
of θ, the so-called constant of polarisation, calculated from the
corresponding observations.

K	θ	K	θ
0·96	8·12	1·98	8·83
1·17	8·42	2·94	9·67
1·47	9·02	3·12	9·67
1·62	8·92	3·99	9·96
1·74	8·65	7·20	11·60

These values of K and θ can of course be only roughly
considered as corresponding values. Apart from several irregularities, we see that θ increases with K within the limits
given, a phenomenon which has already been frequently observed under different circumstances. It was impossible to
extend the observations to stronger currents, owing to the considerable generation of heat in the iron wire.

ON INDUCTION IN ROTATING SPHERES

(*Inaugural Dissertation*, Berlin, 15th March 1880.)

THE interactions between magnets and rotating masses of metals discovered by Arago were first explained by Faraday as phenomena of electromagnetic attraction, and attributed to currents induced by the magnets in the masses of metal. Faraday succeeded in demonstrating the existence of such currents, and in placing the inductive nature of the phenomenon beyond doubt.

In 1853 Felici made the first attempt to apply the theory since developed to some phenomena of this class. He succeeded under simplified conditions in obtaining approximate solutions agreeing with experiment sufficiently for a first approximation.

Great progress was made in 1864 by Jochmann. Starting from Weber's laws he deduced the complete differential equations of the problem, and integrated them for the case when the rotating body is an infinitely extended plane plate or a sphere. His calculations agreed most beautifully with the observations. But he had to make the assumption, for purposes of simplification, that the velocity of rotation was very small, for he was unable to determine the effect of self-induction.

Finally, in 1872 Maxwell gave a very elegant exposition of the theory of the induction in an infinitely extended very thin plate, and showed how it could be applied to the case of Arago's disc.

In the present paper the problem is completely solved for

the case when the body considered is a solid or hollow sphere rotating about a diameter. The inducing magnets may be outside, or in the case of the hollow sphere in the inside space. The solution is also extended to the case where the material of the sphere is capable of magnetisation. Clearly this problem involves those previously solved as special cases.

I have attempted to exhibit the results obtained by means of several drawings.

§ 1. DEFINITION OF THE SYMBOLS.

In this paragraph the symbols to be employed will be defined and some formulæ will be collected together which will be constantly required in the sequel.

Coordinates. 1. The system of coordinates selected is that shown in Fig. 6. The positive directions of rotation are marked in the figure. The axis of z will be taken to coincide with the axis of rotation. Polar coordinates ρ, ω, θ will be used: ω is to correspond to geographical longitude, is to be 0 in the zx-plane for positive x, and is to increase in the direction of positive rotation; θ is to correspond to the complement of the geographical latitude, and is to

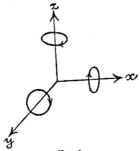

FIG. 6.

be 0 in the positive z-axis. We shall occasionally use the notation

$$x\frac{\partial}{\partial y} - y\frac{\partial}{\partial x} = \frac{\partial}{\partial \omega_z} = \frac{\partial}{\partial \omega},$$

$$z\frac{\partial}{\partial x} - x\frac{\partial}{\partial z} = \frac{\partial}{\partial \omega_y},$$

$$y\frac{\partial}{\partial z} - z\frac{\partial}{\partial y} = \frac{\partial}{\partial \omega_x}.$$

Further, as in Lagrange's notation, differentiation with respect to ω will be denoted by a dash, e.g.

$$\frac{\partial \chi}{\partial \omega} = \chi'.$$

2. The calculations will be carried out in electromagnetic Definition units. In other respects the symbols for electrical magnitudes of the elect-rical quan- will be those used by Helmholtz in vol. lxxvii. of Borchardt's tities. *Journal.*[1]   That is,

$$u,\ v,\ w\frac{\mathrm{mgr}^{\frac{1}{2}}}{\mathrm{mm}^{\frac{3}{2}}\,\mathrm{sec}}$$

are the densities of the current parallel to $x,\ y,\ z$;

$$U,\ V,\ W\frac{\mathrm{mm}^{\frac{1}{2}}\,\mathrm{mgr}^{\frac{1}{2}}}{\mathrm{sec}}$$

are the corresponding components of the vector-potential;

$$\phi\frac{\mathrm{mm}^{\frac{1}{2}}\,\mathrm{mgr}^{\frac{1}{2}}}{\mathrm{sec}}$$

is the potential of free electricity;[2]

$$\kappa\frac{\mathrm{mm}^2}{\mathrm{sec}}$$

is the specific resistance of the material.   The specific resistance of a sheet of infinitesimal thickness δ, viz. $\frac{\kappa}{\delta}$, will, when considered finite, be denoted by

$$k\frac{\mathrm{mm}}{\mathrm{sec}}.$$

Further, let

$$\lambda,\ \mu,\ \nu\frac{\mathrm{mgr}^{\frac{1}{2}}}{\mathrm{mm}^{\frac{1}{2}}\,\mathrm{sec}}$$

be the components of a magnetisation; let

$$L,\ M,\ N\frac{\mathrm{mgr}^{\frac{1}{2}}\,\mathrm{mm}^{\frac{1}{2}}}{\mathrm{sec}}$$

be the potentials of $\lambda,\ \mu,\ \nu$, taken as masses,

$$\theta(0)$$

[1] H. Helmholtz, *Wiss. Abhandl.* vol. i. p. 545.
[2] This is not electromagnetic measure. Measured in the latter units the potential of free electricity is $\phi_m = \phi \mathrm{A}^2$, where $1/\mathrm{A}$ denotes the velocity of light. The above unit avoids the inconvenient factor $1/\mathrm{A}^2$.

be the magnetic permeability, and

$$\chi \frac{\mathrm{mm}^{\frac{1}{2}}\,\mathrm{mgr}^{\frac{1}{2}}}{\sec}$$

the magnetic potential, so far as it is directly due to magnets; the magnetic potential of the currents is to be

$$\Omega \frac{\mathrm{mm}^{\frac{1}{2}}\,\mathrm{mgr}^{\frac{1}{2}}}{\sec}.$$

Ω has no meaning inside the matter of the hollow sphere, and therefore cannot be analytically continued through it, and is one-valued in external and internal space.

We shall denote by

$$\psi \frac{\mathrm{mm}^{\frac{1}{2}}\,\mathrm{mgr}^{\frac{1}{2}}}{\sec}$$

the current function in an infinitely thin spherical shell. To avoid all doubt as to sign we give this as the definition of ψ: when on traversing the space ds ψ increases by $d\psi$, then $d\psi$ is the quantity of electricity which in unit time crosses the element traversed from left to right. In traversing the path the feet are supposed directed to the centre of the shell, the face forwards in the direction of motion.

Since in what follows we shall only deal with currents in concentric spherical shells about the origin, we define

$$\psi \frac{\mathrm{mgr}^{\frac{1}{2}}}{\mathrm{mm}^{\frac{1}{2}}\,\sec}$$

more generally as a function of ρ, θ, ω such that

$$da \cdot \psi_{(\rho=a)}$$

denotes the current-function of the layer between $\rho = a$ and $\rho = a + da$.

For convenience the units have been given along with the magnitudes quoted.

Dimensions of the sphere considered. 3. Let the external radius of the spherical shell considered be R, its internal radius r, the angular velocity of rotation ω.

Development in spherical harmonics. 4. When a function χ, which throughout any given space satisfies the equation $\nabla^2\chi = 0$,[1] is developed in a series of spher-

---

[1] [In the original Δ is used where we use ∇^2.—Tr.]

ical harmonics, then χ_n is to denote the term involving ρ^n as a factor, and this notation is, unless specially excepted, to apply to n negative.

In the further analysis of χ_n let this notation be used :—
for positive n

$$\chi_n = \rho^n Y_n,$$

for negative n

$$\chi_n = \rho^n Y_{-n-1},$$

$$Y_n = \Sigma_i^n (A_{ni} \cos i\omega + B_{ni} \sin i\omega) P_{ni}(\theta);$$

for every n these equations hold :—

$$\nabla^2 \chi_n = 0,$$

$$x\frac{\partial \chi_n}{\partial x} + y\frac{\partial \chi_n}{\partial y} + z\frac{\partial \chi_n}{\partial z} = n\chi_n.$$

The mth differential coefficients with regard to x, y, z of χ_n are spherical harmonics of order $n - m$, unless a preceding one should be of order zero. The expressions

$$\frac{\partial \chi_n}{\partial \omega_x}, \quad \frac{\partial \chi_n}{\partial \omega_y}, \quad \frac{\partial \chi_n}{\partial \omega_z}$$

are spherical harmonics of order n.

Further

$$\nabla^2(\rho^m Y_n) = (m-n)(m+n+1)\rho^{m-2} Y_n,$$

$$x\frac{\partial(\rho^m Y_n)}{\partial x} + y\frac{\partial(\rho^m Y_n)}{\partial y} + z\frac{\partial(\rho^m Y_n)}{\partial z} = m\rho^m Y_n,$$

$$\frac{\partial(\rho^m Y_n)}{\partial \rho} = \frac{m}{\rho}(\rho^m Y_n).$$

5. Let ψ be the current-function of a spherical shell of radius R, and let $\Psi = \int \frac{\psi ds}{r}$ be the potential of a mass of matter distribnted over the shell with density ψ; then the potential of the current sheet is

$$\Omega = -\frac{1}{R}\frac{\partial}{\partial \rho}(\Psi\rho),$$

and the quantities U, V, W are

$$U = \frac{y}{R}\frac{\partial\Psi}{\partial z} - \frac{z}{R}\frac{\partial\Psi}{\partial y} = \frac{1}{R}\frac{\partial\Psi}{\partial\omega_x},$$

$$V = \frac{z}{R}\frac{\partial\Psi}{\partial x} - \frac{x}{R}\frac{\partial\Psi}{\partial z} = \frac{1}{R}\frac{\partial\Psi}{\partial\omega_y},$$

$$W = \frac{x}{R}\frac{\partial\Psi}{\partial y} - \frac{y}{R}\frac{\partial\Psi}{\partial x} = \frac{1}{R}\frac{\partial\Psi}{\partial\omega_z}.$$

If Ψ is a homogeneous function of x, y, z of the nth degree, then

$$\frac{\partial V}{\partial x} - \frac{\partial U}{\partial y} = -\frac{n+1}{R}\frac{\partial\Psi}{\partial z},$$

$$\frac{\partial U}{\partial z} - \frac{\partial W}{\partial x} = -\frac{n+1}{R}\frac{\partial\Psi}{\partial y},$$

$$\frac{\partial W}{\partial y} - \frac{\partial V}{\partial z} = -\frac{n+1}{R}\frac{\partial\Psi}{\partial x}.$$

And we have always

$$\frac{\partial V}{\partial x} - \frac{\partial U}{\partial y} = \frac{\partial\Omega}{dz},$$

$$\frac{\partial U}{\partial z} - \frac{\partial W}{\partial x} = \frac{\partial\Omega}{\partial y},$$

$$\frac{\partial W}{\partial y} - \frac{\partial V}{\partial z} = \frac{\partial\Omega}{\partial x}.$$

These formulæ are developed in Maxwell's *Treatise on Electricity*, vol. ii. p. 276.[1] The signs in part are different, because the system of coordinates there employed is not ours, but a symmetrical one. The system used here is that to which Helmholtz's formulæ apply.

Formulæ for the electromotive-forces.

6. The following are the expressions for the electromotive forces which are produced by the components U, V, W of the vector potential, supposed invariable, due to the element whose component velocities are a, β, γ :—

$$\mathfrak{X} = \beta\left(\frac{\partial V}{\partial x} - \frac{\partial U}{\partial y}\right) - \gamma\left(\frac{\partial U}{\partial z} - \frac{\partial W}{\partial x}\right),$$

[1] 2nd ed. p. 280.

$$\mathfrak{Y} = \gamma\left(\frac{\partial W}{\partial y} - \frac{\partial V}{\partial z}\right) - a\left(\frac{\partial V}{\partial x} - \frac{\partial U}{\partial y}\right),$$

$$\mathfrak{Z} = a\left(\frac{\partial U}{\partial z} - \frac{\partial W}{\partial x}\right) - \beta\left(\frac{\partial W}{\partial y} - \frac{\partial V}{\partial z}\right).$$

These are the expressions given by Jochmann. The change produced in the results by the formulæ of the dynamical theory will be discussed in § 8.

If, in addition to the currents u, v, w, there are components of magnetisation λ, μ, ν, then in this part of the induction in the above formulæ we must replace

$$U, V, W \text{ by } \frac{\partial M}{\partial z} - \frac{\partial N}{\partial y}, \quad \frac{\partial N}{\partial x} - \frac{\partial L}{\partial z}, \quad \frac{\partial L}{\partial y} - \frac{\partial M}{\partial x}.$$

The formulæ thus obtained still hold when the magnets are on the inside of the rotating mass. If the magnets are all outside, since inside the mass

$$\nabla^2 L = 0, \quad \nabla^2 M = 0, \quad \nabla^2 N = 0,$$

we have

$$\mathfrak{X} = \beta\frac{\partial \chi}{\partial z} - \gamma\frac{\partial \chi}{\partial y},$$

$$\mathfrak{Y} = \gamma\frac{\partial \chi}{\partial x} - a\frac{\partial \chi}{\partial z},$$

$$\mathfrak{Z} = a\frac{\partial \chi}{\partial y} - \beta\frac{\partial \chi}{\partial x}.$$

And for the elements of our sphere

$$a = -\omega y, \quad \beta = \omega x, \quad \gamma = 0.$$

§ 2. SOLUTION NEGLECTING SELF-INDUCTION.

In this paragraph the problem will be solved in the case where the effect of self-induction may be neglected. For the components of current u, v, w these equations hold :—

$$\kappa u = -\frac{\partial \phi}{\partial x} + \mathfrak{X},^1$$

$$\kappa v = -\frac{\partial \phi}{\partial y} + \mathfrak{Y},$$

$$\kappa w = -\frac{\partial \phi}{\partial z} + \mathfrak{Z};$$

further, since the currents are steady, we have inside

$$\frac{\partial u}{\partial x} + \frac{\partial v}{\partial y} + \frac{\partial w}{\partial z} = 0,$$

and for $\rho = R$ and $\rho = r$,

$$ux + vy + wz = 0.$$

Hence we have these conditions for ϕ:—
inside,

$$\nabla^2 \phi = \frac{\partial \mathfrak{X}}{\partial x} + \frac{\partial \mathfrak{Y}}{\partial y} + \frac{\partial \mathfrak{Z}}{\partial z},$$

and at the surface,

$$\rho \frac{\partial \phi}{\partial \rho} = x\mathfrak{X} + y\mathfrak{Y} + z\mathfrak{Z},$$

which determine ϕ, with one additive constant arbitrary.

The potential of the magnets in internal and external space we assume to be developed in the series of spherical harmonics

$$\chi = \sum_{-\infty}^{+\infty} {}_n\chi_n .$$

We take each term by itself and thus put the external potential $= \chi_n$.

Then we have

$$\mathfrak{X} = \omega x \frac{\partial \chi_n}{\partial z},$$

$$\mathfrak{Y} = \omega y \frac{\partial \chi_n}{\partial z},$$

$$\mathfrak{Z} = -\omega y \frac{\partial \chi_n}{\partial y} - \omega x \frac{\partial \chi_n}{\partial x} = \omega z \frac{\partial \chi_n}{\partial z} - \omega n \chi_n.$$

---

[1] Using the unit previously employed for ϕ.

Hence these conditions follow for ϕ :—

In the matter of the shell

(a)
$$\nabla^2 \phi = 2\omega \frac{\partial \chi_n}{\partial z} ;$$

for $\rho = r$ and $\rho = R$

(b)
$$\frac{\partial \phi}{\partial \rho} = \frac{\omega}{\rho}\left(\rho^2 \frac{\partial \chi_n}{\partial z} - nz\chi_n \right).$$

A solution of these equations is

$$\phi = \frac{\omega}{n+1}\left(\rho^2 \frac{\partial \chi_n}{\partial z} - nz\chi_n \right).$$

For

$$\nabla^2 \left(\rho^2 \frac{\partial \chi_n}{\partial z} - nz\chi_n \right).$$

$$= 2(2n+1)\frac{\partial \chi_n}{\partial z} - 2n\frac{\partial \chi_n}{\partial z} \qquad (\S 1, 4)$$

$$= 2(n+1)\frac{\partial \chi_n}{\partial z},$$

so that the equation for the interior is satisfied. Further, ϕ is the product of ρ^{n+1} by a function of the angles θ and ω, whence it follows that ϕ satisfies the boundary conditions.

The value of the constant which must be added to the above expression to give the general solution depends in each case on the electrostatic influences to which the shell is subject. We may in any case charge the sphere with so much free electricity as will just make the constant zero, and this we shall in the sequel suppose to have been done.

From ϕ we get at once

$$u = \frac{\omega}{\kappa}\left\{ -\frac{1}{n+1}\frac{\partial}{\partial x}\left(\rho^2 \frac{\partial \chi_n}{\partial z} - nz\chi_n \right) + x\frac{\partial \chi_n}{\partial z} \right\},$$

$$v = \frac{\omega}{\kappa}\left\{ -\frac{1}{n+1}\frac{\partial}{\partial y}\left(\rho^2 \frac{\partial \chi_n}{\partial z} - nz\chi_n \right) + y\frac{\partial \chi_n}{\partial z} \right\},$$

$$w = \frac{\omega}{\kappa}\left\{ -\frac{1}{n+1}\frac{\partial}{\partial z}\left(\rho^2 \frac{\partial \chi_n}{\partial z} - nz\chi_n \right) + z\frac{\partial \chi_n}{\partial z} - n\chi_n \right\}.$$

If we multiply these equations by x, y, z and add we get

$$ux + vy + wz = 0 \, .$$

Thus the current is everywhere perpendicular to the radius and flows in concentric spherical shells about the origin. This is a consequence of the fact that equation (b) is satisfied throughout the mass and not merely at its surfaces.

Further we find

$$\nabla^2 u = \frac{\omega}{\kappa}\left\{ -2\frac{\partial^2 \chi_n}{\partial x \partial z} + 2\frac{\partial^2 \chi_n}{\partial x \partial z} \right\} = 0.$$

$$\nabla^2 v = 0,$$

$$\nabla^2 w = 0, \text{ since also } \nabla^2 \chi_n = 0.$$

In fact u, v, w are homogeneous functions of x, y, z of the nth degree; thus u, v, w are exhibited as spherical harmonics of the nth order. We shall soon find simpler expressions for u, v, w.

Determination of the function Ψ. Since the currents are similar in concentric spherical shells, they are also similar to those which occur in an infinitely thin spherical shell; therefore we first consider such a shell and determine the values of the integrals U, V, W for internal space when n is positive, for external space when n is negative. We shall only work through the first case. κ we replace by k. For U, V, W the conditions hold

$$\nabla^2 U = 0, \quad \nabla^2 V = 0, \quad \nabla^2 W = 0$$

throughout space. At the surface of the shell

$$\frac{\partial U_e}{\partial \rho} - \frac{\partial U_i}{\partial \rho} = -4\pi u \, ,$$

and corresponding equations for V and W; and in addition we have the usual conditions of continuity. All these conditions are satisfied by putting

$$U_i = \frac{4\pi \mathrm{R}}{2n+1}\frac{\omega}{k}\left\{ -\frac{1}{n+1}\frac{\partial}{\partial x}\left(\rho^2\frac{\partial \chi_n}{\partial z} - nz\chi_n\right) + x\frac{\partial \chi_n}{\partial z} \right\}^1$$

$$V_i = \frac{4\pi \mathrm{R}}{2n+1}\frac{\omega}{k}\left\{ -\frac{1}{n+1}\frac{\partial}{\partial y}\left(\rho^2\frac{\partial \chi_n}{\partial z} - nz\chi_n\right) + y\frac{\partial \chi_n}{\partial z} \right\},$$

$$W_i = \frac{4\pi \mathrm{R}}{2n+1}\frac{\omega}{k}\left\{ -\frac{1}{n+1}\frac{\partial}{\partial z}\left(\rho^2\frac{\partial \chi_n}{\partial z} - nz\chi_n\right) + z\frac{\partial \chi_n}{\partial z} - nz\chi_n \right\},$$

[1 U_i, U_e denote respectively U internal, U external.—Tr.]

$$U_e(\rho) = \left(\frac{R}{\rho}\right)^{2n+1} U_i(\rho),$$

$$V_e(\rho) = \left(\frac{R}{\rho}\right)^{2n+1} V_i(\rho),$$

$$W_e(\rho) = \left(\frac{R}{\rho}\right)^{2n+1} W_i(\rho),$$

From these values of U, V, W we calculate the magnetising forces inside, viz:

$$\frac{\partial V}{\partial x} - \frac{\partial U}{\partial y}, \text{ etc.}$$

we put them

$$= -\frac{n+1}{R}\frac{\partial \Psi}{\partial z}, \text{ etc.,}$$

and so obtain the function Ψ (§ 1, 5). We find

$$-\frac{4\pi R}{2n+1}\frac{\omega}{k}\frac{\partial}{\partial z}\left(x\frac{\partial \chi_n}{\partial y} - y\frac{\partial \chi_n}{\partial x}\right) = -\frac{n+1}{R}\frac{\partial}{\partial z}\Psi_i,$$

$$-\frac{4\pi R}{2n+1}\frac{\omega}{k}\frac{\partial}{\partial x}\left(x\frac{\partial \chi_n}{\partial y} - y\frac{\partial \chi_n}{\partial x}\right) = -\frac{n+1}{R}\frac{\partial}{\partial x}\Psi_i,$$

$$-\frac{4\pi R}{2n+1}\frac{\omega}{k}\frac{\partial}{\partial y}\left(x\frac{\partial \chi_n}{\partial y} - y\frac{\partial \chi_n}{\partial x}\right) = -\frac{n+1}{R}\frac{\partial}{\partial y}\Psi_i,$$

whence

$$\Psi_i = \frac{4\pi R^2}{(2n+1)(n+1)}\frac{\omega}{k}\left(x\frac{\partial \chi_n}{\partial y} - y\frac{\partial \chi_n}{\partial x}\right)$$

$$= \frac{4\pi R^2}{(2n+1)(n+1)}\frac{\omega}{k}\chi'_n,$$

and now all the remaining properties of the currents follow at once from Ψ. An arbitrary constant may be added to Ψ, but is of no importance.

We thus obtain the solution of our problem for a spherical shell in the following form (§ 1, 5):— Summary
of formulæ.

Let

$$\chi_n = \left(\frac{\rho}{R}\right)^n Y_n, \quad n > 0,$$

be the inducing potential, then

$$\Psi_i = \frac{4\pi R^2}{(2n+1)(n+1)} \frac{\omega}{k}\left(\frac{\rho}{R}\right)^n Y'_n,$$

$$\Psi_e = \frac{4\pi R^2}{(2n+1)(n+1)} \frac{\omega}{k}\left(\frac{R}{\rho}\right)^{n+1} Y'_n,$$

$$\psi = \frac{\omega}{k} \frac{R}{n+1} Y'_n,$$

$$\Omega_i = - \frac{4\pi R}{2n+1} \frac{\omega}{k}\left(\frac{\rho}{R}\right)^n Y_n',$$

$$\Omega_e = \frac{4\pi R n}{(2n+1)(n+1)} \frac{\omega}{k}\left(\frac{R}{\rho}\right)^{n+1} Y'_n .$$

Again, from the relations

$$U = \frac{1}{R} \frac{\partial}{\partial \omega_x} \Psi, \qquad \frac{\partial U_e}{\partial \rho} - \frac{\partial U_i}{\partial \rho} = - 4\pi u ,$$

and the corresponding ones for V and W, we find

$$u = \frac{1}{R} \frac{\partial \psi}{\partial \omega_x} = \frac{1}{n+1} \frac{\omega}{k} \frac{\partial Y'_n}{\partial \omega_x} ,$$

$$v = \frac{1}{R} \frac{\partial \psi}{\partial \omega_y} = \frac{1}{n+1} \frac{\omega}{k} \frac{\partial Y'_n}{\partial \omega_y} ,$$

$$w = \frac{1}{R} \frac{\partial \psi}{\partial \omega_z} = \frac{1}{n+1} \frac{\omega}{k} \frac{\partial Y'_n}{\partial \omega_z} .$$

Lastly, the expression for the electric potential in the material of the spherical shell may be transformed. Write for the moment $\rho' = \rho \sin \theta$, then

$$\phi = \frac{\omega}{n+1}\left(\rho^2 \frac{\partial \chi_n}{\partial z} - nz\chi_n \right)$$

$$= - \frac{\omega}{n+1} \rho \sin \theta \frac{\partial \chi_n}{\partial \theta} ,$$

and at the surface of the shell

$$\overline{\phi} = - \frac{\omega R}{n+1} \sin \theta \frac{\partial Y_n}{\partial \theta} .$$

Similar calculations may be performed for the case of n negative, where the inducing magnets are inside. They lead to this result :—

If the inducing potential is

$$\chi_n = \left(\frac{R}{\rho}\right)^{n+1} Y'_n ,$$

then

$$\Psi_i = -\frac{4\pi R^2}{(2n+1)n} \frac{\omega}{k} \left(\frac{\rho}{R}\right)^n Y'_n ,$$

$$\Psi_e = -\frac{4\pi R^2}{(2n+1)n} \frac{\omega}{k} \left(\frac{R}{\rho}\right)^{n+1} Y'_n ,$$

$$\Omega_i = \frac{4\pi R(n+1)}{(2n+1)n} \frac{\omega}{k} \left(\frac{\rho}{R}\right)^n Y'_n ,$$

$$\Omega_e = -\frac{4\pi R}{2n+1} \frac{\omega}{k} \left(\frac{R}{\rho}\right)^{n+1} Y'_n ,$$

$$\psi = -\frac{\omega}{k} \frac{R}{n} Y'_n ,$$

$$u = -\frac{1}{n} \frac{\omega}{k} \frac{\partial Y'_n}{\partial \omega_x} ,$$

$$v = -\frac{1}{n} \frac{\omega}{k} \frac{\partial Y'_n}{\partial \omega_y} ,$$

$$w = -\frac{1}{n} \frac{\omega}{k} \frac{\partial Y'_n}{\partial \omega_z} ,$$

$$\bar{\phi} = \frac{\omega}{n} R \sin\theta \frac{\partial Y_n}{\partial \theta} .$$

Of the magnitudes here given, ψ, u, v, w, ϕ are got from their preceding values at once by interchanging n with $-n-1$.

On the solution obtained I make the following remarks :—

1. When a spherical shell of finite thickness rotates under the influence of the potential χ_n (n positive or negative), the induced currents are

$$u = \frac{1}{n+1} \cdot \frac{\omega}{\kappa} \cdot \frac{\partial \chi'_n}{\partial \omega_x},$$

$$v = \frac{1}{n+1} \cdot \frac{\omega}{\kappa} \cdot \frac{\partial \chi'_n}{\partial \omega_y},$$

$$w = \frac{1}{n+1} \cdot \frac{\omega}{\kappa} \cdot \frac{\partial \chi'_n}{\partial \omega_z},$$

and the current-function is

$$\psi = \frac{\rho}{n+1} \cdot \frac{\omega}{\kappa} \cdot \chi'_n.$$

Construction of the lines of flow.

2. We analyse χ_n further and consider the term

$$\chi_{ni} = A_{ni} \left(\frac{\rho}{R} \right)^n \cos i\omega P_{ni}.$$

To this belongs the current-function

$$\psi_{ni} = - \frac{\rho}{n+1} \frac{\omega i}{\kappa} A_{ni} \left(\frac{\rho}{R} \right)^n \sin i\omega P_{ni}.$$

Hence we get the following simple construction for the lines of flow due to such a simple potential:—

Construct on any spherical sheet the equipotential lines and turn the sheet through an angle $\pi/2i$; the lines now represent the lines of flow produced by that potential.

For instance, when the sphere is rotating under the action of a constant force perpendicular to the axis of rotation, the external potential satisfies the required conditions and we have $n = 1$, $i = 1$. The equipotential lines on the sphere are circles, and so also are the lines of flow. The planes of the former are parallel to the axis of rotation and perpendicular to the direction of the force, so that the planes of the latter are parallel both to the axis of rotation and the direction of the force.

Transformation of the solution.

3. We may give to ψ a form which permits of summation for all the spherical harmonics and makes the development of the external potential in a series of them unnecessary.

Let n be positive, then

$$\int_0^\rho \chi_n d\rho = \frac{\rho}{n+1} \chi_n.$$

Secondly, let n be negative, then

$$\int_\infty^\rho \chi_n d\rho = -\frac{\rho}{n}\chi_\nu .$$

Hence, for a positive n,

$$\psi = \frac{\omega}{\kappa}\int_0^\rho \frac{\partial \chi_n}{\partial \omega} d\rho ,$$

and for a negative n,

$$\psi = -\frac{\omega}{\kappa}\int_\rho^\infty \frac{\partial \chi_n}{\partial \omega} d\rho .$$

Summation of spherical harmonics.

These expressions admit of summation at once, and we get the following second form for the solution :—

If χ_i denote the part of the potential due to internal, and χ_e the part due to external magnets, then

$$\psi = \frac{\omega}{\kappa}\frac{\partial}{\partial \omega}\left\{ \int_0^\rho \chi_e \cdot d\rho - \int_\rho^\infty \chi_i \cdot d\rho \right\}$$

Similarly

$$\phi = -\omega \sin \theta \frac{\partial}{\partial \theta}\left\{ \int_0^\rho \chi_e \cdot d\rho - \int_\rho^\infty \chi_i \cdot d\rho \right\} .$$

For an infinitely thin spherical shell of radius R

$$\psi = \frac{\omega}{\kappa}\left\{ \int_0^R \frac{\partial \chi_e}{\partial \omega} d\rho - \int_R^\infty \frac{\partial \chi_i}{\partial \omega} d\rho \right\} ,$$

$$\phi = -\omega \sin \theta \left\{ \int_0^R \frac{\partial \chi_e}{\partial \theta} d\rho - \int_R^\infty \frac{\partial \chi_i}{\partial \theta} d\rho \right\}$$

Hence we get this relation between ϕ and ψ

$$\frac{\partial \phi}{\partial \omega} + \kappa \sin \theta \frac{\partial \psi}{\partial \theta} = 0.$$

§ 3. COMPLETE SOLUTION FOR INFINITELY THIN SPHERICAL SHELLS.

We shall now take into account the effect of self-induction, but in this paragraph we shall confine our considerations to the case of infinitely thin shells. For simplicity n will be supposed positive in the calculations.

In accordance with usual views we regard the total induction as compounded of an infinite series of separate inductions; the current induced by the external magnets induces a second system of currents, this a third, and so on *ad infinitum*. We calculate all these currents and add them together to form a series which, so long as its sum converges to a finite limit, certainly represents the current actually produced.

Let

$$\chi_n = \left(\frac{\rho}{R}\right)^n Y_n$$

represent a part of the external potential. The potential induced by this part is

$$\Omega_i = -\frac{4\pi R}{2n+1}\frac{\omega}{k}\left(\frac{\rho}{R}\right)^n Y'_n,$$

$$\Omega_e = \frac{4\pi Rn}{(2n+1)(n+1)}\frac{\omega}{k}\left(\frac{R}{\rho}\right)^{n+1} Y'_n.$$

Calculation of the successive inductions. In the first place, if inside the spherical shell a second rotate infinitely close to the first and with the same velocity, the currents of the first order (Ω_i) will induce in it a current system whose internal magnetic potential is

$$\Omega'_i = \left(\frac{4\pi R}{2n+1}\frac{\omega}{k}\right)^2\left(\frac{\rho}{R}\right)^n Y''_n.$$

Secondly, if outside the first shell another rotate with the same velocity and infinitely close to the first, the currents of the first order (Ω_e) will induce in it a current system whose potential inside is

$$\Omega'_i = \frac{4\pi \mathrm{R}n}{(2n+1)(n+1)}\frac{\omega}{k} \cdot \frac{4\pi \mathrm{R}(n+1)}{(2n+1)n}\frac{\omega}{k}\left(\frac{\rho}{\mathrm{R}}\right)^n \mathrm{Y}''_n,$$

$$= \left(\frac{4\pi \mathrm{R}}{2n+1} \cdot \frac{\omega}{k}\right)^2 \left(\frac{\rho}{\mathrm{R}}\right)^n \mathrm{Y}''_n.$$

The two expressions for Ω'_i are the same. Hence this is the potential of the current system, which is induced in the spherical shell itself by the currents of the first order. If in the same way we calculate the succeeding inductions and add them together, we get for the whole inductive action

$$\Omega_i = \left(\frac{\rho}{\mathrm{R}}\right)^n \sum_1^{\infty} m\left(-\frac{4\pi \mathrm{R}\omega}{(2n+1)k}\right)^m \frac{\partial^m \mathrm{Y}_n}{\partial \omega^m},$$

$$\Omega_e = -\frac{n}{n+1}\left(\frac{\mathrm{R}}{\rho}\right)^{n+1} \sum_1^{\infty} m\left(-\frac{4\pi \mathrm{R}\omega}{(2n+1)k}\right)^m \frac{\partial^m \mathrm{Y}_n}{\partial \omega^m},$$

$$\psi = -\frac{2n+1}{4\pi(n+1)} \sum_1^{\infty} m\left(-\frac{4\pi \mathrm{R}\omega}{(2n+1)k}\right)^m \frac{\partial^m \mathrm{Y}_n}{\partial \omega^m}.$$

The expressions obtained may be developed still further by analysing Y_n further. We have

$$\mathrm{Y}_n = \sum_1^n i(\mathrm{A}_{ni}\cos i\omega + \mathrm{B}_{ni}\sin i\omega)\mathrm{P}_{ni}.$$

We confine ourselves to one term only of this series. Thus let

$$\mathrm{Y}_n = \mathrm{A}_{ni}\cos i\omega \mathrm{P}_{ni}.$$

Then we have

$$\Omega_i = \mathrm{A}_{ni}\left(\frac{\rho}{\mathrm{R}}\right)^n \mathrm{P}_{ni}\Bigg\{\frac{4\mathrm{R}\omega i}{(2n+1)k}\sin i\omega - \left(\frac{4\pi \mathrm{R}\omega i}{(2n+1)k}\right)^2 \cos i\omega$$

$$-\left(\frac{4\pi \mathrm{R}\omega i}{(2n+1)k}\right)^3 \sin i\omega + \left(\frac{4\pi \mathrm{R}\omega i}{(2n+1)k}\right)^4 \cos i\omega + \ . \ . \ \Bigg\}.$$

Put for shortness

$$\frac{4\pi \mathrm{R}\omega i}{(2n+1)k} = h \ (h \text{ is a pure number});$$

then we find

$$\Omega_i = \mathrm{A}_{ni}\left(\frac{\rho}{\mathrm{R}}\right)^n \mathrm{P}_{ni}(\sin i\omega - h\cos i\omega).h.(1 - h^2 + h^4 - h^6 + \ldots).$$

If h is a proper fraction, the series involved in Ω_i converges and we get

$$\Omega_i = A_{ni}\left(\frac{\rho}{R}\right)^n \frac{h}{1+h^2}(\sin i\omega - h\cos i\omega)P_{ni},$$

$$\Omega_e = -\frac{n}{n+1}A_{ni}\left(\frac{R}{\rho}\right)^{n+1}\frac{h}{1+h^2}(\sin i\omega - h\cos i\omega)P_{ni},$$

$$\psi = -\frac{2n+1}{4\pi(n+1)}A_{ni}\frac{h}{1+h^2}(\sin i\omega - h\cos i\omega)P_{ni}.$$

If $h > 1$,[1] the series occurring in Ω_i diverges and it is no longer allowable to regard the phenomenon as a series of successive inductions, since each one would be larger than the preceding one.

Nevertheless the formulæ given hold for every value of h, as we may easily verify *a posteriori*, and deduce by the same considerations that we shall have to employ in the case of spherical shells of finite thickness. Since I propose again to deduce the above formulæ from the general ones, I shall not now consider them further.

We write

$$h = \tan \delta,$$

and now

$$\Omega_i = A_{ni}\left(\frac{\rho}{R}\right)^n \sin \delta \sin (i\omega - \delta)P_{ni};$$

$$\Omega_e = -\frac{n}{n+1}A_{ni}\left(\frac{R}{\rho}\right)^{n+1} \cdot \sin \delta \sin (i\omega - \delta)P_{ni},$$

$$\psi = -\frac{2n+1}{4\pi(n+1)}A_{ni}\sin \delta \sin (i\omega - \delta)P_{ni}.$$

Hence the result is as follows :—

1. A simple spherical harmonic in the inducing potential induces a current-function which is a surface harmonic of its own type. Hence we may here also retain the construction previously given (§ 2, 2) for the lines of flow, but we must suppose the spherical layer considered to be turned through a certain angle δ/i in the direction of the rotation relative to the

---

[1] A copper spherical shell of 50 mm. radius and 2 mm. thickness would have to make about 87 revolutions per second in order that for $i=1$, $n=1$, h might be equal to 1. [? 62 revolutions per second.—Tr.]

position previously determined. For small velocities of rotation this angle is proportional to the velocity; for large ones
it approaches to the limit $\pi/2i$. The intensity, which at first
increases in proportion to the velocity of rotation, increases
more slowly for larger values and approaches a fixed limit.

2. Finally, when $\omega/k = \infty$, $\delta = \pi/2$, and then

The velocity is infinite

$$\Omega_i = -\chi_n,$$

$$\Omega_c = \frac{n}{n+1}\chi_n,$$

$$\psi = \frac{2n+1}{4\pi(n+1)}\chi_n.$$

This result does not hold for those terms of the development which are symmetrical about the axis of rotation. For
these i, and therefore also h and Ω, vanish for every velocity
of rotation. These terms produce no currents, but merely a
distribution of free electricity in the sphere.

Hence a spherical shell, rotating with infinite velocity,
only allows those portions of the external potential which are
symmetrical about the axis to produce an effect in its interior.
If such terms are absent, the interior of the shell is completely screened from outside influences. If the potential is a
spherical harmonic, the current flows along the equipotential
lines.

3. We found, neglecting self-induction, the following The electric potential.
expression for the electric potential corresponding to χ_n

$$\bar{\phi} = -\frac{\omega}{n+1}R\sin\theta\frac{\partial\chi_n}{\partial\theta}.$$

Taking self-induction into account, we shall have

$$\bar{\phi} = -\frac{\omega}{n+1}R\sin\theta\frac{\partial\overline{\chi_n+\Omega_i}}{\partial\theta}.$$

Hence it follows that the form of the equipotential lines (for
each inducing spherical harmonic) is unaltered by self-induction,
but these lines are turned through the same angle as the lines
of flow. For the parts of the external potential which are

symmetrical about the axis, ϕ increases indefinitely as the velocity increases; for the other parts it approaches a finite limit which is easily calculated.

Limiting Forms of the Spherical Shell.

Plane plate.   We now make the radius of the spherical shell infinite, but keep the variations of the inducing potential finite, and then we examine more closely the electric currents at the equator and at the pole. We thus obtain the theory of plane plates, both rotating and moving in a straight line. The latter may be considered as a special case of the former, but for several reasons it is advisable to treat these cases separately.

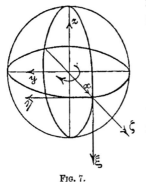

Plates moving in a straight line.

A. *Plates moving in a Straight Line.*

We introduce the co-ordinates ξ, η, ζ, whose connection with x, y, z is shown in Fig. 7.

Fig. 7.

The direction of η is the positive direction of motion. We shall suppose the inducing magnets inside the sphere, *i.e.* on the side of ζ negative. We must examine what form in ξ, η, ζ is assumed by the spherical harmonic

$$A_{ni}\left(\frac{R}{\rho}\right)^{n+1} \cos i\omega . P_{ni} .$$

In order to obtain finite variations we must make n and $i \infty$ of order R. We put

$$\text{for } n, \qquad n\text{R},$$
$$\text{for } i, \qquad r\text{R},$$

and further replace

$$\rho, \ \omega, \ \theta$$

by

$$\text{R}+\zeta, \frac{\eta}{\text{R}}, \frac{\pi}{2}+\frac{\xi}{\text{R}} .$$

Thus

$$\left(\frac{R}{\rho}\right)^{n+1}, \cos i\omega$$

become

$$\epsilon^{-n\zeta}, \cos r\eta.$$

$P_{ni}(\theta)$ must become such a function of ξ that its product by $\epsilon^{-n\zeta}\cos r\eta$ may satisfy the equation $\nabla^2 = 0$. Such a function is $\cos s\xi$ or $\sin s\xi$, provided

$$n^2 = r^2 + s^2.$$

Hence the spherical harmonics formerly used now take the form

$$A_{rs}\,\epsilon^{-n\zeta} \cos r\eta \cos s\xi,$$

and related forms.

The external potential χ must be represented as a series of such forms. This is to be done by means of Fourier's integrals.

For every term (element) of the development the solution is at once obtained from those found before. We now put

$$\tan \delta = \frac{2\pi r}{n}\cdot\frac{a}{k},$$

where a denotes the velocity of the plate, and find

$$\Omega_+ = A_{rs}\epsilon^{-n\zeta}\sin\delta\,\sin(r\eta - \delta)\cos s\xi,$$

$$\Omega_- = -A_{rs}\epsilon^{n\zeta}\sin\delta\,\sin(r\eta - \delta)\cos s\xi, \qquad \text{Solution.}$$

$$\psi = \frac{1}{2\pi}A_{rs}\sin\delta\,\sin(r\eta - \delta)\cos s\xi.$$

By summation of all the terms we obtain the general solution of the problem. The summation may be performed in the case when a/k becomes infinite. Then we have

$$\delta = \frac{\pi}{2}, \qquad \sin\delta = 1,$$

therefore

$$\Omega_+ = -\chi,$$

$$\psi = -\frac{1}{2\pi}\bar{\chi}.$$

On the opposite side to the magnets the potential is zero; the currents flow everywhere along the equipotential lines of the inducing distribution.

Apart from this limiting case the application of the above solution is very cumbersome; we therefore seek approximate methods. In the first place we find such methods by introducing successive inductions. That this method may be permissible it is necessary that $2\pi a/k$ be a proper fraction; if this condition be satisfied the calculation leads to a convergent series, as we have already shown in the general case.

We again start from the infinite spherical shell. The inducing potential χ_{-n-1} produced in the space outside the induced potential

$$\Omega_e = -\frac{4\pi R}{2n+1}\frac{\omega}{k}\cdot\frac{\partial\chi_{-n-1}}{\partial\omega}.$$

We allow R to become infinite while we replace

$$\frac{\partial}{\partial\omega} \text{ by } R\frac{\partial}{\partial\eta},$$

$$n \text{ by } nR,$$

$$\omega R \text{ by } a,$$

$$\chi_{-n-1} \text{ by } \chi_n = A_n e^{-n\zeta}\cos r\eta\cos s\xi,$$

then

$$\Omega_+ = -\frac{2\pi a}{k}\frac{1}{n}\frac{\partial\chi_n}{\partial\eta}.$$

But we have

$$\int_\zeta^\infty \chi_n d\zeta = \frac{\chi_n}{n}.$$

Hence summing for all values of n

$$\Omega_+ = -\frac{2\pi a}{k}\int_\zeta^\infty\frac{\partial\chi}{\partial\eta}\,d\zeta.$$

Now from this potential we can get in the same way the potential of the second order; and proceeding in this way we obtain finally

$$\Omega_+ = -\frac{2\pi a}{k}\int_\zeta^\infty \frac{\partial \chi}{\partial \eta}\,d\zeta + \left(\frac{2\pi a}{k}\right)^2 \int_\zeta^\infty \int_\zeta^\infty \frac{\partial^2 \chi}{\partial \eta^2}\,d\zeta^2 - \cdot\cdot$$

$$\Omega_-(-\zeta) = -\Omega_+(\zeta)$$

$$\psi = \frac{1}{2\pi}\,\overline{\Omega}_+ .$$

Second
form of the
solution.

This series leads to as accurate a result as we please, if only it be carried far enough; in fact it is only the development of the result in ascending powers of $2\pi a/\kappa$, as we may show in the following way.

In the spherical shell the part of Ω_e corresponding to $\chi_{(-n-1)i}$ may be represented in the form (p. 52)

$$\Omega_e = -\frac{1}{1+h^2}\left(\frac{h}{i}\frac{\partial \chi}{\partial \omega} + h^2\chi\right),$$

$$h = \frac{4R\omega i}{(2n+1)k}.$$

If we again introduce the substitutions to be made in the case of a plane plate, develop

$$\frac{1}{1+h^2} = 1 - h^2 + h^4 - h^6 + \cdots,$$

and put for h its value

$$\frac{2\pi a}{k}\cdot\frac{r}{n},$$

we get

$$\Omega_+ = -\frac{2\pi a}{k}\frac{1}{n}\frac{\partial \chi_{rs}}{\partial \eta} - \left(\frac{2\pi a}{k}\right)^2 \frac{r^2}{n^2}\chi_{rs} + \left(\frac{2\pi a}{k}\right)^3 \frac{r^2}{n^3}\frac{\partial \chi_{rs}}{\partial \eta}$$
$$+ \left(\frac{2\pi a}{k}\right)^4 \frac{r^4}{n^4}\chi_{rs} - \cdots,$$

from which development the preceding one follows when we use the relations

$$\int_\zeta^\infty \chi_{rs}\,d\zeta = \frac{\chi_{rs}}{n}, \qquad \frac{\partial^2 \chi_{rs}}{\partial \eta^2} = -r^2\chi_{rs},$$

and sum for all values of r and s.

In this connection it is natural to seek a development in descending powers of $2\pi a/\kappa$ for very large values of this quantity.

When $h>1$, we have

$$\frac{1}{1+h^2} = \frac{1}{h^2}\left(1 - \frac{1}{h^2} + \frac{1}{h^4} - \cdots\right),$$

hence

$$\Omega_+ = -\chi_{rs} - \frac{k}{2\pi a}\frac{n}{r^2}\frac{\partial \chi_{rs}}{\partial \eta} + \left(\frac{k}{2\pi a}\right)^2 \frac{n^2}{r^2}\chi_{rs}$$
$$+ \left(\frac{k}{2\pi a}\right)^3 \frac{n^3}{r^4}\frac{\partial \nu}{\partial \eta} - \cdots.$$

It is true that the terms of this equation cannot, as is shown by trial, be arranged in such a way as to at once permit of summation for all χ_{rs}; but if we suppose χ to be symmetrical with respect to the η-axis, so that in its development only terms in $\cos r\eta$ appear, we have

$$-n\chi_{rs} = \frac{\partial \chi_{rs}}{\partial \zeta}, \quad -\frac{1}{r^2}\frac{\partial \chi_{rs}}{\partial \eta} = \int_0^\eta \chi_{rs}d\eta,$$

and then the summation can be performed, at any rate for the terms of the first order in $\kappa/2\pi a$. If we confine ourselves to these we get

Approximate solution for large values of the velocity.
$$\Omega_+ = -\chi - \frac{k}{2\pi a}\int_0^\eta \frac{\partial \chi}{\partial \zeta}\,d\eta,$$

and the very small resultant potential on the positive side is

$$\Omega_+ + \chi = -\frac{k}{2\pi a}\int_0^\eta \frac{\partial \chi}{\partial \zeta}\,d\eta.$$

But in addition to the condition mentioned, this equation is subject to another one.

However large $2\pi a/\kappa$ may be, yet for certain elements for which r vanishes, $h<1$, and the development employed will be invalid. This circumstance restricts the validity of the expression obtained to a limited region, which however is larger the greater $2\pi a/\kappa$. On this point I refer to an investigation to follow immediately (p. 61).

We determine also the potential ϕ of the free electricity. This follows from the expression for the spherical shell by means of the very same substitutions that we have used all along. We thus find :—

1. Neglecting self-induction,

$$\overline{\phi} = a \int_0^\infty \frac{\partial \chi}{\partial \xi} \, d\zeta \, .$$

2. Taking it into account

$$\overline{\phi} = a \int_0^\infty \frac{\partial(\chi + \Omega)}{\partial \xi} \, d\zeta \, .$$

The case is of interest when the velocity a becomes infinite. If we assume χ to be symmetrical with respect to the η-axis, and restrict our considerations to a limited region, we have for $a = \infty$

$$\Omega + \chi = -\frac{k}{2\pi a} \int_0^\eta \frac{\partial \chi}{\partial \zeta} \, d\eta \, ,$$

and hence

$$\overline{\phi} = -\frac{k}{2\pi} \int_0^\infty \frac{\partial}{\partial \xi} \int_0^\eta \frac{\partial \chi}{\partial \zeta} \, d\eta d\zeta$$

$$= \frac{k}{2\pi} \int_0^\eta \frac{\partial \overline{\chi}}{\partial \xi} d\eta \, .$$

Thus $\overline{\phi}$ approaches a definite finite limit when the velocity increases.

B. *Rotating Discs.*

We next consider the neighbourhood of the pole, and thus obtain the theory of an infinite rotating disc. We again suppose the inducing magnets to be inside the sphere. The propositions we must employ are quite analogous to those of the previous case.

We use ρ, ω, z as co-ordinates, where ρ now denotes the perpendicular distance from the axis of rotation. In the general formulæ we must replace

$$\rho \text{ by } R+z,$$

$$\theta \text{ by } \frac{\rho}{R},$$

ω remains ω,

and after making this substitution we must allow R to become infinite. Then a simple spherical harmonic takes the form

$$A_{ni}e^{-nz} \cos i\omega J_i(n\rho),$$

(and analogous ones), where J_i denotes the Bessel's function of order i. The given χ is to be analysed into terms of this form by means of integrals analogous to those of Fourier.

We treat each term separately.

If we put

$$\tan \delta = \frac{2\pi\omega}{k} \cdot \frac{i}{n},$$

then for the term in question the solution of the problem is

Solution.

$$\Omega_+ = A_{ni}e^{-nz} \sin \delta \sin (i\omega - \delta) J_i(n\rho),$$

$$\Omega_- = - A_{ni}e^{nz} \sin \delta \sin (i\omega - \delta) J_i(n\rho),$$

$$\psi = \frac{1}{2\pi} A_{ni} \sin \delta \sin (i\omega - \delta) J_i(n\rho).$$

By summation we get the complete integrals.

We again attempt to obtain a development in powers of $2\pi\omega/\kappa$ by considering the successive inductions. By the same method as above we get

$$\Omega_+ = - \frac{2\pi\omega}{k} \int_z^\infty \frac{\partial\chi}{\partial\omega} \, dz + \left(\frac{2\pi\omega}{k}\right)^2 \int_z^\infty \int_z^\infty \frac{\partial^2\chi}{\partial\omega^2} \, dz^2 - \cdots,$$

Second form of the solution.

$$\Omega_-(-z) = - \Omega_+(z),$$

$$\psi = \frac{1}{2\pi}\overline{\Omega}_+.$$

But there is a limitation to the validity of these formulæ, which we had not to impose on the previous analogous ones. For their deduction presupposes that for each separate term of the development of χ it is allowable to regard the total induction as the sum of a series of successive inductions. According to the results which we obtained for spheres this condition is only satisfied for those terms for which $2\pi\omega i/kn$ is a proper fraction. Now n may have any value from zero to infinity; thus for a number of terms the necessary condition is not satisfied, and the result can therefore only be approximate. With reference to this point I remark :—

1. At a finite distance the terms for which n is very small vanish relatively to those for which n is finite. The error committed in the above formula must have an appreciable value for large values of ρ.

2. The quantity $2\pi\omega/k$ may always be chosen so small that the approximation may be any desired one within a given region. For by diminishing $2\pi\omega/k$ we diminish the number of those terms which do not satisfy the required condition : a suitable diminution diminishes their number in any desired degree.

There may possibly be difficulties in determining exactly the region of validity for a given value of $2\pi\omega/k$ and a given degree of approximation. For practical applications this determination is of no importance : because, in the first place, we are only concerned here with very small values of $2\pi\omega/k$; and, in the second place, we are only considering plates of limited dimensions, and not infinite plates.

The equation

$$\Omega = -\frac{2\pi\omega}{k}\int_z^\infty \frac{\partial\chi}{\partial\omega}\,dz$$

is exact, apart from self-induction. We see that, in order that we may be allowed to neglect self-induction, it is necessary not only that $2\pi\omega/k$ be small, but also that the investigation be limited to a certain finite region. The extent of this region depends on $2\pi\omega/k$; beyond it not even an approximate determination of the current is possible without taking self-induction into account. We shall meet with an exactly analogous result at the end of § 4.

Approxi-
mation for
large values
of the velo-
city.

A development can also be given for large values of $2\pi\omega/k$. We denote by χ_0 that part of χ which is symmetrical about the axis of rotation, by $\chi_1 = \chi - \chi_0$ the remainder. To χ_0 corresponds for every velocity of rotation the value $\Omega = 0$. Hence, assuming χ to be symmetrical about the x-axis, we get for large values of $2\pi\omega/k$

$$\Omega = -\chi_1 - \frac{k}{2\pi\omega}\int_0^\omega \frac{\partial \chi_1}{\partial z}\, d\omega.$$

The formula is deduced in the same way as above. The series may also be completely developed; and this too for forms of χ which are not symmetrical with respect to the x-axis. I shall not here enter into further detail on the point.

In conclusion let us determine ϕ, the potential of the free electricity. By the proper substitutions we get from the general formulæ :—

Potential of
the free
electricity.

1. Neglecting self-induction,

$$\phi = \omega\rho \int_0^\infty \frac{\partial \chi}{\partial \rho}\, dz.$$

We must add to this value of ϕ a constant, whose value is such as to make ϕ vanish at infinity. The formula which we have found has already been given by Jochmann for the case in which χ is symmetrical with respect to the axis of x. It is seen to be generally true.

2. Taking self-induction into account we have

$$\overline{\phi} = \omega\rho \int_0^\infty \frac{\partial(\chi+\Omega)}{\partial \rho}\, dz.$$

When ω is very large, we find, if χ is symmetrical with respect to the x-axis,

$$\overline{\phi} = \omega\rho \int_0^\infty \frac{\partial \chi_0}{\partial \rho}\, dz + \frac{k}{2\pi}\int_0^\infty \frac{\partial \chi_1}{\partial \rho}\, d\omega.$$

The first term increases indefinitely with ω.

We have in the treatment of plane plates all along assumed that inducing magnets exist only on one side of the plate. This assumption is unnecessary. If it is not true, we divide the total potential into two parts according to its origin, and treat each part separately, as we have shown above for one of the parts.

§ 4. Complete Solution for Spheres and Spherical Shells of Finite Thickness.

We now turn to the consideration of the induction in a spherical shell of finite thickness. To avoid complication we shall at first suppose inducing magnets to exist only outside the shell.

Let U, V, W be the components of a vector potential due to closed currents, wholly or partly inside the shell. The currents u', v', w' induced by U, V, W are given by the equations

$$\kappa u' = -\frac{\partial \phi}{\partial x} + \omega x \left(\frac{\partial V}{\partial x} - \frac{\partial U}{\partial y} \right),$$

$$\kappa v' = -\frac{\partial \phi}{\partial y} + \omega y \left(\frac{\partial V}{\partial x} - \frac{\partial U}{\partial y} \right),$$

$$\kappa w' = -\frac{\partial \phi}{\partial z} - \omega x \left(\frac{\partial W}{\partial y} - \frac{\partial V}{\partial z} \right) - \omega y \left(\frac{\partial U}{\partial z} - \frac{\partial W}{\partial x} \right).$$

Differential equations.

Further, inside we have

$$\frac{\partial u'}{\partial x} + \frac{\partial v'}{\partial y} + \frac{\partial w'}{\partial z} = 0 ,$$

and at the surface

$$u'x + v'y + w'z = 0 .$$

We write for shortness

$$0 = x \left(\frac{\partial W}{\partial y} - \frac{\partial V}{\partial z} \right) + y \left(\frac{\partial U}{\partial z} - \frac{\partial W}{\partial x} \right) + z \left(\frac{\partial V}{\partial x} - \frac{\partial U}{\partial y} \right).$$

If we remember that

$$\frac{\partial U}{\partial x} + \frac{\partial V}{\partial y} + \frac{\partial W}{\partial z} = 0,$$

we get for ϕ these conditions:—
In the material of the shell

$$\nabla^2 \phi = 2\omega\left(\frac{\partial V}{\partial x} - \frac{\partial U}{\partial y}\right) + \omega(x\nabla^2 V - y\nabla^2 U);$$

and at the boundaries

$$\frac{\partial \phi}{\partial \rho} = \frac{\omega}{\rho}\left\{\rho^2\left(\frac{\partial V}{\partial x} - \frac{\partial U}{\partial y}\right) - zO\right\}.$$

Theorem which forms the basis of what follows. We shall first demonstrate the following theorem:—
If U, V, W have the forms

$$U = \rho^m\left(y\frac{\partial \chi_n}{\partial z} - z\frac{\partial \chi_n}{\partial y}\right),$$

$$V = \rho^m\left(z\frac{\partial \chi_n}{\partial x} - x\frac{\partial \chi_n}{\partial z}\right),$$

$$W = \rho^m\left(x\frac{\partial \chi_n}{\partial y} - y\frac{\partial \chi_n}{\partial x}\right),$$

which forms satisfy the equation

$$\frac{\partial U}{\partial x} + \frac{\partial V}{\partial y} + \frac{\partial W}{\partial z} = 0,$$

then the solutions of the preceding differential equations are

$$\phi = -\omega\rho^m\left(\rho^2\frac{\partial \chi_n}{\partial z} - nz\chi_n\right)$$

$$= \omega\rho^{m+1}\sin\theta\frac{\partial \chi_n}{\partial \theta},$$

$$u' = -\frac{\omega}{\kappa}\rho^m\left(y\frac{\partial \chi'_n}{\partial z} - z\frac{\partial \chi'_n}{\partial y}\right),$$

$$v' = -\frac{\omega}{\kappa}\rho^m\left(z\frac{\partial \chi'_n}{\partial x} - x\frac{\partial \chi'_n}{\partial z}\right),$$

$$w' = -\frac{\omega}{\kappa}\rho^m\left(x\frac{\partial\chi'_n}{\partial y} - y\frac{\partial\chi'_n}{\partial x}\right).$$

To verify this we first express the conditions for ϕ in terms of χ_n. We have (§ 1, 4) *Proof.*

$$\nabla^2 U = m(m+2n+1)\rho^{m-2}\left(y\frac{\partial\chi_n}{\partial z} - z\frac{\partial\chi_n}{\partial y}\right),$$

$$\nabla^2 V = m(m+2n+1)\rho^{m-2}\left(z\frac{\partial\chi_n}{\partial x} - x\frac{\partial\chi_n}{\partial z}\right),$$

$$\nabla^2 W = m(m+2n+1)\rho^{m-2}\left(x\frac{\partial\chi_n}{\partial y} - y\frac{\partial\chi_n}{\partial x}\right),$$

$$y\nabla^2 U - x\nabla^2 V = m(m+2n+1)\rho^{m-2}\left(\rho^2\frac{\partial\chi_n}{\partial z} - nz\chi_n\right),$$

$$z\nabla^2 V - y\nabla^2 W = m(m+2n+1)\rho^{m-2}\left(\rho^2\frac{\partial\chi_n}{\partial x} - nx\chi_n\right),$$

$$x\nabla^2 W - z\nabla^2 U = m(m+2n+1)\rho^{m-2}\left(\rho^2\frac{\partial\chi_n}{\partial y} - ny\chi_n\right),$$

And again—

$$\frac{\partial V}{\partial x} - \frac{\partial U}{\partial y} = -m\rho^{m-2}\left(\rho^2\frac{\partial\chi_n}{\partial z} - nz\chi_n\right) - \rho^m(n+1)\frac{\partial\chi_n}{\partial z},$$

$$\frac{\partial W}{\partial y} - \frac{\partial V}{\partial z} = -m\rho^{m-2}\left(\rho^2\frac{\partial\chi_n}{\partial x} - nx\chi_n\right) - \rho^m(n+1)\frac{\partial\chi_n}{\partial x},$$

$$\frac{\partial U}{\partial z} - \frac{\partial W}{\partial x} = -m\rho^{m-2}\left(\rho^2\frac{\partial\chi_n}{\partial y} - ny\chi_n\right) - \rho^m(n+1)\frac{\partial\chi_n}{\partial y}.$$

Hence we get

$$O = -n(n+1)\rho^m\chi_n.$$

The conditions for ϕ become

$$\nabla^2\phi = -\omega m(m+2n+3)\left(\rho^2\frac{\partial\chi_n}{\partial z} - nz\chi_n\right)\rho^{m-2}$$

$$-2\omega(n+1)\rho^m\frac{\partial\chi_n}{\partial z},$$

M. P.   F

and at the boundary

$$\frac{\partial \phi}{\partial \rho} = -(m+n+1)\frac{\omega}{\rho}\rho^m\left(\rho^2\frac{\partial \chi_n}{\partial z} - nz\chi_n\right).$$

Now ϕ satisfies these conditions.   For we have, firstly,

$$\nabla^2\phi = -\omega\left[\nabla^2\left(\rho^{m+2}\frac{\partial\chi_n}{\partial z}\right) - 2n\frac{\partial}{\partial z}(\rho^m\chi_n) - nz\nabla^2(\rho^m\chi_n)\right]$$

$$= -\omega\left[\rho^m\frac{\partial\chi_n}{\partial z}\{(m+2)(m+2n+1)-2n\}\right.$$

$$\left. - nz\rho^{m-2}\chi_n\{m(m+2n+1)+2m\}\right]$$

$$= -\omega\left\{m(m+2n+3)\rho^{m-2}\left(\rho^2\frac{\partial\chi_n}{\partial z} - nz\chi_n\right) + 2(n+1)\rho^m\frac{\partial\chi_n}{\partial z}\right\},$$

so that the first condition is satisfied ; secondly, ϕ is the product of ρ^{m+n+1} by a function of the angles, thus

$$\frac{\partial \phi}{\partial \rho} = \frac{m+n+1}{\rho}\phi,$$

so that the second condition also is satisfied.   From this correct value of ϕ the values of u', v', w' follow by the original differential equations, at first in a more complicated form.   But the same form has already occurred on p. 43, and has already been shown to be identical with the one given above.

This theorem leads to the following propositions :—

1. In the theorem we may replace ρ^m by a series of powers of ρ, each power multiplied by an arbitrary constant, that is, for ρ^m we may substitute any arbitrary function of ρ. And again, we may replace χ_n by a series of spherical harmonics of different degrees with arbitrary coefficients ; for n is without effect on the final result.   Hence we get the following generalisation of the theorem :—

If χ is an arbitrary function, and if

$$U = \frac{\partial\chi}{\partial\omega_x}, \qquad V = \frac{\partial\chi}{\partial\omega_y}, \qquad W = \frac{\partial\chi}{\partial\omega_z},$$

then the currents u', v', w' induced by U, V, W are

$$u' = -\frac{\omega}{\kappa}\frac{\partial\chi'}{\partial\omega_x}, \qquad v' = -\frac{\omega}{\kappa}\frac{\partial\chi'}{\partial\omega_y}, \qquad w' = -\frac{\omega}{\kappa}\frac{\partial\chi'}{\partial\omega_z}.$$

It is not difficult to see the connection between this theorem and the results obtained in preceding paragraphs.

2. The U, V, W which are of the above form are due to currents in concentric spherical shells. For we have

$$x\nabla^2 U + y\nabla^2 V + z\nabla^2 W = 0.$$

And *vice versâ* the U, V, W of such currents may always be expressed in the above form. For if $\chi_n f(\rho)$ is the term involving the nth spherical harmonic in the development of the current function, then the U, V, W belonging to this term are at once seen to have the above form.

On the other hand, the induced currents also flow in concentric spherical shells. For we have

$$ux + vy + wz = 0.$$

Hence we deduce the following conclusion :— The flow is always in concentric spherical shells.
A current which flows in concentric spherical shells induces a current system possessing the same property. Furthermore, the currents which are induced by magnets at rest in a rotating spherical shell always flow in concentric spherical shells about the origin.

3. We find that

$$\phi = \omega(xV - yU)$$

whenever U, V, W have the above form, and the inducing currents the property discussed. This we shall have to make use of in § 8.

There is now no further difficulty in calculating the successive inductions produced by a given external potential. Let χ_n denote the nth term in its development. We found for the currents of the first induction

$$u_1 = \frac{1}{n+1}\frac{\omega}{\kappa}\frac{\partial\chi'}{\partial\omega_x}, \quad v_1 = \frac{1}{n+1}\frac{\omega}{\kappa}\frac{\partial\chi'}{\partial\omega_y}, \quad \omega_1 = \frac{1}{n+1}\frac{\omega}{\kappa}\frac{\partial\chi'}{\partial\omega_z}.$$

The corresponding values of U, V, W are

$$U_1 = \frac{2\pi}{n+1}\frac{\omega}{\kappa}\frac{\partial\chi'}{\partial\omega_x}\left(\frac{R^2}{2n+1} - \frac{\rho^2}{2n+3} - \frac{2r^{2n+3}}{(2n+1)(2n+3)\rho^{2n+1}}\right),$$

$$V_1 = \frac{2\pi}{n+1}\frac{\omega}{\kappa}\frac{\partial \chi'}{\partial \omega_y}\left(\frac{R^2}{2n+1} - \frac{\rho^2}{2n+3} - \frac{2r^{2n+3}}{(2n+1)(2n+3)\rho^{2n+1}}\right),$$

$$W_1 = \frac{2\pi}{n+1}\frac{\omega}{\kappa}\frac{\partial \chi'}{\partial \omega_z}\left(\frac{R^2}{2n+1} - \frac{\rho^2}{2n+3} - \frac{2r^{2n+3}}{(2n+1)(2n+3)\rho^{2n+1}}\right).$$

These values are got by a simple integration; for u, v, w are products of ρ^n by spherical surface harmonics. The potential of each infinitely thin layer is known inside and outside it, and an integration with respect to ρ leads to the given values. Hence follow the currents of the second induction

$$u_2 = -\frac{2\pi}{n+1}\left(\frac{\omega}{\kappa}\right)^2\frac{\partial \chi''}{\partial \omega_x}\left(\frac{R^2}{2n+1} - \frac{\rho^2}{2n+3} - \frac{2r^{2n+3}}{(2n+1)(2n+3)\rho^{2n+1}}\right),$$

$$v_2 = -\frac{2\pi}{n+1}\left(\frac{\omega}{\kappa}\right)^2\frac{\partial \chi''}{\partial \omega_y}\left(\frac{R^2}{2n+1} - \frac{\rho^2}{2n+3} - \frac{2r^{2n+3}}{(2n+1)(2n+3)\rho^{2n+1}}\right),$$

$$w_2 = -\frac{2\pi}{n+1}\left(\frac{\omega}{\kappa}\right)^2\frac{\partial \chi''}{\partial \omega_z}\left(\frac{R^2}{2n+1} - \frac{\rho^2}{2n+3} - \frac{2r^{2n+3}}{(2n+1)(2n+3)\rho^{2n+1}}\right).$$

In this way the calculation may be continued as far as may be desired, but the results continually increase in complication; hence we now proceed to the exact solution of the problem.

General solution.

We have seen that the currents are always perpendicular to the radius, and may therefore again make use of the current-function.

Let $f(\rho) = f$ be any function of ρ whatever, and let

$$\psi = \rho \cdot f \cdot \chi_n$$

be the current-function of a system of currents flowing in the sphere.

The current-densities are

$$u = f\frac{\partial \chi_n}{\partial \omega_x}, \qquad v = f\frac{\partial \chi_n}{\partial \omega_y}, \qquad w = f\frac{\partial \chi_n}{\partial \omega_z}.$$

Let $F(\rho) = F$ be a second function of ρ, which is given in terms of f by the equation

$$F(\rho) = \frac{4\pi}{2n+1}\frac{1}{\rho^{2n+1}}\left\{\int_r^\rho a^{2n+2}f(a)da + \int_\rho^R \rho^{2n+1}af(a)da\right\}.$$

From this we get, by differentiating,

$$\frac{d}{d\rho}\left(\rho^{-2n}\frac{d}{d\rho}(\rho^{2n+1}F)\right) = -4\pi\rho f(\rho).$$

The values of U, V, W corresponding to u, v, w are

$$U = F\frac{\partial \chi_n}{\partial \omega_x}, \quad V = F\frac{\partial \chi_n}{\partial \omega_y}, \quad W = F\frac{\partial \chi_n}{\partial \omega_z}.$$

Hence follow these currents induced by the system ψ

$$u' = -\frac{\omega}{\kappa}F\frac{\partial \chi'_n}{\partial \omega_x}, \quad v' = -\frac{\omega}{\kappa}F\frac{\partial \chi'_n}{\partial \omega_y}, \quad w' = -\frac{\omega}{\kappa}F\frac{\partial \chi'_n}{\partial \omega_z}.$$

The disturbing function belonging to this system is

$$\psi' = -\frac{\omega}{\kappa}\rho F\chi'_n.$$

Hence the function

$$\psi = \rho \cdot f \cdot \chi_n$$

induces the second function

$$\psi' = -\frac{\omega}{\kappa}\rho F\chi'_n.$$

Now let ψ belong to the current-system actually existing in the sphere under the influence of the external potential χ_n; let ψ_0 belong to the current-system directly induced by external magnets. Then clearly the condition for the stationary state is

$$\psi = \psi_0 + \psi'.$$

To develop this equation further we analyse χ_n and consider each term by itself. Let the one considered be

$$\chi_{ni} = A\left(\frac{\rho}{R}\right)^n \cos i\omega \cdot P_{ni}.$$

We have then (p. 48)

$$\psi_0 = -\frac{\omega}{\kappa}A\rho\left(\frac{\rho}{R}\right)^n \frac{i}{n+1} \sin i\omega \cdot P_{ni}.$$

If we write

$$\psi = -\frac{\omega}{\kappa}A\rho\left(\frac{\rho}{R}\right)^n \frac{i}{n+1}\{f_1(\rho)\sin i\omega + f_2(\rho)\cos i\omega\}P_{ni},$$

we get

$$\psi' = \left(\frac{\omega}{\kappa}\right)^2 A\rho \left(\frac{\rho}{R}\right)^n \frac{i^2}{n+1} \{ F_1(\rho) \cos i\omega - F_2(\rho) \sin i\omega \} P_{ni}.$$

The equation $\psi = \psi_0 + \psi'$ is satisfied if f_1 and f_2 satisfy the equations

$$f_1(\rho) = 1 + \frac{i\omega}{\kappa} F_2(\rho),$$

$$f_2(\rho) = - \frac{i\omega}{\kappa} F_1(\rho),$$

by which f_1 and f_2 are completely determined.

If we regard f_1 and f_2 as known, the result of the investigation may be expressed in the following form :—

Self-induction leaves the form of the lines of flow unaltered (for each separate term of the development). Its effect is :—

Firstly, to turn the system in the direction of rotation through an angle δ/i, where the angle δ is different for different layers and is given by the equation $\tan \delta = f_2/f_1$.

Secondly, to change the intensity of the current differently in different layers. The ratio of the intensity actually occurring to that found without taking account of self-induction is $\sqrt{f_1^2 + f_2^2} : 1$.

We shall have to occupy ourselves for some time with the determination of the functions f_1 and f_2.

We introduce the following contractions.   Let

$$\frac{4\pi i\omega}{\kappa} = \mu^2,$$

$$\mu r = s, \qquad \mu R = S,$$

$$f_1(\rho) = \phi_1(\mu\rho) = \phi_1\sigma,$$

$$f_2(\rho) = \phi_2(\mu\rho) = \phi_2\sigma.$$

In the equations which give f_1 and f_2 we put for F_1 and F_2 their values, transform the equations so as to involve ϕ and σ, and thus obtain

$$\phi_1\sigma = 1 + \frac{1}{(2n+1)\sigma^{2n+1}}\left\{\int_s^\sigma a^{2n+2}\phi_2 a \,.\, da + \int_\sigma^S \sigma^{2n+1}a\phi_2 a \,.\, da\right\},$$

$$\phi_2\sigma = -\frac{1}{(2n+1)\sigma^{2n+1}}\left\{\int_s^\sigma a^{2n+2}\phi_1 a \,.\, da + \int_\sigma^S \sigma^{2n+1}a\phi_1 a \,.\, da\right\}.$$

These give by differentiation

$$\frac{d}{d\sigma}\left(\sigma^{-2n}\frac{d}{d\sigma}(\sigma^{2n+1}\phi_1)\right) = -\sigma\phi_2,$$

$$\frac{d}{d\sigma}\left(\sigma^{-2n}\frac{d}{d\sigma}(\sigma^{2n+1}\phi_2)\right) = \sigma\phi_1.$$

The form of the functions ϕ_1, ϕ_2 depends only on n; in the constant of integration μ, s, S are involved.

The above equations may be written

$$\phi''_1 + \frac{2n+2}{\sigma}\phi'_1 = -\phi_2,$$

$$\phi''_2 + \frac{2n+2}{\sigma}\phi'_2 = \phi_1.$$

As differential equations these are exactly equivalent to the following :—

$$\phi_2 = \pm\phi_1\sqrt{-1},$$

$$\phi''_1 + \frac{2n+2}{\sigma}\phi'_1 \pm \phi_1\sqrt{-1} = 0.$$

For all solutions of the latter system satisfy the former, and the general solution of the latter involves 2×2 arbitrary constants, and is therefore also the general solution of the former system.

Let us put $\lambda^4 = -1$, where λ is that root whose real part is positive, so that

$$\lambda_1 = \sqrt{\tfrac{1}{2}} \,.\, (1 + \sqrt{-1}),$$

$$\lambda_2 = \sqrt{\tfrac{1}{2}} \,.\, (1 - \sqrt{-1}).$$

Then our equations become

$$\phi_2 = -\lambda^2 \phi_1,$$

$$\phi''_1 + \frac{2n+2}{\sigma}\phi'_1 - \lambda^2 \phi_1 = 0.$$

The two particular integrals are

$$\int_{-1}^{+1}(1-v^2)^n \epsilon^{\sigma\lambda v}dv, \quad \int_{1}^{\infty}(1-v^2)^n \epsilon^{-\sigma\lambda v}dv,$$

which hold for real positive values of σ.

We shall prove farther on that these integrals satisfy the equations. Since in our case n is a whole number the integrations can be performed, and the solution expressed in a finite form; but for simplicity we may retain the integral form. Let us write

$$p_n(\sigma) = \int_{-1}^{+1}(1-v^2)^n \epsilon^{\sigma v}dv,$$

Definition
of p and q.

$$q_n(\sigma) = \int_{1}^{\infty}(1-v^2)^n \epsilon^{-\sigma v}dv,$$

then clearly the solutions of the differential equations are—

$$\phi_1 = Ap_n(\lambda_1\sigma) + Bp_n(\lambda_2\sigma) + Cq_n(\lambda_1\sigma) + Dq_n(\lambda_2\sigma),$$

$$-\phi_2 = \lambda_1^2 Ap_n(\lambda_1\sigma) + \lambda_2^2 Bp_n(\lambda_2\sigma) + \lambda_1^2 Cq_n(\lambda_1\sigma) + \lambda_2^2 Dq_n(\lambda_2\sigma).$$

These solutions must be substituted in the integral equations so that the constants may be determined. The following formulæ will serve to evaluate the integrals which occur :—

$$p_n(\lambda\sigma) = \int_{-1}^{+1}(1-v^2)^n \epsilon^{\lambda\sigma v}dv,$$

$$\sigma^{-2n}\frac{d}{d\sigma}(\sigma^{2n+1}p_n) = \int_{-1}^{+1}(1-v^2)^n(\sigma\lambda v + 2n + 1)\epsilon^{\lambda\sigma v}dv$$

$$= 2np_{n-1}(\lambda\sigma),^{[1]}$$

---

[1] The last members of the equations are got by transforming the preceding integrals, especially by integration by parts.

$$\frac{d}{d\sigma}\left[\sigma^{-2n}\frac{d}{d\sigma}(\sigma^{2n+1}p_n)\right] = \lambda\int_{-1}^{+1}(1-v^2)^n(\sigma\lambda v^2 + 2(n+1)v)\epsilon^{\lambda\sigma v}dv$$

$$= \lambda^2\sigma p_n(\lambda\sigma).^1$$

The last equation shows that p_n is a solution of the equation under discussion.

The preceding equations when integrated give

$$\int \sigma p_n(\lambda\sigma)d\sigma = \frac{2n}{\lambda^2}p_{n-1}(\lambda\sigma),$$

Integral and recurring formulæ for p and q.

and

$$\int \sigma^{2n}p_{n-1}(\lambda\sigma)d\sigma = \frac{1}{2n}\sigma^{2n+1}p_n(\lambda\sigma),$$

whence by differentiating we get these recurring formulæ

$$p_n(\lambda\sigma) = \frac{2n}{\lambda}\frac{p'_{n-1}(\lambda\sigma)}{\sigma},$$

$$p_{n-1}(\lambda\sigma) = \frac{2n+1}{2n}p_n(\lambda\sigma) + \frac{\lambda\sigma}{2n}p'_n(\lambda\sigma),$$

whence

$$p_{n-1} = \frac{2n+1}{2n}p_n + \frac{\lambda^2\sigma^2}{4n(n+1)}p_{n+1},$$

$$p_n = \frac{2}{\lambda^2\sigma^2}\{2n(n-1)p_{n-2} - n(2n-1)p_{n-1}\}.$$

Exactly similar calculations may be performed for the q's. The results are got by replacing p by q; hence

$$\int \sigma q_n(\lambda\sigma)d\sigma = \frac{2n}{\lambda^2}q_{n-1}(\lambda\sigma),$$

$$\int \sigma^{2n}q_{n-1}(\lambda\sigma)d\sigma = \frac{1}{2n}\sigma^{2n+1}q_n(\lambda\sigma), \text{ etc.}$$

With the use of these formulæ it is easy to perform the necessary integrations; for instance, we get by help of an integration by parts

---

[1] See footnote on p. 72.

$$\int_s^\sigma a^{2n+2} p_n(\lambda a)\, da + \sigma^{2n+1}\int_\sigma^S a p_n(\lambda a)\, da$$

$$= \frac{2n}{\lambda^2}\sigma^{2n+1} p_{n-1}(\lambda S) - \frac{2n}{\lambda^2} s^{2n+1} p_{n-1}(\lambda s) + \frac{2n+1}{\lambda^2} s^{2n+1} p_n(\lambda s)$$

$$- \frac{2n+1}{\lambda^2}\sigma^{2n+1} p_n(\lambda\sigma)$$

$$= \frac{2n}{\lambda^2}\sigma^{2n+1} p_{n-1}(\lambda S) - \frac{s^{2n+3}}{2(n+1)} p_{n+1}(\lambda s) - \frac{2n+1}{\lambda^2}\sigma^{2n+1} p_n(\lambda\sigma).$$

When we substitute these and the similar expressions for q in the equations, and remember that $\phi_2 = -\lambda^2\phi_1$ and $\lambda^4 = -1$, the p's and q's cancel as they must do, and we are left with equations of the form

$$0 = (\text{const})_1 + \frac{(\text{const})_2}{\rho^{2n+1}},$$

which are the solutions of the equation

$$\frac{d}{d\sigma}\left[\sigma^{-2n}\frac{d}{d\sigma}(\sigma^{2n+1}\phi)\right] = 0.$$

The constants occurring here must vanish separately; remembering that $\frac{1}{\lambda_1^2} = -\frac{1}{\lambda_2^2}$ we thus obtain the following four equations for A, B, C, D

$$\frac{2n+1}{2n} = A p_{n-1}(\lambda_1 S) + B p_{n-1}(\lambda_2 S) + C q_{n-1}(\lambda_1 S) + D q_{n-1}(\lambda_2 S),$$

$$0 = A p_{n-1}(\lambda_1 S) - B p_{n-1}(\lambda_2 S) + C q_{n-1}(\lambda_1 S) - D q_{n-1}(\lambda_2 S),$$

$$0 = A p_{n+1}(\lambda_1 s) + B p_{n+1}(\lambda_2 s) + C q_{n+1}(\lambda_1 s) + D q_{n+1}(\lambda_2 s),$$

$$0 = A p_{n+1}(\lambda_1 s) - B p_{n+1}(\lambda_2 s) + C q_{n+1}(\lambda_1 s) - D q_{n+1}(\lambda_2 s).$$

These equations are easily solved and give

$$A = \frac{2n+1}{4n}\cdot\frac{q_{n+1}(\lambda_1 s)}{p_{n-1}(\lambda_1 S) q_{n+1}(\lambda_1 s) - p_{n+1}(\lambda_1 s) q_{n-1}(\lambda_1 S)},$$

$$C = -\frac{2n+1}{4n}\cdot\frac{p_{n+1}(\lambda_1 s)}{p_{n-1}(\lambda_1 S) q_{n+1}(\lambda_1 s) - p_{n+1}(\lambda_1 s) q_{n-1}(\lambda_1 S)},$$

$$B = \frac{2n+1}{4n} \cdot \frac{q_{n+1}(\lambda_2 s)}{p_{n-1}(\lambda_2 S)q_{n+1}(\lambda_2 s) - p_{n+1}(\lambda_2 s)q_{n-1}(\lambda_2 S)},$$

$$D = -\frac{2n+1}{4n} \cdot \frac{p_{n+1}(\lambda_2 s)}{p_{n-1}(\lambda_2 S)q_{n+1}(\lambda_2 s) - p_{n+1}(\lambda_2 s)q_{n-1}(\lambda_2 S)}$$

We get the complete solution by substituting these values in ϕ_1 and ϕ_2. It may be more simply exhibited thus: Since λ_1 and λ_2 are conjugate, $p(\lambda_1 \sigma)$ and $p(\lambda_2 \sigma)$ also are conjugate; in the same way A and B are conjugate, as is easily seen, and hence

$$Ap_n(\lambda_1 \sigma) + Bp_n(\lambda_2 \sigma)$$

is equal to twice the real part of either expression.

In the same way

$$Ap_n(\lambda_1 \sigma) - Bp_n(\lambda_2 \sigma),$$

which expression occurs in ϕ_2, is twice the imaginary part of the first term. Remembering this, and also the values of A and C, we easily recognise the truth of the equation

$$\frac{2n+1}{2n} \cdot \frac{p_n(\lambda_1 \sigma)q_{n+1}(\lambda_1 s) - q_n(\lambda_1 \sigma)p_{n+1}(\lambda_1 s)}{p_{n-1}(\lambda_1 S)q_{n+1}(\lambda_1 s) - q_{n-1}(\lambda_1 S)p_{n+1}(\lambda_1 s)}$$

Solution of the equations for the f's by means of the p's and q's.

$$= \phi_1 + \phi_2 \sqrt{-1} = f_1 + f_2 \sqrt{-1}.$$

This equation is especially simple when $s = 0$, that is in the case of a solid sphere. Then $q_{n+1}(s)$ is infinite, and thus our equation becomes

$$\frac{2n+1}{2n} \frac{p_n(\lambda_1 \sigma)}{p_{n-1}(\lambda_1 S)} = \phi_1 + \phi_2 \sqrt{-1}.$$

The quantities, a knowledge of which is of special interest to us, are the angle $\sigma = \tan^{-1} f_2/f_1$, and the ratio of increase of current, $\sqrt{f_1^2 + f_2^2}$. These have a very simple analytical meaning: they are the amplitude and modulus of the complex quantity on the left-hand side.

The calculation may be carried still further by means of the following remarks:—

The indefinite integrals defining p and q may be evaluated for integral values of n, and thus p and q may be expressed

Further properties of the p's and q's.

in a finite form. We may and will denote by p and q the functions thus calculated. Then also q's with negative arguments are admissible, and this equation holds

$$- p_n(\rho) = q_n(\rho) + q_n(-\rho),$$

whence follows

$$p_n(\rho) = p_n(-\rho).$$

For let the indefinite integral

$$\int (1 - v^2)^n \, \epsilon^{-\sigma v} dv = V(\sigma, v),$$

then we have

$$q_n(\sigma) = V(\sigma, \infty) - V(\sigma, 1),$$

$$p_n(\sigma) = \int_0^1 (1 - v^2)^n \epsilon^{-\sigma v} dv + \int_0^1 (1 - v^2)^n \epsilon^{\sigma v} dv$$

$$= V(-\sigma, 1) - V(-\sigma, 0)$$

$$\qquad + V(\sigma, 1) - V(\sigma, 0).$$

But for integral values of n

$$V(\sigma, \infty) = 0, \quad V(-\sigma, 0) = -V(\sigma, 0),$$

and thus the statement made follows.

Hence the simplest integrals of the original equations are

$$q_n(\sigma) \text{ and } q_n(-\sigma).$$

The following are the expressions for the first few q's; the first one has been determined directly, the others by the recurring formula.

The first
q's.

$$q_0 = \frac{\epsilon^{-\sigma}}{\sigma},$$

$$q_1 = -\frac{2\epsilon^{-\sigma}}{\sigma^2} \left(1 + \frac{1}{\sigma} \right),$$

$$q_2 = \frac{2^2 . \lfloor 2 . \epsilon^{-\sigma}}{\sigma^3} \left(1 + \frac{3}{\sigma} + \frac{3}{\sigma^2} \right),$$

$$q_3 = -\frac{2^3 . \lfloor 3 . \epsilon^{-\sigma}}{\sigma^4} \left(1 + \frac{6}{\sigma} + \frac{15}{\sigma^2} + \frac{15}{\sigma^3} \right), \text{ etc.}$$

Hence follow the equations

$$p_0 = \frac{\epsilon^{\sigma} - \epsilon^{-\sigma}}{\sigma},$$

$$p_1 = \frac{2}{\sigma^2}\left(\epsilon^{\sigma} + \epsilon^{-\sigma} - \frac{\epsilon^{\sigma} - \epsilon^{-\sigma}}{\sigma}\right), \text{ etc.}$$

For large values of σ p and q approach the values

$$q_n = (-2)^n \cdot \underline{|n} \cdot \frac{\epsilon^{-\sigma}}{\sigma^{n+1}},$$

$$p_n(\sigma) = -q_n(-\sigma).$$

The p's and q's for large and small values of the argument.

For very small values of σ we get

$$q_n(\sigma) = \frac{(-2)^n \cdot \underline{|n} \cdot 1 \cdot 3 \dots (2n-1)}{\sigma^{2n+1}}\epsilon^{-\sigma}$$

The equation $-p(\sigma) = q(\sigma) + q(-\sigma)$ here has no longer any meaning; for when $\sigma = 0$, $q = \pm \infty$. In order to find p for very small values of σ also, we expand it in a series of ascending powers of σ. This is easily done by substituting for $\epsilon^{\sigma v}$ its expansion in the integral representing p; integrating each term we obtain

$$p_n(\sigma) = \frac{2^{n+1} \cdot \underline{|n}}{1 \cdot 3 \dots (2n+1)}\left\{1 + \frac{\sigma^2}{2(2n+3)}\right.$$

$$\left. + \frac{\sigma^4}{2 \cdot 4 \cdot (2n+3)(2n+5)} + \dots\right\}$$

The following formula is of importance for our further investigations. We have

$$q_n(\sigma)q_{n-1}(-\sigma) - q_n(-\sigma)q_{n-1}(\sigma)$$

$$(a) \quad = -\frac{4n(n-1)}{\sigma^2}\left\{q_{n-1}(\sigma)q_{n-2}(-\sigma) - q_{n-1}(-\sigma)q_{n-2}(\sigma)\right\}$$

$$= -\frac{\underline{|n} \cdot \underline{|n-1}}{\sigma}\left(-\frac{4}{\sigma^2}\right)^n,$$

which equality is easily demonstrated by means of the recurring formula found for q.

In all the properties of p_n and q_n considered we notice their close relation to Bessel's functions; in fact we may express J_m in terms of $p_{m+\frac{1}{2}}$ and $q_{m+\frac{1}{2}}$.

We may now remove p from the formula expressing our result, and thus we obtain[1]

Final form of the solution.

$$\frac{2n+1}{2n} \cdot \frac{q_{n+1}(\lambda s)q_n(-\lambda \sigma) - q_{n+1}(-\lambda s)q_n{}'(\lambda \sigma)}{q_{n+1}(\lambda s)q_{n-1}(-\lambda S) - q_{n+1}(-\lambda s)q_{n-1}(\lambda S)}$$

$$= \phi_1 + \phi_2 \sqrt{-1}.$$

Its application.

We shall apply this formula, which gives the exact solution, to some special cases which admit of simplifications.

Thin spherical shell.

1. In the first place, let the spherical shell be very thin, and let d be its thickness. Then S is only slightly different from s. Let

$$S = s + \delta, \text{ where now } \delta = \mu d.$$

For σ we may put any convenient value between s and S; suppose $\sigma = S$.

We substitute these values in the above formula. In the denominator we employ the substitution

$$q_{n-1} = \frac{2n+1}{2n}q_n + \frac{\lambda^2 \sigma^2}{4n(n+1)}q_{n+1}$$

and divide by the numerator. Thus we obtain

$$\phi_1 + \phi_2 \sqrt{-1}$$

$$= \frac{1}{1 + \dfrac{\lambda^2 S^2}{2(n+1)(2n+1)} \dfrac{q_{n+1}(\lambda s)q_{n+1}(-\lambda S) - q_{n+1}(-\lambda s)q_{n+1}(\lambda S)}{q_{n+1}(\lambda s)q_n(-\lambda S) - q_{n+1}(-\lambda s)q_n(\lambda S)}}$$

We develop and put

$$q_{n+1}(\lambda S) = q_{n+1}\{\lambda(s+\delta)\}$$

$$= q_{n+1}(\lambda s) + \lambda \delta q'_{n+1}(\lambda s)$$

$$= q_{n+1}(\lambda s) + \frac{\delta \lambda^2 s}{2(n+2)}q_{n+2}(\lambda s),$$

$$q_{n+1}(-\lambda S) = q_{n+1}(-\lambda s) + \frac{\delta \lambda^2 s}{2(n+2)}q_{n+2}(-\lambda s).$$

[1] From this point onwards we write λ instead of λ_1; thus—
$$\lambda = \sqrt{\tfrac{1}{2}(1 \div \sqrt{-1})}.$$

Using formula (a) (p. 77) we may divide out the q's and thus obtain

$$\phi_1 + \phi_2\sqrt{-1} = \dfrac{1}{1 + \dfrac{s\delta\lambda^2}{2n+1}} \cdot$$

But now we have

$$\frac{s\delta}{2n+1} = \frac{4\pi \mathrm{R} i \omega}{(2n+1)k} = h,$$

according to our previous notation, and hence

$$\phi_1 + \phi_2\sqrt{-1} = \frac{1}{1 + h\sqrt{-1}}$$

$$= \frac{1}{1 + h^2} - \frac{h}{1 + h^2}\sqrt{-1},$$

which result agrees with the one previously obtained.

Thus we have on the one hand tested our formula by means of a result already known; on the other hand we have proved that the previously given formulæ hold for all values of h, which proof still remained to be given.

2. Secondly, we apply our formulæ to the case where we need only retain the first power of the angular velocity in f_1 and f_2. For simplicity we restrict the investigation to a solid sphere. In this case we found

$$f_1 + f_2\sqrt{-1} = \frac{2n+1}{2n} \frac{p_n(\lambda\sigma)}{p_{n-1}(\lambda\mathrm{S})}.$$

Expanding the p's and retaining only first powers we get

$$f_1 + f_2\sqrt{-1} = \frac{2 + \dfrac{\sigma^2}{2n+3}\sqrt{-1}}{2 + \dfrac{\mathrm{S}^2}{2n+1}\sqrt{-1}} \cdot$$

A closer consideration of this equation shows that the values of f_1, f_2 thence found when substituted in ψ merely give the inductions of the first and second order, which we have already calculated on p. 68. Here we only consider the angle through which the lines of flow are turned. Retaining only lowest powers we find

$$\tan^{-1}\frac{f_2}{f_1} = \delta = -\frac{2\pi\omega i}{\kappa}\left(\frac{R^2}{2n+1} - \frac{\rho^2}{2n+3}\right),$$

so that the angle in question is

$$\frac{\delta}{i} = -\frac{2\pi\omega}{\kappa}\left(\frac{R^2}{2n+1} - \frac{\rho^2}{2n+3}\right).$$

Thus all the layers appear rotated: the rotation is least at the surface of the sphere and increases continuously inwards. If we imagine a plane section taken through the equator of the sphere and join corresponding points of the different layers we get a system of congruent curves, which is very suitable for representing the state of the sphere. The equation of one of these curves clearly is

$$y = x\tan\frac{\delta}{i}, \quad \rho = \sqrt{x^2 + y^2},$$

or very approximately

$$y = -\frac{2\pi\omega}{\kappa}x\left(\frac{R^2}{2n+1} - \frac{x^2}{2n+3}\right).$$

In Fig. 8 these curves are drawn for a copper sphere for which $R = 50$ mm., $n = 1$, when it makes 1, 2, 3, 4 revolutions per second.

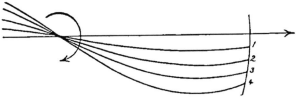

FIG. 8.

Large velocities of rotation.   3. Thirdly, let us assume that μ is so large that for $q(S\lambda)$ and $q(s\lambda)$ we may put their approximate values. Further, assume that the ratio r/R is neither very nearly $= 1$ nor very nearly $= 0$. The former case has been considered already; the latter requires special consideration. Substituting the approximate values in the exact formula we find

$$\phi_1 + \phi_2\sqrt{-1} = \frac{2n+1}{\lambda}\frac{S^n}{\sigma^{n+1}}\frac{\epsilon^{\lambda(\sigma-s)} + \epsilon^{-\lambda(\sigma-s)}}{\epsilon^{\lambda(S-s)} - \epsilon^{-\lambda(S-s)}}.$$

Since S is not nearly equal to s, and both are very great, the second term in the denominator vanishes compared with the first, and we get

$$\phi_1 + \phi_2 \sqrt{-1} = \frac{2n+1}{\lambda S}\left(\frac{R}{\rho}\right)^{n+1} \epsilon^{-\lambda\mu(R-r)}(\epsilon^{\lambda\mu(\rho-r)} + \epsilon^{-\lambda\mu(\rho-r)}).$$

The second term in the bracket vanishes in comparison with the first except when $\rho = r$; if then we are content with an approximate knowledge of the current at the inner surface we may write

$$\phi_1 + \phi_2 \sqrt{-1} = \frac{2n+1}{\lambda S}\left(\frac{R}{\rho}\right)^{n+1} \epsilon^{-\lambda\mu(R-\rho)}.$$

Since s or r has disappeared from this equation, we may assume that it holds also for a solid sphere. In fact it is easily deduced from the exact formulæ which hold for a solid sphere if we make similar approximations to those used above, and do not require an exact knowledge of the currents at the centre (where, as a matter of fact, the current intensity is very small).

In the expressions obtained

$$\lambda = \sqrt{\tfrac{1}{2}}(1 + \sqrt{-1});$$

without performing the separation into real and imaginary parts we easily find

$$\tan^{-1}\frac{f_2}{f_1} = -\frac{\pi}{4} - \frac{\mu}{\sqrt{2}}(R - \rho),$$

$$\sqrt{f_1^2 + f_2^2} = \frac{2n+1}{\mu}\frac{R^n}{\rho^{n+1}}\epsilon^{-\frac{\mu}{\sqrt{2}}(R-\rho)}$$

Substituting these values in ψ we find

$$\psi = -\frac{2n+1}{2(n+1)}A\sqrt{\frac{i\omega}{\kappa\pi}}\epsilon^{-\frac{\mu}{\sqrt{2}}(R-\rho)}\sin\left(i\omega - \frac{\pi}{4}\right.$$

$$\left. -\frac{\mu}{\sqrt{2}}(R - \rho)\right)P_{ni},$$

which is the current-function produced for very large velocities of rotation by the external potential

$$\chi_n = A\left(\frac{\rho}{R}\right)^n \cos i\omega P_{ni}.$$

The meaning of the above formula is easily grasped. If we collect together its result and the results previously obtained we may describe the phenomena, which would be presented by a spherical shell rotating with constantly increasing velocity under the influence of an inducing spherical harmonic function, in the following terms :—

Summary
of the
result. When self-induction begins to be appreciable, it does not alter the form of the lines of flow in the various spherical layers, but these latter commence to undergo an apparent rotation in the direction of rotation; and then the inner layers gain on the outer ones. There is no limit to the rotation of the inner layers; it may increase indefinitely. The angle of rotation of the outermost layer converges to the value $\pi/4i$; moreover, for spherical shells it may in the first instance have exceeded this value. If the velocity of rotation be very great, corresponding points of the different layers lie on spirals of Archimedes, and the number of turns which these make in the sphere increases indefinitely with the velocity of rotation.

At first the intensity increases with the velocity of rotation, but nowhere proportionately to it; more quickly in the outer than in the inner layers. In the outermost layer it constantly increases, ultimately as $\sqrt{\omega}$; in the other layers it reaches a maximum for some definite velocity and then decreases. For large velocities it decreases inwards from the surface in proportion to an exponential, whose argument has $\sqrt{\omega}$ for a factor.

It is of interest to note also the dependence of the phenomenon on the order i (whose square root is involved in μ); for this I refer to the formulæ.

An apparent contradiction between the theory of an infinitely thin spherical shell and that of one of finite thickness may excite notice; it is easily explained when we consider that every spherical shell, however thin, may only be regarded as infinitely thin up to a certain value of the velocity of rotation.

Case where
the mag-
nets are
inside the
shell. I shall deal shortly with the case where the inducing magnets are inside the spherical shell, so that spherical harmonics of negative degree occur.

Let

$$\chi_n = A\left(\frac{r}{\rho}\right)^{n+1}\cos i\omega P_{ni},$$

then

$$\psi_0 = \frac{\omega}{\kappa}A\rho\left(\frac{r}{\rho}\right)^{n+1}\frac{i}{n}\sin i\omega P_{ni}.$$

If we write

$$\psi = \frac{\omega}{\kappa}A\rho\left(\frac{r}{\rho}\right)^{n+1}\frac{i}{n}(f_1\sin i\omega + f_2\cos i\omega)P_{ni},$$

the function ψ' induced by ψ becomes

$$\psi' = -\left(\frac{\omega}{\kappa}\right)^2 A\rho\left(\frac{r}{\rho}\right)^{n+1}\frac{i^2}{n}(F_1\cos i\omega - F_2\sin i\omega)P_{ni}.$$

But here the connection between f and F is somewhat different from what it was before, for we have

$$F(\rho) = \frac{4\pi}{2n+1}\left\{\int_r^\rho af(a)da + \int_\rho^R \rho^{2n+1}\frac{f(a)da}{a^{2n}}\right\}.$$

The condition

$$\psi = \psi_0 + \psi'$$

leads to the same equations as before,

$$f_1 = 1 + \frac{i\omega}{\kappa}F_2,$$

$$f_2 = -\frac{i\omega}{\kappa}F_1.$$

Using the same contractions as before we get

$$\phi_1(\sigma) = 1 + \frac{1}{2n+1}\left\{\int_s^\sigma a\phi_2(a)da + \int_\sigma^s \sigma^{2n+1}a^{-2n}\phi_2(a)da\right\},$$

$$\phi_2(\sigma) = -\frac{1}{2n+1}\left\{\int_s^\sigma a\phi_1(a)da + \int_\sigma^s \sigma^{2n+1}a^{-2n}\phi_1(a)da\right\}.$$

On differentiation these become

$$\frac{d}{d\sigma}\left(\sigma^{2n+2}\frac{d}{d\sigma}(\sigma^{-2n-1}\phi_1)\right) = -\sigma\phi_2,$$

$$\frac{d}{d\sigma}\left(\sigma^{2n+2}\frac{d}{d\sigma}(\sigma^{-2n-1}\phi_2)\right) = \sigma\phi_1,$$

or

$$\phi_1'' - \frac{2n}{\sigma}\phi_1' = -\phi_2,$$

$$\phi_2'' - \frac{2n}{\sigma}\phi_2' = \phi_1.$$

If we put $\phi = \sigma^{2n+1}\overline{\phi}$, we get for $\overline{\phi}$ the equations

$$\overline{\phi}_1'' + \frac{2n+2}{\sigma}\overline{\phi}_1' = -\overline{\phi}_2,$$

$$\overline{\phi}_2'' + \frac{2n+2}{\sigma}\overline{\phi}_2' = \overline{\phi}_1,$$

which equations again lead to the p's and q's.

The constants may be determined in the same way as before, and then we find

$$\phi_1\sqrt{-1} - \phi_2 = -2(n+1)(2n+1)\frac{\sigma^{2n-1}}{s^{2n+3}}$$

$$\frac{q_{n-1}(\lambda S)q_n(-\lambda\sigma) - q_{n-1}(-\lambda S)q_n(\lambda\sigma)}{q_{n-1}(\lambda S)q_{n+1}(-\lambda s) - q_{n-1}(-\lambda S)q_{n+1}(\lambda s)}.$$

The formula becomes especially simple for the case where $S = \infty$, that is, when we have to deal with a spherical hollow in an infinitely extended mass.

Then $q_{n-1}(\lambda S) = 0$, and we get

$$\phi_1\sqrt{-1} - \phi_2 = -2(n+1)(2n+1)\frac{\sigma^{2r+1}}{s^{2n+3}}\cdot\frac{q_n(\lambda\sigma)}{q_{n+1}(\lambda s)}.$$

If we may neglect $\mu\rho = \sigma$ in comparison with unity, on account of the small value of ω, we may put for the q's their values for small arguments (p. 77). We then obtain

$$\phi_1\sqrt{-1} - \phi_2 = \lambda^2\epsilon^{-(\sigma-s)},$$

or since we have in part already neglected quantities of order σ

$$\phi_1 \sqrt{-1} - \phi_2 = \lambda^2 = \sqrt{-1}$$
$$\phi_1 = 1, \quad \phi_2 = 0,$$

as must be the case.

On the other hand, if $\mu\rho$ be large compared with unity, and we put for the q's their approximate values for large arguments (p. 77), we get

$$\phi_1 + \phi_2 \sqrt{-1} = (2n+1)\left(\frac{\rho}{r}\right)^n \frac{1}{\lambda s} \epsilon^{-\lambda(\sigma - s)}.$$

Hence result phenomena similar to those for the spherical shell; the rotation is $\pi/4i$ at the innermost layer, and thence increases indefinitely as ρ increases to infinity.

For ψ we find

$$\psi = \frac{2n+1}{2n} A \sqrt{\frac{i\omega}{\kappa \pi}} \epsilon^{-\frac{\mu}{\sqrt{2}}(\rho - r)} \sin\left(i\omega - \frac{\pi}{4} - \frac{\mu}{\sqrt{2}}(\rho - r)\right) P_{ni},$$

which expression is quite analogous to that obtained for the spherical shell.

Moreover, we easily see that, even for the smallest velocities of rotation, ρ can always be chosen so large in un-limited space that the approximation made may be permissible: Neglecting hence even for the smallest values of ω the induction will pass self-induction. through all possible angles, at distances, it is true, where the intensity is very small.

I here wish to draw attention to the remark I have already made on p. 61 in regard to neglecting self-induction.

It would be very easy to extend the results obtained for spherical shells to plane plates of finite thickness; but in order to avoid complicated calculations I omit the investigation. The chief part of the phenomena can, in fact, be deduced without calculation from what has been already discussed.

§ 5. FORCES WHICH ARE EXERTED BY THE INDUCED CURRENTS.

We shall now calculate the forces exerted by the induced currents and the heat generated by them. The latter is equivalent to the work which must be done in order to main-tain the rotation.

A. *Potential of the Induced Currents.*

1. We first calculate it for external space. The part of it due to the spherical layer between $\rho = a$ and $\rho = a + da$ is

Its value in external space.

$$d\Omega_e = \frac{4\pi n}{2n+1}\left(\frac{a}{\rho}\right)^{n+1}\psi_{ni}(a)da,$$

when we consider the term ψ_{ni} of the whole current-function ψ.
Now

$$\psi_{ni}(a)da = -A\,\frac{\omega}{\kappa}a\left(\frac{a}{R}\right)^n\frac{i}{n+1}(f_1(a)\sin i\omega + f_2(a)\cos i\omega)P_{ni}da.$$

Substituting this value in $d\Omega$, and attempting to perform the integrations, we meet with the integrals

$$\int_r^R a^{2n+2}f(a)da.$$

But we have

$$\int_r^R a^{2n+2}f_1(a)da = \frac{(2n+1)R^{2n+1}}{4\pi}F_1(R)$$

$$= -\frac{(2n+1)\kappa}{4\pi i\omega}f_2(R).R^{2n+1},$$

according to the definition of F (p. 68), and the equations satisfied by f_1, f_2, F_1, F_2 (p. 70); and similarly

$$\int_r^R a^{2n+2}f_2(a)da = -\frac{(2n+1)\kappa}{4\pi i\omega}(1-f_1(R)).R^{2n+1}.$$

Using these expressions we find

$$\Omega_e = \frac{n}{n+1}A\left(\frac{R}{\rho}\right)^{n+1}[f_2(R)\sin i\omega + \{1 - f_1(R)\}\cos i\omega]P_{ni}.$$

For very small angular velocities $f_2 = 0, f_1 = 1$, and thus $\Omega_e = 0$. For very large ones $f_1 = f_2 = 0$, and thus at the surface of the spherical shell

$$\bar{\Omega} = \frac{n}{n+1}\bar{\chi}_n.$$

2. In precisely the same way we may perform the investi- Value in the inside space. gation for the space inside the spherical shell; we find

$$\Omega_i = -\left(\frac{\rho}{R}\right)^n A[f_2(r)\sin i\omega + \{1 - f_1(r)\}\cos i\omega]P_{ni}.$$

Hence for the whole potential

$$\Omega_i + \chi_n = A\left(\frac{\rho}{R}\right)^n [f_1(r)\cos i\omega - f_2(r)\sin i\omega]P_{ni}.$$

For vanishing angular velocities this expression reduces to χ_n, for large ones to zero; more exactly for large values of μ we find by means of a formula which we have employed previously (p. 81)

$$f_1(r) + f_2(r)\sqrt{-1} = \frac{2(2n+1)}{\lambda\mu r}\left(\frac{R}{r}\right)^n \frac{1}{\epsilon^{\lambda(S-s)} - \epsilon^{-\lambda(S-s)}}$$

$$= 2(n+1)\left(\frac{R}{r}\right)^n \frac{1}{\lambda\mu r}\epsilon^{-\lambda\mu(R-r)}.$$

Hence it follows that

$$\Omega_i + \chi_n$$

$$= A\frac{2(2n+1)}{\mu r}\left(\frac{\rho}{r}\right)^n \epsilon^{-\frac{\mu}{\sqrt{2}}(R-r)}\cos\left(i\omega - \frac{\pi}{4} - \frac{\mu}{\sqrt{2}}(R-r)\right)P_{ni}.$$

Thus the internal potential diminishes with exceedingly great rapidity as the velocity increases. At the same time its equipotential surfaces exhibit the peculiarity of appearing turned through an angle proportional to the [square root of Peculiar the] angular velocity. As the velocity gradually increases behaviour of the mag- the forces conditioned by the potential take up successively netic forces all the directions of the compass; and this can be repeated in the inside space. any number of times as the velocity goes on increasing.

B. *Heat Generated.*

Let R be the radius of a very thin spherical shell, and suppose that in it exists the current-function

$$\psi = \Sigma\psi_n.$$

Let the resistance of the shell be k: required the heat W generated in it.

We determine the values of u, v, w belonging to ψ, and in particular to the term

Heat generated in a spherical shell.

$$\psi_{ni} = A \sin i\omega P_{ni}.$$

When u, v, w have been found, the heat generated is

$$W = k \int (u^2 + v^2 + w^2)ds,$$

the integral being extended over the whole surface of the sphere.

Introducing Ω and Θ to denote currents parallel to circles of latitude and to the meridians in the direction of increasing θ and ω, we have

$$\Omega = -\frac{1}{R} \frac{\partial \psi}{\partial \theta},$$

$$\Theta = -\frac{1}{R \sin \theta} \frac{\partial \psi}{\partial \omega},$$

$$u = \Theta \cos \theta \cos \omega + \Omega \sin \omega,$$

$$v = \Theta \cos \theta \sin \omega - \Omega \cos \omega,$$

$$w = -\Theta \sin \theta.$$

Substituting for ψ_{ni} the value given we get

$$u = \frac{A}{R}\{ -\cos i\omega \cos \omega . iP_{ni} . \cot \theta - \sin i\omega \sin \omega P'_{ni}\}$$

$$u = \frac{A}{R}\{ -\cos i\omega \sin \omega . iP_{ni} . \cot \theta + \sin i\omega \cos \omega P'_{ni}\},$$

$$w = \frac{A}{R}i \cos i\omega . P_{ni}.$$

But now

$$iP_{ni} \cot \theta = \tfrac{1}{2}\{P_{n,i+1} + (n+i)(n-i+1)P_{n,i-1}\},$$

$$P'_{ni} = \tfrac{1}{2}\{ -P_{n,i+1} + (n+i)(n-i+1)P_{n,i-1}\}.$$

Substituted in u, v, w these give

$$u = -\frac{A}{2R}\{\cos (i+1)\omega . P_{n,i+1}$$

$$+ (n+i)(n-i+1) \cos (i-1)\omega . P_{n,i-1}\},$$

$$v = -\frac{A}{2R}\{\sin (i+1)\omega . P_{n,i+1}$$
$$- (n+i)(n-i+1) . \sin (i-1)\omega . P_{n,i-1}\},$$
$$w = \frac{A}{R}i \cos i\omega . P_{ni}.$$

Thus u, v, w are developed in terms of spherical harmonics. We suppose the u, v, w expanded in a similar form for all the terms, and then form the expression

$$\int (u^2 + v^2 + w^2)ds.$$

On integration, terms involving products of spherical harmonics of different orders vanish, so that we may determine W_n separately for each ψ_n, and add the results. A closer consideration then shows that we may also determine the heat separately for each ψ_{ni} and again add the results. It is true that all the integrals do not vanish which correspond to combinations of different ψ_{ni}'s; but those integrals in $\int u^2 ds$ for which this occurs will be destroyed by corresponding ones in $\int v^2 ds$.

We now get for the ψ_{ni} above quoted

$$W_{ni} = k\int (u^2 + v^2 + w^2)ds$$

$$= \frac{kA^2}{4R^2}\left\{\int (P_{n,i+1})^2 ds\right.$$

$$+ (n+i)^2(n-i+1)^2\int (P_{n,i-1})^2 ds + 4i^2\int (\cos i\omega P_{ni})^2 ds\right\},$$

which gives, by well-known formulæ and simple reductions

$$W_{ni} = kA^2\frac{2\pi n(n+1)}{2n+1}(n-i+1)(n-i+2)\ldots(n+i)$$
$$= kA^2(n,i),$$

where (n,i) is an easily intelligible abbreviation. Since we have further

$$W = \Sigma\Sigma W_{ni},$$
$$\scriptstyle n \quad i$$

our problem is solved. It is easily seen that the result may be expressed in the forms

$$W = \frac{k}{R^2} \Sigma_n n(n+1) \Sigma_i \int \psi^2_{ni} ds,$$

or

$$W = \frac{k}{R^2} \Sigma_n n(n+1) \int \psi^2_n ds.$$

The preceding theorem might perhaps have been more simply demonstrated by means of reasoning based on Green's theorem. In the proof here given the following formulæ are implicitly involved

Analytical formulæ.

$$\int \left\{ \left(\frac{\partial \psi_n}{\partial \omega_x} \right)^2 + \left(\frac{\partial \psi}{\partial \omega_y} \right)^2 + \left(\frac{\partial \psi}{\partial \omega_z} \right)^2 \right\} ds = n(n+1) \int \psi^2_n ds,$$

$$\frac{\partial}{\partial \omega_x}(\sin i\omega P_{ni}) = -\tfrac{1}{2} \cos (i+1)\omega P_{n,i+1}$$

$$- \tfrac{1}{2}(n+i)(n-i+1) \cos (i-1)\omega P_{n,i-1},$$

$$\frac{\partial}{\partial \omega_y}(\sin i\omega P_{ni}) = -\tfrac{1}{2} \sin (i+1)\omega P_{n,i+1}$$

$$+ \tfrac{1}{2}(n+i)(n-i+1) \sin (i-1)\omega P_{n,i-1},$$

$$\frac{\partial}{\partial \omega_z}(\sin i\omega P_{ni}) = i \cos i\omega P_{ni},$$

and to these similar equations may easily be added. If ω, θ and ω', θ' refer to systems of polar co-ordinates with different axes, the equations last quoted enable us to deduce integrals of the form

$$\int \cos i\omega P_{ni}(\theta) \cos j\omega' P_{nj}(\theta') ds',$$

(in which the integrations are to be performed with respect to ω', θ') from the well-known integral

$$\int P_{n,0}(\theta) \cos j\omega' P_{nj}(\theta') ds' = \frac{4}{2n+1} \cos j\omega P_{nj}(\theta),$$

Generation of heat in the rotating sphere. but, it is true, only by laborious calculation. I now proceed to determine the heat generated in the rotating sphere by the term χ_{ni} of the inducing potential. To χ_{ni} corresponds

$$\psi_{ni} = -\frac{\omega}{\kappa}A\rho\left(\frac{\rho}{R}\right)^n \frac{i}{n+1}(f_1 \sin i\omega + f_2 \cos i\omega)P_{ni},$$

and hence the heat

$$W_{ni} = \frac{\omega^2}{\kappa}A^2\frac{i^2(n,i)}{(n+1)^2}\int_r^R \left(\frac{\rho}{R}\right)^{2n}(f_1^2+f_2^2)\rho^2 d\rho.$$

The integration can be performed for small and for large Small velo-
angular velocities. For the former $f_1 = 1$, $f_2 = 0$, and thus cities.
the heat generated becomes in this case

$$W_{ni} = A^2\frac{R^3\omega^2}{\kappa}\frac{i^2(n,i)}{(n+1)^2(2n+3)}\left(1 - \left(\frac{r}{R}\right)^{2n+3}\right).$$

For very large angular velocities we had

$$f_1^2+f_2^2 = \frac{(2n+1)^2}{\mu^2}\frac{R^{2n}}{\rho^{2n+2}}\epsilon^{-\mu\sqrt{2}(R-\rho)}.$$

Large velo-
cities.

The integral W_{ni} may be taken from $r = 0$, and becomes

$$\int_0^R \frac{(2n+1)^2}{\mu^2}\epsilon^{-\mu\sqrt{2}(R-\rho)}d\rho = \frac{(2n+1)^2}{\mu^3\sqrt{2}},$$

for $R\mu$ may be regarded as infinite. Hence we get for very large values of ω

$$W_{ni} = A^2\frac{(2n+1)^2(n,i)}{8(n+1)^2}\sqrt{\frac{\kappa\omega i}{2\pi^3}},$$

and W depends on R, in so far as A involves R.

Hence the heat generated increases indefinitely as ω increases,[1] and indeed proportionately to $\sqrt{\omega}$. The same holds good for the work which has to be done in order to maintain the rotation. If the inducing magnets form a rigidly connected system, they are subject to a couple about the axis of

---

[1] As regards the apparent contradiction with the result got for infinitely thin spherical shells the remark on p. 82 holds.

rotation which can be calculated from the heat generated. For if we imagine the shell at rest and the inducing magnets rotating with angular velocity ω, then the couple of moment D, which maintains the rotation, does work $2\pi\omega D$ per unit time, and this work is equal to the heat generated. Thus—

$$D = \frac{W}{2\pi\omega}.$$

Couple exerted on the inducing magnets. But this couple is equal to that with which in the reverse case the rotating sphere acts on the magnets at rest. It is easy to see that for small values of ω D increases proportionately to ω/κ, but for large values decreases proportionately to $\sqrt{\chi/\omega}$, ultimately becoming zero. (This does not prevent work being done of the order $\sqrt{\omega}$.) On the other hand we have seen already that for infinitely large values of ω the forces exerted on the inducing magnets are finite, and since now they produce no couple about the axis of rotation their resultant must act in a plane through the axis.

In fact for infinite velocities the sphere behaves as regards the external magnets as a conducting sphere does with regard to electric charges; but a conducting sphere cannot impart to inducing charges any rotation about an axis through its centre.

§ 6. Rotation of Magnetic Spheres.

I now assume that the material of the sphere is capable of magnetisation, but that it is without coercive force.

We must first form the expressions for the electromotive forces in this case. According to the precedent of § 1, 6, in order to find the effect of magnetisation, we must in the general expressions for the electromotive forces replace

$$U \text{ by } \frac{\partial M}{\partial z} - \frac{\partial N}{\partial y},$$

$$V \text{ by } \frac{\partial N}{\partial x} - \frac{\partial L}{\partial z},$$

$$W \text{ by } \frac{\partial L}{\partial y} - \frac{\partial M}{\partial x}.$$

We must accordingly replace—

$$\frac{\partial V}{\partial x} - \frac{\partial U}{\partial y} \text{ by } \nabla^2 N + \frac{\partial \chi}{\partial z}$$

$$\frac{\partial U}{\partial z} - \frac{\partial W}{\partial x} \text{ by } \nabla^2 M + \frac{\partial \chi}{\partial y} \qquad (1),$$

$$\frac{\partial W}{\partial y} - \frac{\partial V}{\partial z} \text{ by } \nabla^2 L + \frac{\partial \chi}{\partial x}$$

since

$$\frac{\partial L}{\partial x} + \frac{\partial M}{\partial y} + \frac{\partial N}{\partial z} = -\chi \qquad (2).$$

But now

$$\nabla^2 L = -4\pi\lambda$$
$$\nabla^2 M = -4\pi\mu \qquad (3),$$
$$\nabla^2 N = -4\pi\nu$$

and

$$\frac{\lambda}{\theta} = \frac{\partial V}{\partial z} - \frac{\partial W}{\partial y} - \frac{\partial \chi}{\partial x}$$

$$\frac{\mu}{\theta} = \frac{\partial W}{\partial x} - \frac{\partial U}{\partial z} - \frac{\partial \chi}{\partial y} \qquad (4).$$

$$\frac{\nu}{\theta} = \frac{\partial U}{\partial y} - \frac{\partial V}{\partial x} - \frac{\partial \chi}{\partial z}$$

If by these equations we eliminate L, M, N from the expressions (1), and add the forces directly exerted by the currents, that is $\frac{\partial V}{\partial x} - \frac{\partial U}{\partial y}$, etc., we get for the expressions, which are now to be substituted for $\frac{\partial V}{\partial x} - \frac{\partial U}{\partial y}$, etc., the following :—

$$\left(1 + 4\pi\theta\right)\left(\frac{\partial V}{\partial x} - \frac{\partial U}{\partial y} + \frac{\partial \chi}{\partial z}\right)$$

$$\left(1 + 4\pi\theta\right)\left(\frac{\partial U}{\partial z} - \frac{\partial W}{\partial x} + \frac{\partial \chi}{\partial y}\right) \qquad (5).$$

$$\left(1 + 4\pi\theta\right)\left(\frac{\partial W}{\partial y} - \frac{\partial V}{\partial z} + \frac{\partial \chi}{\partial x}\right)$$

Here χ denotes the total potential; but this consists—

(a) Of the given external potential of the inducing magnets.

(b) Of the potential χ_θ of the magnetised sphere itself. This last satisfies the conditions:—

Inside

$$\nabla^2 \chi_\theta = 0 \qquad (6),$$

as follows from equation (2) and (4); at the surface—

$$4\pi\theta N_\rho = (1 + 4\pi\theta)\left(\frac{\partial \chi_\theta}{\partial \rho}\right)_i - \left(\frac{\partial \chi_\theta}{\partial \rho}\right)_e, \qquad (7),$$

where $N\rho$ is the radial force exerted by the external magnetism and the induced currents.

In words we may thus express the effect of the magnetisability of the medium:—

The magnetisation firstly alters the internal magnetising force in the manner shown by the general theory of magnetism, and secondly increases the effects of the magnetising force in the ratio $1 + 4\pi\theta : 1$. The two effects are opposed, and the result is that the action is found to be increased in only a finite degree even for large values of θ.

Self-induction neglected.   Let us again, to begin with, neglect self-induction. It is to be remarked that this is allowable only when

$$R\sqrt{\frac{4\pi\omega(1 + 4\pi\theta)}{\kappa}}$$

is very small. When θ and R are large, ω must be very small absolutely to satisfy this condition.

If the external potential be

$$\chi_n = A\rho^n Y_n,$$

the potential of the spherical shell itself may be expressed in the form

$$\chi_\theta = \left(C + \frac{B r^{2n+1}}{\rho^{2n+1}}\right)\chi_n,$$

and the total potential therefore in the form

$$\chi = \left(A + B\left(\frac{r}{\rho}\right)^{2n+1}\right)\chi_n.$$

According to what precedes, the magnetic spherical shell is in exactly the same condition as a non-magnetisable one of equal resistance which is subject to the influence of a potential

$$(1 + 4\pi\theta)\left(A + B\left(\frac{r}{\rho}\right)^{2n+1}\right)\chi_n.$$

Since this potential consists of two spherical harmonics, the currents may by what precedes be regarded as known.

For the current-function we get

$$\psi = -\frac{\omega}{\kappa}(1 + 4\pi\theta)\left(\frac{A}{n+1} - \frac{B}{n}\left(\frac{r}{\rho}\right)^{2n+1}\right)\rho\frac{\partial\chi_n}{\partial\omega}.$$

Under like conditions, only with $\theta = 0$, we should have got the current-function

$$\psi_0 = -\frac{\omega}{\kappa}\frac{\rho}{n+1}\frac{\partial\chi_n}{\partial\omega}.$$

By division we get

$$\psi = (1 + 4\pi\theta)\left(A - \frac{n+1}{n}B\left(\frac{r}{\rho}\right)^{2n+1}\right)\psi_0.$$

The form of the currents in the various layers is unaltered, but the intensity is differently distributed. It is convenient to describe the phenomenon by comparison of ψ and ψ_0. The quantities A, B are given by equations (6), (7); if we write $\frac{r}{R} = \epsilon$, they are found to be

$$A = \frac{(2n+1)\{(2n+1)(1+4\pi\theta) - 4\pi\theta n\}}{n(n+1)16\pi^2\theta^2(1 - \epsilon^{2n+1}) + (2n+1)^2(1+4\pi\theta)},$$

$$B = \frac{4\pi\theta n(2n+1)}{n(n+1)16\pi^2\theta^2(1 - \epsilon^{2n+1}) + (2n+1)^2(1+4\pi\theta)}.$$

As the interpretation of these expressions is not very obvious, we shall apply them to some simple cases.   Special cases.

1. θ is very small.   Expanding we get

$$A = 1 - \frac{n}{2n+1}4\pi\theta, \quad B = \frac{n}{2n+1}4\pi\theta, \qquad \text{θ very small.}$$

and hence

$$\psi = \psi_0 + \frac{n+1}{2n+1}4\pi\theta\left(1-\left(\frac{r}{\rho}\right)^{2n-1}\right)\psi_0.$$

Thus the current intensity is unaltered at the inner surface of the spherical shell; in other portions it is always increased when θ is positive. The increase is directly proportional to θ. In diamagnetic spheres the intensity is everywhere less than in neutral ones. The rotation of magnetic spheres absorbs more work, that of diamagnetic ones less work than that of neutral ones.

θ very large.

2. Let θ be very great and ϵ not nearly equal to unity. Then we have

$$A = \frac{2n+1}{4\pi\theta n\left(1-\epsilon^{2n-1}\right)},$$

$$B = \frac{2n+1}{4\pi\theta\left(n+1\right)\left(1-\epsilon^{2n-1}\right)},$$

and hence

$$\psi = \frac{2n+1}{n}\frac{1-\left(\frac{r}{\rho}\right)^{2n-1}}{1-\left(\frac{r}{R}\right)^{2n+1}}\psi_0.$$

Thus the current in the innermost layer is here zero: thence it increases rapidly outwards and becomes $(2n+1)/n$ times as great at the outer surface as for the neutral sphere. If θ is at all large the increase of current is almost independent of its absolute value.

Thin spherical shells.

3. Let ϵ be infinitely nearly equal to unity. Then

$$A = \frac{(2n+1)(1+4\pi\theta)-4\pi\theta n}{(2n+1)(1+4\pi\theta)},$$

$$B = \frac{4\pi\theta n}{(2n+1)(1+4\pi\theta)}.$$

Thus

$$\psi = \psi_0.$$

In infinitely thin spherical shells the magnetic permeability is without effect on the induced currents (though the magnetisation is not zero, and the magnetic forces in the shell are altered). It may here be noted that this result holds also when self-induction is taken into account.

4. Let $\epsilon = 0$, which is the case of a solid sphere. The Solid sphere. term with a negative power of ρ vanishes, and we get

$$A = \frac{1}{1 + \dfrac{4\pi\theta n}{2n+1}},$$

$$\psi = \frac{1 + 4\pi\theta}{1 + \dfrac{n}{2n+1}4\pi\theta}\psi_0.$$

For large values of θ we have

$$\psi = \frac{2n+1}{n}\psi_0$$

The quantity $2n+1/n$ lies between 2 and 3.

Hence in iron spheres the currents are from two to three times as strong as in a non-magnetic metal of equal resistance; the heat generated, the work used up, and the damping produced are from four to nine times as great as in such a metal.

5. Plane plates.

A very thin plane plate may be looked upon as portion of Plane plates. a very thin spherical shell, hence for such a one

$$\psi = \psi_0.$$

A very thick plate may be regarded as portion of an infinitely large solid sphere; since n is to be put very large we have for such a plate

$$\psi = \frac{1 + 4\pi\theta}{2 + 2\pi\theta}\psi_0.$$

In both limiting cases the total current-function remains unaltered; in the last case for large values of θ the intensity is doubled by the permeability.

For medium thicknesses of the plates intermediate values

hold; the calculations are easily performed, but since they give no very simple results they have been omitted here.

We shall now take into account self-induction, but shall only perform the calculations for a solid sphere. Spherical shells do not offer analytical difficulties of any special kind, but the calculations become exceedingly complicated.

We find the currents by the following reasoning :—

Let the inducing potential be

$$\chi_{ni} = A\left(\frac{\rho}{R}\right)^n \cos i\omega P_{ni}.$$

Let ψ_0 be the current-function directly induced by χ_{ni} then we have

$$\psi_0 = -\frac{1 + 4\pi\theta}{1 + \dfrac{n}{2n+1}4\pi\theta} \cdot \frac{\omega}{\kappa} A\rho\left(\frac{\rho}{R}\right)^n \frac{i}{n+1}\sin i\omega P_{ni}.$$

Let the actual current-function be

$$\psi = -\frac{\omega}{\kappa} A\rho\left(\frac{\rho}{R}\right)^n \frac{i}{n+1}(f_1 \sin i\omega + f_2 \cos i\omega)P_{ni}.$$

We have to find the currents induced by this. For this purpose it is necessary first to know the potential χ_θ induced by ψ in the magnetic mass.

The current-function

$$\psi = \rho\left(\frac{\rho}{R}\right)^n f(\rho)Y_n$$

produces a radial magnetic force

$$N_\rho = \frac{x}{\rho}\left(\frac{\partial W}{\partial y} - \frac{\partial V}{\partial z}\right) + \frac{y}{\rho}\left(\frac{\partial U}{\partial z} - \frac{\partial W}{\partial x}\right) + \frac{z}{\rho}\left(\frac{\partial V}{\partial x} - \frac{\partial U}{\partial y}\right)$$

$$= \frac{O}{\rho} \quad \text{(p. 63)}$$

$$= -\frac{n(n+1)}{\rho}F(\rho)\cdot\left(\frac{\rho}{R}\right)^n Y_n \quad \text{(p. 65),}$$

where F, f are connected by the equation of p. 68.

From these equations and from the equations determining χ_θ (equations (6) and (7), p. 94) we get χ_θ in the general case, and therefore in our particular case we have

$$\chi_\theta = \frac{4\pi\theta n(n+1)}{2n+1+4\pi\theta n}$$

$$\cdot \frac{\omega}{k}A\frac{i}{n+1}\left(\frac{\rho}{R}\right)^n \cdot \left\{F_1(R)\sin i\omega + F_2(R)\cos i\omega\right\}P_{ni}.$$

If now by ψ' we mean that current-function which ψ and χ_θ together would produce in the unmagnetised sphere, then in the magnetic mass they will produce the current-function

$$\psi'_\theta = (1 + 4\pi\theta)\psi',$$

and the condition for the stationary state becomes

$$\psi = \psi_0 + \psi'_\theta.$$

ψ' is to be formed in exactly the same way as before, so that ψ'_θ also is known. If we substitute the values of ψ, ψ_0, ψ'_θ in the last equation and equate coefficients of $\cos i\omega$ and $\sin i\omega$, we get for f_1, f_2, F_1, and F_2 these equations

$$f_1(\rho) = \frac{(2n+1)(1+4\pi\theta)}{2n+1+4\pi\theta n} - \frac{\omega i}{k}\frac{4\pi\theta n(1+4\pi\theta)}{2n+1+4\pi\theta n}F_2(R)$$

$$+ \frac{\omega i}{k}(1+4\pi\theta)F_2(\rho),$$

$$f_2(\rho) = \frac{\omega i}{k}\frac{4\pi\theta n(1+4\pi\theta)}{2n+1+4\pi\theta n}F_1(R) - \frac{\omega i}{k}(1+4\pi\theta)F_1(\rho).$$

If we put

$$\frac{4\pi i\omega}{k}(1+4\pi\theta) = \mu^2,$$

$$f_1(\rho) = \phi_1(\mu\rho) = \phi_1(\sigma),$$

$$f_2(\rho) = \phi_2(\mu\rho) = \phi_2(\sigma),$$

then ϕ_1, ϕ_2 are given by precisely the same differential equations as before (p. 71). Since we are dealing with a solid sphere, we must only retain those solutions which are finite at the centre, and may put

$$\phi_1(\sigma) = A p_n(\lambda_1\sigma) + B p_n(\lambda_2\sigma),$$

$$\phi_2(\sigma) = -\lambda_1^2 A p_n(\lambda_1\sigma) - \lambda_2^2 B p_n(\lambda_2\sigma),$$

$$\lambda = \lambda_1 = \sqrt{\tfrac{1}{2}}(1 + \sqrt{-1}),$$

$$\lambda_2 = \sqrt{\tfrac{1}{2}}(1 - \sqrt{-1}).$$

The constants are determined in precisely the same way as above. The integrals to be formed are not different from those got before, but the calculation is somewhat more intricate, owing to the complicated constants. The result, however, is comparatively simple, namely

The solution.

$$f_1(\rho) + f_2(\rho)\sqrt{-1} = \frac{(2n+1)(1+4\pi\theta)p_n(\lambda\mu\rho)}{2n p_{n-1}(\lambda\mu R) + 4\pi\theta n p_n(\lambda\mu R)}.$$

We first verify this result. For vanishing θ it gives

Comparison with previous results.

$$f_1 + f_2\sqrt{-1} = \frac{2n+1}{2n}\frac{p_n(\lambda\mu\rho)}{p_{n-1}(\lambda\mu R)},$$

which agrees with the result already obtained for a non-magnetic solid sphere (p. 75).

Further, for vanishing ω it gives, since

$$p_n(0) = \frac{2^{n+1}\lfloor n}{1 . 3 \ldots (2n+1)},$$

$$f_1 + f_2\sqrt{-1} = \frac{(2n+1)(1+4\pi\theta)}{2n+1+4\pi\theta n},$$

which result also we have found (p. 97).

In general it appears that the form of the currents in a magnetic sphere is the same as for a non-magnetic sphere of equal resistance which is rotating $(1+4\pi\theta)$ times as fast as the magnetic sphere. But in addition the two current-systems differ in that they are turned as a whole through a certain angle relatively to one another, and that their intensities are different.

Small velocities of rotation.

I apply the formula to two special cases.

1. Let $4\pi\theta$ be very great, but ω sufficiently small that

$\mu^2 R^2$ may be neglected in comparison with unity. We must expand the expression, retaining only the first power of that quantity. We have

$$f_1 + f_2 \sqrt{-1} = \frac{2n+1}{n} \frac{p_n(\mu\rho\lambda)}{p_n(\mu R\lambda)}$$

$$= \frac{2n+1}{n} \cdot \frac{2(2n+3)+\mu^2\rho^2\sqrt{-1}}{2(2n+3)+\mu^2 R^2\sqrt{-1}} \quad \text{(p. 77)}.$$

We get for the angle of rotation, neglecting higher powers than the first

$$\delta = \tan^{-1}\frac{f_2}{f_1} = -\frac{\mu^2}{2(2n+3)}(R^2 - \rho^2),$$

$$\frac{\delta}{i} = -\frac{16\pi^2\omega\theta}{2(2n+3)\kappa}(R^2 - \rho^2).$$

Hence the rotation vanishes at the outer surface;[1] generally it is considerably increased, compared with that for a non-magnetic sphere nearly in the ratio $4\pi\theta : 1$.

In Fig. 9 are given the curves for an iron sphere corresponding to those for a copper sphere represented on p. 80.

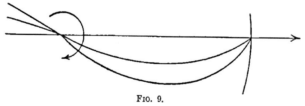

FIG. 9.

The resistance of iron is taken to be six times that of copper, and $4\pi\theta$ is put $= 200$. The velocities represented are exceedingly small ones, namely one revolution in five and one in ten seconds; even here the effect of self-induction is well marked (*cf.* Fig. 15 *b*, p. 123).

2. If ω become very great, whilst θ retains a finite but otherwise arbitrary value, the phenomenon becomes very similar to that in non-magnetic spheres, as may be easily deduced from the formulæ. Here also the angle of rotation

Large velocities.

---

[1] A consequence of the fact that at this surface for large values of θ, according to the equations for χ_θ,

$$N_r = \frac{\partial \chi_\theta}{\partial r}.$$

becomes $\pi/4i$ at the outer surface. The phenomenon is identical with that which occurs in a non-magnetic sphere with $(1+4\pi\theta)$ times the velocity. The heat generated is $\sqrt{1+4\pi\theta}$ times that generated in a non-magnetic sphere rotating with equal velocity.

§ 7. RELATED PROBLEMS.

In this paragraph we shall consider some problems which stand in very close relation to those already treated.

I.

Any solid of revolution.   If we neglect self-induction we may apply our knowledge of the currents in a sphere to find those in a solid of revolution of any form whatever, or at least to reduce their determination to a simpler problem.

Let S be the surface of revolution bounding the solid, n its inward normal. Describe about it a sphere of any radius. Let u_1, v_1, w_1 be the currents which would flow in the latter, and let

$$N = u_1 \cos a + v_1 \cos b + w_1 \cos c$$

be the current in the direction of n at the surface S. If we determine u_2, v_2, w_2 so that

$$\kappa u_2 = -\frac{\partial \phi_2}{\partial x}$$

$$\kappa v_2 = -\frac{\partial \phi_2}{\partial y},$$

$$\kappa w_2 = -\frac{\partial \phi_2}{\partial z},$$

$$\frac{\partial u_2}{\partial x}+\frac{\partial v_2}{\partial y}+\frac{\partial w_2}{\partial z}=0,$$

$$u_2 \cos a + v_2 \cos b + w_2 \cos c = -N,$$

then clearly

$$u_1+u_2,\ v_1+v_2,\ w_1+w_2$$

are the currents sought in S. Hence the problem is reduced to this simpler one :—

To determine such a function ϕ_2 that inside S $\nabla^2\phi_2 = 0$, and at its surface $\partial\phi/\partial n = \kappa N$, a given function.

1. As an example, suppose a plate bounded by the straight line $\xi = b$ to move parallel to a given straight line. Suppose the external potential expanded, and let a term of it be

$$A\epsilon^{-\zeta n} \cos r\eta \cos s\xi$$

Then we found for the current in the infinite plate

$$\psi_1 = A\frac{r}{n}\cdot\frac{a}{\kappa}\cdot\sin r\eta.\cos s\xi.$$

Thus the current perpendicular to the boundary is

$$-\frac{\partial\psi_1}{\partial\eta} = -A\frac{r^2}{n}\cdot\frac{a}{\kappa}\cdot\cos r\eta.\cos sb.$$

Hence we get for ϕ_2 the conditions

$$\frac{\partial^2\phi_2}{\partial\xi^2}+\frac{\partial^2\phi_2}{\partial\eta^2} = 0\ ,$$

and for $\xi = b$

$$\frac{\partial\phi_2}{\partial\xi} = A\frac{r^2}{n}\cdot\frac{a}{\kappa}\cdot\cos r\eta.\cos sb.$$

We have

$$\phi_2 = A\frac{r}{n}\frac{a}{\kappa}\epsilon^{r(\xi-b)}\cos r\eta.\cos sb.$$

To ϕ_2 corresponds the current-function

$$\psi_2 = -A\frac{r}{n}\cdot\frac{a}{\kappa}\cdot\epsilon^{r(\xi-b)}\sin r\eta.\cos sb,$$

and thus the total current-function becomes

$$\psi_1+\psi_2 = A\frac{r}{n}\cdot\frac{a}{\kappa}\cdot\epsilon^{-rb}\sin r\eta(\epsilon^{rb}.\cos s\xi - \epsilon^{r\xi}.\cos sb).$$

By summing for all the terms we get the complete solution. The solution for a band bounded on both sides is similar.

2. In order to determine the currents in a limited rotating disc, let a term of the external potential be

$$A\epsilon^{-n\zeta}\cos i\omega J_i(n\rho).$$

Then we had

$$\psi_1 = A\frac{\omega}{\kappa}\frac{i}{n}\sin i\omega J_i(n\rho).$$

Thus the inward radial current is at the boundary where $\rho = R$

$$\frac{\partial\psi}{R\partial\omega} = A\frac{\omega}{\kappa}\frac{i^2}{n}\cos i\omega\frac{J_i(nR)}{R}.$$

Hence we find as above

$$\phi_2 = -A\frac{\omega}{\kappa}\frac{i}{n}J_i(nR)\left(\frac{\rho}{R}\right)^i\cos i\omega.$$

Determining the corresponding current-function ψ_2 we get for the total current-function

$$\psi_1 + \psi_2 = A\frac{\omega}{\kappa}\cdot\frac{i}{n}\frac{\sin i\omega}{R^i}\{R_i J_i(n\rho) - \rho^i J_i(nR)\}.$$

We again get the complete solution by summing for the various terms. In the same way the currents may be determined in rings bounded by concentric circles.

In general the solution of the problem requires neither the development in a series of separate terms nor the determination of the potential ϕ_2; it is sufficient to determine ψ_2 so that inside the plate

$$\frac{\partial^2\psi_2}{\partial x^2} + \frac{\partial^2\psi_2}{\partial y^2} = 0,$$

and at its boundary $\psi_2 = -\psi_1$. Some simple examples will be given in § 9.

II.

In conductors electromotive forces of electromagnetic origin produce the same effects as numerically equal electrostatic forces. If this is true also of dielectrics, then spheres of dielectric material must become polarised when rotating in a magnetic field.

Let

$$\mathfrak{x},\ \mathfrak{y},\ \mathfrak{z}\frac{\mathrm{mm}^{\frac{1}{2}}\ \mathrm{mgr}^{\frac{1}{2}}\ {}^{1}}{\sec}$$

be the components of the polarisation,

$$\epsilon\ (\text{number})\,{}^{1}$$

the dielectric constant.

For $\mathfrak{x},\ \mathfrak{y},\ \mathfrak{z}$ we have the equations

$$\mathfrak{x} = -\,\epsilon\frac{\partial\phi}{\partial x}+\epsilon\mathfrak{X}\,,$$

$$\underline{\mathfrak{y}} = -\,\epsilon\frac{\partial\phi}{\partial y}+\epsilon\underline{\mathfrak{Y}}\,,$$

$$\mathfrak{z} = -\,\epsilon\frac{\partial\phi}{\partial z}+\epsilon\mathfrak{Z}\,,$$

$$\frac{\partial\mathfrak{x}}{\partial x}+\frac{\partial\underline{\mathfrak{y}}}{\partial y}+\frac{\partial\mathfrak{z}}{\partial z}=\frac{1}{4\pi}\nabla^{2}\phi\,;$$

for $\rho = \mathrm{R}$

$$\mathfrak{x}x+\mathfrak{y}y+\mathfrak{z}z=\frac{\rho}{4\pi}\left(\frac{\partial\phi_{i}}{\partial\rho}-\frac{\partial\phi_{e}}{\partial\rho}\right).$$

Hence we have for ϕ

$$\nabla^{2}\phi=\frac{4\pi\epsilon}{1+4\pi\epsilon}\left(\frac{\partial\mathfrak{X}}{\partial x}+\frac{\partial\underline{\mathfrak{Y}}}{\partial y}+\frac{\partial\mathfrak{Z}}{\partial z}\right),$$

and for $\rho = \mathrm{R}$

$$(1+4\pi\epsilon)\frac{\partial\phi_{i}}{\partial\rho}-\frac{\partial\phi_{e}}{\partial\rho}=\frac{4\pi\epsilon}{\rho}(x\mathfrak{X}+y\underline{\mathfrak{Y}}+z\mathfrak{Z}).$$

In external space we must have $\nabla^{2}\phi = 0$.

If χ_{n} again be the nth term of the external potential we have, as above (p. 43)

$$\frac{\partial\mathfrak{X}}{\partial x}+\frac{\partial\underline{\mathfrak{Y}}}{\partial y}+\frac{\partial\mathfrak{Z}}{\partial z}=2\omega\frac{\partial\chi_{n}}{\partial z}\,,$$

$$x\mathfrak{X}+y\underline{\mathfrak{Y}}+z\mathfrak{Z}=\omega\left(\rho^{2}\frac{\partial\chi_{n}}{\partial z}-nz\chi_{n}\right).$$

---

[1] The units are again such that $1/\Lambda$, the velocity of light, does not occur. The corresponding magnitudes in magnetic measure are $\Lambda^{2}\mathfrak{x}$, $\Lambda^{2}\mathfrak{y}$, $\Lambda^{2}\mathfrak{z}$, $\Lambda^{2}\epsilon$.

To satisfy the equations of condition we put

$$\phi = \phi^0 + \phi',$$

$$\phi_i^0 = \frac{4\pi\epsilon}{1+4\pi\epsilon}\frac{\omega}{n+1}\left(\rho^2\frac{\partial\chi_n}{\partial z} - nz\chi_n\right),$$

$$\phi_e^0 = \frac{4\pi\epsilon}{1+4\pi\epsilon}\frac{\omega}{n+1}\left[\left(\frac{R}{\rho}\right)^{n+2}\frac{n}{n+1}\left(\frac{\rho^2}{2n+1}\frac{\partial\chi_n}{\partial z} - z\chi_n\right)\right.$$

$$\left. + \left(\frac{R}{\rho}\right)^n\frac{R^2}{2n+1}\overline{\frac{\partial\chi_n}{\partial z}}\right].$$

ϕ_i^0 satisfies the partial differential equation which ϕ is to satisfy. ϕ_e^0 is so formed that (1) it satisfies the equation

$$\nabla^2\phi_e^0 = 0,$$

(2) at the surface of the sphere it is equal to ϕ_i^0. That the first condition is satisfied is seen when we notice that the expressions under the straight lines are spherical surface harmonics of degrees $(n+1)$ and $(n-1)$, as is easily proved. Substituting $\phi^0 + \phi'$ in the equations for ϕ, we get for ϕ' these equations

$$\nabla^2\phi' = 0 \text{ everywhere, } \phi' \text{ continuous,}$$

when $\rho = R$

$$(1+4\pi\epsilon)\frac{\partial\phi_i'}{\partial\rho} = \frac{\partial\phi_e'}{\partial\rho} + \frac{\partial\phi_e^0}{\partial\rho}.$$

to satisfy which is not difficult, as we have already expressed ϕ_e^0 as a series of spherical harmonics.

Earth in dielectric space.   A case of especial interest is that in which a spherical magnet rotates in a surrounding dielectric. For the earth is a rotating magnet, and according to many physicists interplanetary space is a dielectric. To determine the electric potential in this case we must remember that the earth is a conductor; hence in it a distribution will form which will react on the dielectric and make the potential constant at the earth's surface.

If $\chi = \Sigma\chi_n$ is the earth's potential the problem reduces to this:—

To determine ϕ so that in external space

$$\nabla^2\phi = \frac{4\pi\epsilon}{1+4\pi\epsilon} \cdot 2\omega\frac{\partial\chi}{\partial z},$$

and at the surface

$$\phi = \text{const.}$$

We easily find

$$\phi = \frac{4\pi\epsilon}{1+4\pi\epsilon}\omega\sum\frac{R^2-\rho^2}{2n+1}\cdot\frac{\partial\chi_n}{\partial z}.$$

Hence follows the rate of increase of potential at the earth's surface

$$\frac{\partial\phi}{\partial\rho} = -\frac{4\pi\epsilon}{1+4\pi\epsilon}2R\omega\sum\frac{1}{2n+1}\frac{\overline{\partial\chi_n}}{\partial z}.$$

Much the greater part of the earth's magnetic force is due to terms for which $n = -2$, or at any rate is small. Therefore we may write approximately

$$\frac{\partial\phi}{\partial\rho} = \frac{4\pi\epsilon}{1+4\pi\epsilon}\tfrac{2}{3}R\omega\cdot\frac{\overline{\partial\chi}}{\partial z}.$$

$\overline{\partial\chi}/\partial z$ is the component of the earth's magnetic force in the direction of the north pole of the heavens.

If we assume that for interplanetary space $4\pi\epsilon/(1+4\pi\epsilon)$ is very nearly 1, we get for the electromotive forces values of the order of 1 Daniell in 50 m., that is, very small values. However, a term of the form const/ρ may have to be added to the above value of ϕ. Its value depends on the quantity of free electricity on the earth, although it does not vanish with this quantity; but the order of magnitude of the calculated forces is not altered by the presence of this term.

III.

When a sphere of any arbitrary magnetic properties rotates in a liquid, which is itself a conductor, and makes electric contact with the surface of the sphere, the sphere will induce currents in the liquid. In general these no longer flow in concentric spherical shells, but traverse the magnet.

Spherical magnet in a liquid.

The determination of these currents presents no further difficulty apart from self-induction. I shall not enter in detail into the calculations. Fig. 10 represents the simplest case. A homogeneous magnetic sphere rotates about its magnetic axis. The figure drawn represents the lines of flow in a

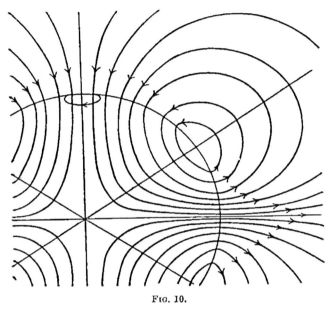

Fig. 10.

meridional section. The form of the lines of flow does not depend upon the resistances of the magnet and the liquid. But the intensity vanishes when either resistance becomes infinitely great.

§ 8. SOLUTION FOR THE FORMULÆ OF THE POTENTIAL LAW.

So far we have assumed for the induced electromotive forces the expressions which Jochmann has deduced for them from Weber's fundamental law. We shall now inquire what changes the results undergo when we use the formulæ which follow from the potential law and are given in vol. lxxviii. of Borchardt's *Journal*.[1]

If $\mathfrak{X}, \mathfrak{Y}, \mathfrak{Z}$ denote the electromotive forces hitherto assumed, $\mathfrak{X}', \mathfrak{Y}', \mathfrak{Z}'$ those which follow from the potential law, we have

---

[1] Helmholtz, *Wiss. Abhandl.* vol. i. p. 702.

$$\mathfrak{X}' = \mathfrak{X} - \omega\frac{\partial}{\partial x}(\mathrm{V}x - \mathrm{U}y),$$

$$\underline{\mathfrak{Y}}' = \underline{\mathfrak{Y}} - \omega\frac{\partial}{\partial y}(\mathrm{V}x - \mathrm{U}y),$$

$$\underset{\sim}{\mathfrak{Z}}' = \underset{\sim}{\mathfrak{Z}} - \omega\frac{\partial}{\partial z}(\mathrm{V}x - \mathrm{U}y).$$

But we saw on p. 67, that for all U, V, W occurring in the investigation

$$\phi = \omega(\mathrm{V}x - \mathrm{U}y).$$

We see at once that we may retain the previous solutions unaltered as regards u, v, w, ψ, Ω. The only alteration which must be made is to put for ϕ', the potential of the free electricity,

$$\phi' = \mathrm{const},$$

and, when free electricity was not present originally,

$$\phi' = 0.$$

On an infinite sphere or plane plate we must have always

$$\phi' = 0.$$

Maxwell obtained the same result, starting from the formulæ of the potential law for conductors at rest. If we reject the terms $a\mathrm{U} + \beta\mathrm{V} + \gamma\mathrm{W}$ in the expressions for the electromotive forces in conductors in motion, the equations for conductors at rest must also be altered, and the equation

$$\phi = 0$$

then no longer holds.

§ 9. Special Cases and Applications.

In conclusion, the formulæ obtained will be applied to some particular cases.

1. A single magnetic pole of strength 1 moves in a straight line parallel to an infinitely thin plane plate. Let the origin of ξ, η, ζ be taken at the foot of the perpendicular from the pole on the plate, and let the negative η-axis be parallel to

Magnetic pole above a plane plate.

the direction of its motion.[1] Let the coordinates of the pole be 0, 0, $-c$; then its potential is

$$\chi = \frac{1}{\sqrt{\xi^2 + \eta^2 + (\zeta + c)^2}} = \frac{1}{r}.$$

Thus the induced potential of the first order becomes for positive ζ

$$\Omega_1 = -\frac{2\pi a}{k} \int_{\zeta}^{\infty} \frac{\partial \chi}{\partial \eta} d\zeta = \frac{2\pi a}{k} \frac{\eta}{\xi^2 + \eta^2} \left(1 - \frac{\zeta + c}{r}\right).$$

Hence we get for the potential of the second order

$$\Omega_2 = -\frac{2\pi a}{k} \int_{\zeta}^{\infty} \frac{\partial \Omega_1}{\partial \eta} d\zeta = \left(\frac{2\pi a}{k}\right)^2 \frac{\partial}{\partial \eta} \left\{ \frac{(\zeta + c - r)\eta}{\xi^2 + \eta^2} \right\}$$

$$= \left(\frac{2\pi a}{k}\right)^2 \frac{1}{\xi^2 + \eta^2} \left\{ \frac{\xi^2 - \eta^2}{\xi^2 + \eta^2}(\zeta + c - r) - \frac{\eta^2}{r} \right\}.$$

In the same way the calculation may be continued.

We get for the current-functions of the first and second orders

$$\psi_1 = \frac{a}{k} \frac{\eta}{\xi^2 + \eta^2} \left(1 - \frac{c}{r}\right) = \frac{a}{k} \frac{\eta}{r(r + c)},$$

$$\psi_2 = -2\pi \left(\frac{a}{k}\right)^2 \frac{r\xi^2 + c\eta^2}{(r^2 - c^2)(r + c)r},$$

where now $r^2 = \xi^2 + \eta^2 + c^2$.

In the η-axis we have (since $\xi = 0$)

$$\psi_2 = -2\pi \left(\frac{a}{k}\right)^2 \frac{c}{(r + c)r},$$

thus

$$\psi = \psi_1 + \psi_2 = \frac{a}{k} \frac{1}{(r + c)r} \left(\eta - \frac{2\pi a c}{k}\right).$$

Displacement of the induced distribution.

We may regard the point $\xi = 0$, $\psi = 0$ as the centre of the distribution: thus it appears displaced through a distance

---

[1] a then becomes positive.

[2] This result agrees exactly with that obtained by Jochmann.

$2\pi ac/k$ in consequence of self-induction, and in fact lags behind the moving pole by this distance. The same is true of the whole distribution near the pole.

For infinite velocities we get

$$\Omega_+ = -\chi = -\frac{1}{r},$$

$$\psi = -\frac{1}{2\pi r};$$

for very large values of $2\pi a/k$

$$\Omega = -\chi - \frac{k}{2\pi a}\int_0^{\eta}\frac{\partial\chi}{\partial\zeta}d\eta$$

$$= -\frac{1}{r} + \frac{k}{2\pi a}\frac{\eta(\zeta+c)}{r(r^2-\eta^2)},$$

$$\psi = -\frac{1}{2\pi r}\left(1 - \frac{k}{2\pi a}\cdot\frac{\eta c}{\xi^2+c^2}\right).$$

Here also the abscissa of the point $\xi = 0$, $\psi = 0$ is

$$\eta = \frac{2\pi ac}{k};$$

but since this value is very large, and our formula holds only for finite values of η, the value of the distance must be regarded as only an approximation.

The potential of the free electricity in the plate is

$$\phi = a\int_0^{\infty}\frac{\partial}{\partial\xi}(\chi+\Omega)d\zeta,$$

so that for small velocities

$$\phi = a\int_0^{\infty}\frac{\partial\chi}{\partial\xi}d\zeta = -a\frac{\xi}{r(r+c)}.$$

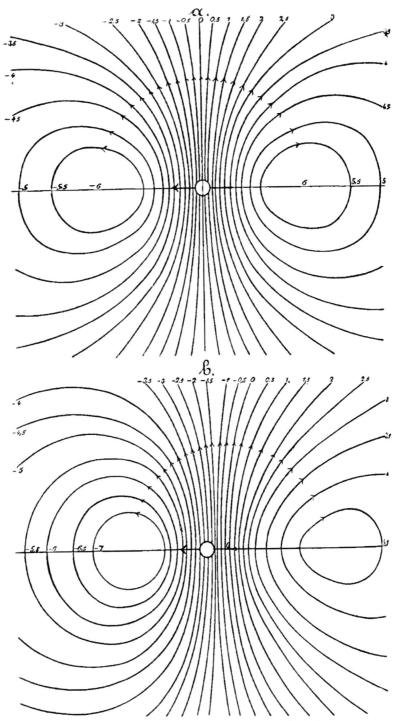

FIG. 11, a and b.—Pole moving in a straight line, $\frac{2}{3}$ nat. size.

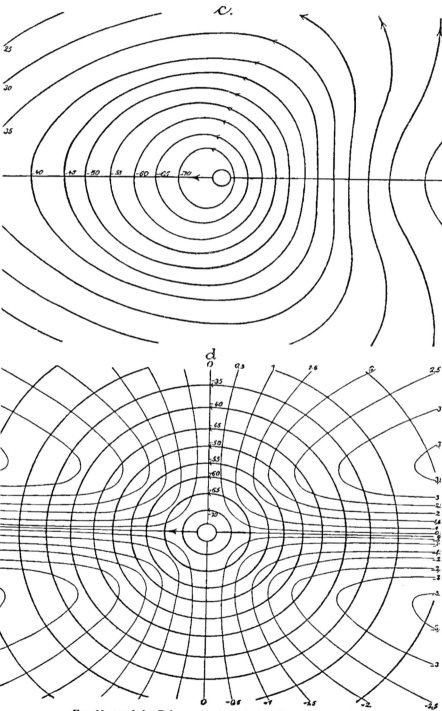

FIG. 11, c and d.—Pole moving in a straight line, ⅔ nat. size.

Thus in this case the equipotential lines have the same form as the lines of flow. For very large velocities we have

$$\phi = \frac{\kappa}{2\pi}\int_0^{\eta}\frac{\partial\chi}{\partial\xi}\eta = d - \frac{\kappa}{2\pi}\frac{\xi\eta}{r(r^2 - \eta^2)},$$

which formula is not applicable at infinity.

See Fig. 11. The formulæ here developed are illustrated by Fig. 11, pp. 112 and 113. The assumptions on which the diagrams are based are the following:—

The plate is made of copper (thus $\kappa = 227,000$) and has a thickness 2 mm. (thus $k = 113,500$). The distance of the pole from it is 30 mm. The values of ψ marked give absolute measure when the strength of the pole is 13,700 mm$^{\frac{3}{2}}$mgr$^{\frac{1}{2}}$/sec.

In Fig. 11, a and b, p. 112, the velocity of the pole is 5 m/sec ($a = 5000$); here a represents the phenomenon when self-induction is neglected, b when it is taken into account.

Fig. 11 c represents the phenomenon for a velocity of 100 m/sec, calculated by means of the formula for large values of $2\pi a/k$. It is true that for the value chosen the approximation is not very close. Fig. 11 d, p. 113, corresponds to an infinite velocity of the pole. The electric equipotential lines are also shown in this diagram. The values of the electric potential marked are in millions of the units employed by us.

The connection between the various states is clearly shown by the diagrams themselves.

Magnetic pole above a rotating disc. 2. A magnetic pole at rest is placed above a rotating infinite disc. Let the xz-plane be taken so as to pass through the pole. In addition to xyz we introduce coordinates $\xi\,\eta\,\zeta$, of which the origin is the foot of the perpendicular let fall from the pole on the disc. Further, let

$$\xi = x - a, \quad \eta = y, \quad \zeta = z;$$

thus

$$\frac{\partial}{\partial\omega} = a\frac{\partial}{\partial\eta} + \xi\frac{\partial}{\partial\eta} - \eta\frac{\partial}{\partial\xi}.$$

a is the distance of the pole from the axis of rotation; let c be its distance from the plate. Then

$$\chi = \frac{1}{\sqrt{\xi^2 + \eta^2 + (\zeta + c)^2}} = \frac{1}{r}.$$

Hence

$$\Omega_1 = -\frac{2\pi\omega}{k}\int_\zeta^\infty \frac{\partial\chi}{\partial\omega}d\zeta,$$

or since

$$\xi\frac{\partial\chi}{\partial\eta} - \eta\frac{\partial\chi}{\partial\xi} = 0 .$$

$$\Omega_1 = -\frac{2\pi\omega a}{k}\int_\zeta^\infty \frac{\partial\chi}{\partial\eta}d\zeta = \frac{2\pi\omega a}{k}\frac{\eta}{\xi^2+\eta^2}\left(1-\frac{\zeta+c}{r}\right),$$

$$\psi_1 = \frac{\omega a}{k}\frac{\eta}{r(r+c)}.$$

Hence the form of the lines of flow is independent of the distance of the pole from the axis.[1] For the induction of the second order we get

$$\Omega_2 = \left(\frac{2\pi\omega}{k}\right)^2 a\frac{\partial}{\partial\omega}\left\{\frac{(\zeta+c-r)\eta}{\xi^2+\eta^2}\right\},$$

$$\psi_2 = -2\pi\left(\frac{\omega}{k}\right)^2 a\frac{\partial}{\partial\omega}\left(\frac{\eta}{r+c}\right)$$

$$= -2\pi\left(\frac{\omega a}{k}\right)^2\left\{\frac{r\xi^2+c\eta^2}{(r^2-c^2)(r+c)r} + \frac{\xi}{a(r+c)}\right\},$$

which formulæ are meaningless at infinity.

When the angular velocity is small, if the inducing pole is not very close to the axis, we may regard the point $\xi=0$, $\psi=0$ as the centre of the distribution. Its ordinate is found to be

$$\eta_0 = \frac{2\pi\omega ac}{k}.$$

Hence in the neighbourhood of the pole the distribution is turned through the angle

$$\frac{2\pi\omega c}{k}$$

in the direction of rotation of the disc.

Rotation of the induced distribution.

[1] As already found by Jochmann.

3. I shall now apply the formulæ to another example. Suppose that above the rotating disc two wires are stretched parallel to the x-axis and are traversed in opposite directions by equal currents of unit intensity. For a single current the currents induced in the unlimited disc would become infinite.

Let the coordinates of the points in which the wires meet the plane yz be $0, a, -c$, and $0, a', -c'$; we then have for positive values of z

$$\chi = \tan^{-1} \frac{y-a}{z+c} - \tan^{-1} \frac{y-a'}{z+c'}.$$

Hence it follows, by means of the formulæ used before, if r, r_1 denote perpendicular distances from the wires, that

$$\Omega_1 = \frac{2\pi\omega}{k} x \log\left(\frac{r}{r_1}\right),$$

$$\psi_1 = \frac{\omega}{k} x \log\left(\frac{r}{r_1}\right).$$

For the potential of the free electricity in the plate we get

$$\phi = \omega y \log\left(\frac{r}{r_1}\right),$$

so that the equipotential lines are straight lines parallel to the wires. In Fig. 12 a the lines of flow are drawn for the case where

See Fig.
12 a.

$$c = c' = 10 \text{ mm}, \qquad a = -a' = 20 \text{ mm}.$$

Since, moreover, at infinity the currents become infinite, we must suppose $2\pi\omega/k$ to be exceedingly small in order to get a sufficient approximation in a finite region.

Further, as all the currents are closed at infinity we cannot, from the case of an unlimited disc, directly draw inferences as to a limited one.

Hence I shall calculate, by the method developed in § 7, the currents in a limited disc under like conditions. Let the radius of the disc be R.

The exact solution of the problem requires us to develop rather complicated functions in series of sines and cosines. I therefore assume that the perpendicular distance of the wires conveying the currents is at a distance from the centre large compared with the radius of the disc, so as to simplify the calculations.

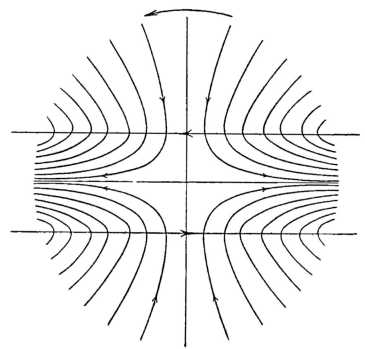

Fig. 12 a.—Rotating disc and rectilinear currents.

In the first place, suppose again

$$c = c', \quad a = -a'.$$

If we develop

$$\psi_1 = \frac{\omega}{k} x \log \left(\frac{r}{r_1} \right)$$

in powers of the coordinates, and neglect higher powers of the expression

$$\frac{y^2}{c^2 + a^2},$$

we get

$$\psi_1 = -\frac{2axy}{c^2 + a^2} + \frac{2ay^3x(3c^2 - a^2)}{3(c^2 + a^2)^3} + \cdots$$

$$= -\frac{a\rho^2 \sin 2\omega}{c^2 + a^2} + \frac{(3c^2 - a^2)a}{6(c^2 + a^2)^3}\rho^4 \left(\sin 2\omega - \tfrac{1}{2} \sin 4\omega \right).$$

The corresponding ψ_2 is (§ 7, I., conclusion)

$$\psi_2 = \frac{a\rho^2 \sin 2\omega}{c^2 + a^2} - \frac{(3c^2 - a^2)a}{6(c^2 + a^2)^3}\rho^2(R^2 \sin 2\omega - \tfrac{1}{2}\rho^2 \sin 4\omega).$$

Hence we have

$$\psi = -\frac{a(3c^2 - a^2)}{6(c^2 + a^2)^3}\rho^2 \sin 2\omega(R^2 - \rho^2).$$

Hence the form of the lines of flow is independent of the ratio $a : c$, but the current is greatly dependent upon it. If $a = 0$ or $a = c\sqrt{3}$, it vanishes. If $a < c\sqrt{3}$, the direction of the current is the same as in the unlimited plate; if $a > c\sqrt{3}$,

See Fig. 12 b.

it is the opposite. When we consider closely the distribution of the forces which act, this at first sight astonishing result is explicable. The form of the distribution is shown in Fig. 12 b.

In the same way the problem may be solved for any desired position of the wires. When one of them moves off to

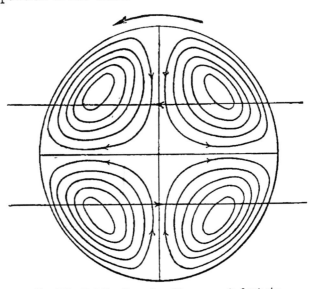

F⎰ɪɢ. 12 b.—Rotating disc and rectilinear currents, ⅔ nat. size.

infinity, the currents remain finite in the limited disc, and we find on retaining the first two powers of the dimensions of the disc

$$\psi = \frac{c^2 - a^2}{8(c^2 + a^2)^2}\rho \cos \omega(R^2 - \rho^2) - \frac{a(3c^2 - a^2)}{12(c^2 + a^2)^3}\rho^2 \sin 2\omega(R^2 - \rho^2).$$

The connection with the previous result is easily seen.

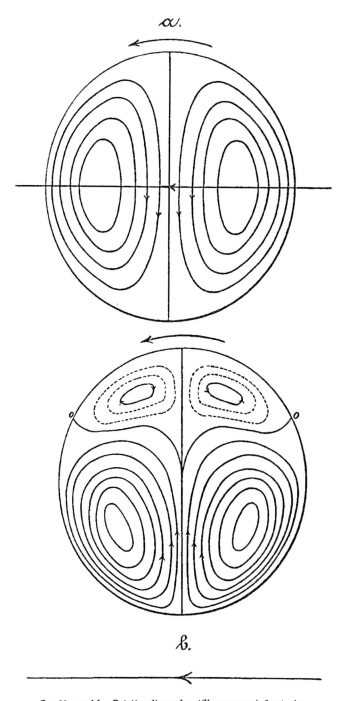

Fig. 13, a and b.—Rotating disc and rectilinear current, ⅔ nat. size.

See Fig. 13. In Fig. 13 two particular cases are represented. In a the straight wire cuts the axis of rotation at a sufficient distance from the disc, and in this case the second term above vanishes. In b the wire lies in the plane of the disc, and in fact at the distance from the disc at which it is represented in the figure itself.

Rotating spherical shells.

4. If measurements are to be made in experiments on the rotatory phenomena of induction, very thin spherical shells should be used; for in their case the calculations can be easily and exactly performed. The simplest form of experiment would be one in which such a spherical shell is made

Execution of experiments.

to rotate under the influence of a constant force. The rotation of the current planes might be demonstrated either by the effect of the currents on a very small magnet, or better by a galvanometric method.

As an example I shall calculate the angle of rotation and the magnetic moment of the rotating spherical shell.

Suppose the shell to be of copper, let its radius be 50 mm., its thickness 2 mm.; since $n = 1$, $i = 1$, we have

$$\tan \delta = \frac{4\pi}{3} \cdot \frac{R\omega}{k},$$

and if T be the inducing force, we find the moment of the shell to be

$$M = T \frac{R^3 \sin \delta}{2}.$$

If q is the number of revolutions per second,

$$\omega = 2\pi q,$$

and since $k = 113,500$, we find

$$\tan \delta = 0 \cdot 0116 \, q.$$

From the above the following table has been calculated:—

q	δ	$\dfrac{M}{T}$	q	δ	$\dfrac{M}{T}$
5	3°19′	3,614	80	42°51′	42,500
10	6°27′	7,178	90	46°13′	45,100
20	13°3′	14,110	100	49°13′	47,310
30	19°10′	20,520	200	66°40′	57,360
40	24°53′	26,290	500	80°15′	61,570
50	30°6′	31,340			
60	34°49′	35,680	∞	90°	62,500
70	39°4′	39,380			

Figs. 14 and 15, pp. 122 and 123, are intended to illustrate Rotating
solid
the distribution of current in solid spheres rotating under spheres and
the influence of a constant force perpendicular to the axis of constant
rotation. force.

Here the closed circuits are all circles whose planes are
parallel to the axis of rotation. Hence if we know the
current-density in the equatorial plane it is very easy to determine it at all other points. But in our case $u = 0$, $v = 0$ in See Figs.
the xy-plane, and thus the current-density $= w$. The diagrams 14 and 15.
represent the density of the current in the plane in question
by means of the curves

$$w = \text{const.}$$

The values of w marked give absolute values when the
influencing force

$$T = 289 \frac{\text{mgr}^{\frac{1}{2}}}{\text{mm}^{\frac{3}{2}}\,\text{sec}}$$

The size of the spheres is that drawn (R = 50 mm.).

In Fig. 14 a copper sphere is illustrated making five
turns a second (in a neglecting self-induction).

In Fig. 15 a the same sphere is illustrated when making
fifty turns a second.

Fig. 15 b shows the currents in an iron sphere making five
turns a second. Here the resistance of iron is taken to be six
times that of copper, and $4\pi\theta = 200$. We see that even with
the very moderate speed chosen an approximate representation
could not be obtained if we neglected self-induction.

6. There is a well-known experiment in which a conduct- Stoppage of
ing sphere rotating between the poles of an electromagnet is rotating
spheres by
brought to rest by suddenly exciting the latter. The theory electro-
of this experiment is very simple if we assume the magnetic magnet.
field to be uniform, neglect self-induction, and at every instant
treat the currents as steady. If T be the magnetic force
parallel to Ox, the external potential is

$$\chi = -\,T\rho \sin\theta \cos\omega\,;$$

thus

$$\psi = \frac{\omega}{2\kappa}T\rho^2 \sin\theta \sin\omega,$$

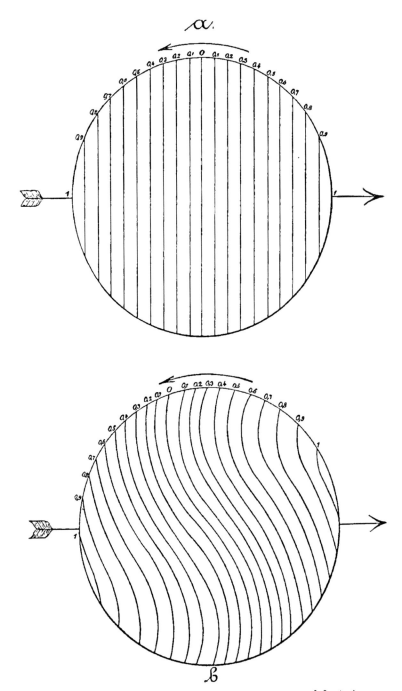

FIG. 14, *a* and *b*.—Rotating copper sphere, five turns per second, $\frac{2}{3}$ nat. size.

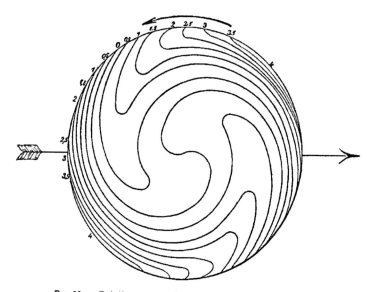

Fig. 15 a.—Rotating copper sphere, 50 turns a second, ⅔ nat. size.

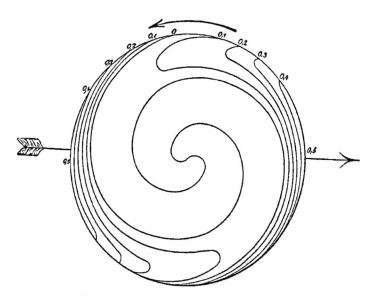

Fig. 15 b.—Rotating iron sphere, five turns a second, ⅔ nat. size.

and hence the heat generated is (§ 6)

$$W = \frac{2\pi R^5}{15} \cdot \frac{T^2 \omega^2}{\kappa} .$$

If F be the moment of inertia of the sphere, ω_0 its velocity at time $t = 0$, and if it rotate under no external forces, the equation of its motion is

$$\frac{F\omega^2}{2} + \frac{2\pi}{15}\frac{T^2 R^5}{\kappa}\int_0^t \omega^2 dt = \frac{F\omega_0^2}{2} ,$$

or

$$\omega = \omega_0 \cdot \epsilon^{-\frac{2\pi}{15} \cdot \frac{T^2 R^5}{F\kappa}t} .$$

If q be the mass of 1 cub. cm. of the material,

$$F = \frac{8}{15}q\pi R^5 ,$$

thus

$$\omega = \omega_0 \cdot \epsilon^{-\frac{T^2}{4q\kappa}t} .$$

An analogous law holds when the sphere is set in motion by the action of rotating magnets.

Spheres of different radii and spherical shells are set in motion and brought to rest with equal velocity. This in fact corresponds with an experiment made by Matteucci.[1]

Matteucci's experiment.

The angle which the sphere traverses after excitation of the electromagnet amounts to

$$\int_0^\infty \omega dt = \frac{4q\kappa}{T^2}\omega_0 .$$

For strongly magnetic spheres we find

$$\int_0^\infty \omega dt = \frac{4q\kappa}{9T^2}\omega_0 .$$

[1] Wiedemann, *Galvanismus*, § 878; *Lehre von der Elektricität*, 1885, vol. iv. § 386, p. 322.

From the above the following table is calculated. In it T is taken $= 5000$, which corresponds to an electromagnet of medium strength. The initial velocity is taken to be one turn (2π) per second. The angles described are given in turns. The relative values hold for every T and every ω_0.

Material.	$\int\limits_{0}^{\infty}\omega\,dt$
Aluminium . .	0·14
Iron . . .	0·16
Silver . .	0·27
Copper	0·31
German silver . . .	3·90
Graphite	27·2
Conc. sol. of copper sulphate	about 544,000

7. Damping in a galvanometer.

Consider a magnet swinging inside a conducting spherical shell; and suppose it to be very small, or to have approximately the form of a uniformly magnetised sphere. If M be its moment, then in the spherical shell

$$\chi = -\frac{M}{\rho^2}\sin\theta\cos\omega.$$

Thus

$$\psi = -\frac{\omega}{\kappa}\frac{M}{\rho}\sin\theta\sin\omega,$$

and the heat generated per second is

$$W = \frac{8\pi}{3}\frac{M^2\omega^2}{\kappa}\left(\frac{1}{r} - \frac{1}{R}\right),$$

where, as before, r denotes the inner and R the outer radius of the spherical shell.

Let now ϕ be the deflection of the needle from its position of rest, and F its moment of inertia; then its vibrations are determined by the equation

$$\frac{d^2\phi}{dt^2} + \frac{MT}{F}\phi + 2\epsilon\frac{dt}{d\phi} = 0,$$

which may be written

$$d\left(\frac{F\left(\frac{d\phi}{dt}\right)^2}{2}\right) + d\left(\frac{MT\phi^2}{2}\right) + 2\epsilon F\left(\frac{d\phi}{dt}\right)^2 dt = 0,$$

so that the rate at which the heat is generated is

$$2\epsilon F\left(\frac{d\phi}{dt}\right)^2,$$

and thus we have

$$\epsilon = \frac{4\pi M^2}{3}\frac{1}{\kappa F}\left(\frac{1}{r} - \frac{1}{R}\right).$$

If ϵ be small, we thence obtain for the logarithmic decrement of the needle

$$\lambda = \frac{4\pi^2}{3\kappa} \cdot \frac{R-r}{Rr}\sqrt{\frac{M^3}{TF}}.$$

Aperiodic
state. In order that the aperiodic state may occur, we must have

$$\epsilon^2 > \frac{MT}{F},$$

or

$$\frac{R-r}{Rr} > \frac{3\kappa}{4\pi}\sqrt{\frac{TF}{M^3}},$$

from which equation, for given values of T, F, M, κ, it is easy to calculate the thickness of the damper necessary to ensure that the aperiodic state may be attained.

III

ON THE DISTRIBUTION OF ELECTRICITY OVER THE SURFACE OF MOVING CONDUCTORS

(*Wiedemann's Annalen*, **13**, pp. 266-275, 1881.)

IF conductors charged with electricity are in motion relatively to one another, the distribution of free electricity at the surface varies from instant to instant. This change produces currents inside the conductors which, on their part again, presuppose differences of potential, unless the specific resistance of the conductors be vanishingly small. Hence we may draw these inferences :—

1. That the distribution of electricity at the surface of moving conductors is at each instant different from that at the surface of similar conductors at rest in similar positions. In particular, the potential at the surface and inside is no longer constant, so that a hollow conductor does not entirely screen its interior from external influence when it is in motion.

2. That the motion of charged conductors is attended by a continual development of heat. Hence continual motions of such conductors are possible only by a supply of external work, and under the sole action of internal forces a system of such conductors must come to rest.

The changes which the motion of conductors compels us to make in the conclusions of electrostatics are especially noticeable in those cases where the geometrical relations between the surfaces are invariable, that is, for surfaces of revolution rotating about their axes. Such bodies will have a tendency to drag with them in their motion electrically-charged bodies near them, and the same is true of charged liquid jets.

The nature and magnitude of the phenomena indicated will in the following be submitted to calculation.

In forming the differential equations we assume that the only possible state of motion of electricity in a conductor is the electric current. Hence if a quantity of electricity disappears at a place A and appears again at a different place B, we postulate a system of currents between A and B, not a motion of the free electricity from A to B. The explicit mention of this assumption is not superfluous, because it contradicts another, not unreasonable, assumption. When an electric pole moves about at a constant distance above a plane plate the induced charge follows it, and the most obvious and perhaps usual assumption is that it is the electricity considered as a substance which follows the pole; but this assumption we reject in favour of the one above mentioned. Further, we leave out of account all inductive actions of the currents generated. This is always permissible, unless the velocity of the moving conductors be comparable with that of light.

Let u, v, w be components of current parallel to the axes of x, y, z; ϕ the total potential, h the surface-density, κ the specific resistance of a conductor, all measured in absolute electrostatic units. Thus κ is a time, in fact the time in which a charge arbitrarily distributed through the conductor diminishes to $1/\epsilon^{4\pi}$ of its original value. If now we refer everything to coordinates fixed in the conductor and consider the motion in this conductor, we have

$$\kappa u = -\frac{\partial \phi}{\partial x}, \quad \kappa v = -\frac{\partial \phi}{\partial y}, \quad \kappa w = -\frac{\partial \phi}{\partial z} \qquad (1),$$

$$\frac{d\Delta\phi}{dt} = 4\pi\left(\frac{\partial u}{\partial x} + \frac{\partial v}{\partial y} + \frac{\partial w}{\partial z}\right) \qquad (2),$$

$$-\frac{dh}{dt} = u\cos a + v\cos b + w\cos c \qquad (3),$$

$$-4\pi h = \frac{\partial \phi_i}{\partial n_i} + \frac{\partial \phi_e}{\partial n_e} \qquad (4),$$

in which equation n_i, n_e denote respectively the internal and external normal, and a, b, c denote the angles which n_i makes with the axes. From (1) and (2) we get

$$\frac{d\nabla^2\phi}{dt} = -\frac{4\pi}{\kappa}\nabla^2\phi, \text{ or } \nabla^2\phi = (\nabla^2\phi)_0 \epsilon^{-\frac{4\pi}{\kappa}t}.$$

Hence, if the density inside is not zero initially, it still continually approaches this value, and cannot be again produced by electrostatic influences. Hence we have here

$$\nabla^2\phi = 0 \tag{5}.$$

Further, from (1) and (3),

$$\kappa\frac{dh}{dt} = \frac{\partial\phi_i}{\partial n_i} \tag{6},$$

or by using equation (4)

$$\frac{\kappa}{4\pi}\frac{d}{dt}\left(\frac{\partial\phi_i}{\partial n_i} + \frac{\partial\phi_c}{\partial n_c}\right) = -\frac{\partial\phi_i}{\partial n_i} \tag{7}.$$

The equations (5) and (7) involve ϕ alone. Equation (5) must be satisfied throughout space; equation (7) at the surfaces of all conductors. ϕ is determined for all time by these equations —which no longer involve a reference to any particular system of coordinates—together with the well-known conditions of continuity and the initial value of ϕ. In the differential coefficient dh/dt, h relates to a definite element of the surface; if the velocities of this element relative to any system of coordinates be a, β, γ, then the above equations will refer to these coordinates, provided dh/dt be replaced by

$$\frac{\partial h}{\partial t} + a\frac{\partial h}{\partial x} + \beta\frac{\partial h}{\partial y} + \gamma\frac{\partial h}{\partial z}.$$

We get for the heat generated in time δt

$$\delta W = \delta t \int \kappa(u^2 + v^2 + w^2)d\tau,$$

$$= -\frac{1}{\kappa}dt\int \phi\frac{\partial\phi_i}{\partial n_i}ds,$$

$$= -\int \phi\delta h ds,$$

where ds denotes an element of surface, and the integrals are to be taken, the first throughout the interior, the others over the surface, of all the conductors.   It is easy to prove in our particular case that the equations used agree with the principle of the conservation of energy, which has, however, been proved true of them in general.

If κ be very small, ϕ may be expanded in ascending powers of κ.   The individual terms of this expansion may be found in the following way, if we regard the ordinary electrostatic problem as solved.

Let ϕ_1 be for all time the potential corresponding to the state of equilibrium for the existing charges and the positions of the bodies at each instant, and let h_1 be the density corresponding to ϕ_1.   Then let ϕ_2 be determined so that $\nabla^2\phi_2 = 0$, that at the surfaces of the inductors $\partial\phi_2/\partial n_i = k\partial h_1/\partial t$, that the conditions of continuity are satisfied, and that the sum of the free electricity may vanish for each conductor.   In the same way in which ϕ_2 is formed from ϕ_1, let ϕ_3 be formed from ϕ_2, ϕ_4 from ϕ_3, and so on ; then clearly $\phi = \phi_1 + \phi_2 + \phi_3 + \cdots$ represents exactly the potential, provided the series converges. The convergence of the series depends on the relation between κ, the dimensions of the conductors, and their velocities ; for any value of κ we can imagine velocities sufficiently small to ensure convergence.   For metallic conductors and terrestrial velocities each term vanishes in comparison with the preceding one.   The special phenomena due to electrical resistance are here inappreciable, and the form of the currents alone is of interest.   Since ϕ_1 is constant inside a conductor, and ϕ_3 vanishes in comparison with ϕ_2, all the currents flow along the lines of force of the potential ϕ_2, and we have

$$\kappa u = -\frac{\partial\phi_2}{\partial x}, \quad \kappa v = -\frac{\phi_2}{\partial y}, \quad \kappa w = -\frac{\partial\phi_2}{\partial z}.$$

We shall now confine ourselves to the case in which only one conductor is in motion, and shall assume this to be a solid of revolution rotating about its axis.   We refer our investigation to a system of coordinates fixed in space, of which the z-axis is the axis of rotation.   In addition, we employ polar coordinates ρ, ω, θ with the same axis.   Let T be the time of one turn.   The conditions which ϕ must satisfy in the conductor are in this case : (1) inside $\nabla^2\phi = 0$; (2) at the surface, $\partial\phi_i/\partial n_i = \kappa(\partial h/\partial t)+(2\pi\kappa/\text{T})(\partial h/\partial \omega)$, where h now refers to a point fixed in space. When the conductor rotates with uniform velocity under the influence of a potential independent of the time, after the lapse of a certain time a stationary state is reached, the condition for which is $\partial h/\partial t = 0$; and thus $\partial\phi_i/\partial n_i = (2\pi\kappa/\text{T})/(\partial h/\partial \omega)$.

As an example we shall consider the case of a spherical shell rotating with constant velocity about a diameter. Let its external radius be R, its internal radius r. Suppose the external potential Φ, under whose influence the motion takes place, developed in a series of spherical harmonics inside the spherical shell. The actions produced by the separate terms may be added, so that we may limit the investigation to one term. Let $\Phi = A_{ni}(\rho/\text{R})^n \cos i\omega P_{ni}(\theta)$. Denote by ϕ the potential of the electrical charge itself, which is induced on the spherical shell; in particular denote it by ϕ_1 in the inside space, by ϕ_2 in the substance of the shell, by ϕ_3 in the outside space. In addition to the general conditions for the potential of electrical charges, ϕ must satisfy the condition that for $\rho = r$ and $\rho = \text{R}$

$$\frac{\partial\Phi}{\partial\rho} + \frac{\partial\phi_i}{\partial\rho} = -\frac{\kappa}{2\text{T}}\frac{\partial}{\partial\omega}\left(\frac{\partial\phi_i}{\partial\rho} - \frac{\partial\phi_e}{\partial\rho}\right).$$

All these requirements are fulfilled when we put

$$\phi_1 =$$
$$\left(\frac{\rho}{\text{R}}\right)^n(A\cos i\omega + B\sin i\omega)P_{ni}(\theta) + \left(\frac{\rho}{r}\right)^n(A'\cos i\omega + B'\sin i\omega)P_{ni}(\theta),$$

$$\phi_2 =$$
$$\left(\frac{\rho}{\text{R}}\right)^n(A\cos i\omega + B\sin i\omega)P_{ni}(\theta) + \left(\frac{r}{\rho}\right)^{n+1}(A'\cos i\omega + B'\sin i\omega)P_{ni}(\theta),$$

$$\phi_3 =$$
$$\left(\frac{\text{R}}{\rho}\right)^{n+1}(A\cos i\omega + B\sin i\omega)P_{ni}(\theta) + \left(\frac{r}{\rho}\right)^{n+1}(A'\cos i\omega + B'\sin i\omega)P_{ni}(\theta).$$

For the general conditions are at once satisfied, and the

two boundary conditions give, when we equate factors of $\cos i\omega$ and $\sin i\omega$, four linear equations for the four constants A, B, A′, B′. If these latter are satisfied, so also will be the former. Using the contractions $\kappa/2\mathrm{T} = a$, $r/\mathrm{R} = \epsilon$, we get for these equations—

$$\mathrm{A}_{ni}\cdot n \quad = -n\mathrm{A} - (2n+1)ai\mathrm{B} + (n+1)\epsilon^{n+1}\mathrm{A}' \quad * \quad ,$$
$$0 \quad = (2n+1)ai\mathrm{A} \quad -n\mathrm{B} \quad * \quad +(n+1)\epsilon^{n+1}\mathrm{B}',$$
$$\mathrm{A}_{ni}\cdot n\epsilon^n = -n\epsilon^n\mathrm{A} \quad * \quad +(n+1)\mathrm{A}' \quad +(2n+1)ai\mathrm{B}',$$
$$0 \quad = \quad * \quad -n\epsilon^n\mathrm{B} - (2n+1)ai\mathrm{A}' + (n+1)\,\mathrm{B}'.$$

These equations determine the four constants uniquely. Without actually performing the somewhat cumbrous solution it is easy to recognise the correctness of the following remarks :—

1. When $a = 0$, $\mathrm{A} = -\mathrm{A}_{ni}$, $\mathrm{A}' = \mathrm{B}' = \mathrm{B} = 0$, as must be the case for a sphere at rest.

2. If a be finite but very small, then $\mathrm{A} + \mathrm{A}_{ni}$ and A' are of order a^2, B, B′ are of order a. Hence it follows that the chief points of the phenomenon are these. The distribution of the charge on the outer surface (the form of the lines of constant density) is not changed by the rotation (of course only for the separate terms of the development); but the charge appears rotated in the direction of the rotation of the sphere through an angle of order a, and the density has diminished by a small quantity of order a^2. In addition a charge makes its appearance on the sphere forming the inner boundary, and its type is similar to that of the first charge; its density is of order a, and it is turned relatively to the first charge through a small angle $\pi/2i$. In the substance of the shell as well as inside we get differences of potential of order a.

3. If a be large, B, B′ are of order $1/a$, A, A′ of order $1/a^2$. As the velocity increases the charge on the external surface finally appears turned through the angle $\pi/2i$; its density is small, of order $1/a$, and the charge on the inner spherical surface is like it as regards type, position, and density. In the ultimate state $\phi = 0$ everywhere, and then we have the external potential in the substance and the interior of the spherical shell; the currents everywhere flow in the lines of

force of that potential. The free electricity, which by the currents is brought to the boundary, is by the rotation of the sphere carried back to its starting-point so quickly that the density remains infinitely small. A screening of the internal space no longer takes place.

In particular cases the calculation itself becomes very simple. In the first place, for a solid sphere $\epsilon = 0$. If we put $\tan \delta = (2n + 1)ai/n$, then δ/i is the angle through which the distribution appears to be turned, and the density of the charge is to that induced on the sphere at rest as $\cos \delta : 1$. When the sphere rotates under the influence of a uniform force perpendicular to the axis of rotation, the distribution on it is represented by a spherical harmonic of the first degree. The lines of flow are parallel straight lines whose direction for small velocities of rotation is perpendicular to the axis and to the direction of the force, but for large velocities appears turned from the latter direction through an angle whose tangent $= 3a = \frac{3}{2}\kappa/T$. For a rotating cylinder the circumstances are quite similar; the angle of rotation is here found to be $2a = \kappa/T$.

Secondly, suppose ϵ nearly unity, that is, the thickness d of the spherical shell infinitely small. We must then suppose the specific resistance κ to be so small that $\kappa/d = k$, the specific superficial resistance, may be a finite quantity. With this assumption the tangent of the angle of rotation becomes generally $\tan \delta = \dfrac{(2n+1)i}{2n(n+1)} \cdot \dfrac{kR}{T}$, and in the particular case of a uniform force $\tan \delta = \frac{3}{4}kR/T$.

Under similar circumstances we find for a thin hollow cylinder $\tan \delta = kR/T$, so that in this case the rotation is greater for the cylinder than for the sphere, although for a solid cylinder it was less. The density in the last case also is to that for the sphere in the ratio $\cos \delta : 1$.

As an illustration of the results of the calculation I have in the accompanying diagram represented the flow of electricity in a rotating hollow cylinder, whose internal is one-half its external radius. The time of one turn is twice the specific resistance of the material. The arrow A marks the direction of the external inducing force, the arrow B that of the force in the inside space; the remaining two arrows indicate the position of the charges on the outer .and inner curved surfaces. The lines occupying the substance of the cylinder represent the lines of flow.

It remains to inquire in what practically realisable cases the effects discussed could become appreciable. Clearly they attain a measurable value when the angle of rotation becomes measurable, and this occurs when for solid bodies the quantity κ/T, or when for very thin shells the quantity $k\mathrm{R}/T$, has a finite value. Here R denotes the mean distance of the shell from the axis of rotation. Since T cannot well become less

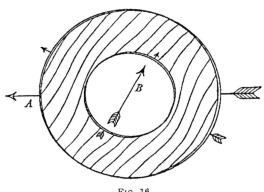

FIG. 16.

than $\frac{1}{100}$ second, κ must reach at least several hundredths of a second. Thus it is obvious that in metallic conductors, for which κ is of the order of trillionths of a second, the rotation phenomenon can never be appreciable. On the other hand, it is obvious that even at moderate velocities no measurable charge can be formed upon insulators such as shellac and paraffin, for which κ is many thousand seconds. But for certain other substances, which lie at the boundary between semi-conductors and bad conductors, the phenomenon should be capable of complete demonstration ; e.g. for ordinary kinds of glass, for mixtures of insulators with conductors in form of powder, for liquids of about the conductivity of petroleum, oil of turpentine, or mixtures of these with better conducting ones, etc. As the specific resistance κ is connected in a simple way with the angle of rotation, measurements of the latter might serve to determine the former. However, in bodies of the necessary resistance the phenomena of residual charge occur, and our differential equations only hold roughly for these. The effect of a residual charge will always be to make the constant κ appear less than it is found to be from observations on steady currents, and less too by an amount increasing with the velocity of rotation. The dielectric displacement acts in the same sense, since it is equivalent to partial conduction without resistance. For very thin shells these disturbing influences disappear.

I know of no previous experiments which might serve to illustrate the effects investigated. Hence I have performed the following one. Above a plate of mirror glass. of relatively high conductivity (by a different method κ had been found to be $= 4$ seconds), a needle 10 cm. long was suspended by a wire and allowed to execute torsional vibrations; the moment of inertia of the needle was sufficiently increased by means of added weights, and at its ends it carried two horizontal brass plates, each 3 cm. long and 2 cm. broad. Their distance a from the glass plate could be varied. When the needle was electrically charged the brass plates acted on the opposing glass surface as condensers; the bound electricity was compelled to follow the motion of the needle, and ought, according to the preceding, to damp the vibration of the needle. Now such a damping actually showed itself. The needle was connected with a Leyden jar, of which the sparking distance was 0·5 mm., whilst a was 2 mm. The needle was found to return to its position of rest without further oscillation, though previously it had vibrated freely; even when a was increased to 35 mm., the increase of the damping at the instant of charging was perceptible to the naked eye. And when I charged the needle by a battery of only 50 Daniell cells, while a was 2 mm., I obtained an increase of damping which could be easily perceived by mirror and scale. It was impossible to submit the experiment to an exact computation, but by making some simplifying assumptions I was able to convince myself that theory led to a value of the logarithmic decrement of the order of magnitude of that observed.

As we have shown, we possess, in a conductor rotating under the influence of external forces, a body at the surface of which the potential has different values, which it again resumes after a slight disturbance. Hence if we connect two points of the surface by a conductor, a current flows through the connection; if we connect the points with two conductors, these may as often as we please be raised to different potentials. If we use metallic discs as the rotating bodies the differences of potential obtainable by means of possible velocities of rotation are indefinitely small; but if we use very bad conductors the differences of potential even for moderate velocities are of the order of the inducing differences. Induction machines without metallic rubbers are based on this principle. The theoretically simplest of such machines consists of a cylinder rotating under the influence of a constant force. How far, however, the explanation here indicated is a complete one must for the present remain a moot question.

UPPER LIMIT FOR THE KINETIC ENERGY OF ELECTRICITY IN MOTION

(*Wiedemann's Annalen*, **14**, pp. 581-590, 1881.)

IN a previous paper[1] I have deduced, from experiments on the strength of extra-currents, the conclusion that the kinetic energy of an electric current of magnetic strength 1 in a copper conductor is less than $0·008$ mg. mm.^{2}/sec.^{2} This conclusion, however, could only be drawn on the supposition that a certain relation did not exist between the specific resistance of metals and the density of electricity in them. In the present paper I propose to describe an experiment which I have made with a view to demonstrating kinetic energy in electrical flow, but equally with a negative result. This experiment, however, has advantages over the previous ones: for, in the first place, it is more direct; secondly, it gives a smaller value of the upper limit; and thirdly, it gives it without limitation of any kind.

Suppose a thin metal plate of the form shown in Fig. 17 to be traversed by as strong a current as possible between the electrodes A and B; further, let the points C and D be connected with a delicate galvanometer, and let the system be so adjusted that no current flows through the galvanometer. Let the plate be made to rotate about an axis through its centre and perpendicular to its plane. The current will now tend to deviate laterally from the direction AB in case electricity in motion exhibits inertia, for the same mechanical reason that the rotation of the earth causes the trade winds to deviate

---

[1] See I. p. 1.

from the direction of the meridian. The consequence of this tendency will be a difference of potential between the points C and D, and a current through the galvanometer. This current must be reversed when the direction of rotation is reversed; when the rotation is clockwise and the current flows in the plate from A to B, then the current through the galvanometer outside the plate must flow from D to C, as shown by the arrows.

An action of the kind mentioned must occur, whatever be the nature of the electric current, provided only that with it a motion of an inert mass is connected, which changes its direction when the current is reversed. The difficulty of the experiment consists in preparing four connections, sufficiently certain and steady, even with rapid rotations; this difficulty I have overcome to such an extent that one of the most delicate galvanometers could be used when the velocity was 30 turns per second, and the difference of potential between A and B was that of 1 Daniell. No deflection of the needle could be detected which would indicate the existence of electric inertia. Basing my calculations on Weber's hypothesis, I am able from my experiments to infer by the method given below that μ, the kinetic energy of a current of magnetic strength 1 in a cubic millimetre of a silver conductor, cannot greatly exceed $0{\cdot}00002$ mg. mm.^{2}'sec^2.

As regards the method of experimenting I may mention the following. The metal plate used was the silvering of a glass plate, produced by Liebig's process. Its form is shown in Fig. 17; the distance AB was about 45 mm., the distance CD 25 mm. The leads were soldered to small platinum plates, and these were pressed into contact with the silvering by small screws penetrating the glass plate; a layer of gold-leaf was introduced between the silvering and the plates, so as to produce a more uniform contact. The electrical resistance was at first $5{\cdot}4$ Siemens units in the direction AB, and $3{\cdot}5$ Siemens units in the direction CD. From some unexplained causes these resistances diminished in time, and after some weeks were found to be $4{\cdot}8$ and $3{\cdot}1$ Siemens units respectively. From the ratio of these resistances and from special experiments, it followed that the resistances of the contacts at the leads did not amount to any appreciable fraction of the whole resistance.   The system was adjusted to bring the needle to zero by scraping off the silver at various points of the edge ; but as a sufficiently accurate adjustment from various causes could not be permanently obtained, shunts of several hundred Siemens units resistance were introduced between *A* and *C* and between *C* and *B*, and by their adjustment the needle could always be brought to zero, in so far as that seemed desirable.

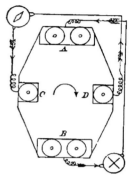

FIG. 17.

The glass plate was fastened to a brass disc so as to permit of a rapid rotation ; the silvered surface faced the disc, and was only separated from it by the thinnest possible air film.   The disc itself was at the end of a horizontal steel spindle, which was set in two bearings in such a way that its two ends were free.   The connection to the galvanometer was made at the glass plate itself; that to the battery, which supplied the current, at the other end of the spindle ; the connections to the points *A* and *B* were formed by the spindle itself and by a wire lying in a canal bored through the spindle. The arrangement by which the last connection was effected between the moving and fixed parts is shown in Fig. 18.   A fine platinum wire passes through a piece of glass tube drawn out to a very fine point and very exactly centred.   A second platinum wire is wound round the tube ; and the latter, together with the wires, passes through one vessel of mercury and enters a second in such a way that the first-mentioned wire rotates in the mercury of the last vessel, and the second wire in the mercury of the first vessel.   The glass tube was

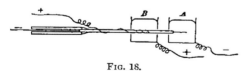

FIG. 18.

fastened at one end of the spindle by sealing-wax to the glass plate ; at the other end to the spindle itself.   As the diameter of the windings of the wire *B* was only about $\frac{1}{2}$ mm., the platinum moved relatively to the surrounding mercury at a speed of only 160 mm/sec, even with a velocity of rotation of 100 revolutions per second.   The result was good, for even with the latter velocity there was no appreciable transition-resistance; and the disturbances due to heating were only just perceptible, and small compared with other unavoidable ones. The spindle was rotated by a cord, which connected it with the quickest spindle of a Becquerel's phosphoroscope, so that it revolved at double the speed of the latter. The crank of the phosphoroscope was turned by hand, one turn of it corresponding to 290 revolutions of the spindle. As the whole apparatus was built as lightly as possible, even large velocities could be rapidly generated and again annulled. The galvanometer used was of Siemens' pattern, with an astatic system of two bell magnets and four coils, with a total resistance of about 7 Siemens units. By aid of external magnets the arrangement could be made as astatic as desired; in the final experiments the sensitiveness was such that a difference of potential of one-millionth of a Daniell between the points D and C gave a deflection of 32 scale divisions. The motion of the needle was aperiodic; a second position of rest was reached in about 8 seconds with an accuracy sufficient for the experiments described. The current was supplied from a Daniell cell and measured by a common tangent galvanometer. A commutator was placed in the connections to both galvanometer and battery.

After the current had been allowed to flow through the plate until no further heating took place, the needle was brought nearly to its natural position of rest by adjusting the external resistances between A, C, and B. Then the crank of the phosphoroscope was made to turn once round as uniformly as possible, an operation which on the average required 8 to 9 seconds, and was terminated by an automatic catch. But after the rotation ceased the needle hardly ever returned to the original position of rest, but to a new position of rest. As soon as this was attained (*i.e.* after 6 to 8 seconds) it was read off. The deviation from the original position of rest I shall call the permanent deflection; by the instantaneous deflection will be meant the distance of the needle at the end of the rotation from the mean of the initial and final resting points. We regard the instantaneous deflection as a measure of the current whose causes act only during the rotation, *e.g.* the influence of inert mass; while we ascribe the permanent deflection to disturbances which continue to act after rotation has ceased. This method of calculation could only lay claim to accuracy if the rotation were uniform and the permanent deflection small; but the disturbances were too various and the deflections too irregular to permit of fuller discussion.

The first experiments already showed that if there was any effect of inertia, it did not much exceed the errors unavoidably introduced by disturbing causes. In order to detect such an effect, and to find as small as possible a value of its upper limit, I took a set of · eight observations together, in which the direction of rotation was changed between every two observations : the connection to the galvanometer was reversed every other observation, and the current in the plate was reversed between the first four and the last four observations. Such a set of eight observations I call an experiment. By suitably combining the observations it would be possible to calculate the mean effect of the various disturbing causes for each experiment. For the deflections must include, and we should be able to eliminate from them :—

1. A part which changes sign only when the connection with the galvanometer is reversed, but not when the direction of rotation or the connection to the battery is changed. It could only be due to an electromotive force generated by the rapid rotation at the point of contact of the galvanometer circuit. In so far as this force was thermoelectric the corresponding deflection must have been permanent.

2. A part whose sign depended on the direction of the galvanometer and battery connections, but not on the direction of rotation. This could be due to various causes :—

(a) The straining of the plate by the considerable centrifugal force, whose effect could only appear in the momentary deflection.

(b) An uniform change of temperature of the whole plate owing to rotation, whose effect would be felt in the permanent deflection.

(c) A change in the ratios of the resistances AC/BC and AD/BD during the experiment, due to external causes. In fact the resting-point of the needle changed slowly even when there was no rotation, but continuously and so much that the error produced was of the order of the others. The effect was felt in the permanent deflection.

3. A part whose sign depended on the direction of rotation as well as on the connections. Thus :—

(*a*) If such a part occurred in the momentary deflection no other cause perhaps could be assigned except the inertia of the electricity moved.

(*b*) In the permanent deflection such a part might be produced, because during rotation two diagonally opposite branches of the bridge moved in front of the other two, and thus were more strongly cooled by the air-currents than the latter. As the conducting layer of silver was very close to the brass disc, I had not anticipated such an effect; but it proved to be very large, and was especially inconvenient, since it only differed from the effect of inertia in lasting for a time after the rotation ceased. By surrounding the plate and brass disc by cotton wool and by a drum of paper I was able to diminish this disturbance considerably; and still further by hermetically sealing the paper drum by a coating of paraffin. But even then the disturbance did not completely disappear.

I performed two series, each of twenty, of the experiments described. They differed in the strength of the current employed, in the sensitiveness of the galvanometer, and especially in this, that in the first series the paraffin coating mentioned was wanting. The second series was by far the better, and what follows refers to it alone. To it also refers the statement made above respecting the sensitiveness of the galvanometer. The strength of the current was $1·17$ mg$^{\frac{1}{2}}$ mm$^{\frac{1}{2}}$/sec magnetic units; the velocity of rotation, according to what has been said above, was on the average $290/8\frac{1}{2} = 34$ turns per second. The galvanometer deflection at the end of the rotation amounted on the average to 10 to 15 scale divisions, and in the succeeding seconds changed mostly by only a few divisions. The greater part of this deflection corresponded to the causes (2 *b*) and (2 *c*), which could no longer be separated : the effect of disturbances (1) and (3 *b*) was found to be 2 to 4 scale divisions ; the disturbance (2 *a*) was small. The practicability of the method followed from the fact that the separate disturbances were found to be of the same sign and of the same order of magnitude in all the experiments, almost without exception. The following are the twenty values, in scale divisions, obtained for the part of the deflection mentioned under the head (3 a) :—

$+3\cdot6,$	$-1\cdot0,$	$-0\cdot0,$	$-2\cdot7,$	$-1\cdot1,$	$+0\cdot1,$	$-0\cdot6,$
$+0\cdot8,$	$-1\cdot1,$	$+0\cdot2,$	$-0\cdot4,$	$+0\cdot5,$	$+0\cdot7,$	$+0\cdot5,$
$+0\cdot8,$	$+1\cdot2,$	$+1\cdot1,$	$+0\cdot7,$	$+0\cdot6,$	$+0\cdot7.$	

The mean of these values is $+0\cdot23$. The difference from zero is somewhat larger than the probable error of the result, but perhaps the cause of the difference is to be looked for in the somewhat arbitrary calculation of the momentary deflection rather than in any physical phenomenon. The effect of inertia should have been a negative deflection, according to the circumstances of the experiment and the sign used; thus such an effect could not be detected at all. If we attribute the constant deflection $0\cdot23$ to some other cause, and calculate the error of the experiments from zero, we still find that the odds are 14 to 1, that no deflection exceeding $\frac{1}{2}$ a scale division, and $3480 : 1$, that no deflection exceeding 1 scale division existed, which could be attributed to an inert mass.

In calculating the experiment on the basis of Weber's hypothesis, for simplicity I assume that the mass of a positive unit is the same as that of a negative unit, and that both electricities flow in the current with equal and opposite velocities. Let m be the mass of the electrostatic unit, v the velocity with which it is compelled to move in the axis of the plate AB or in a parallel straight line; and let ω be the velocity of rotation of the plate. Then the apparent force due to rotation, which acts on the unit perpendicular to its path, is equal to $2mv\omega + C$, where C is the centrifugal force at the position of the unit. The unit of opposite sign in the same position is subject to a force $-2mv\omega + C$. The sum of the two forces, $2C$, represents a ponderomotive force, namely, the increase in the amount of the centrifugal force acting on the material of the conductor, due to increase of its mass by that of the electricity; but the difference, $X = 4mv\omega$, is in fact the electromotive force which we tried to detect by the galvanometer. Now m is equal to M, the mass of all the positive and negative electricity contained in one cubic millimetre, divided by the number of electrostatic units contained in one cubic millimetre; this number again is equal to i, the current-density, measured electrostatically, divided by the velocity v; hence $m = Mv/i$ and $X = 4\omega . Mv^2/i = 4i\omega . Mv^2/i^2$. Now without altering the equation we may use magnetic units on both sides; if we do so, $Mv^2/i^2 = Mv_0^2/i_0^2$ is that quantity which in the introduction is denoted by μ, and thus $X = 4\mu i\omega$. Here we put for the current-density i the quotient of the total current-strength J by q, the cross-section of the conductor, and for the electromotive intensity X the quotient of ϕ, the difference of potential between the points C and D, by b, the breadth of the plate; if we call its mean thickness d, then we get $\phi = 4\mu J\omega b/q = 4\mu J\omega/d$, or, as we require μ,

$$\mu = \frac{\phi q}{4Jb\omega} = \frac{\phi d}{4J\omega}.$$

We may approximately calculate the cross-section q or the thickness d from the amount of silver deposited; but it is more rational, as well as more accurate, to determine it from the electrical resistance of the plate, for this resistance depends directly on the mean velocity with which the electricity flows through the plate, and we are concerned with just this velocity and only indirectly with the cross-section. As the conduction was doubtless metallic we must take for the specific resistance of the conducting material that of silver; from the length of the plate $= 45$ mm., and its mean resistance $= 5\cdot1$ Siemens units, we get the required cross-section $q = 0\cdot00014$ mm^2, and the corresponding thickness $d = 0\cdot6 \times 10^{-6}$ mm. It is true this thickness is only about one-tenth of that deduced from the amount of silver deposited; but this only shows what was very probable before, namely, that the silver is very unequally distributed over the glass. Employing the value thus obtained for the thickness, we put $J = 1\cdot17$ mg$^{\frac{1}{2}}$ mm$^{\frac{1}{2}}$ sec^{-1}, $\omega = 2\pi \times 34$ sec^{-1}, $\phi = 1$ scale division $= 1/32 \times 10^6$ of a Daniell $= 3300$ mg$^{\frac{1}{2}}$ mm$^{\frac{3}{2}}$ sec^{-1}; and thus find $\mu = 0\cdot0000185$ mm^2. Thus μ appears as an area, namely, energy divided by the unit of the square of a magnetic current-density and by the unit of volume. Since the value $\phi = 1$ scale division was found to be extremely improbable, the statement made in the introduction is justified. Even if the assumptions made in calculating the experiments were only very rough approximations, it would still remain unlikely that even a much narrower limit should be exceeded.

It is worth noting that we do know electric currents, which certainly possess kinetic energy [of matter] considerably exceeding in magnitude the limit determined, namely, currents in electrolytes. From the chemical equivalent of a current of strength 1 in magnetic measure, and from the migration number of silver nitrate, it is easy to calculate the velocities with which the atomic groups Ag and NO_3 move in a solution of this salt of given concentration, when a current of unit density flows through the solution. Hence the kinetic energy of this motion follows, and in fact we find approximately for solutions of average concentrations $\mu = 0.0078/n$ mm², when there are n parts by weight of salt to 1 of water. Thus if the experiment described could be performed with an electrolyte under the same conditions as with a metal, it would give a positive result; but as a matter of fact, the resistance and decomposition of the electrolyte prevent our obtaining anything like equally favourable conditions of experiment.

V

ON THE CONTACT OF ELASTIC SOLIDS

(Journal für die reine und angewandte Mathematik, **92,** pp. 156-171, 1881.)

IN the theory of elasticity the causes of the deformations are assumed to be partly forces acting throughout the volume of the body, partly pressures applied to its surface. For both classes of forces it may happen that they become infinitely great in one or more infinitely small portions of the body, but so that the integrals of the forces taken throughout these elements remain finite. If about the singular point we describe a closed surface of small dimensions compared to the whole body, but very large in comparison with the element in which the forces act, the deformations outside and inside this surface may be treated independently of each other. Outside, the deformations depend upon the shape of the whole body, the finite integrals of the force-components at the singular point, and the distribution of the remaining forces; inside, they depend only upon the distribution of the forces acting inside the element. The pressures and deformations inside the surface are infinitely great in comparison with those outside.

In what follows we shall treat of a case which is one of the class referred to above, and which is of practical interest,[1] namely, the case of two elastic isotropic bodies which touch each other over a very small part of their surface and exert upon each other a finite pressure, distributed over the common area of contact. The surfaces in contact are imagined as perfectly smooth, *i.e.* we assume that only a normal pressure

---

[1] *Cf.* Winkler, *Die Lehre von der Elasticität und Festigkeit,* vol. i. p. 43 (Prag. 1867); and Grashof, *Theorie der Elasticität und Festigkeit,* pp. 49-54 (Berlin, 1878).

CONTACT OF ELASTIC SOLIDS

acts between the parts in contact. The portion of the surface which during deformation is common to the two bodies we shall call the surface of pressure, its boundary the curve of pressure. The questions which from the nature of the case first demand an answer are these: What surface is it, of which the surface of pressure forms an infinitesimal part ?[1] What is the form and what is the absolute magnitude of the curve of pressure? How is the normal pressure distributed over the surface of pressure? It is of importance to determine the maximum pressure occurring in the bodies when they are pressed together, since this determines whether the bodies will be without permanent deformation; lastly, it is of interest to know how much the bodies approach each other under the influence of a given total pressure.

We are given the two elastic constants of each of the bodies which touch, the form and relative position of their surfaces near the point of contact, and the total pressure. We shall choose our units so that the surface of pressure may be finite. Our reasoning will then extend to all finite space; the full dimensions of the bodies in contact we must imagine as infinite.

In the first place we shall suppose that the two surfaces are brought into mathematical contact, so that the common normal is parallel to the direction of the pressure which one body is to exert on the other. The common tangent plane is taken as the plane xy, the normal as axis of z, in a rectangular rectilinear system of coordinates. The distance of any point of either surface from the common tangent plane will in the neighbourhood of the point of contact, i.e. throughout all finite space, be represented by a homogeneous quadratic function of x and y. Therefore the distance between two corresponding points of the two surfaces will also be represented by such a function. We shall turn the axes of x and y so that in the last-named function the term involving xy is absent.

---

[1] In general the radii of curvature of the surface of a body in a state of strain are only infinitesimally altered; but in our particular case they are altered by finite amounts, and in this lies the justification of the present question. For instance, when two equal spheres of the same material touch each other, the surface of pressure forms part of a plane, i.e. of a surface which is different in character from both of the surfaces in contact.

Then we may write the equations of the two surfaces

$$z_1 = A_1x^2 + Cxy + B_1y^2, \quad z_2 = A_2x^2 + Cxy + B_2y^2,$$

and we have for the distance between corresponding points of the two surfaces $z_1 - z_2 = Ax^2 + By^2$, where $A = A_1 - A_2$, $B = B_1 - B_2$, and A, B, C are all infinitesimal.[1] From the meaning of the quantity $z_1 - z_2$ it follows that A and B have the like sign, which we shall take positive. This is equivalent to choosing the positive z-axis to fall inside the body to which the index 1 refers.

Further, we imagine in each of the two bodies a rectangular rectilinear system of axes, rigidly connected at infinity with the corresponding body, which system of axes coincides with the previously chosen system of xyz during the mathematical contact of the two surfaces. When a pressure acts on the bodies these systems of coordinates will be shifted parallel to the axis of z relatively to one another; and their relative motion will be the same in amount as the distance by which those parts of the bodies approach each other which are at an infinite distance from the point of contact. The plane $z = 0$ in each of these systems is infinitely near to the part of the surface of the corresponding body which is at a finite distance, and therefore may itself be considered as the surface, and the direction of the z-axis as the direction of the normal to this surface.

Let ξ, η, ζ be the component displacements parallel to the axes of x, y, z; let Y_x denote the component parallel to Oy of the pressure on a plane element whose normal is parallel to Ox, exerted by the portion of the body for which x has smaller values on the portion for which x has larger values, and let a similar notation be used for the remaining com-

[1] Let ρ_{11}, ρ_{12} be the reciprocals of the principal radii of curvature of the surface of the first body, reckoned positive when the corresponding centres of curvature lie inside this body; similarly let ρ_{21}, ρ_{22} be the principal curvatures of the surface of the second body; lastly let ω be the angle which the planes of the curvatures ρ_{11} and ρ_{21} make with each other. Then

$$2(A + B) = \rho_{11} + \rho_{12} + \rho_{21} + \rho_{22},$$

$$2(A - B) = \sqrt{(\rho_{11} - \rho_{12})^2 + 2(\rho_{11} - \rho_{12})(\rho_{21} - \rho_{22})\cos 2\omega + (\rho_{21} - \rho_{22})^2}.$$

If we introduce an auxiliary angle τ by the equation $\cos\tau = (A - B)/(A + B)$, then

$$2A = (\rho_{11} + \rho_{12} + \rho_{21} + \rho_{22})\cos^2\frac{\tau}{2}, \quad 2B = (\rho_{11} + \rho_{12} + \rho_{21} + \rho_{22})\sin^2\frac{\tau}{2}.$$

ponents of pressure; lastly let $K_1\theta_1$ and $K_2\theta_2$[1] be the respective coefficients of elasticity of the bodies. Generally, where the quantities refer to either body, we shall omit the indices. We then have the following conditions for equilibrium:—

1. Inside each body we must have

$$0 = \nabla^2\xi + (1 + 2\theta)\frac{\partial\sigma}{\partial x}, \quad 0 = \nabla^2\eta + (1 + 2\theta)\frac{\partial\sigma}{\partial y},$$

$$0 = \nabla^2\zeta + (1 + 2\theta)\frac{\partial\sigma}{\partial z}, \quad \sigma = \frac{\partial\xi}{\partial x} + \frac{\partial\eta}{\partial y} + \frac{\partial\zeta}{\partial z};$$

and in 1 we have to put θ_1 for θ, in 2 θ_2 for θ.

2. At the boundaries the following conditions must hold:—

(a) At infinity ξ, η, ζ vanish, for our systems of coordinates are rigidly connected with the bodies there.

(b) For $z = 0$, i.e. at the surface of the bodies, the tangential stresses which are perpendicular to the z-axis must vanish, or

$$Y_z = -K\left(\frac{\partial\eta}{\partial z} + \frac{\partial\zeta}{\partial y}\right) = 0, \quad X_z = -K\left(\frac{\partial\zeta}{\partial x} + \frac{\partial\xi}{\partial z}\right) = 0.$$

(c) For $z = 0$, outside a certain portion of this plane, viz. outside the surface of pressure, the normal stress also must vanish, or

$$Z_z = 2K\left(\frac{\partial\zeta}{\partial z} + \theta\sigma\right) = 0.$$

Inside that part

$$Z_{z1} = Z_{z2}.$$

We do not know the distribution of pressure over that part, but instead we have a condition for the displacement ζ over it.

(d) For if a denote the relative displacement of the two systems of coordinates to which we refer the displacements, the distance between corresponding points of the two surfaces after deformation is $Ax^2 + By^2 + \zeta_1 - \zeta_2 - a$, and since this distance vanishes inside the surface of pressure we have

$$\zeta_1 - \zeta_2 = a - Ax^2 - By^2 = a - z_1 + z_2.$$

(e) To the conditions enumerated we must add the con-

---

[1] [Kirchhoff's notation, *Mechanik*, p. 121.—Tr.]

dition that inside the surface of pressure Z_z is everywhere positive, and the condition that outside the surface of pressure $\zeta_1 - \zeta_2 > a - Ax^2 - By^2$, otherwise the one body would overflow into the other.

(f). Lastly the integral $\int Z_z ds$, taken over the part of the surface which is bounded by the curve of pressure, must be equal to the given total pressure, which we shall call p.

The particular form of the surface of the two bodies only occurs in the boundary condition (2 d), apart from which each of the bodies acts as if it were an infinitely extended body occupying all space on one side of the plane $z = 0$, and as if only normal pressures acted on this plane. We therefore consider more closely the equilibrium of such a body. Let P be a function which inside the body satisfies the equation $\nabla^2 P = 0$; in particular, we shall regard P as the potential of a distribution of electricity on the finite part of the plane $z = 0$. Further let

$$\Pi = -\frac{zP}{K} + \frac{1}{K(1 + 2\theta)}\left\{\int_z^i P\,dz - J\right\},$$

where i is an infinitely great quantity, and J is a constant so chosen as to make Π finite. For this purpose J must be equal to the natural logarithm of i multiplied by the total charge of free electricity corresponding to the potential P.

From the definition of Π it follows that

$$\nabla^2 \Pi = -\frac{2}{K}\frac{\partial P}{\partial z}.$$

Introducing the contraction $\vartheta = \frac{2(1 + \theta)}{K(1 + 2\theta)}$ we put

$$\xi = \frac{\partial \Pi}{\partial x}, \quad \eta = \frac{\partial \Pi}{\partial y}, \quad \zeta = \frac{\partial \Pi}{\partial z} + 2\vartheta P,$$

$$\sigma = \nabla^2 \Pi + 2\vartheta \frac{\partial P}{\partial z} = \frac{2}{K(1 + 2\theta)}\frac{\partial P}{\partial z}$$

This system of displacements is easily seen to satisfy the

differential equations given for ξ, η, ζ, and the displacements vanish at infinity. For the pressure components we find

$$X_y = -2K\left\{\frac{\partial^2\Pi}{\partial x^2} + \frac{2\theta}{K(1+2\theta)}\frac{\partial P}{\partial z}\right\},$$

$$X_y = -2K\frac{\partial^2\Pi}{\partial x\partial y},$$

$$Y_y = -2K\left\{\frac{\partial^2\Pi}{\partial y^2} + \frac{2\theta}{K(1+2\theta)}\frac{\partial P}{\partial z}\right\},$$

$$X_z = -2K\left\{\frac{\partial^2\Pi}{\partial x\partial z} + \vartheta\frac{\partial P}{\partial x}\right\} = 2z\frac{\partial^2 P}{\partial x\partial z},$$

$$Z_z = -2K\left\{\frac{\partial^2\Pi}{\partial z^2} + \frac{2(2+3\theta)}{K(1+2\theta)}\frac{\partial P}{\partial z}\right\},$$

$$Y_z = -2K\left\{\frac{\partial^2\Pi}{\partial y\partial z} + \vartheta\frac{\partial P}{\partial y}\right\} = 2z\frac{\partial^2 P}{\partial y\partial z}.$$

The last two formulæ show that for the given system the stress-components perpendicular to the z-axis vanish throughout the plane $z = 0$. We determine the displacement ζ and the normal pressure Z_z at the plane $z = 0$, and find

$$\zeta = \vartheta P, \quad Z_z = -2\frac{\partial P}{\partial z}.$$

The density of the electricity producing the potential P is $-(1/2\pi)(\partial P/\partial z)$, hence we have the following theorem. The displacement ζ in the surface, which corresponds to the normal pressure Z_z, is equal to $\vartheta/4\pi$ times the potential due to an electrical density numerically equal to the pressure Z_z.

We now consider again both bodies : we imagine the electricity whose potential is P to be distributed over a finite portion only of the plane $z = 0$; we make Π_1 and Π_2 equal to the expressions derived from the given expression for Π by giving to the symbols K and θ the index 1 and 2, and put

$$\xi_1 = \frac{\partial\Pi_1}{\partial x}, \quad \eta_1 = \frac{\partial\Pi_1}{\partial y}, \quad \zeta_1 = \frac{\partial\Pi_1}{\partial z} + 2\vartheta_1 P,$$

$$\xi_2 = -\frac{\partial\Pi_2}{\partial x}, \quad \eta_2 = -\frac{\partial\Pi_2}{\partial y}, \quad \zeta_2 = -\frac{\partial\Pi_2}{\partial z} - 2\vartheta_2 P ;$$

whence we have for $z = 0$

$$\zeta_1 = \vartheta_1 P, \quad \zeta_2 = -\vartheta_2 P, \quad Z_{z1} = -2\frac{\partial P}{\partial z}, \quad Z_{z2} = 2\frac{\partial P}{\partial z}$$

This assumption satisfies the conditions (1), (2 a), and (2 b) according to the explanations given. Since $\partial P/\partial z$ has on the two sides of the plane $z = 0$ values equal but of opposite sign, and since it vanishes outside the electrically charged surface whose potential is P, the conditions (2 c) also are fulfilled, provided the surface of pressure coincides with the electrically charged surface. From the fact that P is continuous across the plane $z = 0$, it follows that for $z = 0, \vartheta_2\zeta_1 + \vartheta_1\zeta_2 = 0$. But according to the condition (2 d) we have for the surface of pressure, $\zeta_1 - \zeta_2 = a - z_1 + z_2$; here therefore

$$\zeta_1 = \frac{\vartheta_1}{\vartheta_1 + \vartheta_2}(a - z_1 + z_2), \quad \zeta_2 = -\frac{\vartheta_2}{\vartheta_1 + \vartheta_2}(a - z_1 + z_2).$$

Apart from a constant which depends on the choice of the system of coordinates, and need therefore not be considered, the equation of the surface of pressure is $z = z_1 + \zeta_1 = z_2 + \zeta_2$, or $(\vartheta_1 + \vartheta_2)z = \vartheta_2 z_1 + \vartheta_1 z_2$. Thus the surface of pressure is part of a quadric surface lying between the undeformed positions of the surfaces which touch each other; and is most like the boundary of the body having the greater coefficient of elasticity. If the bodies are composed of the same material it is the mean surface of the surfaces of the two bodies, since then $2z = z_1 + z_2$.

We now make a definite assumption as to the distribution of the electricity whose potential is P. Let it be distributed over an ellipse whose semi-axes a and b coincide with the axes of x and y, with a density $\dfrac{3p}{8\pi^2 ab}\sqrt{1 - \dfrac{x^2}{a^2} - \dfrac{y^2}{b^2}}$, so that it can be regarded as a charge which fills an infinitely flattened ellipsoid with uniform volume density. Then

$$P = \frac{3p}{16\pi}\int_u^\infty \left(1 - \frac{x^2}{a^2 + \lambda} - \frac{y^2}{b^2 + \lambda} - \frac{z^2}{\lambda}\right)\frac{d\lambda}{\sqrt{(a^2 + \lambda)(b^2 + \lambda)\lambda}},$$

where u, the inferior limit of integration, is the positive root of the cubic equation

$$\frac{x_2}{a^2+u}+\frac{y^2}{b^2+u}+\frac{z^2}{u}=1 .$$

Inside the surface of pressure, which is bounded by the given ellipse, we have $u=0$, $P=L-Mx^2-Ny^2$; where L, M, N denote certain positive definite integrals. The condition (2 d) is satisfied by choosing a and b so that

$$(\vartheta_1+\vartheta_2)M = A, \quad (\vartheta_1+\vartheta_2)N = B,$$

which is always possible. The unknown a which occurs in the condition is then determined by the equation

$$(\vartheta_1+\vartheta_2)L = a.$$

It follows directly from the equation

$$Z_z = \frac{3p}{2\pi ab}\sqrt{1-\frac{x^2}{a^2}-\frac{y^2}{b^2}}$$

that the first of the conditions (2 e) is satisfied.

To show that the second also is satisfied is to prove that when $z=0$ and $x^2/a^2+y^2/b^2>1$, $(\vartheta_1+\vartheta_2)P>a-Ax^2-By^2$. For this purpose we observe that here

$$P = L - Mx^2 - Ny^2$$

$$-\frac{3p}{16\pi}\int_0^u\left(1-\frac{x^2}{a^2+\lambda}-\frac{y^2}{b^2+\lambda}\right)\frac{d\lambda}{\sqrt{(a^2+\lambda)(b^2+\lambda)\lambda}},$$

and hence $P>L-Mx^2-Ny^2$, for the numerator of the expression under the sign of integration is negative throughout the region considered. Multiplying by $\vartheta_1+\vartheta_2$ we get the inequality which was to be proved. Finally, a simple integration shows that the last condition (2 f) also is satisfied; therefore we have in the assumed expression for P and the corresponding system ξ, η, ζ a solution which satisfies all the conditions.

The equations for the axes of the ellipse of pressure written explicitly are

$$\int_0^\infty \frac{du}{\sqrt{(a^2+u)^3(b^2+u)u}} = \frac{A}{\vartheta_1+\vartheta_2}\frac{16\pi}{3p}.$$

$$\int_0^\infty \frac{du}{\sqrt{(a^2+u)(b^2+u)^3u}} = \frac{B}{\vartheta_1+\vartheta_2}\frac{16\pi}{3p}.$$

or introducing the ratio $k = a/b$, and transforming,

$$\frac{1}{a^3}\int_0^\infty \frac{dz}{\sqrt{(1+k^2z^2)^3(1+z^2)}} = \frac{8\pi}{3p}\frac{A}{\vartheta_1+\vartheta_2},$$

$$\frac{1}{a^3}\int_0^\infty \frac{dz}{k^2\sqrt{(1+k^2z^2)(1+z^2)^3}} = \frac{8\pi}{3p}\frac{B}{\vartheta_1+\vartheta_2}.$$

By division we obtain a transcendental equation for the ratio k.[1] This depends only on the ratio $A:B$, and it follows at once, from the meaning we have attached to the forces and displacements, that the ellipse of pressure is always more elongated than the ellipses at which the distance between the bodies is constant. As regards the absolute magnitude of the surface of pressure for a given form of the surfaces it varies as

[1] The solution of this equation and the evaluation of the integrals required for the determination of a and b may be performed by the aid of Legendre's tables without necessitating any new quadratures. The calculation, usually somewhat laborious, may in most cases be avoided by the use of the following small table, of which the arrangement is as follows. If we express A and B in the equations for a and b in terms of the principal curvatures and the auxiliary angle τ introduced in a previous note, the solutions of these equations are expressible in the form

$$a = \mu\sqrt{\frac{3p(\varrho_1+\vartheta)}{8(\rho_{11}+\rho_{12}+\rho_{21}+\rho_{22})}}, \quad b = \nu\sqrt{\frac{3p(\varrho_1+\vartheta_2)}{8(\rho_{11}+\rho_{12}+\rho_{21}+\rho_{22})}},$$

where μ, ν are transcendental functions of the angle τ. The table gives the values of these functions for ten values of the argument τ expressed in degrees.

τ	90	80	70	60	50	40	30	20	10	0
μ	1·0000	1·1278	1·2835	1·4858	1·7542	2·1357	2·7307	3·7779	6·6120	∞
ν	1·0000	0·8927	0·8017	0·7171	0·6407	0·5673	0·4930	0·4079	0·3186	0·0000

the cube root of the total pressure and as the cube root of the quantity $\vartheta_1 + \vartheta_2$. By the preceding the distance through which the bodies approach each other under the action of the given pressure is

$$a = \frac{3p}{8\pi} \cdot \frac{\vartheta_1 + \vartheta_2}{a} \int_0^\infty \frac{dz}{\sqrt{(1 + \lambda^2 z^2)(1 + z^2)}}.$$

If we perform the multiplication by $\vartheta_1 + \vartheta_2$, a splits up into two portions which have a special meaning. They denote the distances through which the origin approaches the infinitely distant portions of the respective bodies; we may call them the indentations which the respective bodies have undergone. With a given form of the touching surfaces the distance of approach varies as the pressure raised to the power $\frac{2}{3}$ and also as the same power of the quantity $\vartheta_1 + \vartheta_2$. When A and B alter in magnitude while their ratio remains unchanged, the dimensions of the surface of pressure vary inversely as the cube roots of the absolute values of A and B, and the distance of approach varies directly as these roots. When A and B become infinite, the distance of approach becomes infinite; bodies which touch each other at sharp points penetrate into each other.

In connection with this we shall determine what happens to the element at the origin of our system of coordinates by finding the three displacements $\frac{\partial \xi}{\partial x}$, $\frac{\partial \eta}{\partial y}$, $\frac{\partial \zeta}{\partial z}$. In the first place we have at the origin

$$\sigma = \frac{2}{K(1 + 2\theta)} \frac{\partial P}{\partial z} = -\frac{3p}{2K(1 + 2\theta)\pi} \frac{1}{ab},$$

$$\frac{\partial \zeta}{\partial z} = \frac{1}{K(1 + 2\theta)} \frac{\partial P}{\partial z} = -\frac{3p}{4K(1 + 2\theta)\pi} \frac{1}{ab}.$$

Further, at the plane $z = 0$

$$\xi = \frac{\partial \Pi}{\partial x}, \quad \eta = \frac{\partial \Pi}{\partial y},$$

$$\Pi = \frac{1}{K(1 + 2\theta)} \int_0^\infty P\, dz = \frac{1}{2K(1 + 2\theta)} \int_{-\infty}^\infty P\, dz.$$

We see that in the said plane ξ and η are proportional to
the forces exerted by an infinitely long elliptic cylinder, which
stands on the surface of pressure and whose density increases
inwards, according to the law of increase of the pressure in the
surface of pressure. In general then, ξ and η are given by
complicated functions; but for points close to the axis they
can be easily calculated. Surrounding the axis we describe a
very thin cylindrical surface, similar to the whole cylinder;
this [small] cylinder we may treat as homogeneous, and since
the part outside it has no action at points inside it, the components of the forces in question, and therefore also ξ and η,
must be equal to a constant multiplied respectively by x/a and
by y/b. Hence

$$a\frac{\partial \xi}{\partial x} - b\frac{\partial \eta}{\partial y} = 0.$$

On the other hand we have

$$\frac{\partial \xi}{\partial x} + \frac{\partial \eta}{\partial y} = \sigma - \frac{\partial \zeta}{\partial z} = -\frac{3p}{4K(1+2\theta)\pi}\frac{1}{ab}.$$

From these equations we find for the three quantities
which we sought

$$\frac{\partial \xi}{\partial x} = -\frac{3p}{4K(1+2\theta)\pi}\frac{1}{a(a+b)},$$

$$\frac{\partial \eta}{\partial y} = -\frac{3p}{4K(1+2\theta)\pi}\frac{1}{b(a+b)},$$

$$\frac{\partial \zeta}{\partial z} = -\frac{3p}{4K(1+2\theta)\pi}\frac{1}{ab}.$$

The negative sign of these three quantities shows that the
element in question is compressed in all three directions.
The compressions vary as the cube root of the total pressure.
It is easy to determine from them the pressures at the origin.
These pressures are the most intense of all those occurring
throughout the bodies pressed together; we may therefore
say that the limit of elasticity will not be exceeded until
these pressures become of the order of magnitude required for
transgressing the elastic limit. In plastic bodies, e.g. in the

softer metals, this transgression will at first consist in a lateral
deformation accompanied by a permanent compression ; so that
it will not result in an infinitely increasing disturbance of
equilibrium, but the surface of pressure will increase beyond
the calculated dimensions until the pressure per unit area is
sufficiently small to be sustained. It is more difficult to determine what happens in the case of brittle bodies, as hard
steel, glass, crystals, in which a transgression of the elastic
limit occurs only through the formation of a rent or crack, *i.e.*
only under the influence of tensional forces. Such a crack
cannot start in the element considered above, which is compressed in every direction ; and with our present-day knowledge
of the tenacity of brittle bodies it is indeed impossible exactly
to determine in which element the conditions for the production
of a crack first occur when the pressure is increased. However,
a more detailed discussion shows this much, that in bodies
which in their elastic behaviour resemble glass or hard steel,
much the most intense tensions occur at the surface, and in
fact at the boundary of the surface of pressure. Such a discussion shows it to be probable that the first crack starts at
the ends of the smaller axis of the ellipse of pressure, and
proceeds perpendicularly to this axis along that ellipse.

The formulæ found become especially simple when both
the bodies which touch each other are spheres. In this case
the surface of pressure is part of a sphere. If ρ is the reciprocal of its radius, and if ρ_1 and ρ_2 are the reciprocals of the
radii of the touching spheres, then we have the relation
$(\vartheta_1 + \vartheta_2)\rho = \vartheta_2\rho_1 + \vartheta_1\rho_2$; which for spheres of the same material
takes the simpler form $2\rho = \rho_1 + \rho_2$. The curve of pressure is
a circle whose radius we shall call a. If we put

$$x^2 + y^2 = r^2, \quad \frac{r^2}{a^2+u} + \frac{z^2}{u} = 1,$$

then will

$$P = \frac{3p}{16\pi}\int_u^\infty \left(1 - \frac{r^2}{a^2+u} - \frac{z^2}{u}\right)\frac{du}{(a^2+u)\sqrt{u}}.$$

which may also be expressed in a form free of integrals.

We easily find for a, the radius of the circle of pressure,
and for α, the distance through which the spheres approach

each other, and also for the displacement ζ over the part of the plane $z = 0$ inside the circle of pressure :—

$$a = \sqrt[3]{\frac{3p(\vartheta_1 + \vartheta_2)}{16(\rho_1 + \rho_2)}}, \qquad a = \frac{3p(\vartheta_1 + \vartheta_2)}{16a},$$

$$\zeta = \frac{3p}{32}\vartheta\frac{2a^2 - r^2}{a^3}.$$

Outside the circle of pressure ζ is represented by a somewhat more complicated expression, involving an inverse tangent. Very simple expressions may be got for ξ and η at the plane $z = 0$. For the compression at the plane $z = 0$ we find

$$\sigma = -\frac{3p}{2\mathrm{K}(1 + 2\theta)\pi}\frac{\sqrt{a^2 - r^2}}{a^3}$$

inside the circle of pressure; outside it $\sigma = 0$. For the pressure Z_z inside the circle of pressure we obtain

$$Z_z = \frac{3p}{2\pi}\frac{\sqrt{a^2 - r^2}}{a^3} \; ;$$

at the centre we have

$$Z_z = \frac{3p}{2\pi a^2}, \qquad X_x = Y_y = \frac{1 + 4\theta}{4(1 + 2\theta)}\frac{3p}{\pi a^2}.$$

The formulæ obtained may be directly applied to particular cases. In most bodies θ may with a sufficient approximation be made equal to 1. Then K becomes $\frac{3}{8}$ of the modulus of elasticity ; ϑ becomes equal to $\frac{32}{9}$ times the reciprocal of that modulus ; in all bodies ϑ is between three and four times this reciprocal value. If, for instance, we press a glass lens of 100 metres radius with the weight of 1 kilogramme against a plane glass plate (in which case the first Newton's ring would have a radius of about 5·2 millimetres), we get a surface of pressure which is part of a sphere of radius equal to 200 metres. The radius of the circle of pressure is 2·67 millimetres ; the distance of approach of the glass bodies amounts to only 71 millionths of a millimetre. The pressure Z_z at the centre of the surface of pressure is 0·0669 kilogrammes per square millimetre, and the perpendicular pressures X_x and Y_y have

about $\frac{5}{6}$ that value.   As a second example, consider a number
of steel spheres pressed by their own weight against a rigid
horizontal plane.   We find that the radius of the circle of
pressure in millimetres is very approximately $a = \frac{1}{1000}R^{\frac{2}{3}}$.
Hence for spheres of radii

$$1 \text{ mm.,} \qquad 1 \text{ m.,} \qquad 1 \text{ km.,} \qquad 1000 \text{ km.,}$$

a becomes about

$$\frac{1}{1000} \text{ mm.,} \qquad 10 \text{ mm.} \qquad 100 \text{ m.,} \qquad 1000 \text{ km.,}$$

or $\qquad a = \qquad \frac{1}{1000}, \qquad \frac{1}{100}, \qquad \frac{1}{10}, \qquad \frac{1}{1}$

of the radius.   For spheres whose radius exceeds 1 km.
the radius of the circle of pressure is more than $\frac{1}{10}$ of the
radius of the sphere.   Our calculations do not apply to such
ratios, for we presupposed the ratio to be a small fraction.
But the very fact that for such large spheres equilibrium is
no longer possible with small deformations shows that equilibrium is altogether impossible.   Consider further two steel
spheres of equal radius touching one another and pressed
together only by their mutual gravitational attraction.   In
millimetres we find [1] the radius of the circle of pressure to be
$\rho = 0.000000378R^{\frac{2}{3}}$.   If the radius of the two spheres is 4·3
kilometres, then $\rho = \frac{1}{100}R$; if it is 136 kilometres, then
$\rho = \frac{1}{10}R$.   That value of R, for which the elastic forces cease
to be able to equilibrate gravitational attraction, will lie
between the above values and nearer to the greater.   If steel
spheres of greater radius be placed touching each other, they
will break up into pieces whose dimensions are of the order o:
the values of R just mentioned.

Finally, we shall apply the formulæ we have obtained t(
the impact of elastic bodies.   It follows, both from existing
observations and from the results of the following considerations, that the time of impact, i.e. the time during which th(
impinging bodies remain in contact, is very small in absolut(
value ; yet it is very large compared with the time taken b]
waves of elastic deformation in the bodies in question t(
traverse distances of the order of magnitude of that part o
their surfaces which is common to the two bodies when i]

---

[1] In these calculations the modulus of elasticity of steel is taken to be 20,00·
kg/mm², its density 7·7, and the mean density of the earth 6.

closest contact, and which we shall call the surface of impact. It follows that the elastic state of the two bodies near the point of impact during the whole duration of impact is very nearly the same as the state of equilibrium which would be produced by the total pressure subsisting at any instant between the two bodies, supposing it to act for a long time. If then we determine the pressure between the two bodies by means of the relation which we previously found to hold between this pressure and the distance of approach along the common normal of two bodies at rest, and also throughout the volume of each body make use of the equations of motion of elastic solids, we can trace the progress of the phenomenon very exactly. We cannot in this way expect to obtain general laws; but we may obtain a number of such if we make the further assumption that the time of impact is also large compared with the time taken by elastic waves to traverse the impinging bodies from end to end. When this condition is fulfilled, all parts of the impinging bodies, except those infinitely close to the point of impact, will move as parts of rigid bodies; we shall show from our results that the condition in question may be realised in the case of actual bodies.

We retain our system of axes of xyz. Let a be the resolved part parallel to the axis of z of the distance of two points one in each body, which are chosen so that their distance from the surface of impact is small compared with the dimensions of the bodies as a whole, but large compared with the dimensions of the surface of impact; and let a' denote the differential coefficient of a with regard to the time. If dJ is the momentum lost in time dt by one body and gained by the other, then it follows from the theory of impact of rigid bodies that $da' = -k_1 dJ$, where k_1 is a quantity depending only upon the masses of the impinging bodies, their principal moments of inertia, and the situation of their principal axes of inertia relatively to the normal at the point of impact.[1]   On

---

[1] See Poisson, *Traité de mécanique*, II. chap. vii. In the notation there employed we have for the constant k_1

$$k_1 = \frac{1}{M} + \frac{(b\cos\gamma - c\cos\beta)^2}{A} + \frac{(c\cos\alpha - a\cos\gamma)^2}{B} + \frac{(a\cos\beta - b\cos\alpha)^2}{C}$$

$$+ \frac{1}{M'} + \frac{(b'\cos\gamma' - c'\cos\beta')^2}{A'} + \frac{(c'\cos\alpha' - a'\cos\gamma')^2}{B'} + \frac{(a'\cos\beta' - b'\cos\alpha')^2}{C'}.$$

the other hand, dJ is equal to the element of time dt, multiplied by the pressure which during that time acts between the bodies. This is $k_2 a^{\frac{3}{2}}$, where k_2 is a constant to be determined from what precedes, which constant depends only on the form of the surfaces and the elastic properties quite close to the point of impact. Hence $dJ = k_2 a^{\frac{3}{2}} dt$ and $da' = -k_1 k_2 a^{\frac{3}{2}} dt$; integrating, and denoting by a'_0 the value of a' just before impact, we find

$$a'^2 - a'^2_0 + \tfrac{4}{5} k_1 k_2 a^{\frac{5}{2}} = 0,$$

which equation expresses the principle of the conservation of energy. When the bodies approach as closely as possible a' vanishes; if a_m denote the corresponding value of a, then $a_m = \left(\dfrac{5 a'^2_0}{4 k_1 k_2}\right)^{\frac{2}{5}}$, and the simultaneous maximum pressure is $p_m = k_2 a^{\frac{3}{2}}_m$. From this we at once obtain the dimensions of the surface of impact.

In order to deduce the variation of the phenomenon with the time, we integrate again and obtain

$$t = \int_a^{a_m} \frac{da}{\sqrt{a'^2_0 - \tfrac{4}{5} k_1 k_2 a^{\frac{5}{2}}}}.$$

The upper limit is so chosen that $t = 0$ at the instant of nearest approach. For each value of the lower limit a, the double sign of the radical gives two equal positive and negative values of t. Hence a is an even and a' an odd function of t; immediately after impact the points of impact separate along the normal with the same relative velocity with which they approached each other before impact. And the same transcendental function which represents the variation of a' between its initial and final values, also represents the variations of all the component velocities from their initial to their final values.

In the first place, the bodies touch when $a = 0$; they separate when a again $= 0$. Hence the duration of contact, that is the time of impact, is

$$T = 2 \int_0^{a_m} \frac{da}{\sqrt{a'^2_0 - \tfrac{4}{5} k_1 k_2 a^{\frac{5}{2}}}} = 2\eta \sqrt[5]{\frac{25}{16 a'_0 k_1^2 k_2^2}} = 2\eta \frac{a_m}{a'_0},$$

$$\eta = \int_0^1 \frac{d\epsilon}{\sqrt{1 - \epsilon^{\frac{5}{2}}}} = 1.4716.$$

Thus the time of impact may become infinite in various ways without the time, with which it is to be compared, also becoming infinite. In particular the time of impact becomes infinite when the initial relative velocity of the impinging bodies is infinitely small; so that whatever be the other circumstances of any given impact, provided the velocities are chosen small enough, the given developments will have any accuracy desired. In every case this accuracy will be the same as that of the so-called laws of impact of perfectly elastic bodies for the given case. For the direct impact of two spheres of equal radius R and of the same material of density q the constants k_1 and k_2 are

$$k_1 = \frac{3}{2R^3\pi q}, \qquad k_2 = \frac{8}{3k_1}\sqrt{\frac{R}{2}};$$

hence in the particular case of two equal steel spheres of radius R, taking the millimetre as unit of length, and the weight of one kilogramme as unit of force, we have

$$\log k_1 = 8.78 - 3 \log R,$$
$$\log k_2 = 4.03 + \tfrac{1}{2} \log R.$$

Thus for two such spheres impinging with relative velocity v:

the radius of the surface of impact . $a_m = 0.0020 R v^{\frac{2}{5}} \text{mm},$

the time of impact . $T = 0.000024 R v^{-\frac{1}{5}}\text{sec},$

the total pressure at the instant of
    nearest approach . . . $p_m = 0.00025 R^2 v^{\frac{6}{5}}\text{kg},$

the simultaneous maximum pressure
    at the centre of impact per unit
    area . . . $p'_m = 29.1 v^{\frac{2}{5}}\text{kg/mm}^2.$

For instance, when the radius of the spheres is 25 mm., the velocity 10 mm/sec, then $a_m = 0.13$ mm., $T = 0.00038$ sec., $p_m = 2.47$ kg., $p'_m = 73.0$ kg/mm.[2] For two steel spheres as large as the earth, impinging with an initial velocity of 10 mm/sec, the duration of contact would be nearly 27 hours.

ON THE CONTACT OF RIGID ELASTIC SOLIDS
AND ON HARDNESS

(*Verhandlungen des Vereins zur Beförderung des Gewerbefleisses*, November 1882.)

WHEN two elastic bodies are pressed together, they touch each other not merely in a mathematical point, but over a small but finite part of their surfaces, which part we shall call the surface of pressure. The form and size of this surface and the distribution of the stresses near it have been frequently considered (Winkler, *Lehre von der Elasticität und Festigkeit*, Prag. 1867, I. p. 43; Grashof, *Theorie der Elasticität und Festigkeit*, Berlin, 1878, pp. 49-54); but hitherto the results have either been approximate or have even involved unknown empirical constants. Yet the problem is capable of exact solution, and I have given the investigation of the problem in vol. xcii. of the *Journal für reine und angewandte Mathematik*, p. 156.[1] As some aspects of the subject are of considerable technical interest, I may here treat it more fully, with an addition concerning hardness. I shall first restate briefly the proof of the fundamental formulæ.

We first imagine the two bodies brought into mathematical contact; the common normal coincides with the line of action of the pressure which the one body exerts upon the other. In the common tangent plane we take rectangular rectilinear axes of xy, the origin of which coincides with the point of contact; the third perpendicular axis is that of z. We can confine our attention to that part of each body which is very close to the point of contact, since here the stresses are extremely great compared with those occurring elsewhere, and

[1] See V. p. 146.

consequently depend only to the very smallest extent on the
forces applied to other parts of the bodies. Hence it is sufficient to know the form of the surfaces infinitely near the point
of contact. To a first approximation, if we consider each
body separately, we may even suppose their surfaces to coincide with the common tangent plane $z = 0$, and the common
normal to coincide with the axis of z; to a second approximation, when we wish to consider the space between the bodies,
it is sufficient to retain only the quadratic terms in xy in the
development of the equations of the surfaces. The distance
between opposite points of the two surfaces then becomes a
homogeneous quadratic function of the x and y belonging to
the two points; and we can turn our axes of x and y so that
from this function the term in xy disappears. After completing this operation let the distance between the surfaces
be given by the equation $e = Ax^2 + By^2$. A and B must of
necessity have the same sign, since e cannot vanish; when we
construct the curves for which e has the same value, we obtain
a system of similar ellipses, whose centre is the origin. Our
problem now is to assign such a form to the surface of pressure
and such a system of displacements and stresses to its neighbourhood, that (1) these displacements and stresses may satisfy
the differential equations of equilibrium of elastic bodies, and
the stresses may vanish at a great distance from the surface of
pressure; that (2) the tangential components of stress may
vanish all over both surfaces; that (3) at the surface the
normal pressure also may vanish outside the surface of pressure,
but inside it pressure and counterpressure may be equal;
the integral of this pressure, taken over the whole surface of
pressure, must be equal to the total pressure p fixed before-
hand; that, lastly (4) the distance between the surfaces, which
is altered by the displacements, may vanish in the surface of
pressure, and be greater than zero outside it. To express the
last condition more exactly, let ξ_1, η_1, ζ_1 be the displacements
parallel to the axes of x, y, z in the first body, ξ_2, η_2, ζ_2 those
in the second. In each let them be estimated relatively to
the undeformed parts of the bodies, which are at a distance
from the surface of pressure; and let a denote the distance
by which these parts are caused by the pressure to approach
each other. Then any two points of the two bodies, which

have the same coordinates x, y, have approached each other by a distance $a - \zeta_1 + \zeta_2$ under the action of the pressure; this approach must in the surface of pressure neutralise the original distance $Ax^2 + By^2$ Hence here we must have $\zeta_1 - \zeta_2 = a - Ax^2 - By^2$, whilst elsewhere over the surfaces $\zeta_1 - \zeta_2 > a - Ax^2 - By^2$. All these conditions can be satisfied only by one single system of displacements; I shall give this system, and prove that it satisfies all requirements.

As surface of pressure we take an ellipse, whose axes coincide with those of the ellipses $c = $ constant, but whose shape is more elongated than theirs. We reserve the determination of the lengths of its semi-axes a and b until later. First we define a function P by the equation

$$P = \frac{3p}{16\pi} \int_u^\infty \left(1 - \frac{x^2}{a^2 + \lambda} - \frac{y^2}{b^2 + \lambda} - \frac{z^2}{\lambda}\right) \frac{d\lambda}{\sqrt{(a^2 + \lambda)(b^2 + \lambda)\lambda}},$$

where the lower limit of integration is the positive root of the cubic equation

$$0 = 1 - \frac{x^2}{a^2 + u} - \frac{y^2}{b^2 + u} - \frac{z^2}{u}.$$

The quantity u is an elliptic coordinate of the point xyz; it is constant over certain ellipsoids, which are confocal with the ellipse of pressure, and vanishes at all points which are infinitely close to the surface of pressure. The function P has a simple meaning in the theory of potential. It is the potential of an infinitely flattened gravitating ellipsoid, which would just fill the surface of pressure; in that theory it is proved that P satisfies the differential equation

$$\nabla^2 P = \frac{\partial^2 P}{\partial x^2} + \frac{\partial^2 P}{\partial y^2} + \frac{\partial^2 P}{\partial z^2} = 0.$$

Now from this P we deduce two functions Π, one of which refers to the one body, the second to the other, and we make

$$\Pi_1 = -\frac{1}{K_1}\left(zP - \frac{1}{1 + 2\Theta_1}\int_z^\infty P dz\right),$$

$$\Pi_2 = -\frac{1}{K_2}\left(zP - \frac{1}{1 + 2\Theta_2}\int_z^\infty P dz\right).$$

Here K, Θ denote the coefficients of elasticity in Kirchhoff's notation. Young's modulus of elasticity is expressed in terms of these coefficients by the equation

$$E = 2K\frac{1 + 3\Theta}{1 + 2\Theta}.$$

The ratio between lateral contraction and longitudinal extension is

$$\mu = \frac{\Theta}{1 + 2\Theta}.$$

For bodies like glass or steel, this ratio is nearly $\frac{1}{3}$, or Θ nearly 1, and K is nearly $\frac{3}{8}$ E. For slightly compressible bodies the ratio is nearly $\frac{1}{2}$; here then $\Theta = \infty$, $K = \frac{1}{3}E$. As a matter of fact a particular combination of K and Θ will play the principal part in our formulæ, for which we shall therefore introduce a special symbol. We put

$$\vartheta = \frac{2(1 + \Theta)}{K(1 + 2\Theta)}.$$

In bodies like glass, $\vartheta = 4/3K = 32/9E$; in all bodies ϑ lies between $3/E$ and $4/E$, since Θ lies between 0 and ∞. In regard to the Π's we must note that calculated by the above formulæ they have infinite values; but their differential coefficients, which alone concern us, are finite. It would only be necessary to add to the Π's infinite constants of suitable magnitude to make them finite. By a simple differentiation, remembering that $\nabla^2 P = 0$, we find

$$\nabla^2\Pi_1 = -\frac{2}{K_1}\frac{\partial P}{\partial z}, \quad \nabla^2\Pi_2 = -\frac{2}{K_2}\frac{\partial P}{\partial z}.$$

We now assume the following expressions for the displacements in the two bodies :—

$$\xi_1 = \frac{\partial\Pi_1}{\partial x}, \quad \eta_1 = \frac{\partial\Pi_1}{dy}, \quad \zeta_1 = \frac{\partial\Pi_1}{dz} + 2\vartheta_1 P,$$

$$\xi_2 = -\frac{\partial\Pi_2}{\partial x}, \quad \eta_2 = -\frac{\partial\Pi_2}{dy}, \quad \zeta_2 = -\frac{\partial\Pi_2}{dz} - 2\vartheta_2 P,$$

whence follow

$$\sigma_1 = \frac{\partial\xi_1}{\partial x} + \frac{\partial\eta_1}{\partial y} + \frac{\partial\zeta_1}{\partial z} = \nabla^2\Pi_1 + 2\vartheta_1\frac{\partial P}{\partial z} = \frac{2}{K_1(1 + 2\Theta_1)}\frac{\partial P}{\partial z},$$

$$\sigma_2 = -\frac{2}{K_2(1+2\Theta_2)}\frac{\partial P}{\partial z}.$$

In the first place, this system satisfies the equations of equilibrium, for we have

$$\nabla^2 \xi_1 + (1+2\Theta_1)\frac{\partial \sigma_1}{\partial x} = \frac{\partial \nabla^2 \Pi_1}{\partial x} + \frac{2}{K_1}\frac{\partial^2 P}{\partial z \partial x} = 0,$$

and similar equations hold for ξ_2, η_1, η_2; for the ζs we get the same result, remembering that $\nabla^2 P = 0$. For the tangential stress components at the surface ($z = 0$) we find, leaving out the indices :—

$$X_z = -K\left(\frac{\partial \zeta}{\partial x} + \frac{\partial \xi}{\partial z}\right) = -K\left(2\frac{\partial^2 \Pi}{\partial z \partial x} + 2\vartheta\frac{\partial P}{\partial x}\right) = 2z\frac{\partial^2 P}{\partial x \partial z} = 0,$$

$$Y_z = -K\left(\frac{\partial \eta}{\partial z} + \frac{\partial \zeta}{\partial y}\right) = -K\left(2\frac{\partial^2 \Pi}{\partial y \partial z} + 2\vartheta\frac{\partial P}{\partial x}\right) = 2z\frac{\partial^2 P}{\partial y \partial z} = 0,$$

as the second condition requires.

It is more troublesome to prove that the third condition is satisfied. We again omit indices, as the calculation applies equally to both bodies. We have generally

$$Z_z = -2K\left(\frac{\partial \zeta}{\partial z} + \Theta\sigma\right) = -2K\left\{\frac{\partial^2 \Pi}{\partial z^2} + \frac{2(2+3\Theta)}{K(1+2\Theta)}\frac{\partial P}{\partial z}\right\}$$

$$= 2z\frac{\partial^2 P}{\partial z^2} - 2\frac{\partial P}{\partial z};$$

therefore at the surface $Z_z = -2\frac{\partial P}{\partial z}$. Now, using the equation for u, we have generally

$$\frac{\partial P}{\partial z} = -\frac{3p}{8\pi}z\int_u^\infty \frac{d\lambda}{\lambda\sqrt{(a^2+\lambda)(b^2+\lambda)\lambda}},$$

and therefore at the surface $\frac{\partial P}{\partial z}$ vanishes, as it must do, and with it Z_z, at any rate outside the surface of pressure. In the compressed surface, where $u = 0$, the expression takes the form $0 . \infty$; the ordinary procedure for the evaluation of such an indeterminate form gives

$$\frac{\partial P}{\partial z} = - \frac{3p}{8\pi ab} \frac{z^2 \dfrac{\partial u}{\partial z}}{u \sqrt{u}},$$

that is, since for $u = 0$ we have

$$z^2 = u\left(1 - \frac{x^2}{a^2} - \frac{y^2}{b^2}\right),$$

$$Z_z = -2\frac{\partial P}{\partial z} = \frac{3p}{2\pi ab}\sqrt{1 - \frac{x^2}{a^2} - \frac{y^2}{b^2}}.$$

Here no quantity occurs which could be affected by an index. Hence in the surface of pressure Z_z is the same for both bodies; pressure and counter-pressure are equal. Lastly, the integral of Z_z over the surface of pressure is $3p/4\pi ab$ times the volume of an ellipsoid whose semi-axes are 1, a, b; *i.e.* it equals p, and therefore the total pressure has the required value.

It remains to be shown that the fourth condition can be satisfied by a suitable choice of the semi-axes a and b. For this purpose we remark that

$$\zeta_1 = \frac{\partial \Pi_1}{\partial z} + 2\vartheta_1 P = -\frac{z}{K_1}\frac{\partial P}{\partial z} + \vartheta_1 P,$$

so that at the surface $\zeta_1 = \vartheta_1 P$ and $\zeta_2 = \vartheta_2 P$. Since inside the surface of pressure the lower limit u of the integral is constantly zero, inside that surface P has the form $P = L - Mx^2 - Ny^2$; and therefore it is necessary so to determine a, b and a that $(\vartheta_1 + \vartheta_2)M = A$, $(\vartheta_1 + \vartheta_2)N = B$, $(\vartheta_1 + \vartheta_2)L = a$, so as to satisfy the equation $\zeta_1 - \zeta_2 = a - Ax^2 - By^2$, and this determination is always possible. Written explicitly the equations for a and b are

$$\int_0^\infty \frac{du}{\sqrt{(a^2 + u)^3(b^2 + u)u}} = \frac{A}{\vartheta_1 + \vartheta_2}\frac{16\pi}{3p},$$

$$\int_0^\infty \frac{du}{\sqrt{(a^2 + u)(b^2 + u)^3 u}} = \frac{B}{\vartheta_1 + \vartheta_2}\frac{16\pi}{3p}.$$

(I)

Finally, it is easily shown that the very essential inequality, which must be fulfilled outside the surface of
pressure, is actually satisfied; but I omit the proof, since it
requires the repetition of complicated integrals.

Thus our formulæ express the correct solution of the
proposed problem, and we may use them to answer the chief
questions which may be asked concerning the subject. It is
necessary to carry the evaluation of the quantities a and b a
step further; for the equations hitherto found for them cannot
straightway be solved, and in general not even the quantities
A and B are explicitly known. I assume that we are given the
four principal curvatures (reciprocals of the principal radii of
curvature) of the two surfaces, as well as the relative position
of their planes; let the former be ρ_{11} and ρ_{12} for the one
body, ρ_{21} and ρ_{22} for the other, and let ω be the angle
between the planes of ρ_{11} and of ρ_{21}. Let the ρ's be reckoned
positive when the corresponding centres of curvature lie
inside the body considered. Let our axes of xy be placed so
that the xz-plane makes with the plane of ρ_{11} the angle ω', so
far unknown. Then the equations of the surfaces are

$$2z_1 = \rho_{11}(x \cos \omega' + y \sin \omega')^2 + \rho_{12}(y \cos \omega' - x \sin \omega')^2,$$

$$2z_2 = - \rho_{21}\{x \cos (\omega' - \omega) + y \sin (\omega' - \omega)\}^2$$
$$- \rho_{22}\{y \cos (\omega' - \omega) - x \sin (\omega' - \omega)\}^2.$$

The difference $z_1 - z_2$ gives the distance between the surfaces.
Putting it $= Ax^2 + By^2$, and equating coefficients of x^2, xy, y^2
on both sides, we obtain three equations for ω', A and B;
their solution gives for the angle ω', which evidently determines the position of the axes of the ellipse of pressure
relatively to the surfaces, the equation

$$\tan 2\omega' = \frac{(\rho_{21} - \rho_{22})\sin 2\omega}{\rho_{11} - \rho_{12} + (\rho_{21} - \rho_{22})\cos 2\omega},$$

for A and B

$$2(A + B) = \rho_{11} + \rho_{12} + \rho_{21} + \rho_{22},$$

$$2(A - B) =$$
$$- \sqrt{(\rho_{11} - \rho_{12})^2 + 2(\rho_{11} - \rho_{12})(\rho_{21} - \rho_{22})\cos 2\omega + (\rho_{21} - \rho_{22})^2}.$$

For the purpose of what follows it is convenient to introduce an auxiliary angle τ by the equation

$$\cos \tau = -\frac{A - B}{A + B},$$

and then

$$2A = (\rho_{11} + \rho_{12} + \rho_{21} + \rho_{22})\sin^2\frac{\tau}{2},$$

$$2B = (\rho_{11} + \rho_{12} + \rho_{21} + \rho_{22})\cos^2\frac{\tau}{2}.$$

We shall introduce these values into the equations for a and b, and at the same time transform the integrals occurring there by putting in the first $u = b^2z^2$, in the second $u = a^2z^2$. Denoting the ratio b/a by k we get

$$\frac{1}{a^3}\int_0^\infty \frac{dz}{\sqrt{(1 + k^2z^2)^3(1 + z^2)}} = \frac{4\pi}{3p}\frac{\rho_{11} + \rho_{12} + \rho_{21} + \rho_{22}}{\vartheta_1 + \vartheta_2}\sin^2\frac{\tau}{2},$$

$$\frac{1}{b^3}\int_0^\infty \frac{dz}{\sqrt{\left(1 + \frac{z^2}{k^2}\right)^3(1 + z^2)}} = \frac{4\pi}{3p}\frac{\rho_{11} + \rho_{12} + \rho_{21} + \rho_{22}}{\vartheta_1 + \vartheta_2}\cos^2\frac{\tau}{2}.$$

Dividing the one equation by the other we get a new one, involving only k and τ, so that k is a function of τ alone; and the same is true of the integrals occurring in the equations. If we solve them by writing

$$a = \mu\sqrt[3]{\frac{3p(\vartheta_1 + \vartheta_2)}{8(\rho_{11} + \rho_{12} + \rho_{21} + \rho_{22})}},$$

$$b = \nu\sqrt[3]{\frac{3p(\vartheta_1 + \vartheta_2)}{8(\rho_{11} + \rho_{12} + \rho_{21} + \rho_{22})}},$$

then μ and ν depend only on τ, that is on the ratio of the axes of the ellipse $e = $ constant. The integrals in question may all be reduced to complete elliptic integrals of the first species and their differential coefficients with respect to the modulus, and can therefore be found by means of Legendre's tables without further quadratures. But the calculations are wearisome, and I have therefore calculated the table given below,[1] in which are found the values of μ and ν for ten values of the argument τ; presumably interpolation between these values will always yield a sufficiently near approximation. We may sum up our results thus: The form of the ellipse of pressure is conditioned solely by the form of the ellipses $e =$ constant. With a given shape its linear dimensions vary as the cube root of the pressure, inversely as the cube root of the arithmetical mean of the curvatures, and also directly as the cube root of the mean value of the elastic coefficients ϑ; that is, very nearly as the cube root of the mean value of the reciprocals of the moduli of elasticity. It is to be noted that the area of the ellipse of pressure increases, other things being equal, the more elongated its form. If we imagine that of two bodies touching each other one be rotated about the common normal while the total pressure is kept the same, then the area of the surface of pressure will be a maximum and the mean pressure per unit area a minimum in that position in which the ratio of the axes of the ellipse of pressure differs most from 1.

Our next inquiry concerns the indentations experienced by the bodies and the distance by which they approach each other in consequence of the pressure; the latter we called a and found its value to be $(\vartheta_1 + \vartheta_2)L$. Transforming the integral L a little, we get

$$a = \frac{3p}{8\pi} \frac{\vartheta_1 + \vartheta_2}{a} \int_0^\infty \frac{dz}{\sqrt{(1 + k^2 z^2)(1 + z^2)}}.$$

The distances by which the origin approaches the distant

1

τ	90	80	70	60	50	40	30	20	10	0
μ	1·000	1·128	1·284	1·486	1·754	2·136	2·731	3·778	6·612	∞
ν	1·000	0·893	0·802	0·717	0·641	0·567	0·493	0·408	0·319	0

parts of the bodies may be suitably denoted as indentations. Their values are easily found by multiplying by $\vartheta_1 + \vartheta_2$ and thus separating a into two portions. Substituting for a its value, we see that a involves a numerical factor which depends on the form of the ellipse of pressure; and that for a given value of this factor a varies as the $\frac{2}{3}$ power of the pressure, as the $\frac{2}{3}$ power of the mean value of the coefficients ϑ, and as the cube root of the mean value of the curvatures. If one or more of these curvatures become infinitely great, then distance of approach and indentations become infinitely great—a result sufficiently illustrated by the penetrating action of points and edges.

We assumed the surface of pressure to be so small that the deformed surfaces could be represented by quadric surfaces throughout a region large compared with the surface of pressure. Such an assumption can no longer be made after application of the pressure; in fact outside the surface of pressure the surface can only be represented by a complicated function. But we find that inside the surface of pressure the surface remains a quadric surface to the same approximation as before. Here we have $\zeta_1 - \zeta_2 = a - Ax^2 - By^2 = a - z_1 + z_2$, again $\zeta_1 = \vartheta_1 P$, $\zeta_2 = \vartheta_2 P$, or $\zeta_1 : \zeta_2 = \vartheta_1 : \vartheta_2$, and lastly, the equation of the deformed surface is $z = z_1 + \zeta_1 = z_2 + \zeta_2$; whence neglecting a constant, we easily deduce $(\vartheta_1 + \vartheta_2)z = \vartheta_2 z_1 + \vartheta_1 z_2$. This equation expresses what we wished to demonstrate; it also shows that the common surface after deformation lies between the two original surfaces, and most nearly resembles the body which has the greater modulus of elasticity. When spheres are in contact the surface of pressure also forms part of a sphere: when cylinders touch with axes crossed it forms part of a hyperbolic paraboloid.

So far we have spoken of the changes of form, now we will consider the stresses. We have already found for the normal pressure in the compressed surface

$$Z_z = \frac{3p}{2ab\pi}\sqrt{1 - \frac{x^2}{a^2} - \frac{y^2}{b^2}}.$$

This increases from the periphery to the centre, as do the ordinates of an ellipsoid constructed on the ellipse of pressure; it vanishes at the edge, and at the centre is one and a half times as great as it would be if the total pressure were equally distributed over the surface of pressure. Besides Z_z the remaining two principal tensions at the origin can be expressed in a finite form. It may be sufficient to state that they are also pressures of the same order of magnitude as Z_z, and are of such intensity that, provided the material is at all compressible, it will suffer compression in all three directions. When the curve of pressure is a circle, these forces are to Z_z in the ratio of $(1 + 4\Theta)/2(1 + 2\Theta) : 1$; for glass about as $5/6 : 1$. The distribution of stress inside depends not only on the form of the ellipse of pressure, but also essentially on the elastic coefficient Θ ; so that it may be entirely different in the two bodies which are in contact. When we compare the stresses in the same material for the same form but different sizes of the ellipse of pressure and different total pressures, we see that the stresses at points similarly situated with regard to the surface of pressure are proportional to each other. To get the pressures for one case at given points we must multiply the pressures at similarly situated points in the other case by the ratio of the total pressures, and divide by the ratio of the compressed areas. If we suppose two given bodies in contact and only the pressure between them to vary, the deformation of the material varies as the cube root of this total pressure.

It is desirable to obtain a clear view of the distribution

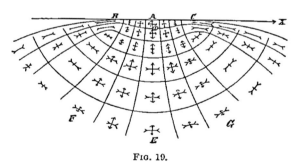

Fig. 19.

of stress in the interior ; but the formulæ are far too complicated to allow of our doing this directly. But by considering the stresses near the z-axis and near the surface we can form a rough notion of this distribution. The result may be expressed by the following description and the accompanying diagram (Fig. 19), which represents a section through the axis of

z and an axis of the ellipse of pressure; arrow-heads pointing towards each other denote a tension, those pointing away from each other a pressure. The figure relates to the case in which $\Theta = 1$. The portion $ABDC$ of the body, which originally formed an elevation above the surface of pressure, is now pressed into the body like a wedge; hence the pressure is transmitted not only in the direct line AE, but also, though with less intensity, in the inclined directions AF and AG. The consequence is that the element is also powerfully compressed laterally; while the parts at F and G are pressed apart and the intervening portions stretched. Hence at A on the element of area perpendicular to the x-axis there is pressure, which diminishes inwards, and changes to a tension which rapidly attains a maximum, and then, with increasing distance, diminishes to zero. Since the part near A is also laterally compressed, all points of the surface must approach the origin, and must therefore give rise to stretching in a line with the origin. In fact the pressure which acts at A parallel to the axis of x already changes to a tension inside the surface of pressure as we proceed along the x-axis; it attains a maximum near its boundary and then diminishes to zero. Calculation shows that for $\Theta = 1$ this tension is much greater than that in the interior. As regards the third principal pressure which acts perpendicular to the plane of the diagram, it of course behaves like the one parallel to the x-axis; at the surface it is a pressure, since here all points approach the origin. If the material is incompressible the diagram is simplified, for since the parts near A do not approach each other, the tensions at the surface disappear.

We shall briefly mention the simplifications occurring in the formulæ, when the bodies in contact are spheres, or are cylinders which touch along a generating line. In the first case we have simply $k = \mu = \nu = 1$, $\rho_{11} = \rho_{12} = \rho_1$, $\rho_{21} = \rho_{22} = \rho_2$; hence

$$a = b = \sqrt{\frac{3p(\vartheta_1 + \vartheta_2)}{16(\rho_1 + \rho_2)}}, \quad a = \frac{3p(\vartheta_1 + \vartheta_2)}{16a}.$$

The formulæ for the case of cylinders in contact are not got so directly. Here the major semi-axis a of the ellipse becomes infinitely great; we must also make the total pressure

p infinite, if the pressure per unit length of the cylinder is to be finite. We then have in the second of equations (I) $B = \frac{1}{2}(\rho_1 + \rho_2)$. Further, we may neglect u compared with a^2, take a outside the sign of integration, and put for the indeterminate quantity $p/a = \infty / \infty$ an arbitrary finite constant, say $\frac{4}{3}p'$; then, as we shall see directly, p' is the pressure per unit length of the cylinder. The integration of the equation can now be performed, and gives

$$b = \sqrt{\frac{p'(\vartheta_1 + \vartheta_2)}{\pi(\rho_1 + \rho_2)}}.$$

For the pressure Z_z we find

$$Z_z = \frac{2p'}{\pi b^2}\sqrt{b^2 - y^2},$$

and it is easy to see that p' has the meaning stated. The distance of approach a, according to our general formula, becomes logarithmically infinite. This means that it depends not merely on what happens at the place of contact, but also on the shape of the body as a whole; and thus its determination no longer forms part of the problem we are dealing with.

I shall now describe some experiments that I have performed with a view to comparing the formulæ obtained with experience; partly that I may give a proof of the reliability of the consequences deduced, and their applicability to actual circumstances, and partly to serve as an example of their application. The experiments were performed in such a way that the bodies used were pressed together by a horizontal one-armed lever. From its free end were suspended the weights which determined the pressure, and to it the one body was fastened close to the fulcrum. The other body, which formed the basis of support, was covered by the thinnest possible layer of lamp-black, which was intended to record the form of the surface of pressure. If the experiment succeeded, the lampblack was not rubbed away, but only squeezed flat; in transmitted light the places of action of the pressure could hardly be detected; but in reflected light they showed as small brilliant circles or ellipses, which could be measured fairly accurately by the microscope. The following numbers are the means of from 5 to 8 measurements.

I first examined whether the dimensions of the surface of pressure increased as the cube root of the pressure. To this end a glass lens of 28·0 mm. radius was fastened to the lever; the small arm of the lever measured 114·0 mm., the large one 930 mm. The basis of support was a plane glass plate; the Young's modulus was determined for a bar of the same glass and found to be 6201 kg/mm². According to Wertheim, Poisson's ratio for glass is 0·32, whence $\Theta = \frac{8}{9}$, K $= 2349$ kg/mm,² and $\vartheta = 0005790$ mm²/kg. Hence our formula gives for the diameter of the circle of pressure in mm., $d = 0\cdot3650 p^{\frac{1}{3}}$, where p is measured in kilogrammes weight. In the following table the first row gives in kilogrammes the weight suspended from the long arm of the lever, the second the measured diameter of the surface of pressure in turns of the micrometer screw of pitch 0·2737 mm. Lastly, the third row gives the quotient $d : \sqrt[3]{p}$, which should, according to the preceding, be a constant.

p	0·2	0·4	0·6	0·8	1·0	1·5	2·0	2·5	3·0	3·5
d	1·56	2·03	2·19	2·59	2·68	3·13	3·52	3·69	3·97	4·02
$d:\sqrt[3]{p}$	2·67	2·75	2·60	2·79	2·68	2·73	2·79	2·71	2·70	2·65

The ratio in question does indeed remain constant, apart from irregularities, though the weights vary up to fifteen times their initial value. To get the theoretical value of the ratio we must divide the factor ·3650 calculated above by the pitch in millimetres of the screw, and multiply by the cube root of the ratio of the long to the short arm of the lever; we thus obtain 2·685, a number almost exactly coincident with 2·707, the mean of the experimental numbers.

Secondly, I have tested the laws relating to the form of the curve of pressure by pressing together two glass cylinders, of equal diameter 7·37 mm., with their axes inclined at different angles to each other. If this angle be called ω, using former equations we get $\rho_{11} = \rho_{12} = \rho$, $\rho_{21} = \rho_{22} = 0$, A + B = ρ. A − B = − ρ cos ω, and therefore the auxiliary angle $\tau = \omega$ Hence if we determine the large and small axes of the ellipse of pressure for one and the same pressure but different inclinations, divide the major axes by the function μ belonging to the inclination used and the minor axes by the corresponding function ν, the quotient of all these divisions must be one and the same constant, namely, the quantity $2(3p\vartheta/8\rho)^{\frac{1}{3}}$. The following table gives in the first column the inclination ω in degrees, in the next two the values of $2\,a$ and $2\,b$ as measured in parts of the scale of the micrometer eye-piece, of which 96 equal one millimetre, and in the last two the quotients $2a/\mu$ and $2b/\nu$:—

ω	$2\,a$	$2\,b$	$\dfrac{2\,a}{\mu}$	$\dfrac{2\,b}{\nu}$
90	40·6	40·6	40·6	40·6
80	45·4	36·6	40·2	41·0
70	52·8	31·0	41·3	38·7
60	59·6	27·6	40·0	38·5
50	72·2	26·4	41·2	41·2
40	90·4	23·8	42·2	42·0
30	110·0	21·0	40·3	42·6
20	156·2	18·4	41·3	45·3
10	274·6	15·0	41·6	47·0

The quotients are fairly constant, excepting those for the minor axes at small inclinations. But at such an inclination it is extremely difficult to bring the cylinders together so as to make the common tangent plane exactly horizontal; and in any other position a slight slipping of one cylinder on the other occurs, which unduly magnifies the minor axis. In all these measurements the pressure was 12 kg. weight. Taking for ϑ the value ·0005790 already used, we get from the given values the value of the constant to be 40·80, which agrees almost exactly with 40·97, the mean resulting from the values for a; whilst it differs slightly, for the reasons explained, from 41·88, the mean resulting from the value for b.

Lastly, I have attempted to examine the effect of the moduli of elasticity by pressing a steel lens against planes of different metals. But here I encountered difficulties in the observation. In the first place, it is not so easy to obtain quite plane and smooth surfaces as for glass; secondly, the metallic surfaces cannot so easily be covered with lamp-black; thirdly, we have to confine ourselves to very small pressures so as not to exceed the elastic limits. All these causes together preclude our obtaining any but very imperfect curves of pressure, and in measuring these there is room for discretion. I obtained values which were always of the order of magnitude of those calculated, but were too uncertain to be of use in accurately testing the theory. However, the numbers given show conclusively that our formulæ are in no sense speculations, and so will justify the application now to be made of them. The object of this is to gain a clearer notion and an exact measure of that property of bodies which we call hardness.

The hardness of a body is usually defined as the resistance it opposes to the penetration of points and edges into it. Mineralogists are satisfied in recognising in it a merely comparative property; they call one body harder than another when it scratches the other. The condition that a series of bodies may be arranged in order of hardness according to this definition is that, if A scratches B and B scratches C, then A should scratch C and not *vice versâ*; further, if a point of A scratches a plane plate of B, then a point of B should not penetrate into a plane of A. The necessity of the concurrence of these presuppositions is not directly manifest. Although experience has justified them, the method cannot give a quantitative determination of hardness of any value. Several attempts have been made to find one. Muschenbroek measured hardness by the number of blows on a chisel which were necessary to cut through a small bar of given dimensions of the material to be examined. About the year 1850 Crace-Calvert and Johnson measured hardness by the weight which was necessary to drive a blunt steel cone with a plane end 1·25 mm. in diameter to a depth of 3·5 mm. into the given material in half an hour. According to a book published in 1865,[1] Hugueny measured the same property by the weight necessary to drive a perfectly determinate point 0·1 mm. deep into the material. More recent attempts at a definition I have not met with. To all these attempts we may urge the following objections: (1) The measure obtained is not only not absolute, since a harder body is essential for the determination, but it is also entirely dependent on a point selected at random. From the results obtained we can draw no conclusions at all

---

[1] F. Hugueny, *Recherches expérimentales sur la dureté des corps.*

as to the force necessary to drive in another point. (2) Since finite and permanent changes of form are employed, elastic after-effects, which have nothing to do with hardness, enter into the results of measurement to a degree quite beyond estimation. This is shown only too plainly by the introduction of the time into the definition of Crace-Calvert and Johnson, and it is therefore doubtful whether the hardness of bodies thus measured is always in the order of the ordinary scale. (3) We cannot maintain that hardness thus measured is a property of the bodies in their original state (although without doubt it is dependent upon that state). For in the position in the experiment the point already rests upon permanently stretched or compressed layers of the body.

I shall now try to substitute for these another definition, against which the same objections cannot be urged. In the first place I look upon the strength of a material as determined, not by forces producing certain permanent deformations, but by the greatest forces which can act without producing deviations from perfect elasticity, to a certain predetermined accuracy of measurement. Since the substance after the action and removal of such forces returns to its original state, the strength thus defined is a quantity really relating to the original substance, which we cannot say is true for any other definition. The most general problem of the strength of isotropic bodies would clearly consist in answering the question—Within what limits may the principal stresses X_x, Y_y, Z_z in any element lie so that the limit of elasticity may not be exceeded? If we represent X_x, Y_y, Z_z as rectangular rectilinear coordinates of a point, then in this system there will be for every material a certain surface, closed or in part extending to infinity, round the origin, which represents the limit of elasticity; those values of X_x, Y_y, Z_z which correspond to internal points can be borne, the others not so. In the first place it is clear that if we knew this surface or the corresponding function ψ (X_x, Y_y, Z_z) = 0 for the given material, we could answer all the questions to the solution of which hardness is to lead us. For suppose a point of given form and given material pressed against a second body. According to what precedes we know all the stresses occurring in the body; we need therefore only see whether amongst them there is one corresponding to a point outside the surface ψ (X_x, Y_y, Z_z) $= 0$, to be enabled to tell whether a permanent deformation will ensue and, if so, in which of the two bodies. But so far there has not even been an attempt made to determine that surface. We only know isolated points of it: thus the points of section by the positive axes correspond to resistance to compression; those by the negative axes to tenacity; other points to resistance to torsion. In general we may say that to each point of the surface of strength corresponds a particular kind of strength of material. As long as the whole of the surface is not known to us, we shall let a definite discoverable point of the surface correspond to hardness, and be satisfied with finding out its position. This object we attain by the following definition,—*Hardness is the strength of a body relative to the kind of deformation which corresponds to contact with a circular surface of pressure.* And we get an absolute measure of the hardness if we decide that—*The hardness of a body is to be measured by the normal pressure per unit area which must act at the centre of a circular surface of pressure in order that in some point of the body the stress may just reach the limit consistent with perfect elasticity.* To justify this definition we must show (1) that the neglected circumstances are without effect; (2) that the order into which it brings bodies according to hardness coincides with the common scale of hardness. To prove the first point, suppose a body of material A in contact with one of material B, and a second body made of A in contact with one made of C. The form of the surfaces may be arbitrary near the point of contact, but we assume that the surface of pressure is circular, and that B and C are harder or as hard as A. Then we may simultaneously allow the total pressures at both contacts to increase from zero, so that the normal pressure at the centre of the circle of pressure may be the same in both cases. We know that then the same system of stresses occurs in both cases, therefore the elastic limit will first be exceeded at the same time and at points similarly situated with respect to the surface of pressure. We should from both cases get the same value for the hardness, and this hardness would correspond to the same point of the surface of strength. It is obvious that the elements in which the elastic limit is first exceeded may have very different positions relatively to the surface of pressure in different materials, and that the positions of the points of hardness in the surface of strength may be very dissimilar. We have to remark that the second body which was used to determine the hardness of A might have been of the same material A; we therefore do not require a second material at all to determine the hardness of a given one. This circumstance justifies us in designating the above as an absolute measurement. To prove the second point, suppose two bodies of different materials pressed together; let the surface of pressure be circular; let the hardness, defined as above, be for one body H, for the second softer one h. If now we increase the pressure between them until the normal pressure at the origin just exceeds h, the body of hardness h will experience a permanent indentation, whilst the other one is nowhere strained beyond its elastic limit; by moving one body over the other with a suitable pressure we can in the former produce a series of permanent indentations, whilst the latter remains intact. If the latter body have a sharp point we can describe the process as a scratching of the softer by the harder body, and thus our scale of hardness agrees with the mineralogical one. It is true that our theory does not say whether the same holds good for all contacts, for which the compressed surface is elliptical : but this silence is justifiable. It is easy to see that just as hardness has been defined by reference to a circular surface of pressure, so it could have been defined by assuming for it any definite ellipticity. The hardnesses thus diversely defined will show slight numerical variations. Now the order of the bodies in the different scales of hardness is either the same, or it is not. In the first case, our definition agrees generally with the mineralogical one. In the second case, the fault lies with the mineralogical definition, since it cannot then give a definite scale of hardness at all. It is indeed probable that the deviations from one another of the variously defined hardnesses would be found only very small; so that with a slight sacrifice of accuracy we might omit the limitation to a circular surface of pressure both in the above and in what follows. Experiments alone can decide with certainty.

Now let H be the hardness of a body which is in contact with another of hardness greater than H. Then by help of this value we can make this assertion, that all contacts with a circular surface of pressure for which

$$Z = \frac{3p}{2\pi a^2} = \frac{2}{\pi} \sqrt[3]{\frac{3p(\overline{\rho_{11} + \rho_{12} + \rho_{21} + \rho_{22}})^2}{(\vartheta_1 + \vartheta_2)^2}} \leqq H,$$

or for which

$$\frac{p(\rho_{11} + \rho_{12} + \rho_{21} + {}_{22})^2}{(\vartheta_1 + \vartheta_2)^2} \leqq \frac{\pi^3 H^3}{24}$$

can be borne, and only these.

The force which is just sufficient to drive a point with spherical end into the plane surface of a softer body, is proportional to the cube of the hardness of this latter body, to the square of the radius of curvature of the end of the point, and also to the square of the mean of the coefficients ϑ for the two bodies. To bring this assertion into better accord with the usual determinations of hardness we might be tempted to measure the latter not by the normal pressure itself, but rather by its cube. Apart from the fact that the analogy thus produced would be fictitious (for the force necessary to drive one and the same point into different bodies would not even then be proportionate to the hardness of the bodies), this proceeding would be irrational, since it would remove hardness from its place in the series of strengths of material.

Though our deductions rest on results which are satisfactorily verified by experience, still they themselves stand much in need of experimental verification. For it might be that actual bodies correspond very slightly with the assumptions of homogeneity which we have made our basis. Indeed, it is sufficiently well known that the conditions as to strength near the surface, with which we are here concerned, are quite different from those inside the bodies. I have made only a few experiments on glass. In glass and all similar bodies the first transgression beyond the elastic limit shows itself as a circular crack which arises in the surface at the edge of the compressed surface, and is propagated inwards along a surface conical outwards when the pressure increases. When the pressure increases still further, a second crack encircles the first and similarly propagates itself inwards; then a third appears, and so on, the phenomenon naturally becoming more and more irregular.

From the pressures necessary to produce the first crack under given circumstances, as well as from the size of this crack, we get the hardness of the glass. Thus experiments in which I pressed a hard steel lens against mirror glass gave the value 130 to 140 kg/mm^2 for the hardness of the latter. From the phenomena accompanying the impact of two glass spheres, I estimated the hardness at 150; whilst a much larger value, 180 to 200, was deduced from the cracks produced in pressing together two thin glass bars with natural surfaces. These differences may in part be due to the deficiencies of the methods of experimenting (since the same method gave rise to considerable variations in the various results); but in part they are undoubtedly caused by want of homogeneity and by differences in the value of the surface-strength. If variations as large as the above are found to be the rule, then of course the numerical results drawn from our theory lose their meaning; even then the considerations advanced above afford us an estimate of the value which is to be attributed to exact measurements of hardness.

VII

ON A NEW HYGROMETER

(Verhandlungen der physikalischen Gesellschaft zu Berlin, 20th January 1882.)

In this hygrometer, and others constructed on the same principle, the humidity is measured by the weight of water absorbed from the air by a hygroscopic inorganic substance, such as a solution of calcium chloride. Such a solution will absorb water from the air, or will give up water to the air, until such a concentration is attained that the pressure of the saturated water-vapour above it at the temperature of the air is equal to the pressure of the (unsaturated) water-vapour actually present in the air. If the temperature and humidity change so slowly as to allow the state of equilibrium to be attained, the absolute humidity can be deduced from the temperature and the weight of the solution. But it appears that for most salts, and at any rate for calcium chloride (and sulphuric acid), the pressure of the saturated vapour above the salt solution at the temperatures under consideration is approximately a constant fraction of the pressure of saturated water-vapour. Hence the relative humidity can be deduced directly from the weight with sufficient accuracy for many purposes. And if great accuracy is required, the effect of temperature can be introduced as a correcting factor, which need only be approximately known.

The idea suggested can be realised in two ways. The instrument may either be adapted for rapidly following changes of humidity, when great accuracy is not required, as in balance-rooms; or it may be adapted for accurate measurements, if we

only require the average humidity over a lengthened period
(days, weeks, or months), as in meteorological investigations.
An instrument of the first kind was exhibited to the Society.
The hygroscopic substance was a piece of tissue-paper of 1
sq. cm. surface, saturated with calcium chloride, and attached
to one arm of a lever (glass fibre) about 10 cm. long. The
latter was supported on a very thin silver wire stretched
horizontally, so that the whole formed a very delicate torsion
balance. The hygrometer was calibrated by means of a series
of mixtures of sulphuric acid and water by Regnault's method.
In dry air the fibre stood about 45° above the horizontal. In
air of relative humidity 10, 20, . . . 90 per cent it sank
downwards through 18, 31, 40, 47, 55, 62, 72, 86, 112 degrees. In saturated water-vapour it naturally stood vertically
downwards. The only thing ascertained as to the effect of
temperature was that it is very small. For equal relative
humidities the pointer stood 1 to 2 degrees lower at 0° than
at 25°. When brought into a room of different humidity, the
instrument attained its position of equilibrium so rapidly that
it could be read off after 10 to 15 minutes. The instrument
has the disadvantage that when the humidity is very great
(85 per cent and upwards), visible drops are formed on the
paper, and if it be carelessly handled these may be wiped or
even shaken off.

In instruments of the second kind the calcium chloride
would be contained in glass vessels of a size adapted to the
interval of time for which the mean humidity is required.
These vessels would be weighed from time to time, or placed
on a self-registering balance.

VIII

ON THE EVAPORATION OF LIQUIDS, AND ESPECIALLY OF MERCURY, IN VACUO

(*Wiedemann's Annalen*, **17**, pp. 177-193, 1882.)

WHEN a liquid evaporates into a gas whose pressure is greater than the pressure of the saturated vapour of the liquid, the vapour near the surface is always exceedingly near the state of saturation ; and the rate of evaporation is chiefly determined by the rate at which the vapour formed is removed. The removal of the vapour, at any rate through the layers nearest the surface, takes place by diffusion. Starting with this conception, the evaporation of a liquid into a gas has been frequently discussed. But hitherto no attention seems to have been paid to the conditions which determine the rate of evaporation in a space which contains nothing but the liquid and its vapour. In this paper evaporation under these conditions will be considered. In the first place evaporation in vacuo is affected by the rate at which the vapour formed can escape, in so far as this escape may under certain circumstances be greatly retarded by viscosity ; but clearly this is a matter of very little importance. For if we imagine the evaporation to take place between two plane parallel liquid surfaces, then as far as this is concerned the rate of evaporation might be infinite. Again we may specify the rate at which heat is supplied to the surface of the liquid as the condition of evaporation. When the stationary state is attained, the amount of liquid which evaporates is just so much that its latent heat is equal to the amount of heat supplied. But this explanation is incomplete, since we might equally well regard the supply of heat, conversely, as being determined by the evaporation. For both depend upon the temperature of the outermost layer of liquid; and this again is determined by the relation between the possible supply of heat by conduction and the possible loss of heat by evaporation. Now one of two things must happen. Either (*a*) evaporation has no limit beyond that which is involved in the supply of heat; so that if sufficient heat is supplied, an unlimited amount of liquid can evaporate from a given surface in unit time, and the temperature, density, and pressure of the vapour produced will not differ perceptibly from that of saturated vapour. In this case all liquid surfaces in the same space must assume the same temperature; and this temperature as well as the amounts of liquid which evaporate are determined by the relation between the possible supply of heat and the different areas. Or (*b*) only a limited quantity of liquid can evaporate from a liquid surface at a given temperature. In this case there may be surfaces at different temperatures in the same space, and the pressure and density of the vapour arising must differ by a finite amount from the pressure and density of the saturated vapour of at least one of these surfaces: the rate of evaporation will depend upon a number of circumstances, but chiefly upon the nature of the liquid; so that there will be for every liquid a specific evaporative power. It will be seen that the alternative (*a*) can be regarded as a limiting case of (*b*). Hence in the absence of any hypothesis or experimental information we should have to assume the latter, which is the more general, to be correct. But we shall presently show by a more detailed discussion that the first-mentioned alternative is an extremely improbable one.

I have made a number of experiments on evaporation in vacuo in the hope of arriving at an experimental decision between these two alternatives, if possible by exact measurements of the evaporative power of any liquid under different conditions. The experiments have only partly achieved their aim: nevertheless I describe them here, because they throw light upon the problem, and may clear up the way for better methods. The experiments are described in the first section: in the second section is given a theoretical discussion, which justifies the view adopted and establishes limits for the quantities under consideration.

I. I started the experiments on the assumption that the rate of evaporation of a liquid is at all events determined by the temperature of the surface and the pressure exerted upon it by the vapour which arises. In the course of the investigation I began to doubt, not whether these magnitudes were necessary conditions, but whether they were sufficient conditions for determining the amount of liquid which evaporates: in the second section it will be shown that there was no reason for this doubt. Hence I first set to work at the following problem:—To find for any fluid simultaneous values of the temperature t of the surface, the pressure P upon it, and the height h of the layer of liquid which evaporates from it in unit time. The difficulty experienced in solving this apparently simple problem arises in the determination of t and P. Even when the evaporation only goes on at a moderate rate very considerable quantities of heat are required to keep it up; the result of which is that the temperature increases very rapidly from the surface towards the interior. Hence if we dip a thermometer the least bit into the liquid it does not show the true surface temperature. The experiments further showed that at moderate rates of evaporation there was only a slight difference between the pressure and the pressure of saturated vapour. As it is just this difference that we wish to examine, it follows that both pressures must be very accurately measured. Lastly, the interior of the liquids in these experiments is necessarily in the superheated state; and since boiling with bumping would render the experiments impracticable, one is restricted to a very narrow range of temperature and pressure.

I pass over certain experiments made with water, for I soon observed that water, on account of its high latent heat and low conductivity, was ill suited for my purpose. Mercury appeared to be the most suitable liquid, for it has a relatively small latent heat and a conductivity similar to that of metals; and on account of its cohesion and the low pressure of its vapour, it can be superheated strongly without boiling. The first experiments were carried out with the apparatus shown in Fig. 20.   Into the retort A, placed inside a heating vessel, was fused a glass tube open above and closed below; inside this and just under the surface of the mercury was the thermometer which indicated the temperature.   To the neck of the retort was attached the vertical tube B, which was immersed in a fairly large cooling vessel, and could thus be maintained at 0° or any other temperature.   By brisk boiling and simultaneous use of a mercury pump all perceptible traces of air were removed from the apparatus.   The rate of evaporation was now measured by the rate at which the mercury rose in the tube B.   The pressure P was not to be directly measured.   I supposed, as is frequently done, that P could not exceed the pressure of the saturated vapour at the lower temperature, viz. that

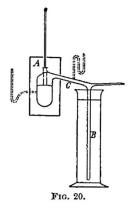

FIG. 20.

of B; and assumed that it would suffice to vary the latter temperature only in order to obtain corresponding values of the pressure.   It soon became clear that this assumption was erroneous; for when the temperature began to exceed 100°, and the evaporation became fairly rapid, the vapour did not condense in the cold tube B, but in the neck or connecting tube at C.   This became so hot that one could not touch it; its temperature was at least 60° to 80°.   This cannot be explained on the assumption that the vapour inside has the exceedingly low pressure corresponding to 0°; for in that case it could only be superheated by contact with a surface at 60°, and could not possibly suffer condensation.   In order to measure the pressure I introduced at C the manometer tube shown in the figure.   But this did not show any change from its initial position when the rate of evaporation was increased.   It was certain that the vapour moved with a certain velocity, so that its pressure upon the surface from which it arose must be different from the pressure which it would naturally possess. It could easily be seen that this velocity was very considerable; for when the drops of mercury on the glass attained a certain size they did not fall downwards from their weight, but were carried along nearly parallel to the direction of the tube.   In order to see whether the vapour exerted a pressure upon the

evaporating surface (for this pressure is really the interesting
point), I now fused the manometer on at *A*, as shown in the
figure, so that the retort itself formed the open limb.   It
turned out that there was a very perceptible pressure ; it
amounted to 2 to 3 mm. when the thermometer stood at.160° to
170°, and the evaporation went on at such a rate that a layer
0·8 mm. deep evaporated per minute.   Hence there was no
difficulty in seeing that in its condensation the vapour might
produce a temperature exceeding 100° ; however, it became
clear that the simple method which had been tried would not
lead to the desired result, but that direct measurements would be
necessary.   The apparatus shown in Fig. 21 was therefore used.
A is again the retort.   The heating vessel (only indicated in
the diagram) in which it was contained consisted of a hollow brass
cylinder 1·5 cm. thick, closely surrounding the retort and covered
over with asbestos.   It was heated by a ring gas-burner, and
had in it a vertical slit through which the level of the mercury
could be observed. *B* is again the tube in which the condensation takes place ; the manometer tube is shown in perspective
at *C*.   The magnifying power of the cathetometer telescope

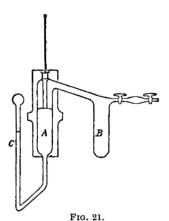

used was such that it could be set with
certainty to within 0·02 mm.   The pressure, *i.e.* the difference of level between
the two surfaces, was measured by a
micrometer eye-piece with two threads :
the absolute height of the surface, *i.e.*
the rate of evaporation, was read off
on the scale of the instrument.   The
temperature was varied by altering the
gas supply.   The apparatus was at
first quite free from air : by admitting
varying, but always small, quantities of
air different pressures could be obtained

FIG. 21.

at the same temperature.   If the pressure of the air
introduced amounted, say, to 1 mm. no evaporation in the
sense here considered could take place so long as the pressure
of the saturated vapour above the surface did not exceed 1
mm., *i.e.* so long as the temperature of the surface did not
exceed 120° ; but when this temperature was exceeded the air
retreated into the condensing tube, and evaporation began ;

but of course it now took place under greater pressure than it
did at the same temperature before the air was introduced.[1]
Three quantities, h, P, and t, had to be measured. In determining the first there was no difficulty. The determination
of P was not simply a case of measuring accurately the
difference of level; large corrections on account of the expansion of the mercury, etc. had to be applied, and some of
these were much larger than the quantity whose value was
sought. But by a careful application of theory and by special
experiments these corrections could be so far determined that
the final measurement could be relied upon to about 0·1 mm.
The outstanding error was so small that the greater part of
the observations would not be injuriously affected by it. The
most uncertain element was the determination of t. I thought
it was safe to assume that the true mean temperature of the
surface could not differ by more than a few degrees from the
temperature indicated by the thermometer when the upper
end of its bulb (about 18 mm. long) was just level with the
surface; and it seemed probable that of the two the true
temperature would be the higher. For the bulk of the heat
was conveyed by the rapid convection currents; these seemed
first to rise upwards from the heated walls of the vessel, then to
pass along the surface, and finally, after cooling, down along the
thermometer tube. If this correctly describes the process, the
bulb of the thermometer was at the coolest place in the liquid.

With this apparatus I carried out a large number of experiments at temperatures between 100° and 200°, and at nine
different pressures (*i.e.* with nine different admissions of air).
The separate observations naturally showed irregularities; but
unless some constant error was present, they undoubtedly point
to the following result :—The observed pressure P was always
smaller than the pressure P_t of the saturated vapour corresponding to the temperature t; at a given temperature the depth
of the layer which evaporated in unit time was proportional
to the difference $P_t - P$; when this difference was 1 mm. the
depth of the layer which evaporated per minute was 0·5 mm.

---

[1] During the observations there was no air in the retort or the connecting
tube. Thus the introduction of the air does not invalidate the title of this
paper. The title, indeed, has only been used for brevity in place of a more
precise one.

at $120°$, $0·35$ at $150°$, and $0·25$ mm. at $180°$ to $200°$. As an example may be given the case in which the highest rate of evaporation was observed. In this case the vessel was quite free from air, the temperature was $183°·3$, the pressure $3·32$ mm., and the level of the mercury sank uniformly at the rate of $1·80$ mm. per minute. Now, since the pressure of the saturated vapour[1] is $10·35$ mm. at $183·3°$, and $3·32$ mm. at $153°·0$, we must assume that there was an error of 7 mm. in the measurement of pressure, or of $30°$ in the measurement of temperature, if we are unwilling to admit that this proves the existence of a limited rate of evaporation peculiar to the liquid. The first-mentioned error could not have occurred; nor do I believe that the second could. But I could not conceal from myself that the results, from the quantitative point of view, were very uncertain; and so I endeavoured to support them by further experiments. For this purpose I made observations with the apparatus shown in Fig. 22, a.

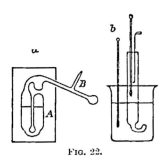

FIG. 22.

The glass vessel A, shaped like a mano-meter and completely free from air, is contained in a thick cast-iron heating vessel in a paraffin bath. The level of the mercury in both limbs is observed from the outside through a plane glass plate. The open arm communicates with the cold receiver B; the communicating tube is not too wide, in order that the evaporation may take place slowly. The small condenser inside the heating vessel is intended to prevent condensed mercury from flowing back into the retort. There is now no difficulty in observing the rate of evaporation or the pressure, at any rate if we regard the pressure of the saturated vapour in the closed limb as known; the uncertainty comes in again in determining the temperature of the evaporating surface. This temperature is equal to that of the bath, less a correction which for a given apparatus is a function of the convection current only which supplies heat to the surface. The known rate of evaporation gives us the required supply of heat; from this again we can deduce the difference of temperature when the above-mentioned

---

[1] For all data as to the pressure of saturated mercury vapour here used, see the determinations given in the next paper (IX. p. 200).

function has been determined. In order to find this, special experiments were made with the apparatus shown in Fig. 22, *b*. A piece of the same tube from which the manometer was made, was bent at its lower end into the shape of the manometer limb. This was filled with mercury to the same depth as the manometer tube; above the mercury was a layer of water about 10 cm. deep, and in this a thermometer and stirrer were placed. This tube was immersed up to the level of the mercury in a warm linseed-oil bath, the temperature of which was indicated by a second thermometer. A steady flow of heat soon set in from the bath through the mercury to the water. The difference between the two thermometers gave the difference between the temperatures of the bath and of the mercury surface; the increase of the temperature gave the corresponding flow of heat. Of course a number of corrections were necessary; after applying these it was found that the flow of heat increased somewhat more rapidly than the difference of temperature. For example, a difference of $10°\cdot0$ was necessary in order to convey to the surface per minute sufficient heat to warm a layer of water 117 mm. high (lying above the surface) through $0°\cdot48$. 1 shall make use of these data for calculating out an experiment made with the evaporation apparatus. When the temperature of the bath was $118°\cdot0$ and the difference of level was $0\cdot26$ mm., it was found that in $3\cdot66$ minutes the mercury in both limbs sank $0\cdot105$ mm. (this was the mean of measurements in both limbs). As the evaporation took place only in one limb, the depth of the layer removed from this in a minute was $2 \times 0\cdot105/3\cdot66 = 0\cdot057$ mm. In order to vaporise unit weight of mercury at $118°$ under the pressure of its saturated vapour, an amount of heat is required which would raise $72\cdot8$ units of water through $1°$. This value may be used with a near approach to accuracy in calculating the results of our experiment. Thus there must have been conveyed to the surface per minute enough heat to raise a layer of water $0\cdot057 \times 13\cdot6 \times 72\cdot8 = 56\cdot4$ mm. high through $1°$, or a layer of water 117 mm. high through $56\cdot4/117 = 0°\cdot48$. For this, according to what precedes, there must have been a difference of temperature of $10°\cdot0$ between the bath and the surface; so that the true temperature of the evaporating surface was $108°\cdot0$. Since the mercury in the open limb was

colder than that in the closed limb, the measured difference
of level (0·26 mm.) was somewhat smaller than it would
have been if both limbs were at the same temperature. An
examination of the distribution of heat in the interior gives
0·03 mm. as the necessary correction; thus the difference of
pressure in the two limbs was equal to 0·29 mm. of mercury at
118°, or 0·28 mm. of mercury at 0°. If we subtract from this
pressure the difference between the saturation-pressures at 118°
and 108°, we obtain the divergence between the pressure upon
the evaporating surface and the saturation-pressure. The
difference to be subtracted amounts to 0·27 mm.; so that
only 0·01 mm. is left. This shows that the pressure of the
vapour does not differ perceptibly from the saturation-pressure;
and the same result follows from all the observations made by
this method. At lower temperatures (90° to 100°) deviations
of a few hundredths of a millimetre, in the direction anticipated, were found; but at high temperatures, on the other
hand, pressures were calculated which slightly exceeded the
saturation-pressure. Clearly there must have been slight
errors in the corrections, as indeed might have been expected
from the method of determination. But the experiments
undoubtedly prove two things. In the first place, that the
method is not well adapted for giving quantitative results,
because the constant errors of experiment are of the same
order as the quantities to be observed. In the second place,
that the positive results obtained by the earlier method had
their origin partly, if not entirely, in the errors made in
measuring the temperature.[1] For, if they had been correct,
deviations of pressure of 0·10 to 0·20 mm. must have manifested themselves in the last experiments, and these could not
have escaped observation.

Thus the net result of the experiments is a very modest
one. They show that the pressure exerted upon the liquid
by the vapour arising from it is practically equal to the
saturation-pressure at the temperature of the surface; and
hence that of the two alternatives mentioned in the introduction, the first is to be regarded as correct. But they do
not show definitely the existence of the small deviation from

[1] That very large errors are possible can be easily seen by calculating those
which would arise if the surface were only supplied with heat by conduction.

this rule which probably occurs, and which is of interest from the theoretical point of view.

II. Let us now consider a process of steady evaporation taking place between two infinite, plane, parallel liquid surfaces kept at constant, but different temperatures. We shall suppose that the liquid which evaporates over can return to its starting-point by means of canals or similar contrivances. All the particles of vapour will move from the one surface to the other in the direction of the common normal and, neglecting radiation, we may with sufficient accuracy assume that in passing over they neither absorb nor give out heat. On this assumption it follows from the hydrodynamic equations of motion that during the whole passage from the one surface to the other, whatever the distance between them may be, the pressure, temperature, density, and velocity of the vapour must remain constant. From this it follows that the process is completely known to us when we know the following quantities :—

1. The temperatures T_1 and T_2 of the two surfaces.

2. The temperature T, the pressure p, and the density d of the vapour which passes over. We must suppose the temperature to be measured by means of a thermometer which moves forward with the vapour and with the same velocity. In the same way the pressure p is to be supposed measured by a manometer moving with the vapour, or determined by the equation of condition of the vapour. We may approximately take as the latter the equation of a perfect gas, $RT = p/d$.

3. The velocity u and the weight m which passes over in unit time from unit area of the one surface to the other. Clearly $m = ud$.

4. The pressure P which the vapour exerts upon the liquid surfaces. This is necessarily the same for both surfaces, and is different from the proper pressure p of the vapour itself. But we can calculate P if the other quantities mentioned are known. For let us suppose the quantity m spread over unit surface, the pressure upon one side of it being P and on the other side p, and its temperature T maintained constant. It will evaporate just as before; after unit time it will be completely converted into vapour, which will occupy

the space u and have the velocity u. Hence its kinetic energy is $\frac{1}{2}mu^2/g$; this is attained by the force $P - p$ acting upon its centre of mass through the distance $u/2$, so that an amount of work $(P - p)u/2$ is done by the external forces. From this follows the equation $P - p = mu/g$; or, since $m = ud$, $m^2 = gd(P - p)$.

Now the problem which evaporation places before us is to find the relations between these quantities for all possible values of them. Two of the eight quantities T_1, T_2, T, p, d, u, m, and P, namely T_1 and T_2, are independent variables; so also are any two of the others. The other six are connected with these by six equations. Of these we have already given three; in order to solve the problem completely we have to find, from theory or experiment, three more. But if we choose, as in the experiments, T_1 and P as the independent variables, and consider only evaporation in the narrower sense, we are no longer interested in T_2, and the problem resolves itself into representing two of the quantities T, p, d, u, m as functions of T_1 and P. But now the functions to be determined do not apply only to the case of evaporation between parallel walls; they hold good for any vapour which arises from a plane element of a liquid, and exerts upon it a pressure P. For we can imagine such evaporation taking place as if we allowed a piston to rest upon the surface at temperature T_1, and at a given instant removed it from the surface with velocity u. The result of this experiment must be singly determined by T_1 and u. But the two above-mentioned functions give us one possible result, and hence this result is the only possible one.

Thus the quantities relating to an element of the evaporating surface are completely determined by two of them, and the assumption upon which the experiments were based is justified; on the other hand, our discussion shows that the experiments, even if they had been successful, would not have completely solved the problem.

We can assign limits to the quantities in question if we make use of the two following assertions which, according to general experience, are at any rate exceedingly likely to be correct. (1) If we lower the temperature of one of several liquid surfaces in the same space while the others remain at the original temperature, the mean pressure upon these surfaces can only be diminished, not increased. (2) The vapour arising from an evaporating surface is either saturated or unsaturated, never supersaturated. For it appears perfectly transparent, which could not be the case if it carried with it substances in a liquid state. The first statement asserts that $P < p_1$, the second that $d < d_p$, if we denote by p_1 the pressure of the saturated vapour at the temperature T_1, and by d_p the density of the saturated vapour at the pressure p. Now $m = \sqrt{gd(P-p)}$, and therefore $m < \sqrt{gd_p(p_1-p)}$. But the right-hand side of this inequality is zero when $p = 0$ and when $p = p_1$; between these it attains a maximum value which m cannot under any circumstances exceed for a surface-temperature T_1. But if in spite of an adequate supply of heat the evaporation cannot exceed a finite limit, the hindrance can only lie in the nature of the fluid; and hence every fluid must have a specific evaporative power. The existence of such a constant is therefore as probable as the assumptions on which our reasoning is based. From the above equation I have calculated the limits for m, assuming the Gay - Lussac - Boyle law to be applicable to the vapour, and taking for the relation between the pressure and temperature of the saturated vapour the equation $\log p = 10\cdot59271 - 0\cdot847 \log T - 3342/T$, which is established elsewhere.[1] By dividing the values of m by the density of mercury we get values for the maximum depth of the layer of liquid which can evaporate in unit time from a surface at the given temperature.

T =	100	110	120	130	140	150	160	170	180	°C
$h <$	0·70	1·11	1·86	3·01	4·50	6·73	9·82	14·31	20·42	$\frac{\text{mm.}}{\text{min.}}$
$u <$	2110	2192	2294	2400	2522	2668	2823	2980	3145	$\frac{\text{m.}}{\text{sec.}}$
$P >$	0·046	0·07	0·09	0·14	0·20	0·27	0·38	0·53	0·71	mm.
$d/d_1 >$	0·0034	32	30	28	26	24	22	20	18	
$h >$	0·08	0·13	0·21	0·32	0·47	0·65	0·88	1·21	1·67	$\frac{\text{mm.}}{\text{min.}}$
$u >$	7·5	7·4	7·3	7·1	6·9	6·8	6·6	6·5	6·2	$\frac{\text{m.}}{\text{sec.}}$
$P-p)/p_1 >$	0·0034	32	30	28	26	24	22	20	18	

[1] See IX. p. 204.

These values, reckoned in mm./min., are given in the second row of the above table; they are about ten times greater than the highest values observed at the corresponding temperatures. The latter are given in the sixth row as lower limits. They are not lower limits for evaporation in general, for this can fall to zero; but they are lower limits for the greatest possible rate of evaporation. The other limits given in the table hold good also for the case in which the evaporation has reached its greatest value. Those given in the third, fourth, and fifth rows also hold good in general; for we may assume that the maximum of u and the minimum of P and d occur simultaneously with the maximum of m. In deducing these limits we have first $u = (P - p)/mg = m/d$; and since $m > m_{min}$, $P - p < p_1$, and $d < d_1$, it follows that $p/m_{min} > u > m_{min}/d_1$. Again $P = p + m^2/d$, and since $m > m_{min}$ and $d < d_p$, it follows that $P > p + m^2_{min}/d_p$. But the expression on the right hand has a minimum, since it becomes infinite when $p = 0$, and when $p = \infty$; this minimum value is given in the table. Finally $d = m^2/(P - p)$ and $P - p = m^2/d$. Hence $d/d_1 > m^2_{min}/d_1 p_1$, and $(P - p)/p_1 > m^2_{min}/d_1 p_1$.

The meaning of the table may be illustrated by an example of what it asserts, such as the following. From a mercury surface at 100° C. we cannot cause a layer of more than 0·7 mm. to evaporate per minute; its vapour will not issue from the surface with a greater velocity than 2110 m./sec.; the pressure upon the surface will not be less than 4 to 5 hundredths of a millimetre, nor will the density of the vapour which issues from it be less than $\frac{1}{300}$ of the density of the saturated vapour. On the other hand, we can in any case cause the evaporation to exceed 0·08 mm. per minute; the velocity of the vapour to exceed 7·3 m./sec.; and the pressure of the issuing vapour to differ from the saturation-pressure by more than $\frac{1}{300}$ of the latter.

In conclusion, I would further point out that the existence of a limited rate of evaporation, peculiar to each fluid, is also in accordance with the kinetic theory of gases; and that with the aid of this conception a fairly reliable upper limit for this rate can be deduced. Let T, p, and d denote the temperature, pressure, and density of the saturated vapour. Then the weight which impinges in unit time upon unit area of a solid surface bounding the vapour is $m = \sqrt{pdg/2\pi}$. And in greatly rarefied vapours nearly the same amount will impinge upon the liquid boundary-surface, for the molecules at their mean distance from the surface will be removed from the influence of the latter. Now, as the amount of the saturated vapour neither increases nor decreases, we may conclude that an equal amount is emitted from the liquid into the vapour. The amount thus emitted from the liquid will be approximately independent of the amount absorbed; thus evaporation, *i.e.* diminution of the amount of liquid, takes place when for any cause a smaller amount than that above mentioned returns from the vapour to the liquid. In the extreme case in which no single molecule is returned to the liquid, the latter must lose the above amount in unit time from unit surface. This amount is therefore an upper limit for the rate of evaporation. It is somewhat narrower than the one first deduced. Calculation shows that for mercury at $100°$ this limit is $0·54$ mm./min., whereas from our earlier assumptions we could only conclude that the rate of evaporation must be less than $0·70$ mm./min. Similar reasoning can be applied to the maximum amount of energy which can proceed from an evaporating surface; we thus find that the velocity of the issuing vapour can never exceed the mean molecular velocity of the saturated vapour corresponding to the temperature of the surface, *e.g.* for mercury at $100°$ it cannot exceed 215 m./sec. Finally, since the pressure of a saturated vapour upon its liquid arises half from the impact of the molecules entering the liquid and half from the reaction of those which leave the surface, and since the number and mean velocity of the latter approximately retain their original values, it follows that the pressure upon an evaporating surface cannot be much smaller than half the saturation-pressure.

These considerations enable us to fix limiting values, but they will not carry us further unless we are willing to accept the assistance of very doubtful hypotheses.

IX

ON THE PRESSURE OF SATURATED MERCURY-VAPOUR

(*Wiedemann's Annalen*, **17**, pp. 193-200, 1882.)

THE following determinations of the pressure of saturated mercury-vapour suggested themselves as a continuation of previous experiments [1] on evaporation. In working out the latter I at first used the data given by Regnault; but these did not prove suitable, as the following will show. I plotted out the results of the experiments made by the second method,[2] taking as abscissæ the amounts which evaporated in unit time from a surface at a given temperature, and as ordinates the corresponding pressures, and thus obtained series of points lying approximately on straight lines. By prolonging these straight lines a very little beyond the observed interval, I found the pressures which corresponded to zero evaporation, and which must therefore have represented the saturation-pressures. The numbers thus found were always smaller than Regnault's. That this might be explained by errors in the latter was first suggested to me by Hagen's experiments;[3] but his data, again, did not agree well with my results. Hagen himself suspected that his values were too small at temperatures above 100°; and as these were just the temperatures which interested me, I decided to investigate the matter myself.

The experiments were first carried on as a continuation of the experiments on evaporation. The measurements were

[1] See VIII. p. 186.   [2] See p. 191.   [3] See *Wied. Ann.* **16**, p. 610, 1882.

made with the U-shaped manometer of the evaporation
apparatus shown in Fig. 21 (p. 190); but as there was now
no evaporation, the condenser and connecting tube were not
required. By boiling and pumping out with a mercury pump,
all air was removed from both limbs of the apparatus. The
temperature of the heated limb was indicated by a thermometer dipping right into the mercury; the thermometer
was calibrated and its readings were reduced to those of an
air-thermometer. In determining the pressure the difference
of level between the two limbs was read off, and then a considerable correction had to be applied. The major part of
this depended upon the expansion of the mercury with heat.
In calculating this, care was taken to ascertain the distribution of temperature, as determined by the law of conduction,
in the tube connecting the two limbs; and the constants
required for ascertaining this distribution were determined by
special experiment. A smaller part of the correction arose
from the difference in the capillary depressions in the two
limbs. It seemed safe to assume that this correction would
be constant for all the temperatures under consideration; so
that it was simply determined by measuring the difference
of level when both limbs were at the same temperature. Of
the pressures measured by this method, only those which
relate to temperatures above 150° were retained for the final
calculations: these were reduced to three mean values, which
are given in the table below and are marked by asterisks.
The observations below 150° were rejected because the corrections were here much larger than the quantities to be observed,
so that the results were uncertain. For example, at 137°·4
the pressure was found to be 1·91 mm.; but here the correction was + 2·49 mm. and the amount directly observed
only − 0·58 mm. Allowing for these unfavourable conditions the rejected observations are found to agree sufficiently
well with the values obtained by the second method and
given as correct. They never differed from the latter by more
than 0·2 or 0·3 mm. They lay between these and Regnault's
values; but were twice or three times as far from Regnault's
values as from my own final ones.

The following method was adopted as much more suitable
for measuring the lower pressures. The open limbs of two

manometers A and B (Fig. 23) communicate with one another.

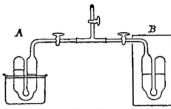

FIG. 23.

They contain air of low pressure, —about 10 to 20 mm. The closed limbs are quite free of air. The manometer A is kept in a water-bath at the temperature of the room. The manometer B was heated in a vessel of thick cast-iron in a paraffin bath, but never so far as to allow the mercury in the closed limb to sink below the level in the open limb. Thus the pressure of the mercury-vapour was smaller than the pressure of the air present (at the time) in the open limb; so that no evaporation, excepting by diffusion, could take place. Hence the pressure in the open limbs of both manometers was the same; and the difference of the readings of the two mano-meters, reduced to mercury at 0°, gave the difference between the saturation-pressure at the temperature of the hot mano-meter and that of the cold one. But, according to the results of this investigation, the pressure of the mercury-vapour in the latter can be put equal to zero. The temperature of the bath was read off on a very good Geissler thermometer; and I compared the indications of this with a Jolly air thermo-meter. The difference of level was measured by means of a micrometer eye-piece in the cathetometer microscope. The adjustment of the cross-wires upon the top of the meniscus was facilitated by means of a wire grating placed behind it, the wires being inclined at 45° to the horizontal. The manometer tube had a clear bore of 20 mm. The pressure of the air in the open limbs was varied. Lastly, after each heating, I convinced myself afresh of the absence of air in the closed limbs by producing electric discharges in them; the tubes then exhibited a green phosphorescence, and only this, so that the pressure of the air in them could not have exceeded one to two hundredths of a millimetre. The result of the experi-ments was as follows. Up to 50° I could perceive no pres-sure exceeding the limits of error (0·02 mm.) of a single experiment. At 60° the pressure was about 0·03 mm., at 70° 0·05 mm., at 80° 0·09 mm. From here on the errors were small compared with the whole values. From 120° to 130° the observed pressures can be taken as correct, since

their errors were negligible compared with those which arose
in determining the temperatures. Groups of eight to twelve
separate observations, lying sufficiently close to each other,
were then formed, the mean temperature being simply associ-
ated with the mean pressure. The six principal values thus
obtained, together with the three determined by the first
method, are given in the first two columns of the following
table. The subsequent calculations are based upon the results
given in these columns.

t	p	Δp	Δt	t	p	Δp	Δt
89·4	0·16	0·00	0·0	*184·7	11·04	+0·15	+0·4
117·0	0·71	+0·04	+1·1	190·4	12·89	−0·37	−0·8
154·2	3·49	+0·01	+0·1	203·0	20·35	+0·23	+0·3
*165·3	5·52	+0·04	+0·2	*206·9	22·58	−0·20	−0·3
177·4	8·20	−0·22	−0·7				

In calculating out the experiments I have made use of a
formula which has not hitherto been employed for the same
purpose.[1] It can be theoretically justified and must be
correct to the same degree of approximation that the laws of
Gay-Lussac and Boyle, which apply to very dilute vapours, are
correct for saturated vapours. On the assumption that this
law holds good, the vapour possesses a constant specific heat
at constant volume. Let this be denoted by c ; further let s
denote the specific heat of the liquid, and ρ_T the internal heat
of vaporisation at the absolute temperature T. Then it
necessarily follows from our assumption that $\rho_T = \text{const} -$
$(s - c)T$. This can be proved as follows. Let a quantity of
the liquid at temperature T be brought to any other temperature. At this temperature it is converted into vapour with-

[1] An analogous formula, deduced by similar reasoning, has indeed been
used by Koláček (*Wied. Ann.* 15, p. 38, 1882) for representing the pressure of
unsaturated water-vapour upon salt solutions. In that case the theoretical
justification of the formula is much stronger than in ours, where its applicability is only really proved by comparing it with the results of experiment.
With regard to Koláček's investigation, I may remark that all the experimental
data are known for applying the above formula to the pressure of vapour above
ice and above water cooled below its freezing-point down to the absolute zero.
Such an application would have to be justified by proving that the formula
obtained represents with satisfactory approximation the pressure of the vapour
for a considerable interval above 0°. For if the formula holds good for a given
interval of temperature, it must hold good for all temperatures below this interval,
inasmuch as a saturated vapour approximates more and more to a perfect gas as
the temperature diminishes.

out any external work. The vapour, again without external work, is brought back to the temperature T and reduced to liquid. During these processes the fluid can neither have absorbed nor given out heat. Now according to the laws of the mechanical theory of heat $\rho_\tau = Au(Tdp/dT - p)$, where p denotes the pressure of the saturated vapour and u its specific volume. Hence we can put $u = RT/p$. If we eliminate ρ_τ and u from the above three equations, we obtain for the curve of the vapour pressure a differential equation which gives the following integral

$$p = k_1 T^{1 - \frac{s-c}{AR}} e^{-\frac{k_2}{T}}.$$

For mercury s is known. From his own experiments, and from a result given by Regnault, Winkelmann[1] finds that this quantity decreases slightly as the temperature increases; the mean value of s between 0 and 100° is 0·0330. Experiments made by Dr. Ronkar of Liège in the Berlin Physical Institute have shown that the change between − 20° and + 200° is exceedingly small. These experiments give 0·0332 as the mean value of s, and I shall use this value in the calculation. Kundt and Warburg have shown that the ratio of the specific heats for mercury is $\frac{5}{3}$: hence it follows that the quantity c is equal to 0·0149. From this it follows that the exponent of T is equal to − 0·847. The two remaining constants are to be determined from the observations. Two of them are sufficient for this: if we choose from the first series the observation at 206°, and from the second series the observation at 154°, we obtain a formula which represents all the observations satisfactorily. The constants thus determined can be improved by applying the method of least squares. In doing this we naturally assume the pressures to be correct, and therefore make the sum of the squares of the temperature-errors a minimum. In this way I find that

$$\log k_1 = 10·59271, \qquad \log k_2 = 3·88623.$$

Introducing these constants into the formula, and throwing it into a form more convenient for calculation, we get

$$\log p = 10·59271 - 0·847 \log T - 3342/T.$$

[1] See *Poggendorff's Ann.* **159**, p. 152, 1876.

In the above table the third and fourth columns are added so as to make it possible to compare the values calculated by the formula with the observed values. The third column gives the errors which must have occurred in the pressure measurements if the observed temperatures are correct. The fourth column gives the errors which must be attributed to the temperature measurements if the pressures are to be regarded as correct. It will be seen that the formula represents the observations completely, if we admit an uncertainty of $0\cdot02$ mm. in the pressure measurements and of $0°\cdot6$ in the temperature measurements; and the disposition of the deviations shows that such uncertainties must be admitted. The measurements made below $89°$ agree perfectly with the formula, as far as a comparison is possible. The following table is calculated by means of the formula, and gives the pressure of the vapour for every $10°$ between $0°$ and $220°$—

t	p	t	p	t	p	t	p
$0°$	$0\cdot00019$	$60°$	$0\cdot026$	$120°$	$0\cdot779$	$180°$	$9\cdot23$
10	$0\cdot00050$	70	$0\cdot050$	130	$1\cdot24$	190	$13\cdot07$
20	$0\cdot0013$	80	$0\cdot093$	140	$1\cdot93$	200	$18\cdot25$
30	$0\cdot0029$	90	$0\cdot165$	150	$2\cdot93$	210	$25\cdot12$
40	$0\cdot0063$	100	$0\cdot285$	160	$4\cdot38$	220	$34\cdot90$
50	$0\cdot013$	110	$0\cdot478$	170	$6\cdot41$		

It should be noted that $p = 0$ when $t = -273°$; and that the formula gives for the internal latent heat of the vapour the value $\rho_T = 76\cdot15 - 0\cdot0183T$. The values given above differ considerably from Regnault's as well as from Hagen's. They are always smaller than Regnault's, but approach the latter as the temperature rises, and almost coincide with them at $220°$. Compared with Hagen's they are smaller below $80°$, nearly coincide between $80°$ and $100°$, and above this are larger.

The most interesting point is the pressure of the vapour at the ordinary temperature of the air. According to the results of our investigation this amounts to less than a thousandth of a millimetre.[1] Hence no correction need be

[1] It might be objected that this value is only calculated; whereas both the previous observers made observations at the temperature of the air, and both believed that they perceived a pressure of a few hundredths of a millimetre. But the

applied on account of this pressure to readings of barometers and manometers. And it is the smallness of this pressure, and not any special property of mercury itself, that explains why the influence of mercury-vapour is negligible in discharge-phenomena, although it is always present in Geissler tubes.

formula used appears to be satisfactorily established, and to be sufficiently tested as far as the single hypothesis contained in it is concerned ; so that it merits at least as much confidence as an observation of such small quantities, which must be difficult and deceptive. In addition to this, I may add that up to 50° I could discover no perceptible pressure ; whereas 0·10 mm., as given by Regnault, or even 0·04 mm., as given by Hagen, could not have escaped observation.

ON THE CONTINUOUS CURRENTS WHICH THE TIDAL ACTION OF THE HEAVENLY BODIES MUST PRODUCE IN THE OCEAN.

(*Verhandlungen der physikalischen Gesellschaft zu Berlin*, 5th January 1883.)

IN consequence of the friction of the water of the sea, internal as well as against its bed, the tidal skin whose axis in the absence of friction would lie in the direction of the tide-generating body or in a perpendicular direction, will be turned through a certain angle out of the positions named. Hence the attraction of the tide-generating body on the protuberances of the tidal ellipsoid gives rise to a couple opposed to the earth's rotation. The work done by the earth against this couple as it keeps rotating is that energy at whose expense the tidal motion is continually maintained in spite of the friction. It would be impossible to transfer to the solid nucleus of the earth this couple, which directly acts on the liquid, if the motion of the liquid relative to the nucleus were purely oscillatory, and if the mean ocean level coincided with the mean level surface. The transference becomes possible only because the mass of liquid constantly lags a little behind the rotating nucleus; or because there is a continual elevation above the mean level at the western coasts of the ocean; or because both phenomena occur together. I have attempted to deduce from the theory of the motion of a viscous fluid an estimate of the character and order of magnitude of the currents generated in this way. The results of the investigation are as follows.

Consider a closed canal. Let l be the distance along it from the origin, L its whole length, h its depth, t the time,

T the length of a day. Let ζ denote the elevation of the water above the mean level, and let

$$\zeta = \zeta_0 \cos 4\pi\left(\frac{l}{L} - \frac{t}{T}\right)$$

be a bidiurnal tidal wave which would traverse the canal under the action of a heavenly body, on the equilibrium theory. Then the tidal wave which is actually produced is given by the equation

$$\zeta = \zeta_1 \cos 4\pi\left(\frac{l}{L} - \frac{t}{T} - \epsilon\right),$$

where

$$\tan 4\pi\epsilon = \frac{kAL}{2\pi\mu h^2(gh - A^2)},$$

and

$$\zeta_1 = \frac{2\pi g\mu h^3}{kAL}\zeta_0 \sin 4\pi\epsilon.$$

Here k denotes the coefficient of viscosity of water, and $A = \dfrac{L}{T}$ denotes the velocity of propagation of the wave, μ the density of water, and g the acceleration of gravity. In the calculation squares and products of small quantities are neglected. For instance, at the free surface the tangential component of pressure is taken to be zero for the mean level; whilst in reality it is zero for the actual level. We find that this error of the second order may be compensated by supposing a tension τ to act at the surface in the direction of propagation of the wave, of which the magnitude is the mean of the values of $\mu\zeta X$ at different times, where X denotes the component of gravitational attraction along the canal. For the tidal wave considered above, we have

$$\tau = \frac{4\pi^2\mu^2 g^2 h^3 \zeta_0^2}{kAL^2} \sin{}^2 4\pi\epsilon = \frac{Ak}{h^3}\zeta_1^2,$$

This tension corresponds to a current flowing along the canal in the direction of the tidal wave, and increasing in velocity uniformly from the bed of the canal to the velocity

$$\mu = \frac{4\pi^2 h^4 g^2 \mu^2}{k^2 AL^2}\zeta_0^2 \sin^2 4\pi\epsilon = A\frac{\zeta_1^2}{h^2}$$

at the surface.

If we apply this result to the case of the earth we see that
generally the tidal wave in its progress must be followed by a
current in the same direction.   In a canal encircling the earth
along a parallel of latitude the current would flow everywhere
from east to west ; in a canal situated in any way whatever
it would be from east to west near the equator, in the opposite
direction at a distance from it.   In general the current is very
small, but it may become very appreciable when the length and
depth of the canal are such that the period of the oscillation
of the water in it is one day, in which case without friction
the tides would be infinitely great.   The formulæ given are
not suitable for getting numerical values, as the differential
equations used are not applicable to the motion of deep seas.
In fact, if we substitute for the coefficient of viscosity the very
small value obtained from experiments with capillary tubes,
we get ridiculously high tides and ridiculously violent currents.
On the other hand we get currents of only about 100 metres
per hour if we use the formula

$$u = A\frac{\zeta_1^2}{h^2},$$

and substitute for ζ_1 values corresponding to actually occurring
tides.

A posteriori, we can from the magnitude of tidal friction
as approximately known draw a conclusion as to the order
of magnitude of the currents caused by gravitation.   In one
century the earth lags twenty-two seconds behind a correct
chronometer.[1]   To produce such a retardation a force must be
constantly applied at the equator equal to 530 million kilogrammes' weight and acting from east to west.   If we imagine
this force distributed along a system of coast-lines which run
parallel to the meridian, bound the ocean on the west, and
have a total length of one earth-quadrant, then we get a
pressure of 53 kilogrammes' weight for each metre length of
coast.   To produce this pressure the sea must at these western
coasts be elevated 0·3 metre above the level surface with which it
coincides at the eastern coasts.   In so far then as the retardation
mentioned of the earth's rotation has its origin in tidal friction,
we can conclude that in consequence of the tide-generating

[1] Thomson and Tait, *Natural Philosophy*, § 830.

M. P.   P

action of the heavenly bodies we get deviations of the mean sea-level from the mean level surface amounting to $\frac{1}{4}$ to $\frac{1}{3}$ metre, and currents of such magnitude as can be produced by these differences of level. Though we are unable to state the magnitude of these currents, yet we can conclude that they are about equal in magnitude to those which are due to differences of temperature. For the differences of temperature may indeed cause variations of the sea-level from the mean level surface up to several metres; but only a small fraction of this height will give rise to currents at all, and only a small part of this fraction will cause currents flowing from east to west.

HOT-WIRE AMMETER[1] OF SMALL RESISTANCE AND NEGLIGIBLE INDUCTANCE

(*Zeitschrift für Instrumentenkunde*, 3, pp. 17-19, 1883.)

ALL the forms of the electro-dynamometer invented by Wilhelm Weber which are intended for weak currents suffer from two defects which are very inconvenient in many investigations. In the first place, the resistance is high, usually amounting to many hundred Siemens units; in the second place, the self-inductance is large. In many respects the second defect restricts the use of the instrument more than the first; for it causes the instrument to offer an apparently increased resistance to alternating currents, and in the case of very rapidly alternating currents this increase can be very considerable. If r is the resistance of the instrument, P its self-inductance, and T the period of the alternating current, the apparent resistance to this current is to the actual resistance r as $\sqrt{1 + P^2\pi^2/T^2 r^2} : 1$. For the instrument described by Wilhelm Weber, and similar ones which are actually in use, the self-inductance P can be estimated as being of the order of one to two earth-quadrants. If we take r as 200 Siemens units, or approximately 200 earth-quadrants per second, it follows that for a current which alters its direction 50 times per second the resistance is apparently increased in the ratio of $\sqrt{2} : 1$; and a current which altered its direction 500,000 times per second would encounter in the instrument an apparent resistance of 20,000 S.U. As to the

---

[1] [*Dynamometrische Vorrichtung.*]

presence or absence of currents alternating more rapidly than 10,000 times per second, the dynamometer could tell us nothing; for its introduction into the circuit would prevent the establishment of such currents. For example, it could not be used for investigating the discharge of a Leyden jar through a short metallic circuit.

In pursuing an investigation[1] which depended upon detecting unusually rapid alternating currents, I found it necessary to have a fairly delicate instrument of small resistance and negligible self-inductance; and it occurred to me to use the heating effect of the current in thin metallic wires as a means of detecting it. The attempt succeeded much better than was to be expected, and I may here be allowed to describe the simple instrument which I used. For a given current it certainly gives a much smaller deflection than the

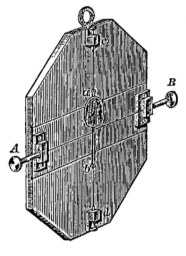

usual dynamometers. But it is much more delicate than any instrument of comparable resistance, its self-inductance is negligible, and it is as easily handled as any other instrument which gives equally accurate results.

The apparatus is shown in Fig. 24. The essential part of it consists of a very thin silver wire, 80 mm. long and 0·06 mm. in diameter, stretched between the screws A and B; the wire does not run right across from the one screw to the other, but is attached by a little solder to the vertical steel wire ab and twisted round this, as shown in Fig. 24, b. The steel wire ab has a diameter of 0·8 mm., and is as smooth and round as possible; the twisting of the silver wire can easily be

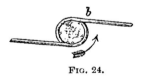

Fig. 24.

managed by first stretching it loosely and then turning the steel wire in the direction of the arrow. The silver wire being now well stretched, ab is held in position by the torsion which it produces in the thinner steel wires ac and bd; these

[1] See XIII. p. 224.

are 0·1 to 0·2 mm. in diameter, and 25 mm. long.   It is now clear that any warming of the silver wire must tend to untwist the wires ac and bd and cause the wire ab to turn around its axis; by means of a mirror attached to the axis this motion is read off through a telescope on a scale at a distance of about 2 metres.   In order to prevent any deflection of the mirror through a general change of temperature, the screws A and B are not fixed directly upon the wooden frame, but upon a strong strap of brass (from which they are of course insulated).   Since brass and silver have very nearly the same expansion, changes of temperature of the whole apparatus have but a very slight effect upon the position of rest.   The instrument is protected from air-currents by a case, which is not shown in the figure.   The apparatus can either stand on a table or hang by a hook from a wall; in the former case levelling-screws are unnecessary.

If we suppose the wire to be warmed 1° above its surroundings, its expansion would amount to 19 millionths of its length, so that each half of it would expand by 760 millionths of a millimetre.   On the scale this expansion appears magnified in the ratio of $2 \times 2000/0\cdot4 : 1 = 10,000 : 1$, and therefore causes a deviation of 7·6 mm.   Hence an elevation of temperature of $\frac{1}{30}°$ C. would correspond to a deviation of about $\frac{1}{4}$ mm. which should be clearly perceptible.

The following are the results of my observations :—

1. The resistance of the instrument is 0·85 S.U.

2. The instrument can be used in any position and requires no special care in adjustment.   The image of the scale remains perfectly quiet, even in a place where a delicate galvanometer or dynamometer keeps continually moving on account of ground-tremors.   When the mirror is thrown into vibration, the vibrations are so rapid that the motion of the image of the scale cannot be followed: but the air-damping is sufficient to bring the image completely to rest in a second or less.

3. When a current of suitable strength is passed through the silver wire, the image moves with a jerk into its new position of rest, and the latter can be read off after 1 or 2 seconds.   When the current is stopped the image jerks back again to its first position of rest.   If the deflection is large, there remains a certain amount of after-effect, but this appears

to be an elastic rather than a thermal after-effect, and is not greater than in other instruments in which forces are measured by the elasticity of wires. After a few minutes, at the outside, the image returns to the original position of rest.

4. The following data indicate the sensitiveness of the instrument. It was included in a circuit containing a Daniell cell and a resistance of r Siemens units. In the following table a denotes the deflection in scale-divisions, and b the square root of this deflection multiplied by the total resistance of the circuit (consisting of r S.U. together with 0·85 S.U. for the instrument, and 0·77 S.U. for the Daniell cell) and divided by 10.

$r =$	100	50	30	20	10	5	3	2
$a =$	0·25	0·9	2·2	4·9	16·9	52·1	106·8	173·8
$b =$	4·94	4·89	4·68	4·77	4·77	4·78	4·77	4·77

The numbers in the third row, excepting those corresponding to the smallest deflections, are all equal: this shows that the deflections are proportional to the square of the current, and that the instrument is well adapted for measurements. The current sent by 1 Daniell through 100 to 150 S.U. can be easily detected: currents sent by 1 Daniell through 30 S.U. and, by means of shunts, all stronger currents, can be measured.

5. When currents alternating a few hundred times per second are sent through the instrument, there arises a difficulty which is due to the small period of vibration of the mirror. The wire absorbs and emits heat very rapidly, and the mirror oscillates in accordance, following every impulse. In itself this is an advantage: but as the eye cannot follow the oscillations, the image of the scale becomes indistinct and the mean deflection cannot be accurately read off. This difficulty is much reduced by using the objective instead of the subjective method of observation; the scale then remains at rest, and although the spot of light oscillates backward and forward, its mean position can be accurately determined. Furthermore, without diminishing the sensitiveness, the period of vibration can be increased at will by increasing the moment of inertia about the axis.

It appeared that the sensitiveness of the instrument was

only limited by the accuracy with which the rotation of the axis could be read off. I therefore made experiments with the object of rendering visible even smaller extensions of the wire by further magnification. This was done partly by applying to the axis of the instrument a lever which rotated other axes; and partly by quite different arrangements of the stretched wire. In this way I succeeded in obtaining deflections ten times as large as those given above: but I cannot recommend those modifications, because they do not admit of the same ease in handling and the same certainty of adjustment. The sensitiveness is best increased by using a thinner silver wire, diminishing the diameter of the axis ab, and increasing the length of the silver wire; for it is rarely that one requires a dynamometer of such small resistance as the one here described.

If we further investigate the theory of the instrument, assuming that *ceteris paribus* the amount of heat emitted by the wire is proportional to its surface but approximately independent of the nature of the metal, we obtain the following rule for the most appropriate construction of the instrument:—Of the metals which appear to be suitable, choose that which expands most on heating: use as thin a wire as can be procured, and choose its length so that the internal resistance of the instrument is equal to the external resistance for which the maximum sensitiveness is required.

XII

ON A PHENOMENON WHICH ACCOMPANIES THE ELECTRIC DISCHARGE

(*Wiedemann's Annalen,* **19**, pp. 78-86, 1883.)

In the following a phenomenon is described which often accompanies the electric discharge, and in particular the Leyden jar spark, in air and other gases, when the density is not too small. It is true that in most circumstances it is so trivial as not to have appeared worthy of mention, but the first time I noticed it its appearance was so striking as to induce me to make several investigations as to its nature. I remark at once that in the experiments a somewhat large induction coil was used, which in the open air gave sparks 4 to 5 cm. long; the Leyden jar mentioned had a coating of some two square feet in area, and it was simply joined up with one coating connected to each pole of the induction coil, without making any other alteration whatever in the circuit.

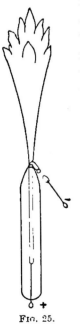

Fig. 25.

1. Fig. 25 represents a discharging apparatus, which consists of a glass tube, not too finely drawn out, and of two electrodes, one inside the tube, the other attached to it outside near the opening. When this apparatus is placed under the receiver of an air pump, the receiver filled with well-dried air and exhausted down to 30 to 50 mm. pressure, and the discharge from the induction coil then sent through, the following phenomenon is observed: Near the cathode is the blue glow; it is succeeded towards

the anode by the dark space, one or more millimetres wide, and from its end to the anode the path of the current is marked by a red band 1 to 2 mm. in diameter. For both directions of the current this band occupies the greater part of the length of the glass tube, and at its opening bends round sharply towards the electrode outside. But in addition I observed a jet, brownish-yellow in colour, and sharply defined, which projected in a straight line from the mouth of the tube; it was some 4 cm. long, and its form was like that shown in the drawing, Fig. 25. The greater portion of the jet appears to be at rest, and only at the tip does it split into a few flickering tongues. The jet does not change its shape appreciably when the current is reversed. But when a Leyden jar is joined up, an important change occurs: the jet becomes brighter, and is straight for a distance of only 1 to 2 cm.; then it splits up into a brush of many branches, which are violently agitated and separate in all directions, in the way shown in Fig. 26.

FIG. 26.

2. If we increase or diminish the pressure of the air, neglecting for the present the effect of the jar, then in both cases the jet becomes less striking, but in different ways. If the pressure be increased, the path of the spark no longer completely fills the cross-section of the mouth of the tube, neither does the escaping jet do so, but it only emerges at that side of the mouth where the spark appears; it becomes narrower, shorter, and assumes a darker, reddish-brown tint. If the pressure be diminished, the jet is again shortened, but at the same time it widens out, and assumes a lighter yellow tint and becomes less bright. When the first striæ form in the tube, it is only just perceptible, and then occupies a small hemispherical space just outside the mouth of the tube. When a Leyden jar is used, a similar succession of appearances is observed, but the greatest development occurs at smaller pressures, and it is advisable to choose a wider-mouthed tube. I obtained the most striking forms in air with the following arrangement. The glass tube was 5 mm. wide and 3 cm. long, and without any contraction at the mouth: the air was

exhausted down to 10 to 20 mm. pressure, and was kept well dried by placing under the receiver a small dish with sulphuric acid or phosphorus pentoxide; a large Leyden jar was joined up, and the glare of the discharge itself screened off by using as outside electrode a metal tube placed round the glass tube, and projecting slightly beyond it. Under these conditions the jet was in form like a tree, which reached up to 12 cm. in height; the part corresponding to the stem projected up straight from the tube a distance of 1 to 5 cm., while the top consisted of flames, which shot violently apart in all directions. The brightness may be judged from the fact that the appearance was still visible in a lighted room, but all details could be observed only in a darkened room.

3. When the wall opposite to the jet is too close, so that the jet cannot be fully developed, it spreads out over the wall. When it meets it perpendicularly, it forms a circular mound round the point of impact; but when it is inclined at an angle, it creeps along the wall in the direction in which a body would be reflected after impinging on the wall (in the direction of the flame). The phenomena which here occur may be most simply described by saying that the jets behave as liquid jets would do if they emerged from the mouth of the tube.

4. A magnet has no action on the jet. Neither have conductors, when brought near, not even when they are charged, e.g. when they are connected with one of the two electrodes.

5. The jet generates much heat in the bodies which it encounters. A thermometer brought into the jet shows a rise of ten or more degrees according to circumstances. When the jet encounters the glass receiver it heats it perceptibly; small objects are melted off from wires on which they have been stuck by wax. When the jet is produced in the open air (see § 10) the heat generated may be felt directly. On the other hand it was found impossible to cause a platinum wire, however thin, to glow when hung in the current.

6. The jet exerts considerable mechanical force. A wire suspended in it is set in violent oscillation, so also is a mica plate, used to deflect the jet. A mica plate, placed on the mouth of the tube, is violently thrown to a distance by the

first discharge. Radiometer-like vanes of various kinds may be set revolving continuously by the jet. But the impulse does not act in one direction only—away from the mouth. A mica plate set up before the mouth, so as to be only movable towards the mouth, is also set in vibration, which fact shows that each impulse directed away from the mouth is followed by a return impulse, though one of less strength.

7. The jet does not appear instantaneously, but takes a conveniently measurable time to develop. I have examined its time-changes, first with a rotating mirror, and secondly with an apparatus specially constructed for the purpose; this has, however, been already described by others, and is arranged as follows: A disc with a narrow radial slit is fixed to the axis of a Becquerel's phosphoroscope; at every revolution of the disc in one particular position of it the apparatus breaks the primary circuit. When the disc is rapidly rotated it appears to be transparent, but if we look through it at different places, we see the phenomena as they occur at certain definite different times after break. This apparatus usually gives better results than the rotating mirror, but in this case the latter is sufficient. Both methods of observation lead to the following results. The phenomenon is not instantaneous, but lasts about $\frac{1}{20}$ sec. The different parts of the jet do not all appear at once; the lower portions emit light before the upper ones commence; the upper parts are visible after the lower ones have gone out. Thus the phenomenon is a jet only to the unaided eye; in reality it consists of a luminous cloud, which is emitted from the tube with a finite velocity. When no Leyden jar is used, this velocity is for the whole path of the order of 2 m. per second, but it appears to be much greater at the commencement of the phenomenon: so also it seemed much greater for Leyden jar sparks; for such sparks it may be that often only the after-glow of the gas and not the development of the jet was observed.

8. Analogous phenomena to those described occur in other gases, but the jets show characteristic differences as regards colour, form, effect of density, etc. In oxygen the jet is very beautiful, much like that in air, but the tint is a purer yellow. The appearance in nitrous oxide resembles that in oxygen almost exactly. In nitrogen it was possible to produce only

very faint jets; the colour was nearest to a dark red. In hydrogen the jets are best developed at about 100 mm. pressure with the help of red Leyden jar sparks: the tint is a fine blue indigo; the brightness is not great. But the size is much larger than in air, so that even in a glass receiver 20 cm. high the jet cannot fully develop itself, but spreads out along the top. In the vapour of turpentine, and of ether, and in coal gas, the jets are greenish-white, short, sharply defined. The spectrum of the light is in air and oxygen continuous, especially bright in the red, yellow, and green; in vapours containing carbon it is a band spectrum, which could with certainty be recognised as one of carbon; in hydrogen it was difficult to observe, owing to the faint light, yet at various times I recognised several bands with certainty, of which the most conspicuous was at any rate very close to the greenish-blue hydrogen line, the others being situated more towards the violet; in nitrogen a spectrum could not be obtained.

9. In the gases mentioned it is always possible to detect the presence of a jet by its mechanical effects, but the jet is by no means clearly visible under all conditions, and its visibility seems to depend on very curious conditions. The air of a room when moist gives a very much weaker appearance than when it has been dried. When we place a dish containing sulphuric acid or phosphorus pentoxide or calcium chloride under the receiver of the air pump, we see the appearance become more distinct as the air becomes drier. The behaviour of hydrogen is still more incomprehensible. When the receiver was filled with this gas the discharges of the Ruhmkorff coil did not at once produce the appearance,—Leyden jar sparks were necessary; but when the jet had once been rendered visible, it could be maintained without using the Leyden jar. But it lasted only a few minutes and then went out, without my being able to reproduce it. I have not succeeded in finding out the conditions necessary for visibility. Greater or less humidity seemed without effect; equally without effect was the presence of a small quantity of oxygen. When the hydrogen was kept for several hours under the air pump without being used, it did not lose its power of becoming luminous; but when this power had once been destroyed by the discharges, it was not restored even after hours of rest. I should attribute

the luminosity to impurities,[1] did I not feel confident that I had recognised the spectrum of the emitted light to be a hydrogen spectrum. However, the vibrations of a plate of mica placed across the jet are just as lively in moist as in dry air, in freshly prepared hydrogen as in that which has ceased to become luminous; so that the visibility of the jet seems to be only an accidental property.

10. The jets may also be produced in gases at atmospheric pressure; it is advisable for this purpose to use a discharge apparatus similar to but smaller than that used before. The appearance, it is true, is only a few millimetres long and not very striking, but further experiments may conveniently be made on it. The heating effect and impact of the jet can be directly felt. The jet scatters smoke and small flames at a distance 2 to 3 cm. from the mouth of the glass tube. A strong current of air bends the jet and drives it to one side. When we blow through the opening at which the jet is formed, it lengthens out; when we suck in air, it shortens. When we pass another gas through the opening and invert a test-tube over it, we get the appearance corresponding to that gas; so with hydrogen we may obtain a very distinct blue jet, only a few millimetres long. If coal gas is passed through and lighted, the flame oscillates violently when the sparks pass; the apparatus described in § 7 shows that each spark drives out a small cloud of gas, which burns above the mouth of the tube and apart from the remaining portion of gas.

11. According to all that has been said, there can hardly be any doubt that the jet is formed by a luminous portion of gas escaping from the tube, and it is natural to assume that the projective impulse is the force of expansion occasioned by the rise in the temperature of the gaseous content. But if we place the electrode, which previously was outside the tube, close to the mouth of the tube inside it, or if we allow sparks to pass inside a glass tube sealed at both ends and possessing a lateral opening, in these cases also jets escape from the mouth of the tube; but they are much weaker than those which would be produced if the spark also passed through the opening. If rise of temperature were the cause of the emission, such a difference could not exist. The above assumption is con-

---

[1] The hydrogen was prepared from pure zinc and dilute sulphuric acid.

tradicted, more directly than by these somewhat ambiguous experiments, by the shapes which the jet takes up when the discharge apparatus is completely altered.

12. By shortening the tube more and more, and changing the distance and form of the electrodes, we may continuously change the discharge apparatus so far used into any other form we please; the jet then changes its shape, but does not disappear, rather passes continuously into other forms. It is to be observed that the discharge apparatus hitherto used has the advantage of all others, only because it separates the appearance considered from the mass of the luminous effects of the discharge. The forms which occur are very various and often very elegant; my observations do not suffice to represent them in order. In general their shape appears to depend on the direction of the current, and it is clearly seen that the portions of gas set in motion have velocities along the path of the current, of which the cause cannot be sought merely in the rise of temperature. A sufficient confirmation is afforded by the single example which I will mention here. When we allow the jar discharge to pass between spherical electrodes not too far apart, the appearance analogous to the jet is a bulge surrounding the centre of the spark path (Fig. 27 *a, a*). Its colour, like that of the jet, is yellow at low pressure, reddish-brown at atmospheric pressure. With this last tint the bulge can, with some care, be seen on every spark which passes between the electrodes of a Holtz machine, when its condensers (which must not be too small) are used. The apparatus described in § 7 gives interesting information as to the production of the bulge. First the bright straight spark appears, and during its presence the yellow is still absent or

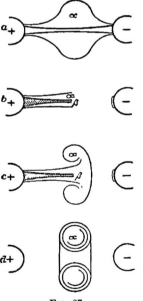

FIG. 27.

cannot be seen owing to the dazzling of the eye; it is followed by the aureole (Fig. 27, *b, β*), which proceeds from the positive electrode as a red band surrounded by the yellow light *a*; the latter, somewhat more than halfway, banks itself up into a wall opposite the cathode, and forms a vortex (Fig. 27, c), and this vortex maintains itself for some time in the air between the electrodes (Fig. 27, d) after the rest of the appearance has died away, but the whole only lasts about $\frac{1}{40}$ second.

I have not found any mention of the above phenomena in the literature of the subject. Dr. Goldstein has often noticed analogous appearances in his numerous experiments on the discharge in rarefied gases, and he was also the first to bring to my notice the favourable effect which a careful drying of the air has on the brightness of the yellow light.

XIII

EXPERIMENTS ON THE CATHODE DISCHARGE

(*Wiedemann's Annalen*, **19**, pp. 782-816, 1883.)

As sources of electricity for experiments on the cathode discharge in gases under diminished pressure, induction machines, induction coils and batteries of many cells have usually been employed. G. Wiedemann and Rühlmann, E. Wiedemann and Spottiswoode in many researches preferred the induction machine; Plücker, Hittorf in his earlier experiments, Goldstein and Crookes used mainly the induction coil. In addition to the early experiments of Gassiot with large batteries we have the more recent ones carried out by Hittorf with his chromic-acid battery,—the silver chloride battery of Warren de la Rue and Müller, and the researches carried out with it are the most famous of all.[1] It appeared to me that certain experiments, which are of importance for a proper understanding of the nature of the cathode discharge, could only be successfully performed with a battery: I therefore set up for these experiments a battery of 1000 secondary Planté cells. The battery as set up did not last well; but it sufficed for carrying out part of the experiments which I had in mind. These experiments will now be described.

---

[1] I was first induced to undertake these experiments by conversations which I had with Dr. E. Goldstein as to the nature of the cathode discharge, which he had so frequently investigated. My best thanks are due to Dr. Goldstein for the ready way in which he placed at my disposal his knowledge of the subject and of its literature while I was carrying out the experiments.

DESCRIPTION OF THE BATTERY

The battery was based on the principle employed by Poggendorff in his polarisation battery, and applied by Planté to the cells which bear his name. The cells are arranged in parallel, charged by a battery of comparatively small electromotive force, and then arranged in series. In this way very high electromotive forces may be attained. It is not necessary to deal singly with each cell thus: groups of five or ten or more cells can be set up permanently in series; and during the charging only these groups need be placed in parallel. The larger the number of cells in each group, the simpler does the commutating mechanism become; of course the electromotive force required for charging increases at the same time. I arranged my cells in groups of five in series. The cells were made of test-tubes, 125 mm. high, 14-15 mm. in diameter, and were filled two-thirds deep with sulphuric acid diluted with nine times its volume of water. The electrodes were strips of lead of suitable length, 10 mm. broad and 1 mm. thick, varnished at the top with asphalt varnish. The neighbouring pairs of electrodes within each group of five cells were formed by bending a single strip of lead (so that no connecting wire was necessary); copper wires soldered to the outer electrodes led to two glass mercury cups which formed the poles of the group. The cells were cemented in fifties on boards, of which five (or 250 cells) went in a box 84 cm. long, 12 cm. wide, and 17 cm. high. The 100 glass cups forming the corresponding poles lay in a row on the front side of the box. The commutation was effected by two interchangeable commutators, of which one was used in charging and the other in discharging. These were made of bent wires attached to a strip of wood; the construction was simple and does not require special explanation.

So long as the battery remained in good condition, it worked as follows. Ten Bunsen or Grove cells were required to charge it. When these had been in action for an hour the battery was charged sufficiently for a day's work. The difference of potential between its poles was about equal to that of 1800 Daniell cells. Its internal resistance, as deduced partly from the behaviour of single cells and partly from experiments in which the current from the whole battery was sent through very high resistances, was about 600 Siemens units. This potential difference kept up, when the battery was on open circuit or only very slightly used, for twelve to fourteen hours; after which there was loss of charge (mainly through chemical action, but partly also through short-circuiting), and the potential difference sank rapidly to lower values. If the circuit was only closed from time to time through rather large resistances, as was usually the case in these experiments, the battery remained in good working order for about six hours. It could supply for two or three hours the current required for continuously lighting a Geissler tube: but if it was closed through a small resistance or short-circuited, it became exhausted in a few minutes or even in a fraction of a minute. It then exhibited the well-known partial recovery of charge. On closing the circuit in free air the battery gave a spark nearly half a millimetre long. It lit up Geissler tubes of the usual form (without capillary) through an interval of pressure from $1\frac{1}{2}$ mm. to a few hundredths of a millimetre; at the former limit the blue glow-light surrounded the cathode as a thin layer; at the latter the cathode rays attained a length of 120-150 mm. In general the connecting wires should not be attached to the electrodes of a Geissler tube without introducing a resistance of several thousand Siemens units; otherwise the cathode discharge passes into an arc discharge, and generally the tube breaks and the battery becomes exhausted in a few moments.

This battery came to grief in the following way. The sulphuric acid crept up in the capillary space between the lead strips and the layer of varnish, and went on spreading farther and farther in this space. If the apparently uninjured varnish was scraped away at any point, it was easy to detect the presence of the acid by its taste. Thus the acid worked its way to the copper wires of the end strips and produced upon these growths of copper sulphate which spread along the wires. After the battery had been in use for three or four weeks, these growths on the wires of the front row of end strips reached to the mercury in the commutator-cups. The mercury then amalgamated the wire along its whole length, and as the inner end of the wire lay lower than the level of the mercury in the cups, the mercury flowed along the amalgamated wire just as if it were a siphon, and emptied each newly-filled cup in a few hours. This emptying could be prevented by heating the wires to redness and coating them for some distance with melted shellac; but the destruction of the copper wires went on, and after four or five months a number of them broke off at the soldered joints. A few of the wires remained quite unattacked, probably because they happened to have been tinned for some distance from the joint.

The general nature of the battery discharge in gases under diminished pressure is now sufficiently well known; I shall, therefore, pass this by and proceed to the description of certain special experiments.

I. Is the Battery Discharge in Gases under diminished pressure continuous or discontinuous?

When Gassiot first produced the cathode discharge by means of a large battery, and examined its appearance— apparently quite continuous—in a rotating mirror, he found that it could be decomposed into a number of partial discharges following each other very rapidly. On this result is based the view held by physicists, that the cathode discharge is of a disruptive nature, and that every apparently continuous discharge must consist of a series of separate disruptive discharges. Most physicists approved of this view until Hittorf, in 1879, showed that Gassiot's experiments do not warrant any such general conclusions; that with a battery of sufficiently small resistance a cathode discharge can be produced which cannot be decomposed into partial discharges, at any rate by a rotating mirror; and that various circumstances indicate that a mirror, however rapidly rotated, could not effect such a resolution. On the other hand, according to a calculation made by E. Wiedemann,[1] the rotating mirror would fail to perform its function if the number of successive discharges in a second were to attain to even a hundred thousand. Hence certain physicists, who for other reasons

---

[1] *Wied. Ann.* **10**, p. 244, 1880.

felt compelled to assume a discontinuity, were not convinced by Hittorf, although they were willing to admit that the current might be made up of hundreds of thousands, or even millions, of separate discharges per second. Among these were E. Wiedemann,[1] Goldstein,[2] and Warren de la Rue.[3] The latter had also described experiments by which he had demonstrated the discontinuity of an apparently continuous discharge otherwise than with a rotating mirror ; but this demonstration could only be carried out under special conditions, and these conditions appeared to be just those under which the rotating mirror would have proved discontinuity.

The point in question may therefore be regarded as still an open one. The question is not whether an apparently continuous discharge may under certain circumstances be shown to be discontinuous ; there is no doubt that this would have to be answered in the affirmative. The question should rather be put in the following form :—Can we establish the existence of a discharge which is undoubtedly a cathode discharge, but in which, nevertheless, no trace of discontinuity can be detected, even by the most delicate methods ?

The discharge, which was tested by the following methods, was produced in a tube of length 340 mm., and clear width 20 mm., between a steel plate (serving as the cathode) 18 mm. in diameter and a steel wire. It took place in air under such a pressure that the blue glow-light extended to a distance of 50 to 60 mm. from the cathode ; furthermore, from six to nine positive red striæ were formed in the tube. The current used lay between $\frac{1}{100}$ and $\frac{1}{400}$ of that sent by a Daniell cell through a Siemens unit, and was regulated by introducing a large liquid resistance. Only in the method which will last be described was a stronger current necessary, and this was $\frac{1}{15}$ to $\frac{1}{30}$ Dan./S.U. In this case it was found advisable to use a somewhat wider and shorter tube, so that only one positive stria was visible, and this only indistinctly. But at the same time there could be no doubt that the discharge was of the nature of a cathode discharge. Of course the discharges investigated showed none of the ordinary

---

[1] *Wied. Ann.* **10**, p. 245, 1880.   [2] *Loc. cit.* **12**, p. 101, 1881.
[3] *Ann. de Chim. et de Phys.*, series 5, **24**, p. 461, 1881 ; and *Phil. Trans.* **169**, p. 225, 1878.

symptoms of intermittence.   They were in no way affected by
the approach of a conductor ; a telephone introduced into the
circuit did not sound ; the tubes themselves gave out no
sound, nor could the image of the discharge be decomposed by
a rotating mirror into separate images.

1. The above-mentioned experiments of Warren de la Rue [1]
were first repeated.   The battery-current, in addition to passing through the gas-tube, was sent through the primary or
secondary coil of various small induction-coils, the free coil
being closed through a dynamometer or galvanometer.   In
no case did I obtain a deflection of these instruments, such as
would indicate a surging induction current due to intermittence of the battery current.   However, this does not
prove much.   Consider first the dynamometric effect of the
induced currents.   At first this certainly increases with the
number of interruptions of the inducing current ; but if this
number becomes very large, the dynamometric effect does not
become infinite.   Since the separate induction impulses are
impeded by self-induction, the dynamometric effect approaches
a fixed limit ; but even this maximum effect could scarcely be
perceived with the dynamometer which I used.   And as far
as the effect on the galvanometer is concerned, the accepted
theory of induction does not indicate that any effect should be
expected, even if the current at each separate discharge sinks
more rapidly than it rises.   I was only induced to perform
these experiments by the fact that results to the contrary had
been obtained by Warren de la Rue and Müller.   Unfortunately I did not succeed in reproducing the phenomenon
observed by them.   When the galvanometer had been removed
from the direct magnetic action of the coil through which the
current flowed, no permanent deflection could be perceived
after the battery current was closed, although the induction
impulse on opening and closing the current drove the needle
beyond the visible scale.[2]

2. In addition to the tube and a large liquid resistance,

[1] *Ann. de Chim. et de Phys.*, series 5, **24**, p. 461, 1881 ; and *Phil. Trans.*
169, p. 225, 1878.

[2] It is certain that any deflection of the needle produced cannot be regarded
as due to any normal galvanometric action.   More probably it was of the nature
of " *doppelsinnige Ablenkung*," in which case the galvanometer would be acting
as a very delicate dynamometer.

a galvanometer and a dynamometer were simultaneously introduced into the circuit, and the deflections produced in both instruments were read off. The battery, gas-tube, and liquid resistance were then separated from the two measuring instruments, and replaced by a Daniell cell, and such a metallic resistance as gave the same galvanometer deflection as before. It was found that the dynamometer reading also was precisely the same as before. But if the current sent by the large battery through the gas-tube had been an intermittent current, it would for a given magnetic effect have produced a much larger dynamometric effect. Suppose, for example, that the duration of one of the partial discharges was equal to a fourth of the time from the beginning of such a discharge to the beginning of the next. While this current lasted it would be four times as strong as a continuous current capable of exerting an equal magnetic effect. While it lasted, its dynamometric effect would be sixteen times as great, or, on an average over the whole time, four times as great as that of the continuous current. Hence this experiment indicates that the discharge is continuous.

3. The current was led to the tube through a Wheatstone bridge arrangement. One arm of this consisted of the secondary of a small induction-coil, having a resistance of 1700 S.U., and a coefficient of self-induction of ten earth-quadrants. The other three arms consisted of equivalent metallic resistances of negligible self-induction. In the actual bridge a dynamometer was introduced, and the arrangement was so adjusted that when a continuous current flowed through it there was no deflection of the dynamometer. It was then found that no deflection was produced by the battery current flowing through the Geissler tube, although this was strong enough to produce a very marked effect as soon as the equilibrium was destroyed by inserting a resistance of 100 S.U. in one of the branches. This experiment tells against discontinuity. For we may regard an intermittent current as composed of a part which flows continuously, and another part which continually changes its direction. The bridge was only adjusted for the former: to the latter the coil, on account of its high self-induction, would certainly offer a far higher apparent resistance than the other branches.

Hence if an alternating part had been present, an oscillating current would have flowed through the dynamometer, and would have been strong enough to produce a perceptible deflection.

The preceding experiments prove that the current flows continuously through the greater part of the metallic circuit even when an air-gap is introduced. They only enable us to form a conclusion as to the current in the tube itself if we assume that the current is uniform in all its parts. But if the number of the partial discharges amounts to 100,000 or more per second, the assumption is unsafe; indeed there is no doubt that the current-variations can only penetrate a small distance into the coil, on account of its large self-induction, and that inside it they must be effaced. Thus only a fraction, and probably a very small fraction, of the effect under consideration would actually occur. On this account coils are avoided in the following experiments.

4. The current was sent through a Wheatstone bridge (Fig. 28) of which the four arms consisted of equal liquid resistances of 700,000 S.U. each. These were made by filling thin glass tubes 30 cm. long with a dilute solution

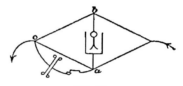

Fig. 28.

of zinc sulphate. The mean potential difference at the points a and b—more accurately the mean square of this difference—could be observed by means of a gold-leaf electroscope: this was enclosed in a metal case connected to the point a, while the leaves themselves were connected to the point b. In this and the following experiments the gold leaves were observed under a microscope. The difference of potential which could just be observed was about one-tenth of that which existed between a and c when the current was flowing. By means of short metallic conductors the points a and c could be connected with the two coatings of a condenser of very large capacity. The resistances were so adjusted that the gold leaves showed no divergence when the current was allowed to pass in the absence of the condenser. On introducing the condenser it was again found that not the slightest divergence could be perceived. This result again tells against discontinuity. For let us suppose that a very rapid intermittent current flows through the apparatus, and let us, as before, conceive of this as being composed of a part which flows continuously and an alternating part. Our bridge is only adjusted for the former; for the latter the arm ac has apparently a vanishing resistance, for the condenser is capable of taking in and giving out the quantities of electricity conditioned by the alternating current without any appreciable change of the potential difference between its coatings. It follows that for the alternating part the potential difference between a and c must be very small, and that between a and b must become large enough to be detected. It seemed advisable to test the correctness of this conclusion by experiment. Into the external circuit was introduced a toothed wheel having a large number of teeth, by which the current could be broken artificially up to 2000 times per second. When the current was thus interrupted the gold leaves still remained at rest, provided that the condenser was not in action. When the condenser was introduced they diverged immediately; the divergence increased with the rate of interruption, and was very considerable at the above-mentioned rate. A single opening and closing of the current could be recognised, when the condenser was introduced, by a slight twitching of the gold leaves. I estimate that the number of partial discharges per second would have to amount to many hundred thousand before the method of testing here used would become ineffective. Of course it would become ineffective if the intermittence was so rapid that in the intervals the electric waves could only travel along a small fraction of the lengths of the liquid resistances used.

5. The leaves of a gold-leaf electroscope were connected by a short copper wire to the negative electrode; these leaves were suspended in a metallic case which could either be connected to the positive electrode by a metallic wire or to the negative electrode through a large resistance of a few million S.U. When the current was passed through the tube and the metal case connected to the positive electrode, the gold leaves diverged strongly; they showed no trace of divergence when the metal case was connected to the negative electrode through the above-mentioned resistance. This result tells against discontinuity of the discharge. For if the potential at the cathode fluctuated very rapidly between that necessary for the

discharge and a much lower potential, the potential of the gold leaves would be able to follow these fluctuations, but the potential of the metal case would not; the quantity of electricity upon the latter would always be that corresponding to the mean potential value, and the divergence of the gold leaves would therefore be proportional to the square of the difference between the potential and its mean value. That an intermittent discharge does actually produce such divergence was shown as follows. The resistance through which the battery-current flowed was gradually increased more and more; when it had attained a certain very high value the discharge began to exhibit the criteria of discontinuity given by Hittorf; and at the same time the gold leaves began to diverge distinctly. The same result was attained by artificial interruption of the battery-current. Here again the method of testing used must fail as soon as the number of interruptions per second reaches a certain value, but this value can be approximately calculated. The partial discharges, if any such were present, could only consist in discharges of the electricity accumulated on the cathode and the gold leaves in metallic connection with it. The capacity of this system was certainly not greater than that of a sphere of 20 mm. radius. The fluctuation of potential at each discharge could not exceed the value of 90 Daniells, for it was found that such a difference of potential between the gold leaves and the surrounding case could be recognised by a perceptible divergence. Now a thousand discharges per second of a sphere of 20 mm. radius, charged each time to a potential of 90 Daniells, would just correspond to the current produced by 1 Daniell through about 5,000,000 S.U. But the currents used in the experiments were about equal to that sent by a Daniell through 100 S.U. Hence if they consisted of partial discharges, the frequency of the latter must have amounted to at least 50 millions per second.

6. The anode of the gas-tube used was connected by a thick metallic wire with one plate of a Kohlrausch condenser, and the cathode was connected with the other plate by a very thin silver wire of 8 cm. length and about 0·8 S.U. resistance. To the latter was attached an arrangement with mirror and scale, by means of which an exceedingly small extension, and there-

fore a very slight elevation of temperature produced in the wire by a current traversing it, could be detected. A rise of temperature of $\frac{1}{30}$° C. could be perceived; the current producing this rise was equal to $\frac{1}{100}$ Daniell/S.U. The wire thus formed a sort of dynamometer without any coil, and will in future be referred to as such.[1] Now the battery-current, which in these experiments was as strong as $\frac{1}{20}$ Daniell/S.U., could be conducted to the cathode in either of two ways. Either it flowed in between the condenser and the dynamometer, in which case it flowed through the latter, and produced in it a deflection of four to five scale-divisions; or else it flowed in between the dynamometer and the gas-tube, in which case not the slightest deflection of the dynamometer could be perceived, —certainly not a deflection of quarter of a scale-division. Now if the current had been composed of partial discharges, a continual charging and discharging of the condenser would have taken place, and therefore an alternating current would have flowed through the dynamometer. The deflection produced by this alternating current would certainly have amounted to a half of that produced by the whole current. Here again I caused intermittence by an artificial interruption of the external circuit. The result was that the dynamometer was deflected whether the current flowed in the one way or the other; and the deflections were even larger (six to eight scale-divisions) than when the current was not interrupted. The explanation of this paradox is that the artificial interruption produces condenser-discharges which act more strongly upon the dynamometer. The criterion here used only ceases to be applicable when the separate partial discharges follow each other so rapidly that the electric waves corresponding to them are no longer able to traverse the silver wire of the dynamometer in the interval. The requisite rapidity can be estimated in various ways; even the lowest estimate gives many thousand millions per second. The following is perhaps the simplest way. If the electric wave does not traverse the dynamometer wire, then each partial discharge consists simply of a discharge of the electricity stored upon the cathode. The capacity of the cathode was less than that of a sphere of 2 cm. radius. During a single discharge the variation of potential

[1] See description of the apparatus in XI. p. 211.

of the cathode could not have exceeded $\frac{1}{100}$ of a Daniell;
for there was a perceptible deflection when the mean potential
difference of the terminals of the dynamometer attained this
value.   Thus in order that the successive discharges should be
equivalent to a current of $\frac{1}{20}$ Daniell/S.U., they must have
amounted to two billions per second.   This mode of estimat-
ing is open to criticism, and I do not wish to insist strongly
on the large number to which it leads.   But I would ask
whether it is likely that an electric current could traverse a
gas-tube 20 cm. long as a fully formed partial discharge with
all its striæ, in a time which would not allow of its traversing
as a steady current 8 cm. of a metallic conductor ?

7. I have not discovered any more decisive methods of
testing.   But a few further experiments may be mentioned
which, although not in themselves decisive, tend in the same
direction as those already described.

(a) If the observer closes the circuit, containing the gas-
tube and a sufficient liquid resistance, through his own body,
he feels a shock on closing and a much weaker shock on opening.   By frequent opening and closing, the sensation can be
heightened until it becomes unbearable.   But while the tube
glows uniformly nothing is perceived beyond a burning at the
points where the current enters and leaves.

(b) The battery-discharge never gives rise to the auxiliary
phenomenon of oscillatory currents, even under conditions which
are very favourable for their production, and under which
the Ruhmkorff discharge produces very powerful currents of
this kind.

(c) The following phenomena have already been mentioned
by Hittorf: When a sufficiently large resistance is introduced,
the discharge is certainly discontinuous.   The tube then frequently gives out a note, the pitch of which indicates the rate
at which the discharges succeed each other.   When the
resistance is diminished, the note becomes higher and the
tube less bright.   But it does not gradually pass over
into the quiet indifferent discharge; when the resistance is
reduced to a certain value the note stops suddenly, the tube
becomes three times as bright, and no further indications
whatever of discontinuity can be obtained.   The sudden
change is still more striking when the electrodes of the tube

are connected with the coatings of a large condenser; for it then often takes place from a state of things in which the separate discharges can be distinguished by the eye. Once the change has taken place, the switching of the condenser in or out of circuit has not the slightest effect upon the appearance of the discharge.

The general conclusion which I draw from the experiments described is that the discharges tested were continuous: from this I further conclude that the battery-discharge in general is to be regarded as continuous, excepting when it exhibits the known criteria of discontinuity; further, that the discharges of an induction-coil, whose period may, be between $\frac{1}{1000}$ and $\frac{1}{60}$ of a second according to the size of the apparatus, are to be regarded as being continuous during this interval.

In order to establish these conclusions fully, it is necessary to show that the considerations which lead to the opposite conclusion cannot be regarded as decisive. These conclusions appear chiefly to depend upon the following experimental results: (1) that a weak current (*e.g.* such as an induction-machine gives) is always discontinuous, and does not become continuous even when the partial discharges succeed each other at the rate of several thousand per second; (2) that the heating effect in a gas-tube is not proportional to the square of the current, but to the current itself; and (3) that in accordance with this the potential difference at the ends of the tube does not increase with increasing current, but persists at the value which enables the weakest current to traverse the tube. In order to show that these results do not necessarily prove discontinuity, I shall make use of a simple mechanical analogue. The arrangement which I shall describe is such that it might in many respects, —and at any rate in those under consideration, —replace a gas-tube as a conductor of electricity,

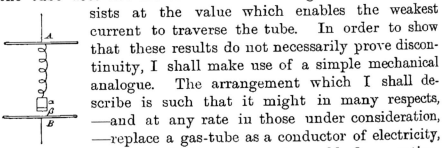

FIG. 29.

and nevertheless a current would flow continuously through it under certain conditions. Let A (Fig. 29) represent the anode, and let this be connected by a metallic spring or other elastic good conductor with the weight a

which lies close to the cathode B.   If there is a difference of potential between A and B, a will be attracted by B.   But a is prevented from coming directly into contact with B by an under layer β of relatively high resistance r.   Between A and B there may exist any number more of these spring-carriers, only differing from the first in that the resistance corresponding to β is for each very large.   A certain potential difference must exist between A and B in order to bring the weight a of the first spring-carrier up against B, and so for all the other spring-carriers.   Suppose this potential difference to be very nearly the same for all of them, and equal to p. The whole arrangement may now replace a gas-tube as follows. It does not allow any current to pass unless the potential difference between A and B attains the value p.   It allows an intermittent current to pass when A and B are connected with a source of electricity which can produce a potential difference p, but is not at the same time able to produce a current of strength p/r.   If, however, the source is capable of yielding such a current, then a and B remain permanently in contact and the current flows continuously.   Whatever the strength of the current may be, the potential difference cannot exceed p, for more and more of the spring-carriers would come into action.   The whole heating effect would therefore be proportional to the current itself, and not to its square.   This proves our point.

Another circumstance seems to have influenced the opinions of previous writers.   The position and development of each stria of the glow-light depends upon the preceding stria (in the direction of the cathode): upon this is founded the legitimate view that from the cathode outwards there must be a time-development from one stria to the next.   But such a time-development is not conceivable, if the discharge in all parts persists continuously.   Perhaps we shall form a correct conception of the circumstances in question if we admit that the discharge as a whole is continuous, but assume that its course along the separate current-lines (*Stromfäden*) is a function of the time.   For example, if the contact of a gas-molecule with the cathode gave rise to an electric disturbance travelling in waves through the medium, the successive production of striæ would be easily intelligible without necessitating any splitting up of the discharge into partial discharges. This would still be a continuous discharge in the sense in which we have used the word.

II. Do the Cathode Rays indicate the Path of the Current ?

As is well known, the cathode rays spread outwards in straight lines, approximately perpendicular to the cathode and without reference to the position of the anode. According to the density of the gas, they proceed in the medium for a few millimetres, centimetres, or even up to lengths of the order of a metre. In air they are blue, but at low densities their luminosity is exceedingly feeble ; they are then most noticeable on account of the phosphorescence which they excite when they strike the glass. If a magnet is brought near the tube they appear bent, much as an elastic wire attached to the cathode and traversed by a current would become bent under the influence of the magnet. This is universally regarded as an electromagnetic action, and, excepting that passing doubts were expressed, the view that used to be held by physicists was as follows : The cathode rays indicate the path of the current, and their blue light arises from the glowing or phosphorescence of the gas-particles under the action of the current. As a fuller knowledge of the facts was attained this view appeared less probable, and more recent experimenters express themselves very reservedly as to the relation between the cathode rays and the actual process of discharge.[1] Under these circumstances it appeared advisable to obtain by experiment a decisive answer to the question—Does the current travel along the cathode rays before it turns towards the anode ? If this question was to be answered in the negative it would become clear that the path of the current could not be recognised by the naked eye, and a fresh question would arise, namely, What is the path

[1] See, e.g. W. Spottiswoode and J. Fletcher Moulton, *Phil. Trans.* 171, p. 649, 1880.

of the current in a space in which various paths are open to it? I have tried to answer both questions for a space containing gas and traversed by a current by determining experimentally the current-lines from the deflections produced by the discharge in a small magnet in its neighbourhood.

Before attacking this problem it was necessary to solve a preliminary one. Whether the cathode rays form the path of the current or not, there is no doubt that they are affected by a magnet. Conversely, it was not improbable that the cathode rays would in any case produce a deflection of the magnet; and this effect might be other than an electromagnetic effect. If such an effect existed, the proposed experiment would be useless. The following experiments show that no such effect occurs.

In a tube 300 mm. long and 28 mm. wide was introduced a cathode consisting of a circular turned brass disc which just filled the cross-section of the tube. Through a hole bored in the centre of the disc was passed a thermometer tube; inside this, and quite centrically with reference to the disc, was a wire of non-magnetic metal. The ends of the wire, projecting but little beyond the disc in the gas-space, formed the anode. The wires used to carry the current in and out were twisted around one another. Now the current-lines must at all events be symmetrical with reference to the axis of the tube; if we suppose the currents replaced by magnetic surfaces, these would be closed ring-magnets which would have no external action. But the cathode rays were fully developed and, according to the density, filled either the whole tube or a part of it with blue light. If they have any action peculiar to themselves upon a magnet outside the tube, it would here exhibit itself apart from any electromagnetic effect. In order to avoid any electrostatic effects the tube was surrounded with tinfoil which was connected to earth; without this precaution the experiments could not have been carried out. The magnet upon which the cathode rays were to act was the one which was used in the subsequent experiments; it was a strongly magnetised piece of watch-spring, 12 mm. long, and was attached to a small mirror of very thin glass. This was hung by a single spider-thread in a very narrow space between two plates of plate-glass. Thus the arrangement was the

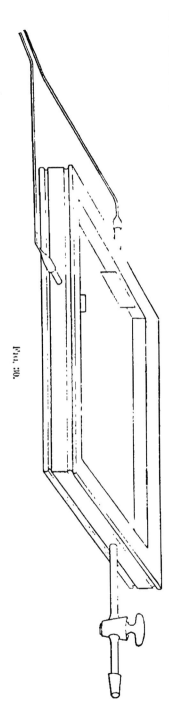

FIG. 30.

same as in a Thomson galvanometer. In all the following experiments it was made strongly astatic by external magnets; this, with the air-damping, made it dead-beat, and in all other respects its behaviour was most satisfactory. The tube was now brought as near as possible to the magnet, first in such a position that the magnet would indicate a force tangential to the tube, then radial, and lastly, parallel to the tube. But there was never any deflection,— none amounting to even one-tenth of a scale-division in the telescope. The strength of the current was from $\frac{1}{100}$ to $\frac{1}{200}$ Daniell S.U. By using a second anode the same current could be made to traverse the length of the tube; it then produced deflections of thirty to forty scale-divisions. Similar deflections were obtained when the first anode was retained and portions of the circuit outside the tube were brought within a few centimetres of the magnet. It was thus proved that, if there was any specific action of the cathode rays upon the magnet, this could not amount to $\frac{1}{300}$ part of the effect produced by the cathode rays as current-carriers.

In the principal experiments the discharge was investigated in an air-space of the form of a flat parallel-epipedon, 12 cm. long, 12 cm. broad, and 1 cm. deep. The case enclosing it is shown in Fig. 30. It was made of a strong brass casting, which formed the side walls and framing, and of two sheets of plate-glass 4 to 5 mm. thick, applied air-tight to this frame. The plates sustained safely the powerful pres-

sure of the air, and could be heated while this pressure was on ;
but they bent under it so strongly that the curvature could
easily be observed on looking at them sideways.   Through the
brass frame were inserted a tube with stopcock for pumping
out, and also several aluminium electrodes ;   the latter were
cemented in glass tubes so as to be insulated from the frame.
It was only after several fruitless attempts that the case was
made air-tight.   One difficulty arose from the bending of the
glass ; this made any accurate grinding impossible, and every
solid cement cracked on pumping out.   Another difficulty
arose from the fact that no trace of any decomposable organic
substance could be allowed
inside the case, so that a
free use of any fatty substance would have been
fatal.   Fig. 31 explains
how a tight joint was
at last secured.   On the

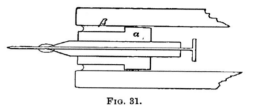

FIG. 31.

ground projecting inner rim a of the frame was laid a thin
strip of rolled gutta-percha, which was kept about a millimetre
away from its inner edge.   The glass plates were then heated
and applied, and the case was exhausted as far as the leakage
would admit ; at the same time a mixture of four parts of
rosin and one part of olive oil was poured into the hollow
space β.   This mixture proved, after cooling, sufficiently fluid
to follow the movements of the glass plates, and was yet so
tough that only after several months did it begin to flow out
of the hollow space on account of its own weight.   The case
could be kept exhausted for days together.   If the current
was sent through it for a considerable time, the pressure of
the gas increased slightly, but not so much as to interfere
with the experiments.   The case was next enclosed in a tinfoil covering, connected to earth but insulated from the brass
frame and the electrodes.   After exhausting it to a pressure
of a few hundredths of a millimetre, it was placed upon a
board covered with co-ordinate paper (squared paper) and
provided with levelling screws.   Exactly over the zero point
of this co-ordinate system hung the magnetic needle which
has been already described, at such a height that the exhausted
case could be moved about underneath without touching it.

M. P.   R

It was only 2 mm. above the surface of the upper glass plate, and therefore 12 mm. above the mean stria of gas through which the current passed. When the current was turned on, the magnet was deflected, the deflection depending upon the strength of the current and the direction of its path with reference to the needle. The total current used was from $\frac{1}{100}$ to $\frac{1}{200}$ Daniell, S.U. In favourable positions of the needle this gave deflections up to eighty scale-divisions. As one-tenth of a division could be read off, the measurements could be made accurately. With the help of the squared paper the position of the plate with reference to the magnet could be altered and accurately read off. Such an arrangement enables us to determine with considerable accuracy the distribution of magnetic force which the current in the stria of air produces just above and parallel to itself. But what we have to do is to deduce from this distribution the distribution of the current in the air-stria itself.

This can be done with the aid of the following proposition: The current-function of the electric current in a plane stria is equal to the potential function of the magnetic force excited by the current in the immediate neighbourhood of the stria, multiplied by a constant. The current-lines therefore coincide with the magnetic equipotential lines, and the current-strengths between every two equipotential lines, between which the potential increases by the same amount, are equal. A proof of this proposition may be found in Maxwell's *Treatise on Electricity and Magnetism*.[1] But it can easily be seen to be true if we consider the case of a magnetic pole brought infinitely near to a plate traversed by a current; for only those parts of the current which are in its immediate neighbourhood can exert upon the pole a force parallel to the plate.

The current-stria which we have to investigate is not infinitely thin, and the testing magnet does not lie in the immediate neighbourhood of its mean plane, but 12 mm. above it. Hence it only enables us to investigate the distribution of the potential in a plane which is 12 mm. above the mean plane of the stria of air. But the magnetic force in this plane will be approximately the same as that inside the stria of air; and hence the equipotential lines on the plane in which the magnet moves will be very similar to the current-lines. The most elegant way of investigating these equipotential lines would be to move the plate beneath the magnet in such a way that the latter always remains undeflected. The curve then described by the projection of the magnet on the plate is an equipotential line, and therefore a current-line. But as the deflection of the magnet had to be read off from a distance with mirror and scale, this method could not be carried out without elaborate mechanism. Hence the following method was adopted. The case was moved under the magnet in such a way that the projection of the latter upon it described a parallel to one side of the square case, and so that the magnet in its undeflected position was perpendicular to this parallel. The current being maintained constant, the deflections for a series of points along this straight line were determined. These were proportional to the differential co-efficients of the potential along this straight line. These differential coefficients were plotted graphically and carefully interpolated; the area of the curve, obtained by a mechanical quadrature, gave the changes of potential along the straight line examined. The same process was carried out for a series of straight lines parallel to the first, and for *one* straight line perpendicular to them. Thus the potential for all points in the plane investigated could be specified, and it was easy to connect the equipotential points and draw the connecting lines at such distances that the potential increased by a constant amount in passing from each one to the next. In consequence of the method followed there was bound to be some uncertainty as to the values obtained, and it was necessary to get an estimate of this. For this purpose the potential was measured along several straight lines perpendicular to the parallel ones, instead of along one only. Thus the value of the potential at every point could be determined in a corresponding number of independent ways. By adjusting these we obtain not only a trustworthy result, but a measure of the uncertainty attaching to the method. It turned out that this was not large enough to interfere much with the results.

These results can best be represented by Fig. 32, *a*, *b*, and *c*.

In these a denotes the blue cathode light, β the positive striæ; the curved lines are equidistant equipotential lines. In a and c the pressure amounted to one-tenth of a millimetre;

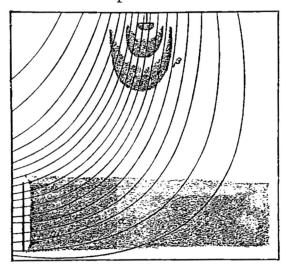

FIG. 32, c (½ nat. size).

hence in these the cathode rays have free ends. In b the pressure was reduced so much that the battery could only barely keep up a continuous discharge; hence in this the cathode rays end perpendicularly upon the opposite side. With regard to these equipotential curves we have to remark: (1) That in constructing each figure some fifty to sixty deflections were used; these were not distributed uniformly over the whole surface, but were mostly taken in the places which seemed most important. (2) The uncertainty which remained is indicated by the number of equipotential curves drawn. For just so many were drawn that the uncertainty as to the position of any single one was equal to the interval between two neighbouring ones. (3) In order to obtain the actual current-lines from the equipotential lines here drawn, we

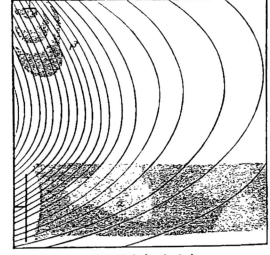

FIG. 32, b (½ nat. size).

must imagine the end-points of the latter joined to the electrodes, and the lines themselves compressed somewhat more together towards those places in which they are closest. It is clear that the actual current-lines could never cut the sides of the vessel, as the lines in our drawings do.

The figures show without any doubt that the direction of the cathode rays does not coincide with the direction of the current. In some places the current-lines are almost perpendicular to the direction of the cathode rays. Some parts of the gas-space are lit up brilliantly by the cathode light, although the current in them is vanishingly small. Roughly speaking, the distribution of the current in its flow from pole to pole is similar to what it would be in a solid or liquid conductor. From this it follows that the cathode rays have nothing in common with the path of the current.

1. Against the preliminary experiment the objection may be raised that since a magnet deflects the cathode rays, conversely the cathode rays must deflect the magnet. But when we come to consider the expression " a magnet deflects this or that ray," and the comparison thus set up with the deflection of an elastic wire traversed by a current, we may well doubt whether these are so suitably chosen as at first sight they appear

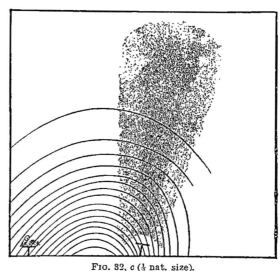

Fig. 32, c (½ nat. size).

to be. Such a wire when the current starts would be straight, and would only be brought into its deflected position after a finite time. But we know that cathode rays, even when the corresponding discharges last less than a millionth of a second, appear completely bent.[1] De la Rive's experiment in which the discharge is made to rotate about a magnetic pole tells against the supposition that electromagnetic action can set gaseous discharges in motion with such speed as this. In De la Rive's experiment the action is undoubtedly electromagnetic; but it takes place at a

[1] See Goldstein, *Über eine Form der elektr. Abstossung*, iii. Teil.

speed which is very easily measurable. And in every actual electromagnetic effect the ponderable substratum of the current is set in motion; which is not the case with the deflection of the discharge.[1] Hence this deflection corresponds much more nearly to Hall's phenomenon. But this analogy again is seen to be defective when we recollect that the cathode rays are not to be regarded as the path of the current. Lastly, it is known that the battery-discharge can be extinguished by bringing a powerful magnet near it; and after the magnet is removed the discharge immediately starts off again. This shows that the action of the magnet upon the discharge cannot be purely electromagnetic. The action of the magnet, which prevents the current from starting, certainly cannot be an action upon the current itself; it can only be an action upon the medium through which the current has to pass. On account of these difficulties, and the fact that the cathode rays do not react upon the magnet, it seems to me probable that the analogy between the deflection of the cathode rays and the electromagnetic action is quite superficial. Without attempting any explanation for the present, we may say that the magnet acts upon the medium, and that in the magnetised medium the cathode rays are not propagated in the same way as in the unmagnetised medium. This statement is in accordance with the above-mentioned fact, and avoids the difficulties. It makes no comparison with the deflection of a wire carrying a current, but rather suggests an analogy with the rotation of the plane of polarisation of light in a magnetised medium.

2. E. Wiedemann and Goldstein have expressed the opinion that the discharge consists of an ether-disturbance, of itself invisible, and only converted into light by imparting its energy to the gas-particles. This view seems to me to be based upon convincing arguments. I should, however, like to see the word ' discharge ' replaced by ' cathode rays ': the two things are quite distinct, although the physicists referred to do not observe the distinction. If we consider carefully the following experiment, it will be difficult to resist the view that the cathode rays themselves are invisible, and that they only produce light by their absorption in the gas. The tube

[1] See Goldstein, *Wied. Ann.* **12**, p. 262, 1881.

already described, which was used in the preliminary experiment of this section, was exhausted so far that the discharges of a large induction coil could only just traverse it : under the action of such discharges there was a brilliant phosphorescence at the end opposite the cathode. After what we have already said, there can be no doubt that the current-paths are restricted to the immediate neighbourhood of the electrodes, which are quite near to one another, and that only the cathode rays traverse the length of the tube. Now at the phosphorescing end of this tube there happened to be a drop of mercury. When that part of the tube was heated, so as to vapourise the mercury and produce there a gas of comparatively high density, the end of the tube became filled with crimson light, which showed the spectrum of mercury. The green phosphorescence of the glass then faded away, and ceased entirely when the stria of mercury vapour attained a certain thickness. By means of a magnet the cathode rays could be made to follow a path iu which they had not to traverse the vapour ; the luminescence of the latter then ceased, and was replaced by a green phosphorescence on the glass at the side of the tube, where the rays now fell. In this way one could at will produce a luminescence of the glass or of the mercury vapour. By further heating and distilling, a larger portion of the tube could be filled with the heavy vapour ; it was then found that the luminescence only extended to the 5 or 6 cm. of the portion which lay nearest to the cathode, the part of the tube behind it remaining dark. Finally, when the whole tube was filled with the heavy vapour, the luminescence—in the form of the ordinary cathode light—filled the space about the cathode for a distance of a few centimetres. Thus the cathode rays first excite luminescence when they enter a denser medium and are themselves absorbed by it. For this absorption an infinitely thin stria of a solid suffices, but a finite stria of a gas is requisite. The denser the gas the shorter the distance through which the cathode rays can penetrate into it. This is probably one reason why the cathode light in comparatively dense gases is restricted to the immediate neighbourhood of the cathode.

3. There can be no doubt that in the preceding experiment the luminescence of the gas, even in the immediate

neighbourhood of the cathode, was not due to the direct action of the current, but to the action of the cathode rays. For without any sudden change it could be gradually transformed into a quite similar luminescence, situated at a great distance from the cathode and in a space where the current was zero. And if we admit that in this special case the cathode light is not directly produced by the current, we can scarcely assume that in the general case it is so produced. According to Goldstein's researches, the cathode light has so many analogies with the separate positive striæ that it can be regarded as a degenerated form of such a stria. It is therefore very improbable that the luminescence of the gas in the positive striæ is due to any causes other than those which produce the luminescence in the cathode light. We are thus led to the assumption, which at first seemed hazardous, that the luminescence of the gas in the glow discharge is not a direct effect of the current, but arises indirectly through an absorption of the cathode rays [1] which are produced by the current. If we could prevent the production of the cathode rays, the gas would everywhere be as dark as it is in the dark intervals between the striæ (although the current flows through these intervening spaces). Conversely, if we could produce the cathode rays in some other way than by the discharge, we could get luminescence of the gas without any current. For the present such a separation can only be carried out ideally.

4. A number of phenomena, which otherwise can only be explained with difficulty, are seen to follow almost as a matter of course when we regard the cathode rays as a disturbance which is quite independent of the actual discharge, and no more connected with it than the light which radiates from the discharge. I shall only mention the penetration of the striæ, the reflection of cathode rays from the anode, and the way in which these rays pass out through anodes consisting of close metal gratings completely surrounding the cathode. With respect to the latter, I may say that I have seen fully developed cathode rays pass through wire-gauze containing not less than thirty-six meshes to the square millimetre.

---

[1] *i.e.* of rays which in their nature are identical with the cathode rays. The name obviously becomes unsuitable if it has also to include the rays of the positive striæ.

III. Have the Cathode Rays Electrostatic Properties?

If we admit that cathode rays are only a subsidiary phenomenon accompanying the actual current, and that they do not
exert electromagnetic effects, then the next question that arises is
as to their electrostatic behaviour. For the experiments relating
to this the battery, unfortunately, was no longer available, and
I had to make use of the discharges of a small induction coil.
On account of their irregularity and suddenness these are very
ill adapted for electrostatic measurements. Hence the experimental results are not so sharp as they otherwise might have
been; but the conclusion to
which they lead may certainly
be regarded as correct. The
question at the head of this
section may be split up into
two simpler ones. Firstly:
Do the cathode rays give
rise to electrostatic forces in
their neighbourhood? Sec-
ondly: In their course are
they affected by external
electrostatic forces? By
cathode rays are here meant
such as are separated from
the path of the current
which produces them: to
prevent confusion we shall
call these pure cathode rays.

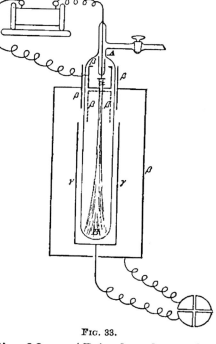

Fig. 33.

A. In seeking an answer
to the first question I made
use of the apparatus shown in Fig. 33. *AB* is the glass tube,
25 mm. wide and 250 mm. long, in which the rays were
produced. *a* is the cathode. All the parts marked β are in
good metallic connection with each other, and such of them as
lie inside the tube form the anode. They consist, in the first
place, of a brass tube which nearly surrounds the cathode, and
only opposite it has a circular opening 10 mm. in diameter,

through which the cathode rays can pass; secondly, of wire-gauze, about 1 sq. mm. in mesh, through which the cathode rays have to pass; thirdly, of a protecting metallic case, which completely surrounds the greater part of the tube and screens that part of the gas-space which lies beyond the wire-gauze from any electrostatic forces which might be produced by induction from without, e.g. from the cathode. If the results which we have already obtained have any meaning, the cathode rays are to be regarded as pure after they have passed through the opening in the metal cylinder and the wire-gauze beyond it. They are none the less vivid; at low densities they cause the glass at B to shine with a brilliant green phosphorescence, upon which the shadow of the wire-gauze is plainly marked. The part of the glass tube which lay within the protecting case was now enclosed in a metallic mantle γ, which was connected with one pair of quadrants of a delicate electrometer; the protecting case and the other quadrants were connected to earth. When even a small quantity of electricity was brought inside this mantle, it attracted by induction electricity of the opposite sign from the electrometer, so that a deflection was produced. The electricity could, e.g., be introduced by replacing the tube AB inside the protected space and the mantle γ by a metal rod which had about the same size and position as the cathode rays. This was placed in metallic connection with the cathode, while the current from the induction coil passed, as it did in the actual experiments, through the tube. The deflection then produced in the electrometer was too great to be measured, but could be estimated at two to three thousand scale-divisions. When the current was stopped the electrometer needle went back to about its old position; and this could be repeated at will. Now if the cathode rays consisted of a stream of particles charged to the potential of the cathode, they would produce effects quantitatively similar to the above, or qualitatively similar if they produced any electrostatic forces whatever in their neighbourhood. On trying the experiment the following results were obtained. When the quadrants of the electrometer were connected together and the induction coil started, the needle naturally remained at rest. When the connection between the quadrants was broken, the needle, in consequence of irregularities in the discharge, began to vibrate through ten or twenty scale-divisions from its position of rest.   When the induction coil was stopped, the needle remained at rest in its zero-position, and again began to vibrate as above when the current was started.   As far as the accuracy of the experiment allows, we can conclude with certainty that no electrostatic effect due to the cathode rays can be perceived; and that if they consist of streams of electrified particles, the potential on their outer surface is at most one-hundredth of that of the cathode.   And this conclusion remains correct even if we now find that there are complications in the part of the tube beyond the wire-gauze, viz. that this part of it is by no means unelectrified. If we start the induction coil after the apparatus has been long at rest, and is therefore free from electricity, a consider-able deflection (150 to 200 scale-divisions), showing a negative charge on the tube, is produced in the electrometer.   But this charge and deflection remain constant, however often the coil is put in and out of action.   They remain for an hour after the discharge has been stopped.   But while the discharge is on, the position of the needle changes instantaneously when a magnet is brought near the tube, and the needle remains constant in its new position so long as the magnet is not moved.   As a matter of fact, then, electricity does penetrate through the wire-gauze into the protected part of the tube until its entrance is prevented by the rise of potential.   We shall not here establish the laws which underlie this penetration of the electricity; it is enough that it has nothing to do with the cathode rays.   For the passage of these latter is in no way influenced when the further penetration of the electricity is prevented; nor, as the first experiment shows, is the amount of electricity in the tube appreciably increased when the cathode rays again begin to enter it.

B. In order to find out whether pure cathode rays are affected by electrostatic forces, the following experiments were made.   The rays were produced in a glass tube 26 cm. long, provided with a circular aluminium cathode 5 mm. in diameter.   As in the preceding experiments, the cathode was almost completely surrounded by the anode, and the cathode rays had to pass out through the wire-gauze.   Further on in their path was a fine wire; the sharp shadow of this, appearing on the phosphorescent patch at a distance of 12 cm., served as an accurate indicator of any deflection. A magnetic force only half as strong as the horizontal intensity of the earth's magnetism, acting perpendicular to the direction of the ray, was sufficient to change quite notably the position of this shadow. The tube was now placed between two strongly and oppositely electrified plates : no effect could be observed in the phosphorescent image. But here there was a doubt whether the large electrostatic force to which the tube was subjected might not be compensated by an electrical distribution produced inside it. In order to remove this doubt, two metallic strips were placed inside the tube at a distance of 2 cm. from one another, and were connected to external conductors by which they could be maintained at different potentials. After passing the wire which produced the shadow, the rays had to travel a distance of 12 cm. between these strips. The latter were first connected with the poles of a battery of twenty small Daniell cells. Opening and closing this connection produced not the slightest effect upon the phosphorescent image. Hence no effect is produced upon the ray by an electromotive force of one Daniell per millimetre acting upon it perpendicular to its length. 240 Planté cells of the large battery were next charged and connected with the two metallic strips. By themselves these 240 cells were not able to discharge across the strips ; but as soon as the induction coil was set to work and the cathode rays filled the space between the strips, the battery also began to discharge between them; and, as there was no liquid resistance in the circuit, this at once changed into an arc discharge. The same phenomenon could be produced with a much smaller number of cells—down to twenty or thirty. This is in accordance with Hittorf's discovery that very small electromotive forces can break through a space already filled with cathode rays. The 240 cells were next connected up through a large liquid resistance : during each separate discharge of the induction coil there was now only a weak battery-discharge lasting for an equally short time. The phosphorescent image of the Ruhmkorff discharge appeared somewhat distorted through deflection in the neighbourhood of the negative strip ; but the part of the shadow in the middle between the two strips was not visibly displaced.

The result may therefore be expressed as follows. Under the conditions of the experiment the cathode rays were not deflected by any electromotive force existing in the space traversed by them, at any rate not by an electromotive force of one to two Daniells per millimetre. Upon this we may make the following remarks :——

1. As far as the imperfect experiments described under III. enable us to decide, the cathode rays cannot be recognised as possessing any electrostatic properties. Under II. we have partly proved, and partly shown it to be probable, that they do not produce any strictly electromagnetic effects. Thus the question arises : are we justified in regarding the cathode rays as being in themselves an electrical phenomenon ? It does not appear improbable that, as far as their nature is concerned, they have no closer relation to electricity than has the light produced by an electric lamp.

2. The experiments described under II. can quite well be reconciled with the view, which has received support in many directions, that the cathode rays consist of streams of electrified material particles. But the results described under III. do not appear to be in accordance with such a view. For we find that the cathode rays behave quite unlike a rod of the same shape connected with the cathode, which is pretty well the opposite of what one would expect, according to this conception. We may also ask with what speed electrified particles would have to move in order that they should be more strongly deflected by a magnetic force of absolute strength unity, acting perpendicularly to their path, than by an electrostatic force of 1 Daniell per millimetre. The requisite speed would exceed eleven earth-quadrants per second,——a speed which will scarcely be regarded as probable. But unless we assume such a speed, the conception here referred to cannot, in accordance with the experiments described under B, account for the action of the magnet upon the rays.

CONCLUSION

By the experiments here described I believe I have proved :——

1. That until stronger proofs to the contrary are adduced,

we may regard the battery discharge as being continuous, and therefore the glow discharge as not being necessarily disruptive.

2. That the cathode rays are only a phenomenon accompanying the discharge, and have nothing directly to do with the path of the current.[1]

3. That the electrostatic and electromagnetic properties of the cathode rays are either *nil* or very feeble.

I have also endeavoured to bring forward a definite conception as to how the glow discharge takes place. The following are the principal features of this :—

The luminescence of the gas in the glow discharge is not a phosphorescence under the direct action of the current, but a phosphorescence under the influence of cathode rays produced by the current. These cathode rays are electrically indifferent, and amongst known agents the phenomenon most nearly allied to them is light. The rotation of the plane of polarisation of light is the nearest analogue to the bending of cathode rays by a magnet.

If this conception is correct, we are forced by the phenomena to assume that there are different kinds of cathode rays whose properties merge into each other and correspond to the colours of light. They differ amongst themselves in respect of exciting phosphorescence, of being absorbed, and of being deflected by a magnet.

The views which most nearly coincide with these are those which have been expressed by E. Wiedemann [2] and E. Goldstein.[3] By comparing this paper with those below referred to, it will be easy to recognise the points of agreement and difference. The experiments here described were carried out in the Physical Institute of the University of Berlin.

---

[1] Since the presence of cathode rays in a gas-space modifies considerably the possibility of passing a discharge through it, there can scarcely be any doubt that the position and development of the cathode rays do indirectly affect the path of the current.

[2] See *Wied. Ann.* **10**, p. 249, 1880.

[3] *Loc. cit.* **12**, p. 265, 1881.

XIV

ON THE BEHAVIOUR OF BENZENE WITH RESPECT TO INSULATION AND RESIDUAL CHARGE

(*Wiedemann's Annalen*, **20**, pp. 279-284, 1883.)

ROWLAND and Nichols have shown[1] that in certain insulating crystals dielectric polarisation is not accompanied by any electric after-effect or formation of a residual charge. They interpret this result as supporting the view that the formation of a residual charge is simply a necessary consequence of imperfect homogeneity in an insulator. Some years ago I wanted to find whether the formation of a residual charge could be detected in a conductor undoubtedly homogeneous; and with this object I tested various liquids. The conductivity of most of these proved to be too high for such experiments; but commercial pure benzene exhibited a sufficiently high resistance, and also a distinct residual charge. A closer investigation disclosed certain peculiarities in the behaviour of benzene which are described below, and these can be interpreted in the same way as the behaviour of crystals. I had not kept the numerical results of my experiments; but Herr E. Heins has been good enough to repeat the experiments, and to allow me to make use of his results. The numerical data given below are taken from Herr Heins' experiments.

1. The method adopted is copied from that of Herr W. Giese.[2] The benzene is contained in a zinc canister (*B*, Fig. 34). In this, and entirely surrounded by it, a zinc plate about 12 cm. long and 8 cm. broad was hung by two wires. This plate

---

[1] *Phil. Mag.* (Series 5) **11**, p. 414, 1881.
[2] *Wied. Ann.* **9**, p. 160, 1880.

formed the inner coating, and the zinc canister the outer coating of a Leyden jar, of which the benzene formed the dielectric. The inner coating was connected with one pair of quadrants—not earthed—of an electrometer; and by means of the key a this coating could be con-

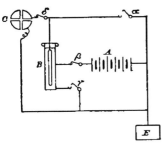

FIG. 34.

nected to earth. The outer coating could either be connected by γ to the earth as well, or by β to one pole of a constant battery of 100 small Daniell cells, the other pole of which was kept at zero potential by an earth-connection. If we now suppose the circuit to be closed at a and β, and open at γ, the needle of the electrometer will clearly stand at zero, and the circuit will be traversed by a current whose strength will depend upon the resistance of the benzene. If the circuit is now broken at a, the inner coating strives to charge itself to the potential of the outer, and hence the electrometer needle is deflected in the direction in which it would move if the unearthed quadrants were directly connected with the insulated pole of the battery. This we shall call the positive direction. The rate of deflection of the needle enables us to measure the resistance of the benzene. The capacity of the electrometer was to that of the benzene condenser in the ratio of $4.5 : 1.$[1] The whole potential of the battery would have deflected the needle 5500 scale-divisions from its position of rest. Now suppose that the connection to the electrometer at δ was broken one second after opening the circuit at a, and that the electrometer was found to give a deflection of a scale-divisions. The difference of potential of the coatings would then have sunk in a second through $a/5500$ of its value. In the absence of the electrometer it would have fallen $(4.5 + 1)$ times as rapidly, $i.e.$ through $a/1000$ in a second, or to $1/e^{4\pi}$ of its value in $4\pi . 1000/a$ seconds. This latter time is to be divided by the specific inductive capacity of benzene in order to obtain the specific resistance in absolute electrostatic measure. In this way, then, we can measure the resistance. In order to observe

[1] The large apparent capacity of the quadrants is due to the strong charge on the electrometer needle.

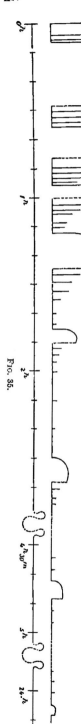

the residual charge the outer coating was disconnected by the key β from the battery, and connected by γ with the earth ; just a second after closing γ the current was broken at a. The residual charge present then produced a negative deflection of the electrometer ; this rapidly increased, reached a maximum, and then, owing to loss of charge by conduction, slowly fell off. An exact measure of the residual charge could only be deduced by complicated calculations from the course of the deflections ; but an estimate of its magnitude can be obtained directly from the maximum deflection.

2. The canister was filled with commercial benzene, and the current was closed, excepting when the resistance and residual charge were from time to time tested. The results were as follows. At first the resistance was so small that in a few moments after opening a the scale moved quite out of the field of view. The residual charge was fairly considerable ; its maximum value was more than 10 per cent of the original charge, but in consequence of the high conductivity it soon disappeared. Twenty to thirty minutes later the resistance was found to have increased to a conveniently measurable value ;[1] at the same time the residual charge had become much smaller. The same changes went on without interruption ; after twenty-four hours the benzene had become almost a perfect insulator, and scarcely any residual charge could be detected. Fig. 35 represents correctly the numerical results of one of the experiments. The abscissæ give the time in hours and minutes from the beginning of the experiment. The vertical ordinates give the

[1] It had increased for both directions of the current.

M. P.

conductivities measured at the corresponding times. The progress of formation of the residual charge, as far as it was followed, is shown by the curves. The measurements are only relative; the conductivity at time 0 was too great to be measured.[1]

3. The conductivity and residual charge at the beginning are certainly due to impurities. For, in the first place, they could be reproduced, after they had once disappeared, by any action which introduced fresh impurities, *e.g.*, by pouring the benzene into other vessels, by stirring it up, blowing in moist air, dipping in a wire of oxidisable metal, or mixing any powder with it. The effects thus produced could again be destroyed as before. In the second place, if a sample of benzene having a high conductivity was carefully distilled over calcium chloride, and only allowed to come in contact with vessels which had been rinsed out with purified benzene, its conductivity was very much reduced. But the highest grade of insulation could never be attained in this way.

4. The reduction of both of these effects is due, at any rate in part, to the action of the current. They certainly fell off even when the benzene was simply allowed to stand; but neither so rapidly nor so far as when the coatings of the jar were connected to the poles of a battery. In this respect different samples of benzene seem to behave differently. The resistance of the sample which I investigated only changed very slightly when no current was used, whereas the conductivity of that examined by Herr Heins fell to very low values simply by standing. It may have been that the former contained chiefly soluble impurities and the latter matter in suspension. Experiments made with the intention of finding out the nature of the active impurities were unsuccessful. I shall only remark that in such experiments the benzene can be tested between glass electrodes; for the resistance of the latter is negligible in comparison with that of the benzene.

5. In its behaviour electrically purified benzene comes extraordinarily near to that of an ideal liquid insulator.

---

[1] In Fig. 35 it will be noticed that after every considerable interruption of the current the flow to the condenser becomes greater than it had been before. This is only very slightly, if at all, due to a decrease in the resistance; it rather expresses the fact that for a short time after each interruption the flow proper is reinforced by that due to the residual charge.

Scarcely a trace of residual charge can be detected, and its insulating power is not far short of that of our best insulators. On account of the evaporation which took place, the experiments could not be extended much beyond twenty-four hours, and at the end of this time a definite limit to the resistance had not yet been reached. But the insulating power may be judged from the fact that in a minute after breaking the earth-connection at a, the electrometer needle had only moved six scale divisions from its position of rest. From this, and from the ratio of the capacities given above, it follows that a Leyden jar containing this benzene as dielectric would require two hours to lose half its charge.

6. The residual charge exhibited by impure benzene arises from polarisation, which produces some kind of after-effect, and not from an absorption of free electricity. This can be proved by the following experiments. After breaking the circuit at a, just at the instant when the residual charge begins to exhibit itself, the benzene is allowed to run out through an opening in the bottom as quickly and quietly as possible; the residual charge now makes its appearance suddenly, and its sign is the same as it would have been if the benzene had not been run out. If the residual charge were due to an absorption of electricity by the dielectric, the removal of this dielectric would certainly be followed by a sudden deflection; but the sign of this would have been opposite to that of the electricity removed with the dielectric, and therefore opposite to that of the original residual charge. In another experiment I polarised impure benzene in a large vessel between two plates, A and B, which were several centimetres apart. A and B were then brought to the potential zero; and a system of three other plates, 1, 2, and 3, was immediately introduced into the space between them. The outer plates 1 and 3 were connected to earth and to one pair of quadrants of an electrometer. Plate 2, which was connected to the other pair of quadrants, was closely attached to 3, but insulated from it. Thus no benzene could enter between 2 and 3, whereas there was a layer a few centimetres thick between 1 and 2. On introducing this system there was an immediate deflection in the galvanometer, the direction of which changed with the direction of polarisation of the benzene;

this corresponded to a portion of the residual charge which otherwise would have developed upon the plates A and B. Now, it is easily seen that if the residual charge is an after-effect of polarisation, the sign of this deflection must be opposite to what it would be if it were due to electric absorption from the plates; for the electrical double stria produced between plates 1 and 2 would have opposite signs in these two cases. The result of the experiment indicated that the effect was due to polarisation. It is not surprising that the results of such experiments are somewhat irregular; for it is impossible to prevent friction and irregular motions which disturb the polarised elements. As a matter of fact, the magnitude of the deflection varied very considerably, and now and again an experiment even gave a result in the opposite direction. But the results of the large majority of the experiments were such as to justify the statement above made.

ON THE DISTRIBUTION OF STRESS IN AN ELASTIC RIGHT CIRCULAR CYLINDER

(*Schlömilch's Zeitschrift für Math. u. Physik*, **28**, pp. 125-128, 1884.)

A HOMOGENEOUS elastic right circular cylinder is bounded by two rigid planes perpendicular to its axis. Let pressures be applied to its curved surface at any desired inclination to it, and let them be independent of the coordinate parallel to the axis and act perpendicularly to that axis. Then the distribution of stress in the interior can be expressed in a finite form so remarkably simple that it may be of interest in spite of the narrow limits of the problem.

Let F be the pressure on the element ds of the curved surface, and f its direction. Further, let M_n be the component in direction n of the pressure on a plane element parallel to the axis of the cylinder, and the normal to which has the direction n. Let (m, n) denote the angle between the directions m and n; r the radius vector joining the element considered to the element ds of the curved surface; p the perpendicular let fall on the axis of the cylinder from the element ds; and R the radius of the cylinder. With this notation

$$M_n = -p \cos(n,m) + \frac{2}{\pi} \int F \frac{\cos(f,r) \cos(n,r) \cos(m,r)}{r} ds,$$

$$p = \frac{1}{2R\pi} \int F \cos(f,r) ds. \tag{1}$$

The integrations extend all round the circumference of the cylinder.

Proof.—We shall first show that the expression (1) represents a possible system of stress. Let x and y be rectangular coordinates in a plane perpendicular to the axis of the cylinder; then the pressures X_x, Y_y, Y_x, which are independent of the third coordinate, form a possible system if they satisfy these differential equations

$$0 = \frac{\partial X_x}{\partial x} + \frac{\partial Y_x}{\partial y}, \quad 0 = \frac{\partial Y_x}{\partial x} + \frac{\partial Y_y}{\partial y}, \quad \frac{\partial^2 X_x}{\partial y^2} + \frac{\partial^2 Y_y}{\partial x^2} = 2\frac{\partial^2 Y_x}{\partial y \partial x} \qquad (2).$$

Let ρ, ω be polar coordinates, $\rho \cos \omega = x$, $\rho \sin \omega = y$, and in the stress-components P_ρ, P_ω, Ω_ω let ω denote the direction perpendicular to ω; then the system of stress

$$P_\rho = \frac{\cos \omega}{\rho}, \quad P_\omega = 0, \quad \Omega_\omega = 0 \qquad (3)$$

satisfies the equations (2). This is proved by calculating the values of X_x, Y_y, Y_x, which follow from (3), and substituting them in (1). The three equations (3) may be replaced by the one equation

$$M_n = \frac{\cos \omega \cos (n,\rho) \cos (m,\rho)}{\rho} = \frac{\cos (x,\rho) \cos (n,\rho) \cos (m,\rho)}{\rho}$$

A sum of such M_n with different poles and multiplied by arbitrary constants will represent a system which satisfies the differential equations (2). Now the integral which occurs in (1) is such a sum, and as the expression in front of the integral merely represents a constant pressure p uniformly distributed through the cylinder, it follows that the system expressed by the equation (1) is a possible one.

We shall prove secondly that when we approach infinitely near to the curved surface and make the direction n coincide with that of the radius ρ, then M_n coincides with the component of F in the direction m; so that $M_n = \text{F} \cos (m,n)$. For this purpose we separate the integral into two parts, one relating to the portion of the boundary infinitely near the element considered, the other to the remaining more distant portion. For this latter, and for it alone, we have

$$r = 2\mathrm{R}\cos{(\rho,r)}, \quad \frac{\cos{(\rho,r)}}{r} = \frac{\cos{(n,r)}}{r} = \frac{1}{2\mathrm{R}};$$

so that this part of the integral

$$= \frac{1}{\mathrm{R}\pi}\int \mathrm{F}\cos{(f,r)}\cos{(m,r)}ds$$

$$= \frac{1}{2\mathrm{R}\pi}\int \{\mathrm{F}\cos{(f,m)} + \mathrm{F}\cos{[(f,\rho)-(m,\rho)]}\}ds,$$

since $(f,\rho)+(m,r)=(f,m)$; $(f,r)-(m,r)=(f,\rho)-(m,\rho)$.

Now since the forces F must not produce a displacement of the cylinder in the direction m, nor a rotation round the axis,

$$\int \mathrm{F}\cos{(f,m)}ds = 0, \quad \int \mathrm{F}\sin{(f,\rho)}ds = 0.$$

Hence the part of the integral examined is equal to

$$\frac{1}{2\mathrm{R}\pi}\cos{(m,\rho)}\int \mathrm{F}\cos{(f,\rho)}ds,$$

and thus cancels the first term in M_n; and M_n reduces to that part of the integral which is due to the part of the curved surface near the element considered. Here we have $rd(\rho,r) = ds\cos{(\rho,r)}$. Hence

$$\frac{\cos{(n,r)}}{r}ds = \frac{\cos{(\rho,r)}}{r}ds = d(\rho,r),$$

and as F, f may be regarded as constant over the smal. portion of surface considered, we have

$$\mathrm{M}_n = \frac{2}{\pi}\mathrm{F}\int_{-\frac{\pi}{2}}^{+\frac{\pi}{2}}\cos{(f,r)}\cos{(m,r)}d(\rho,r)$$

$$= \frac{2}{\pi}\mathrm{F}\int_{-\frac{\pi}{2}}^{+\frac{\pi}{2}}\cos{[(r,\rho)-(f,\rho)]}\cos{[(r,\rho)-(m,\rho)]}d(\rho,r)$$

$$= \frac{F}{\pi} \int_{-\frac{\pi}{2}}^{+\frac{\pi}{2}} \cos \, [2(r,\rho) - (f,\rho)] d(\rho,r) + \frac{F}{\pi} \cos \, (f,m) \int_{-\frac{\pi}{2}}^{+\frac{\pi}{2}} d(r,\rho)$$

$$= F \cos \, (f,m),$$

which was to be proved.

In calculating the first of the parts into which we separated the integral we ought strictly to have excluded from the integration the portion of the curved surface lying close to the element considered; but a simple investigation shows that the error thus committed is infinitesimal.

Example.—Particular applications of our formula may be made to cases where pressures are applied at isolated points of the curved surface. Imagine, for instance, a cylinder placed between two parallel plane plates which are pressed together with a pressure P. This is approximately the position of the rollers which frequently form the basis of support of iron bridges. We take the axis of x to be the line joining the points of contact of the cylinder with the planes; its intersection with the axis of the cylinder we take as origin. The coordinate perpendicular to x we call y, and denote by r_1, r_2 the distances of the element considered from the points of contact. Then the component of stress normal to the element considered is

$$N_n = - \frac{P}{R\pi} + \frac{2P}{\pi} \left\{ \frac{\cos \, (r_1 x) \cos^2 \, (r_1 n)}{r_1} + \frac{\cos \, (r_2 x) \cos^2 \, (r_2 n)}{r_2} \right\}.$$

If we determine the direction n so that N_n becomes a maximum or minimum, keeping r_1, r_2 the same, we get the values and directions of the principal stresses at the point (r_1, r_2). This calculation can be performed. For the axes of x and y the principal stresses are parallel to the axes, whence we easily obtain, for the axis of x

$$X_x = \frac{P}{R\pi} \frac{3R^2 + x^2}{R^2 - x^2}, \quad Y_y = - \frac{P}{R\pi},$$

and for the axis of y

$$X_y = \frac{P}{R\pi} \frac{3R^4 - 2R^2 y^2 - y^4}{R^4 + 2R^2 y^2 + y^4}, \quad Y_y = -\frac{P}{R\pi}\left(\frac{R^2 - y^2}{R^2 + y^2}\right)^2.$$

All the elements of the axes suffer compression in the direction of x, and extension in the perpendicular direction. At the centre the pressure in the direction of x is $6/\pi$ times what it would be if the pressure P were distributed uniformly over the whole section 2R. Even in this simplest case it appears that the distribution of stress is extremely complicated.

XVI

ON THE EQUILIBRIUM OF FLOATING ELASTIC PLATES

(*Wiedemann's Annalen*, 22, pp. 449-455, 1884.)

SUPPOSE an infinitely extended elastic plate, *e.g.* of ice, to float on an infinitely extended heavy liquid, *e.g.* water ; on the plate rest a number of weights without production of lateral tension; the position of equilibrium of the plate is required. The solution of this problem leads to certain paradoxical results, on account of which it is given here.

If we confine ourselves to small displacements, we may regard the effects of the separate weights as superposed, and need only consider the case of a single weight P. We suppose it placed at the origin of coordinates of x, y, of which the plane coincides with the plate, supposed infinitely thin. Further we write $\nabla^2 = \partial^2/\partial x^2 + \partial^2/\partial y^2$, $\rho^2 = x^2 + y^2$, and denote by E and μ in the usual notation the elastic constants of the material of the plate, by h its thickness, and by s the density of the liquid. Let z denote the vertical displacement of the deformed plate from the plane of x, y, reckoned positive when downwards ; then on the one hand $\{Eh^3/12(1 - \mu^2)\}\nabla^4 z$ is the upward pressure per unit area due to the elastic stresses,[1] on the other hand sz is the upward hydrostatic pressure per unit area. The sum of both pressures must vanish everywhere except at the origin. Here the integral of that sum taken over a very small area must be equal to P. But since the integral of the hydrostatic pressure over such an area is infinitesimal, that condition must be satisfied by the integral of the elastic reaction alone. If we write for shortness

[1] Clebsch, *Theorie der Elasticität*, § 73, 1862.

$$\frac{12(1 - \mu^2)s}{Eh^3} = a^4 = \frac{1}{a^4},$$

our problem may be stated mathematically thus: Required an integral of the equation $\nabla^4 z + a^4 z = 0$, which vanishes at infinity, is finite at the origin, and is such that the integral of $sa^4 f \nabla^4 z dw$ taken throughout the neighbourhood of the origin may be equal to P.

With Heine [1] we write

$$K(\rho) = \int_0^\infty e^{i\rho \cos iu}\, du,$$

then $K(\rho)$ is a solution of the equation $\nabla^2 z = -z$, and therefore $K(\rho \sqrt[4]{-a^4})$ is a solution of our equation. And

$$z = \frac{a^2 P}{4\pi si}\left\{ K[a\rho \sqrt{\tfrac{1}{2}}(1 + i)] - K[a\rho \sqrt{\tfrac{1}{2}}(1 - i)] \right\} \quad (1)$$

is also a solution. It is real, and if we bring it into a real form we get by transforming the integral

$$z = \frac{a^2 P}{4\pi s}\int_1^\infty \frac{\epsilon^{-a\rho\sqrt{\frac{1}{2}v}}\sin a\rho \sqrt{\tfrac{1}{2}}v\, dv}{\sqrt{v^2 - 1}} \quad (2),$$

which form shows that the solution assumed vanishes at infinity. In order to examine its value near the origin, we employ an expansion of the function K given by H. Weber,[2] first in a series of Bessel's functions, then of powers of ρ, and thus obtain

$$z = \frac{a^2 P}{2\pi s}\left\{ \frac{a^2\rho^2}{2^2}\log a\rho - \frac{a^6\rho^6}{2^2\, 4^2\,.\,6^2}(\log a\rho - \tfrac{5}{6}) + \dots \right.$$

$$+ \frac{\pi}{4}\left(1 - \frac{a^4\rho^4}{2^2\,.\,4^2} + \frac{a^8\rho^8}{2^2\,.\,4^2\,.\,6^2\,.\,8^2} - \dots\right) \quad (3).$$

$$\left. - (1 + \log 2 - C)\left(\frac{a^2\rho^2}{2^2} - \frac{a^6\rho^6}{2^2\,.\,4^2\,.\,6^2} + \dots\right) \right\}$$

[1] Heine, *Handbuch der Kugelfunktionen*, vol. i. p. 192, 1878.
[2] *l.c.* p. 244. The sign of C is wrongly quoted here.

C is equal to ·57721. The rows are so arranged that each horizontal row by itself represents a particular integral of the given differential equation. This form shows that z remains finite when $\rho = 0$; further, the integral over a small circular area surrounding the origin is

$$\int \nabla^4 z \, dw = 2\pi \int \rho \nabla^4 z \, d\rho = 2\pi \mathrm{L}t \left(\rho \frac{\partial \nabla^2 z}{\partial \rho} \right)_0 = \frac{a^4}{s} \mathrm{P}.$$

Hence the integral considered is the required one; at the same time the form (3) is one very suitable for the numerical calculation of z for small values of ρ. For large values we use a semi-convergent series which one gets from (2) by expanding the root and integrating the separate terms, and whose first terms are

$$z = \frac{a^2 \mathrm{P}}{2\pi s} \sqrt{\frac{\pi}{2}} \frac{e^{-a\rho\sqrt{\frac{1}{4}}}}{\sqrt{a\rho}} \Big\{ \sin \left(a\rho \sqrt{\tfrac{1}{2}} + \frac{\pi}{8} \right)$$

$$- \frac{1}{8\rho} \sin \left(a\rho \sqrt{\tfrac{1}{2}} + \frac{3\pi}{8} \right) + \dots \Big\} \qquad (4).$$

The solution can be expressed in several additional forms. We shall interpret the above in the following remarks.

1. At the place where the weight is put, the indentation of the plate has its greatest value $z = z_0 = a^2 \mathrm{P}/8s$. The plate rises from there in all directions towards the level zero; at first slowly, then faster, then again more slowly. At the distance $\rho = a$, $z = ·646 z_0$; for $\rho = 2a$, $z = ·258 z_0$; for $\rho = 3a$, $z = ·066 z_0$. Near the distance $\rho = \frac{7}{8}\pi \sqrt{2} a = 3·887a$, z changes sign and thus the plate appears raised into a ridge round the central depression. But it is extraordinary that at further distances from the origin ridges and hollows follow each other with the period $\pi \sqrt{2} . a$. The plate is thrown into a series of circular waves; it is true that they diminish so rapidly in height as we go outwards that we need not wonder at being unable to see them without special arrangements. The quantity a, which is characteristic of the system of waves, is a length. To calculate it for the case of ice floating on water, we notice that $s = 10^{-6} \mathrm{kg/mm^3}$; μ can be taken as $\frac{1}{4}$; and,

according to Reusch,[1] E is equal to 236 kg/mm². We thus obtain for different thicknesses h—

$$h = 10 \qquad 20 \qquad 50 \qquad 100 \qquad 200 \text{ mm.}$$
$$a = 0\text{·}38 \qquad 0\text{·}64 \qquad 1\text{·}27 \qquad 2\text{·}14 \qquad 3\text{·}60 \text{ m.,}$$

whence we easily get the depression produced by 100 kg.

$$z_0 = 86\text{·}4 \qquad 30\text{·}5 \qquad 7\text{·}72 \qquad 2\text{·}73 \qquad 0\text{·}96 \text{ mm.}$$

2. The strain produced in the plate depends on the second differential coefficients of z with respect to x and y; hence it becomes infinite at the origin. This shows that the greatest strain cannot be found without a knowledge of the distribution of the weight. We shall calculate the maximum tension in the simple case when the weight P is uniformly distributed over a circular area of radius R, where R is supposed small compared with a. For this purpose we calculate $\nabla^2 z_0$ at the origin. If we call the distance from the origin of the element at which dP rests ρ, then the portion of $\nabla^2 z_0$ due to this element is, by equation (3),

$$\frac{a^4 d\text{P}}{2\pi s} (\log a\rho - \log 2 + \text{C}), \cdot$$

where the terms which vanish with ρ have been neglected. A simple integration now gives

$$\nabla^2 z_0 = 2\frac{\partial^2 z}{\partial x^2} = 2\frac{\partial^2 z}{\partial y^2} = \frac{a^4 \text{P}}{2\pi s} (\log a\text{R} - \tfrac{1}{2} - \log 2 + \text{C})$$

$$= \frac{a^4 \text{P}}{2\pi s} (\log a\text{R} - 0\text{·}6519).$$

The maximum tension at the centre of the curved plate is $p = (\text{E}h/2)\partial^2 z/\partial x^2$; by forming the expression for p and substituting for a^4 its value we find

$$p = \frac{3(1 - \mu^2)\text{P}}{2\pi h^2} (\log a\text{R} - 0\text{·}6519).$$

It would be a mistake to attempt to apply this formula even when R is of the order of the thickness of the plate or

[1] Reusch, *Wied. Ann.* 9, p. 329, 1880.

smaller still. In this case the pressure inside the plate will still be distributed over a circular area whose diameter is approximately equal to the thickness of the plate. We may roughly represent the case when the weight is as far as possible concentrated at a point by making R equal $\frac{1}{2}h$ in the preceding formula; thus we get for the greatest tension which the weight P can produce at all in the plate

$$p = \frac{3(1 - \mu^2)\mathrm{P}}{2\pi h^2}\left(\log\frac{h}{a} - 1\cdot3090\right).$$

For example, in the case of the plates of ice just considered, we get for a weight of 100 kg. the values

$$p = 221, 53, 8\cdot1, 1\cdot9, 0\cdot47 \text{ kg/cm}^2.$$

The plate 100 mm. thick would certainly bear the weight, that 50 mm. thick probably not.

3. The force with which the water buoys up the weight owing to its deformation is

$$2\pi\int_0^\infty sz\rho\,d\rho = -\frac{2\pi s}{a^4}\int_0^\infty \nabla^4 z \cdot \rho\,d\rho = -\mathrm{P},$$

and is therefore equal to the load applied. However great the load, it will always be supported; the force with which the plane unloaded plate is buoyed up is immaterial. If we place a small circular disc of stiff paper on the surface of water, we may put at its centre a load of several hundred grammes, although the force buoying up the paper alone is but a few grammes. Hence when a man floats ou top of a large sheet of ice, it is in strictness more correct to say that he floats because by his weight he has hollowed the ice into a very shallow boat, than to say that he floats because the ice is light enough to support him in addition to its own weight. For he would float just as well if the ice were no lighter than the water; and if instead of the man we placed weights as large as we pleased upon the ice, they might break through, but could never sink with the ice. The limit of the load depends on the strength, not on the density of the ice. The case is different when men or weights are uniformly distributed over the surface, or when the radius of the plate is not very large, that is, not many times a.

4. If we consider the latter case, that of a finite plate, more closely, we get the above-mentioned paradoxical result. For the free edge of the circular plate these conditions[1] must hold

$$(a) \quad \nabla^2 z - \frac{1-\mu}{\rho} \frac{\partial z}{\partial \rho} = 0, \qquad (b) \quad \frac{\partial}{\partial \rho} \nabla^2 z = 0.$$

At the centre we have the same condition as before. The solution is to be compounded of the three integrals of the equation $\nabla^4 z + a^4 z = 0$, which are finite at the origin; and is completely determined by the given conditions. According as at the edge of the plate z is negative or positive, that is, according as the edge is above or below the surface of the water, the plate will or will not float without further aids (without buoyancy of its own). The case (c) when $z = 0$ at the edge, is a limiting case. When we enquire under what conditions the equations (a) (b) (c) are simultaneously possible, we are led to the vanishing of a determinant involving the radius of the plate as the unknown. This determinant in fact vanishes for certain values of R, and with a little patience we find that the least value of R for which this occurs lies between $2 \cdot 5a$ and $2 \cdot 8a$. It is equal to $2 \cdot 5a$ when $\mu = 0$, and to $2 \cdot 8a$ when $\mu = \frac{1}{2}$. If we suppose the plate to be of the same density as water, then, so long as the radius is less than the above value, for every load the edge must be below the surface of the water in the position of equilibrium, and the plate will be unable to support even the slightest load. When the radius just has the critical value, then for every load the edge is at the surface of the water, and thus the plate suddenly becomes able to support every weight which does not exceed the elastic limit. When the radius is still larger, z is negative at the edge and we can now distribute a certain additional weight uniformly over the plate without lowering the edge below the surface of the water; *i.e.* we may suppose the plate somewhat heavier than water to begin with. If we suppose such a plate, which by itself could not float, to be loaded at the centre with a sufficient weight and

[1] Clebsch, *Theorie der Elasticität*, § 73.

then placed on the surface of the water, it will float.   The
certainty with which it floats is increased by adding more
weight at the centre, it is diminished by removing weights
from the centre ; and if in this removal we exceed a certain
limit, floating will cease to be possible and the plate will sink
together with the remaining weights.

ON THE RELATIONS BETWEEN MAXWELL'S FUNDAMENTAL ELECTROMAGNETIC EQUATIONS AND THE FUNDAMENTAL EQUATIONS OF THE OPPOSING ELECTROMAGNETICS.

(*Wiedemann's Annalen*, **23**, pp. 84-103, 1884.)

WHEN Ampère heard of Oerstedt's discovery that the electric current sets a magnetic needle in motion, he suspected that electric currents would exhibit moving forces between themselves. Clearly his train of reasoning was somewhat as follows :—The current exerts magnetic force, for a magnetic pole moves when submitted to the action of the current ; and the current is set in motion by magnetic forces, for by the principle of action and reaction a current-carrier will also move under the influence of a magnet. Unless we make the improbable assumption that different kinds of magnetic force exist, a current-carrier must also move under the action of the magnetic forces which a second current exerts, and thus the interaction between currents follows.

The essential step in this reasoning is the assumption that only *one* kind of magnetic force exists; that therefore the magnetic forces exerted by currents are in all their effects equivalent to equal and equally directed forces produced by magnetic poles. But this assumption is well known to be sufficient to deduce not only the existence but also the precise magnitude of the electromagnetic actions of closed currents from their magnetic actions. Whether Ampère actually started from this principle or not, he certainly stated it at the close of his investigations when he reduced the action of magnets directly to the action of supposed closed currents. At a

later stage the principle was hardly mentioned, but was taken
for granted as self-evident.   After the discovery of the electric
forces exerted by variable currents or moving magnets, a similar
principle was added relative to these electric forces, and this,
too, was not definitely expressed.   It has perhaps nowhere
been explicitly stated that the electric forces, which have their
origin in inductive actions, are in every way equivalent to
equal and equally directed electric forces of electrostatic origin ;
but this principle is the necessary presupposition and conclusion
of the chief notions which we have formed of electromagnetic
phenomena generally.   According to Faraday's idea the electric
field exists in space independently of and without reference to
the method of its production ; whatever therefore be the cause
which has produced an electric field, the actions which the
field produces are always the same.   On the other hand, by
those physicists who favour Weber's and similar views, electrostatic and electromagnetic actions are represented as special
cases of one and the same action-at-a-distance emanating from
electric particles.   The statement that these forces are special
cases of a more general force would be without meaning if we
admitted that they could differ otherwise than in direction
and magnitude, that is, according to nature and method of
action.   But, apart from all theory, the assumption we are
speaking of is implicitly made in most electric calculations;
it has never been directly rejected, and may thus be regarded
as one of the fundamental ideas of all existing electromagnetics.
Nevertheless, to my knowledge no one has yet drawn attention
to certain consequences to which it leads, and which will be
developed in what follows.   As premises we in the first place
employ the two principles referred to, which we might desig-
nate as the principle of the unity of electric force and that
of the unity of magnetic force.   These may be regarded as
generally accepted, even if not as self-evident.   In the second
place, we use the principle of the conservation of energy ; that
of action and reaction as applied to systems of closed currents;
that of the superposition of electric and magnetic actions;
and lastly, the well-known laws of the magnetic and electromotive actions of closed currents and of magnets.   The investigation throughout refers to closed currents, even where
this is not specially stated.

1. Suppose a ring-magnet, whose cross-section we shall for simplicity take as small compared with its other dimensions, to lose its magnetism.   Then it will exert a force on all electricity in its neighbourhood which causes this electricity to circulate round the body of the magnet.   The magnitude of this force is proportional to the rate of loss of magnetisation, and may be constant during a short but finite time, if during this time the magnetisation diminishes at a constant rate.   The distribution of force in space is precisely the same as that which would be produced by a current flowing in the body of the magnet.   Like the latter the electric force considered has a potential which is many-valued, and, apart from its multiplicity, is the same as that due to an electric double layer of uniform moment bounded by the axis of the magnet. The potential of the ring-magnet on an electric pole can, apart from its multiplicity, be represented by the potential of the double layer on the pole; or, taking the multiplicity into account, it can be represented by the solid angle subtended by the magnet at the pole, multiplied by a suitable constant.

Now this potential determines the action of the magnet on the pole as well as of the pole on the magnet.   If we have not a single pole but a whole system of electric charges, the potential of the diminishing magnetisation on it can be found by a simple summation.   In particular, when the electric forces which act on the ring-magnet are due, not to electric charges, but to a second ring-magnet of diminishing moment, their distribution is the same as if they were due to an electric double layer.   Hence, according to our assumption of the unity of electric force, interaction occurs between our two ring-magnets of diminishing moment; and the potential determining this interaction is the mutual potential of two electric double layers which are bounded by the bodies of the magnets. As in electromagnetics the mutual potential of two magnetic double layers is reduced to an integral to be taken along their boundaries, so here we can bring into the same form the potential of the electric layers, that is, of the two magnets of diminishing moment.   We thus find that this potential is the product of the factor [1] A^2 of the rates of diminution of the

---

[1] A is, as usual, the reciprocal of the velocity of light. We get this factor by a quantitative investigation of the case which above is only considered qualitatively. *Cf.* in this respect paragraph 2, p. 278.

moments of the magnets per unit length measured in electro-magnetic units, and of the integral $\int (\cos \epsilon / r) \, de \, de'$, where de, de' denote elements of the axes of the magnets, ϵ the inclination of these elements to one another.

The potential thus determined is of the same form as the mutual potential of electric currents, and therefore represents the same actions. Two ring-magnets, which are placed close together and side by side, will attract each other at the moment when they both lose their magnetism, if they are magnetised in the same direction ; they will repel each other if oppositely magnetised. In the usual [1] electromagnetics this action is missing. To describe it more simply we shall introduce a new name. We call the change of magnetic polarisation a magnetic current, and take as unit that magnetic current intensity which corresponds to unit change per unit time of the polarisation per unit volume measured in absolute magnetic units. So far as we can conclude from the phenomena of unipolar induction as yet known, magnetic poles distributed continuously along a closed curve and moving along it exert the same electromagnetic action at outside points as a ring-magnet coinciding with that curve and of suitably changing moment. If this relation can be looked upon as true in general, the name "magnetic current" includes all the different cases of magnetism in motion ; and we may speak of constant magnetic currents just as we speak of constant electric currents. But here that name is only to be regarded as a simple contraction for "changing polarisation." Our result may now be stated in this form :—Magnetic currents act on each other according to the same laws as electric currents ; in absolute magnitude the action between magnetic currents of S magnetic units is equal to that between electric currents of S electrical units. This theorem may not be capable of experimental verification. It may be possible to show that electrically charged bodies are set in motion by a ring-magnet whose moment is diminishing ; perhaps even that the magnet itself is turned by electrostatic force so that its plane sets itself

---

[1] By usual I mean, here and in what follows, that electromagnetics which regards the forces deduced from Neumann's laws of the potential as exactly applicable, even when we consider the attraction of variable currents. Every such system of electromagnetics is necessarily opposed to Maxwell's.

normally to that force; but even with very powerful electrostatic forces these actions will lie at the limits of observation,
and hence it is hopeless to expect to see a ring-magnet set itself
under the action of the weak forces produced by a second ring-
magnet when the moments of both are diminishing.

But our premises permit of our drawing further inferences
It is known that a knowledge of the mutual electromagnetic
potential of two currents, together with the principle of the
conservation of energy, enables us to predict the existence and
absolute value of the inductive action.   Similar conclusions
may be drawn for magnetic circuits (rings of soft iron).   A
determinate expenditure of work is necessary to maintain in
such a circuit a magnetic current, which we may suppose to
be alternating.   If the amount of this work were the same,
whether the magnet were at rest free from any electrical
influence, or did work in moving through the electric field,
nothing could be simpler than the infinite production of work
from this motion.   Hence such an independence is impossible.
The work done must depend on the nature and velocity of the
circuit's motion and on the changes in the electric field; and
thus the magnetic (magnetomotive) force which produces this
uniform current must also depend upon these circumstances.
This may be expressed by saying that a magnetic force,
produced by the motion and the changes in the field, is super-
imposed upon the magnetic forces due to other causes; this
added force we may describe as induced.   Its magnitude is
given by the condition that for any displacement whatever of
the circuit the external work done in this displacement must
be compensated by an equal additional amount of work which
in consequence of the displacement must be done in the
circuit.   This reasoning is in form the same as that used to
deduce the inductive actions in electric circuits; and since
also the forces between magnetic circuits are of the same form
as those between electric circuits, the final result must in form
be the same in both cases.   In the laws of electric induction
we need only interchange the words " electric " and " magnetic "
throughout in order to obtain the inductive actions in
magnetic circuits.   Thus we find that a plane magnetic
circuit, e.g., a plane ring of soft iron, whose plane is perpendicular to the lines of force in an electric field, is traversed by

a magnetising force at the instant when the intensity of the field is reduced to zero; and that the same ring is subject to an alternating polarisation when we turn it about an axis which is perpendicular to the direction of the electric force. It does not appear impossible that such actions may become capable of experimental detection. Again, a ring-magnet whose polarisation is continually changing its direction must by induction call forth alternating polarisations in all neighbouring iron rings; but this action is certainly too small to reach an observable value.

2. It may at first sight seem as if the actions here deduced from generally accepted premises permitted of incorporation without disturbance into the usual system of electromagnetics; but this is not the case. In fact, suppose that in place of the ring-magnets so far considered we have endless electric solenoids, in which the current-intensity is variable; then the induced electric forces produced by these solenoids are certainly quite analogous to those exerted by the variable magnets. From these latter forces we deduced magneto-dynamic attractions, and we must therefore infer corresponding electrodynamic attractions between the variable solenoids. But as long as the currents in them are constant no action takes place. Hence in general the electromagnetic attraction between currents must depend on their variations and not merely on their momentary intensities. This statement is in opposition to an assumption uniformly accepted in the usual electromagnetics.[1] The correction which must be made in the laws of the magnetic actions of constant currents to make them applicable to variable currents may be calculated from our premises. But this correction requires, on account of the principle of the conservation of energy, a correction in the induced electrical forces as well. This again requires a second correction in the magnetic forces, and so on; so that we obtain an infinite series of successive approximations. We shall now calculate these separate terms. We assume that they are simply to be added to the total result, and that, if only the infinite sums converge to definite limits, then these limiting values are those corresponding to the

---

[1] *Cf.* v. Helmholtz, "Über die Theorie der Elektrodynamik," *Wissenschaftliche Abhandlungen*, vol. i. p. 729.

actual case.   In the calculation we use the following special notation. $\bar{u}$ is to denote a function U for which throughout infinitely extended space $\nabla^2 U = -4\pi u$; hence generally

$$U = \bar{u} = \int \frac{u}{r}\, d\tau,$$

the integral being taken throughout all space.

As regards the electric currents, let u, v, w be the components.   As we only consider closed circuits we have

$$\frac{\partial u}{\partial x} + \frac{\partial v}{\partial y} + \frac{\partial w}{\partial z} = 0.$$

Further let $U_1 = \bar{u}$, $V_1 = \bar{v}$, $W_1 = \bar{w}$.   Then the components L_1 M_1 N_1 of the magnetic force exerted by the currents are, according to the usual electromagnetics, given by the equations

$$L_1 = A\left(\frac{\partial V_1}{\partial z} - \frac{\partial W_1}{\partial y}\right)$$

$$M_1 = A\left(\frac{\partial W_1}{\partial x} - \frac{\partial U_1}{\partial z}\right), \quad \frac{\partial U_1}{\partial x} + \frac{\partial V_1}{\partial y} + \frac{\partial W_1}{\partial z} = 0 \quad (1).$$

$$N_1 = A\left(\frac{\partial U_1}{\partial y} - \frac{\partial V_1}{\partial x}\right)$$

From the existence of these forces, and from the principle of the conservation of energy, it may be, and has been, concluded that changes of u, v, w produce electrical forces whose components X_1 Y_1 Z_1 are

$$X_1 = -A^2\frac{dU_1}{dt}, \quad Y_1 = -A^2\frac{dV_1}{dt}, \quad Z_1 = -A^2\frac{dW_1}{dt} \quad (2).$$

These expressions hold good inside the conductors conveying the currents u, v, w as well as for the space outside.   The forces (2) have been deduced from the forces (1) on the assumption that the latter were due to electric currents.   But on account of our premises we may affirm that even if the forces (1) are caused by any system whatever of variable currents and variable magnets, then their variation must equally give rise to the forces (2).   Let A denote the system which produces the forces (1).   We superpose a system B

consisting only of electric currents which still neutralises the
forces of system A everywhere.   Such a system is possible;
we need only choose as current-components u, v, w where
$4\pi u = \nabla^2 U_1$, $4\pi v = \nabla^2 V_1$, $4\pi w = \nabla^2 W_1$.   If we now move
electric currents about under the action of both systems A and
B, there is no work done in this motion.   Hence the electromotive force necessary to maintain the currents must be
independent of the motion, so that the induced electromotive
force is zero.   But the system B by itself exerts inductive
actions; hence the system A must exert inductive actions
equal and opposite to those of B, and therefore equal to
those of a purely electrical system which exerts the same
magnetic forces as A.   What is true of inductive actions due
to motion must also be true of those due to variations of
intensity; both are most simply determined in terms of each
other by the principle of the conservation of energy.   Hence
from the existence of magnetic forces of the form (1) we may
directly infer that of electric forces of the form (2), whatever
may be the origin of those magnetic forces.

Let us now consider magnetic currents.   Let λ, μ, ν be
the components of magnetisation throughout space, and let

$$\frac{\partial \lambda}{\partial x} + \frac{\partial \mu}{\partial y} + \frac{\partial \nu}{\partial z} = 0, \text{ and } \Lambda = \bar{\lambda}, \text{ M} = \bar{\mu}, \text{ N} = \bar{\nu}.$$

These quantities are to be measured in absolute magnetic
units.   It follows from the forces (1) by the principle of the
conservation of energy, and is indeed generally accepted in
electromagnetics, that the electric force produced by variations
of λ, μ, ν has for components

$$X_1 = A \frac{d}{dt}\left(\frac{\partial N}{\partial y} - \frac{\partial M}{\partial z}\right), \quad Y_1 = A \frac{d}{dt}\left(\frac{\partial \Lambda}{\partial z} - \frac{\partial N}{\partial x}\right),$$

$$Z_1 = A \frac{d}{dt}\left(\frac{\partial M}{\partial x} - \frac{\partial \Lambda}{\partial y}\right).^1$$

We now put, in accordance with our notation,

$$p = \frac{d\lambda}{dt}, \quad q = \frac{d\mu}{dt}, \quad r = \frac{d\nu}{dt},$$

---

[1] *Cf.* v. Helmholtz, *Wissenschaftliche Abhandlungen*, vol. i. p. 619.

and call p, q, r the components of the magnetic current. Further we put $P_1 = \bar{p}$, $Q_1 = \bar{q}$, $R_1 = \bar{r}$ and call P_1, Q_1, R_1 the components of the vector-potential of this current. Then the electric forces produced by the magnetic current are

$$X_1 = A\left(\frac{\partial R_1}{\partial y} - \frac{\partial Q_1}{\partial z}\right)$$

$$Y_1 = A\left(\frac{\partial P_1}{\partial z} - \frac{\partial R_1}{\partial x}\right), \quad \frac{\partial P_1}{\partial x} + \frac{\partial Q_1}{\partial y} + \frac{\partial R_1}{\partial z} = 0 \qquad (3).$$

$$Z_1 = A\left(\frac{\partial Q_1}{\partial x} - \frac{\partial P_1}{\partial y}\right)$$

The reasoning which allows us to infer from the forces (1) that the mutual potential of two electric current-systems u_1, v_1, w_1 and u_2, v_2, w_2 has the form

$$A^2\int\int \frac{1}{r}(u_1u_2 + v_1v_2 + w_1w_2)d\tau_1 d\tau_2,$$

leads to the conclusion, using forces (3), that the magnetic current-systems p_1, q_1, r_1 and p_2, q_2, r_2 have the mutual potential

$$A^2\int\int \frac{1}{r}(p_1p_2 + q_1q_2 + r_1r_2)d\tau_1 d\tau_2.$$

The same considerations which led us from that potential of electric currents to the inductive forces (2) allow us from the potential of magnetic currents to infer the existence of induced magnetic forces of the form

$$L_1 = -A^2\frac{dP_1}{dt}, \quad M_1 = -A^2\frac{dQ_1}{dt}, \quad N_1 = -A^2\frac{dR_1}{dt} \qquad (4).$$

Here also we may affirm that these forces act inside the magnetic bodies as well as in the space outside; and we easily convince ourselves that we cannot well confine the connection between the force (3) and (4) to the case where the forces (3) are due to magnetic currents alone. We must conclude that when a system of currents or magnets gives rise to electrical forces of the form (3), then a variation of this system will give rise to magnetic forces of the form (4).

So far we have merely repeated in precise form the results of the preceding paragraph. We now go further and conclude that a system of variable currents exerts electric forces of the form (2). These may be represented in the form (3). Hence unless they are constant they will give rise to magnetic forces of form (4). And these must be added as a correction to the known magnetic forces of form (1). To arrive at the expression of the forces (2) in the form (3) we put

$$- A^2 \frac{dU_1}{dt} = A\left(\frac{\partial R}{\partial y} - \frac{\partial Q}{\partial z}\right),$$

$$- A^2 \frac{dV_1}{dt} = A\left(\frac{\partial P}{\partial z} - \frac{\partial R}{\partial x}\right),$$

$$- A^2 \frac{dW_1}{dt} = A\left(\frac{\partial Q}{\partial x} - \frac{\partial P}{\partial y}\right).$$

Assuming for the present that

$$\frac{\partial P}{\partial x} + \frac{\partial Q}{\partial y} + \frac{\partial R}{\partial z} = 0 \qquad (a)$$

we get, by differentiating the second equation with respect to z, the third with respect to y, and subtracting the results,

$$- A \frac{d}{dt}\left(\frac{\partial V_1}{\partial z} - \frac{\partial W_1}{\partial y}\right) = \nabla^2 P,$$

and thence

$$P = \frac{1}{4\pi} A \frac{d}{dt}\left(\frac{\partial}{\partial z}\overline{V}_1 - \frac{\partial}{\partial y}\overline{W}_1\right).$$

We get similar expressions for Q and R. It is easy to see that these satisfy the equation (a); and the assumption of the truth of this equation is justified.

From the values of P, Q, R follow the magnetic forces produced by their variation. The x-component is

$$- A^2 \frac{dP}{dt} = - \frac{1}{4\pi} A^3 \frac{d^2}{dt^2}\left(\frac{\partial}{\partial z}\overline{V}_1 - \frac{\partial}{\partial y}\overline{W}_1\right).$$

This term we must add to the component L_1 of the previously assumed magnetic force. Let us call the component thus

XVII FUNDAMENTAL EQUATIONS OF ELECTROMAGNETICS 283

corrected L_2 and form the similarly corrected components M_2, N_2; then these forces may be represented by the system

$$L_2 = A\left(\frac{\partial V_2}{\partial z} - \frac{\partial W_2}{\partial y}\right),$$

$$M_2 = A\left(\frac{\partial W_2}{\partial x} - \frac{\partial U_2}{\partial z}\right), \quad \frac{\partial U_2}{\partial x} + \frac{\partial V_2}{\partial y} + \frac{\partial W_2}{\partial z} = 0 \qquad (5),$$

$$N_2 = A\left(\frac{\partial U_2}{\partial y} - \frac{\partial V_2}{\partial x}\right),$$

where we have put

$$U_2 = U_1 - \frac{1}{4\pi}A^2\frac{d^2}{dt^2}\overline{U}_1, \quad V_2 = V_1 - \frac{1}{4\pi}A^2\frac{d^2}{dt^2}\overline{V}_1,$$

$$W_2 = W_1 - \frac{1}{4\pi}A^2\frac{d^2}{dt^2}\overline{W}_1.$$

From what precedes we may at once conclude that the electromotive forces produced by a variation of the current-system no longer have exactly the form (2), but have these corrected values

$$X_2 = -A^2\frac{dU_2}{dt}, \quad Y_2 = -A^2\frac{dV_2}{dt}, \quad Z_2 = -A^2\frac{dW_2}{dt} \qquad (6).$$

Exactly similar reasoning compels us to correct the actions of magnetic systems presented by the equations (3) and (4). The results may be represented by the following sample equations

$$X_2 = A\left(\frac{\partial R_2}{\partial y} - \frac{\partial Q_2}{\partial z}\right), \text{ etc.} \qquad (7),$$

$$L_2 = -A^2\frac{dP_2}{dt}, \text{ etc.} \qquad (8),$$

where $\qquad P_2 = P_1 - \frac{1}{4\pi}A^2\frac{d^2}{dt^2}\overline{P}_1$, etc.

If we wish to represent the forces by which the corrected equations (5) and (7) differ from the usually accepted ones (1) and (3), as distinct from these latter in nature, we need only form a system of electric or magnetic currents in which the forces (1) or (3), as the case may be, are zero. Any endless electric or magnetic solenoid will serve as an example.

We see at once that we cannot regard the result obtained as final. Indeed we deduced forces (5) from forces (2); but now the forces (2) have been found inexact and have been replaced by the forces (6). Hence we must repeat our reasoning with these latter forces. The result is easily seen; we obtain it if we everywhere replace the index 2 by 3 and put

$$U_3 = U_1 - \frac{A^2}{4\pi} \frac{d^2}{dt^2} \overline{U}_2 = U_1 - \frac{A^2}{4\pi} \frac{d^2}{dt^2}\overline{U}_1 + \frac{A^4}{16\pi^2} \frac{d^4}{dt^4}\overline{\overline{U}}_1,$$

and similar expressions for the other components of the vector-potential. The terms in A^5 which here appear in the expressions for the magnetic forces of electric currents, and the electric forces of magnetic currents, may be perceived apart from the terms of lower order. We need only take an ordinary electric or magnetic solenoid, which may be called a solenoid of the first order, and roll it up into a solenoid which may be called a solenoid of the second order, in order to get a system in which the forces here calculated are the largest of those occurring. From the consideration of such solenoids we may demonstrate the existence of the separate terms, independently of the fact of our admitting or not admitting that they are simply added together to give the final result.

Our reasoning prevents us from stopping at any stage and constantly adds, as before, more and more terms, thus leading to an infinite series. To represent the final result we denote by L, M, N, X, Y, Z the completely corrected forces and obtain

$$L = A\left(\frac{\partial V}{\partial z} - \frac{\partial W}{\partial y}\right) \qquad X = -A^2\frac{dU}{dt}$$

$$M = A\left(\frac{\partial W}{\partial x} - \frac{\partial U}{\partial z}\right) \text{ (9)}, \qquad Y = -A^2\frac{dV}{dt} \qquad \text{(10)}.$$

$$N = A\left(\frac{\partial U}{\partial y} - \frac{\partial V}{\partial x}\right) \qquad Z = -A^2\frac{dW}{dt}$$

where we now have for U, V, W

$$U = \bar{u} - \frac{A^2}{4\pi} \frac{d^2}{dt^2}\overline{\bar{u}} + \frac{A^4}{16\pi^2} \frac{d^4}{dt^4}\overline{\overline{\bar{u}}} - \ldots$$

$$V = \bar{v} - \frac{A^2}{4\pi} \frac{d^2}{dt^2}\overline{\bar{v}} + \frac{A^4}{16\pi^2} \frac{d^4}{dt^4}\overline{\overline{\bar{v}}} - \ldots$$

$$W = \bar{w} - \frac{A^2}{4\pi} \frac{d^2}{dt^2}\overline{\bar{w}} + \frac{A^4}{16\pi^2} \frac{d^4}{dt^4}\overline{\overline{\bar{w}}} - \ldots$$

$$\frac{\partial U}{\partial x} + \frac{\partial V}{\partial y} + \frac{\partial W}{\partial z} = 0.$$

Corresponding equations hold for the magnetic currents. If the series are convergent, there is no reason to doubt that they give us the true values. But in general they will converge. For let us consider that element of the integral U which is due to the current u in a certain element of space. We resolve this current into a series of simple harmonic functions of the time and suppose $u_0 \sin nt$ to be the term involving $\sin nt$. Then the element of U due to this term will be given by the equation

$$dU = d\tau \frac{u_0 \sin nt}{r}\left(1 - \frac{1}{1 \cdot 2} \frac{A^2}{4\pi}n^2 r^2 \right.$$

$$\left. + \frac{1}{1 \cdot 2 \cdot 3 \cdot 4} \frac{A^4}{16\pi^2}n^4 r^4 + \ldots\right).$$

This series converges to a limit easily found. If n and r are not very large, then every term after the first few will be infinitesimal compared with the preceding one. Hence also the integral of the elements of U will have a determinate value. Since the same is true of V, W, P, Q, and R, we may expect to find, in the equations (9) (10) and the corresponding ones for magnetic currents, a system of forces in complete agreement with all our requirements.

3. It is obvious that this system may be represented, or in technical terms described, more simply than by the equations (9) and (10). By these equations we have

$$\nabla^2 U = - 4\pi u + A^2 \frac{d^2}{dt^2}\bar{u} - \ldots$$

and

$$A^2\frac{d^2U}{dt^2} = A^2\frac{d^2}{dt^2}\overline{u} - \quad \cdot \,,$$

hence

$$\nabla^2 U - A^2\frac{d^2U}{dt^2} = -4\pi u.$$

The other components of the vector-potentials, both of electric and magnetic currents, satisfy analogous differential equations. Since u, v, w, p, q, r vanish in empty space, the distribution of these potentials is there given by the equations

$$\nabla^2 U - A^2\frac{d^2U}{dt^2} = 0, \qquad\qquad \nabla^2 P - A^2\frac{d^2P}{dt^2} = 0$$

$$\nabla^2 V - A^2\frac{d^2V}{dt^2} = 0, \qquad\qquad \nabla^2 Q - A^2\frac{d^2Q}{dt^2} = 0$$

$$\nabla^2 W - A^2\frac{d^2W}{dt^2} = 0, \qquad\qquad \nabla^2 R - A^2\frac{d^2R}{dt^2} = 0$$

$$\frac{\partial U}{\partial x} + \frac{\partial V}{\partial y} + \frac{\partial W}{\partial z} = 0, \qquad\qquad \frac{\partial P}{\partial x} + \frac{\partial Q}{\partial y} + \frac{\partial R}{\partial z} = 0$$

$$(11).$$

The vector-potentials now show themselves to be quantities which are propagated with finite velocity—the velocity of light —and indeed according to the same laws as the vibrations of light and of radiant heat. Riemann in 1858 and Lorenz in 1867, with a view to associating optical and electrical phenomena with one another, postulated the same or quite similar laws for the propagation of the potentials. These investigators recognised that these laws involve the addition of new terms to the forces which actually occur in electromagnetics; and they justify this by pointing out that these new terms are too small to be experimentally observable. But we see that the addition of these terms is far from needing any apology. Indeed their absence would necessarily involve a contradiction of principles which are quite generally accepted.

The vector-potentials of electric and magnetic currents have hitherto occurred as quite separate, and from them the electric and magnetic forces were deduced in an unsymmetric manner. This contrast between the two kinds of forces disappears as soon as we attempt to determine the propagation of these forces themselves, *i.e.* as soon as we eliminate the vector-potentials from the equations. This may be performed by differentiating equations (9) with respect to t and removing the differential coefficients of U, V, W with respect to t by equations (10). It may also be performed by differentiating equations (10) with respect to t, remembering that, *e.g.*

$$A^2\frac{d^2U}{dt^2} = \nabla^2U = \frac{\partial}{\partial y}\left(\frac{\partial U}{\partial y} - \frac{\partial V}{\partial x}\right) - \frac{\partial}{\partial z}\left(\frac{\partial W}{\partial x} - \frac{\partial U}{\partial z}\right),$$

and removing the functions of U, V, W in the brackets by means of equations (9). In this way we get six equations connecting together the values of L, M, N, X, Y, Z in empty space, viz. the following :—

$$A\frac{dL}{dt} = \frac{\partial Z}{\partial y} - \frac{\partial Y}{\partial z}, \qquad A\frac{dX}{dt} = \frac{\partial M}{\partial z} - \frac{\partial N}{\partial y}$$

$$A\frac{dM}{dt} = \frac{\partial X}{\partial z} - \frac{\partial Z}{\partial x}, \qquad A\frac{dY}{dt} = \frac{\partial N}{\partial x} - \frac{\partial L}{\partial z} \qquad (12).$$

$$A\frac{dN}{dt} = \frac{\partial Y}{\partial x} - \frac{\partial X}{\partial y}, \qquad A\frac{dZ}{\partial t} = \frac{\partial L}{\partial y} - \frac{\partial M}{\partial x}$$

These same equations connect together the forces produced by magnetic currents, for they are got by eliminating P, Q, R as well as U, V, W. Hence they connect together the electric and magnetic forces in empty space quite generally, whatever the origin of these forces. The electric and magnetic forces are now interchangeable. If we eliminate first one set and then the other we obtain the following system, which, however, does not completely represent the system (12):—

$$\nabla^2L - A^2\frac{d^2L}{dt^2} = 0, \qquad \nabla^2X - A^2\frac{d^2X}{dt^2} = 0$$

$$\nabla^2M - A^2\frac{d^2M}{dt^2} = 0, \qquad \nabla^2Y - A^2\frac{d^2Y}{dt^2} = 0$$

$$\nabla^2N - A^2\frac{d^2N}{dt^2} = 0, \qquad \nabla^2Z - A^2\frac{d^2Z}{dt^2} = 0 \qquad (13).$$

$$\frac{\partial L}{\partial x} + \frac{\partial M}{\partial y} + \frac{\partial N}{\partial z} = 0, \qquad \frac{X}{\partial x} + \frac{\partial Y}{\partial y} + \frac{\partial Z}{\partial z} = 0$$

Now the system of forces given by the equations (12) and (13) is just that given by Maxwell. Maxwell found it by considering the ether to be a dielectric in which a changing polarisation produces the same effect as an electric current. We have reached it by means of other premises, generally accepted even by opponents of the Faraday-Maxwell view. The equations (12) and (13) appear to us to be a necessary complement of the equations (1), (2), (3), which are usually regarded as exact. From our point of view, the Faraday-Maxwell view does not furnish the basis of the system of equations (12) and (13), although it affords the simplest interpretation of them. In Maxwell's theory the equations (12) and (13) apply not merely to empty space but also to any other dielectric. Starting from our premises we can also show these laws to hold in every homogeneous medium. We must assume the fact as experimentally demonstrated that the magnetic forces which surround a current-system placed in a homogeneous medium are distributed according to the equations (1) in the same way as in empty space. Hence we need only imagine the conductors and masses of iron which we have considered to be completely immersed in the given medium. In this medium we must define the units of electricity and magnetism in the same terms as in empty space. We must then determine the constant A, which gives the absolute value of the magnetic force produced by unit current in the new electrostatic measure. All further forces follow from the assumed experimental fact and the general premises; and since all the propositions are the same as those for empty space, the final result is the same. It is true that the value of the constant A will not be the same as in empty space, and that it will have different values in different media. Its reciprocal is always the velocity of propagation of electric and magnetic changes. It is an internal constant, but the only internal electromagnetic constant of the medium. The two constants of which it is generally built up, viz. the specific inductive capacity and the magnetic permeability, should in contrast to it be termed external constants. Not only the measurement, but even the definition of these latter constants, requires the specification of at least two media (one of which may be empty space).

In what precedes I have attempted to demonstrate the truth of Maxwell's equations by starting from premises which are generally admitted in the opposing system of electromagnetics, and by using propositions which are familiar in it. Consequently I have made use of the conceptions of the latter system ; but, excepting in this connection, the deduction given is in no sense to be regarded as a rigid proof that Maxwell's system is the only possible one. It does not seem possible to deduce such a proof from our premises. The exact may be deduced from the inexact as the most fitting from a given point of view, but never as the necessary.[1] I think, however, that from the preceding we may infer without error that if the choice rests only between the usual system of electromagnetics and Maxwell's, the latter is certainly to be preferred ; and that for the following reasons :—

1. The system of the electromagnetic action of closed currents founded on direct action-at-a-distance is in its present state certainly incomplete. Either it must introduce different kinds of electric force, which it has never done, or it must admit the existence of actions which hitherto it has not taken into account. Maxwell's system does not in the same way contain within itself the proof of its incompleteness.

2. When we attempt to complete the usual system of electromagnetics, we always arrive at laws which are very complicated and very difficult to handle. And either we refuse to admit the accumulated results of paragraph 2, in which case we end with an unfruitful declaration of incompetence ; or, as from the standpoint of the system seems more reasonable, we accept them as being valid, and so arrive at forces which in fact are the same as those demanded by Maxwell's system. But then the latter offers by far the simplest exposition of the results.

[1] The mode in which we have deduced conclusions from the principle of the conservation of energy clearly marks at each stage the point at which our deductions are only the most fitting, and not the necessary ones. This mode is the most fitting from the standpoint of the usual system of electromagnetics, for it corresponds exactly to the accepted proposition in which Helmholtz in 1847 and Sir W. Thomson in 1848 deduced induction from electromagnetic action. But perhaps it may not be the only possible method ; for just as in that proposition, so we have in ours made tacit assumptions besides the principle of the conservation of energy. That proposition also is not valid if we admit the possibility that the motion of metals in the magnetic field may of itself generate heat ; that the resistance of conductors may depend on that motion ; and other such possibilities.

M. P.   U

3. The objections which may perhaps be raised to the further conclusions of paragraph 2 do not apply to the reasoning specially exhibited in paragraph 1, which proved the attraction between magnetic currents. This latter depends directly on the premises : it stands or falls with them alone. But it is sufficient to show the superiority of Maxwell's system ; for it is predicted in the latter, whereas it is unknown in the opposing system.

XVIII

ON THE DIMENSIONS OF MAGNETIC POLE IN DIFFERENT SYSTEMS OF UNITS

(*Wiedemann's Annalen*, **24**, pp. 114-118, 1885.)

Two years ago this subject was discussed in the *Annalen*,[1] and even more vigorously in the *Philosophical Magazine*. In general we may now regard the matter as settled ; but I think there is still one point which admits of a more complete explanation, and as the question is one of principle it is worthy of attention. Between the electromagnetic[2] and electrostatic systems of units there appeared to be a certain discrepancy. In the former there was agreement as to the starting-point, viz. the magnetic pole, and also as to the electrical pole whose dimensions were deduced ; whereas in the latter a difference of opinion was possible, not indeed as to the starting-point, viz. the electrical pole, but as to the magnetic pole deduced from it. Side by side with Maxwell's electrostatic system there appeared that of Clausius. Now even if it is shown that neither of these is necessarily incorrect—that the only question is, which of the two is preferable—there may yet remain in the minds of many physicists a feeling that both of them, and therefore the electrostatic system generally, are inferior to the magnetic system, respecting which no doubt has been raised ;

---

[1] *Cf.* Clausius, *Wied. Ann.* **16**, p. 529, 1882, and **17**, p. 713, 1882 ; v. Helmholtz, *Wied. Ann.* **17**, p. 42 ; also a series of papers in the *Phil. Mag.* (Ser. 5) **13**, and **14**, 1882. [*Phil. Mag.* **13**, pp. 376, 427, 429, 431, 530 ; **14**, 124, 225, 357. Translations of Clausius' two papers will be found in the same journal, **13**, pp. 381-398, and **15**, pp. 79-83 ; and of Helmholtz's paper in **14**, pp. 430-440.—Tr.]

[2] Called by Clausius electrodynamic. [In this volume, as in the *Electric Waves*, "*elektrodynamisch*" is generally rendered as "electromagnetic."—Tr.]

and that by using the latter one may avoid the pitfalls which undoubtedly beset the former. I shall endeavour to show that such a conception would be incorrect, by comparing with the assumptions from which Maxwell and Clausius start two others; theoretically, although not practically, the latter are as well established as the former, and by using them we can make the magnetic and electrostatic systems change places. If these new assumptions had originally been adopted instead of the old ones, there would have been agreement as to the electrostatic system, but discussion as to the magnetic system. This shows clearly *a posteriori* (and the same can be proved *a priori*) that neither of the two systems is in general preferable to the other or more reliable than it; only one of the two may be preferable in a given department of electromagnetics, or more reliable in its application to a given electromagnetic calculation. In a sense it is simply a matter of chance that the discussion arose in connection with the electrostatic and not the magnetic system. I shall compare, as thesis and antithesis, the old and the new assumptions, together with the deductions from them.

The thesis then is :—

(*a*) The work which must be done in order to move a magnetic pole m in a closed path once around a constant electric current, which in the time t conveys the quantity e, is proportional to the strength m of the pole and the strength e/t of the current: it is independent of geometrical relations. If then we put $A = k_1 me/t$, k_1 is a constant whose magnitude and dimensions depend only upon the system of units chosen. Maxwell considers it best to connect electrical and magnetic quantities in such a way that this constant becomes a number of no dimensions. Thus, using the usual notation

$$[m][e] = \mathsf{M L^2 T^{-1}} \qquad (\mathrm{M}).$$

(*b*) The moment $m\delta$ of a magnetic doublet, which for purposes of calculation can be completely replaced by a small circular current, is proportional to the strength e/t of the current and the area f enclosed by it. Hence $m\delta = k_2 ef/t$, where again k_2 is a constant which depends only upon the units chosen. If k_1 is a pure number, k_2 in general will not be so; and conversely. Now Clausius holds that according to Ampère's theory it is necessary to connect magnetic and electrical quantities in such a way that k_2 shall be a number of no dimensions; from which it follows that

$$[m] = [e] \, \mathsf{LT}^{-1} \qquad \text{(C)}.$$

The consequences of the assumptions (M) and (C) are as follows :—

1. In the magnetic system we start with the dimensions $[m] = \mathrm{M}^{\frac{1}{2}}\mathrm{L}^{\frac{3}{2}}\mathrm{T}^{-1}$. From this we deduce, as the dimensions of electric pole,

$\mathrm{M}^{\frac{1}{2}}\mathrm{L}^{\frac{1}{2}}$, according to (M); $\mathrm{M}^{\frac{1}{2}}\mathrm{L}^{\frac{1}{2}}$, according to (C).

Hence there is agreement.

2. In the electrostatic system we start with the dimensions of electric pole $[e] = \mathrm{M}^{\frac{1}{2}}\mathrm{L}^{\frac{3}{2}}\mathrm{T}^{-1}$. From this we deduce, as the dimensions of magnetic pole,

$\mathrm{M}^{\frac{1}{2}}\mathrm{L}^{\frac{1}{2}}$, according to (M); $\mathrm{M}^{\frac{1}{2}}\mathrm{L}^{\frac{3}{2}}\mathrm{T}^{-2}$, according to (C).

The two expressions are different, and this is the objection urged against the electrostatic system.

In setting forth the antithesis I shall make use of the expression "magnetic current."[1]   A constant magnetic current is represented by a wire-shaped ring-magnet which gains or loses equal quantities of magnetism in equal times. For sufficiently short periods we can produce such currents of any desired strength, and for periods of any length if we make them sufficiently weak. The electrical forces exerted by such a current are known, and every system of electromagnetics contains the following propositions, although they may be differently expressed :—

(a) The work which must be done in order to move an electric pole e in a closed path once around a constant magnetic current, which in the time t conveys the quantity m, is proportional to the strength e of the pole and the strength m/t of the current; it is independent of geometrical relations. If then we put $A = k_1' e.m/t$, what has been stated for k_1 and k_2

will hold good for k_1'. Now we may regard it as advantageous, say with respect to the theory of unipolar induction, to take this very equation as the fundamental equation for the connection and to make k_1' a pure number. We thus arrive at the assumption :—

$$[m][e] = \mathsf{M}\mathsf{L}^2\mathsf{T}^{-1} \qquad (\mathrm{M}'),$$

which also coincides with (M).

(b) For purposes of calculation an electrical doublet can be completely replaced by a small magnetic circular current, whose plane is perpendicular to the axis of the doublet. Thus the moment $e\delta$ of the doublet must be proportional to the strength m/t of the current and the area which it embraces. Hence we put $e\delta = k_2'fm/t$. Theoretically there would be nothing wrong—although from the standpoint of present theories and applications it would be unpractical— if we started from this equation and made k_2' a pure number. We should then have :—

$$[e] = [m]\mathsf{L}\mathsf{T}^{-1} \qquad (\mathrm{C}').$$

The consequences of the assumptions (M') and (C') are as follows :—

1. In the magnetic system we still have

$$[m] = \mathsf{M}^{\frac{1}{2}}\mathsf{L}^{\frac{3}{2}}\mathsf{T}^{-1}.$$

Hence the dimensions of electric pole would be deduced as

$\mathsf{M}^{\frac{1}{2}}\mathsf{L}^{\frac{1}{2}}$, according to (M'); $\quad \mathsf{M}^{\frac{1}{2}}\mathsf{L}^{\frac{3}{2}}\mathsf{T}^{-2}$, according to (C').

Thus there is now the inconvenience that in the magnetic system different assumptions lead to different results.

2. In the electrostatic system we still have

$$[e] = \mathsf{M}^{\frac{1}{2}}\mathsf{L}^{\frac{3}{2}}\mathsf{T}^{-1}.$$

Hence in this the dimensions of magnetic pole are

$\mathsf{M}^{\frac{1}{2}}\mathsf{L}^{\frac{1}{2}}$, according to (M'); $\quad \mathsf{M}^{\frac{1}{2}}\mathsf{L}^{\frac{1}{2}}$, according to (C'),

and the electrostatic system has the advantage previously assigned to the magnetic system.

The thesis and antithesis together show that, regarded purely from the standpoint of calculation, neither system has any advantage over the other.   From the practical point of view the forms based upon (M) and (M') have the advantage of being most easily remembered.   If we regard magnetism simply as a phenomenon of electricity in motion, the electrostatic system in the form (C) will appear preferable ; for according to this view it alone renders the physical as well as the mathematical connections.   For my own part I always feel safest from errors of calculation when I use, according to v. Helmholtz's advice,[1] none of these apparently consistent systems, but adhere to what he calls Gauss's system.   This defines the units of electricity and magnetism separately with the same dimensions $[e] = [m] = M^{\frac{1}{2}}L^{\frac{3}{2}}T^{-1}$, and introduces factors with the dimensions whenever electrical and magnetic quantities occur together.

[1] *Wied. Ann.* **17**, p. 48, 1882.   [*Phil. Mag.* (5) **14**, p. 436, 1882.]

XIX

A GRAPHICAL METHOD OF DETERMINING THE ADIABATIC CHANGES OF MOIST AIR

(*Meteorologische Zeitschrift*, 1, pp. 421-431, 1884.)

(With diagram at end of book.)

In the course of theoretical discussions meteorologists frequently have to consider the changes of state which take place in moist air when it is compressed or expanded without any supply of heat. They wish to obtain solutions of such problems as quickly as possible, and do not care to be referred to complicated thermodynamic formulæ. In practice they generally refer to the small but useful table published by Prof. Hann in 1874.[1] But it seems possible to attain greater completeness, with at least equal facility, by using the graphical method, and the accompanying table constitutes an attempt in this direction. It contains nothing theoretically new except in so far as it takes fully into account the peculiar behaviour of moist air at 0^0; this, to the best of my knowledge, has not been treated of before.[2] As the exact formulæ of the problem do not seem to have been collected, I shall state them completely under A. Under B I shall explain how the formulæ are represented in the diagram. Under C I shall explain fully, by means of a numerical example, the use of the diagram (which may be purely mechanical). By following this example

---

[1] Hann, *Zeitschrift der österreichischen Gesellschaft für Meteorologie*, 9, p. 328, 1874.

[2] The editor of the *Met. Zeitschr.* gives a reference to Guldberg and Mohn, *Études sur les mouvements de l'atmosphère*, 1, pp. 9-16, and *Österr. Zeitschrift*, 1878, pp. 117-122. See also the supplementary note on p. 311 of this volume.

with the diagram in hand, we shall be able to judge of its utility and to see how it is used, without needing to wade through the calculations in A and B.

A. Suppose that 1 kilogramme of a mixture of air and water-vapour contains λ parts by weight of dry air, and μ parts by weight of unsaturated water-vapour. Let the pressure of the mixture be p, its absolute temperature T. The question is:—What changes will the mixture undergo as the pressure gradually diminishes to zero without heat being supplied? We must distinguish several stages.

Stage 1. The vapour is unsaturated, and no liquid water is present. We assume that the unsaturated mixture obeys the laws of Gay-Lussac and Boyle. If then e be the partial pressure of the water-vapour, $p - e$ that of the dry air, v the volume of 1 kilogramme of the mixture, we have

$$p - e = \lambda \frac{RT}{v}, \qquad e = \mu \frac{R_1 T}{v},$$

where R, R_1 are constants of known meaning and magnitude. Since the total pressure is the sum of these two values, we get $pv = (\lambda R + \mu R_1)T$, and this is the so-called characteristic equation of the mixture. Further, let c_v denote the specific heat at constant volume of the air, c_v' that of water-vapour; then in order to produce the changes dv and dT, we must supply the dry air with an amount of heat

$$dQ_1 = \lambda \left(c_v dT + ART \frac{dv}{v} \right),$$

and the water-vapour with

$$dQ_2 = \mu \left(c_v' dT + AR_1 T \frac{dv}{v} \right),[1]$$

or both together with the amount of heat

$$dQ = (\lambda c_v + \mu c_v')dT + A(\lambda R + \mu R_1)T \frac{dv}{v}.$$

But this amount of heat vanishes for the change we are considering. In order to integrate the differential equation

[1] Clausius, *Mechanische Wärmethcorie*, vol. i. p. 51, 1876.

resulting from putting $dQ = 0$, we divide it by T.   We know
a priori from the theory of heat that this operation renders
the equation integrable, and we find it confirmed *a posteriori.*
Performing the integration, eliminating v by the characteristic
equation, and remembering that $c_v + AR$ equals c_p the specific
heat at constant pressure,[1] we obtain

$$0 = (\lambda c_p + \mu c_p{}') \log \frac{T}{T_0} - A(\lambda R + \mu R_1) \log \frac{p}{p_0} \qquad (I).$$

The right-hand member of this equation has a physical meaning; it is the difference of the entropy of the mixture in the
two states defined by the quantities p, T and p_0, T_0.   Clearly
the mixture behaves like a gas, whose density and specific
heat have values which are the means of those of the water-
vapour and of the air.

We must now calculate the limiting value of p down to
which equation (I) may be used.   Now and in what follows
let e denote the pressure of saturated aqueous vapour at the
temperature T. e is a function of T, but of T alone.   Then
the quantity ν of saturated aqueous vapour contained in the
volume v at temperature T, is

$$\nu = \frac{vc}{R_1 T} \qquad (a).$$

and this quantity must exceed μ, as long as the vapour remains
unsaturated.   Thus the limit is reached as soon as $\mu = \nu$.   If
we introduce the value of v from the characteristic equation,
this condition takes the form

$$p = \frac{\lambda R + \mu R_1}{\mu R_1} \cdot e \qquad (b).$$

As soon as p and T reach values satisfying this condition, we
must leave equation 1, and enter on—

Stage 2. The air is saturated with aqueous vapour, and
contains liquid water in addition.   We neglect the volume of
the latter.   Then we may here also consider the air by itself,
and the water with its vapour by themselves, in each case as
if the other were absent.   Both have the same volume v and

---

[1] Clausius, *Mechanische Wärmetheorie*, vol. i. p. 51, 1876.

temperature T as the mixture; but the pressure p of the mixture is the sum of the partial pressures $P_1 = \lambda \dfrac{RT}{v}$ of the air, and $p_2 = e$ of the water vapour. The equation

$$p = \lambda \frac{RT}{v} + e, \quad \text{or} \quad (p - e)v = \lambda RT$$

is now the characteristic equation of the mixture. The amount of heat necessary to produce the changes dT and dv is for the air as before

$$dQ_1 = \lambda \left(c_v dT + ART \frac{dv}{v} \right),$$

but the amount of heat to be supplied to the water in order to produce the change dT, and at the same time to increase the amount ν of water-vapour by $d\nu$, while pressure and volume suffer corresponding changes, is

$$dQ_2 = Td\left(\frac{\nu r}{T}\right) + \mu c dT.$$

The equation is deduced by Clausius in his *Mechanische Wärmetheorie*, vol. i. part vi. § 11. c is the specific heat of liquid water and r the external latent heat of steam, both being measured in heat units. Hence the whole amount of heat to be supplied is

$$dQ = \lambda \left(c_v dT + ART \frac{dv}{v} \right) + Td\left(\frac{\nu r}{T}\right) + \mu c dT.$$

Here again we put $dQ = 0$, divide by T, and integrate. From the integral equation we eliminate v and ν by means of the characteristic equation and equation (a), and obtain

$$0 = (\lambda c_p + \mu c) \log \frac{T}{T_0} + \lambda AR \log \frac{p_0 - e_0}{p - e}$$

$$+ \lambda \frac{R}{R_1} \left(\frac{r}{T} \frac{e}{p - e} - \frac{r_0}{T_0} \frac{e_0}{p_0 - c_0} \right) \qquad \text{(II)}.$$

The quantity equated to zero again represents the difference

of entropy between the initial and final states.   We may use
the equation obtained until the temperature falls to the freezing-
point ; then we pass to —

Stage 3, in which the air contains ice, as well as vapour
and liquid water.   Now the temperature will not at once
fall any further with further expansion, for the latent heat
developed by the freezing water will, without any lowering of
temperature, yield the work necessary to overcome the external
pressure.   But the latent heat will not be spent ᷿in this work
alone, but also in evaporating a portion of the water already
condensed.   For since during the expansion the volume
increases without fall of temperature, at the end of the process there will be more aqueous vapour than before, and the
weight of ice formed will be less than that of the liquid water
initially present.   Let v again denote that portion of μ which
exists as vapour, σ the portion existing as ice, and let q be
the latent heat of fusion of 1 kilogramme of ice.   T, e, r are
constants.   Since then $d\mathrm{T} = 0$, we need only supply the air with
the heat $\lambda \mathrm{ART} dv/v$, the water which is evaporated with the
heat $r dv$, and the water which is frozen with the heat $- q d\sigma$.
Hence the whole of the mixture is supplied with the heat

$$dQ = \lambda \mathrm{ART} \frac{dv}{v} + r dv - q d\sigma.$$

As before we put $dQ = 0$, divide by T, and integrate, and
thus get

$$0 = \lambda \mathrm{AR} \log \frac{v}{v_0} + \frac{r}{\mathrm{T}} (v - v_0) - \frac{q}{\mathrm{T}} (\sigma - \sigma_0).$$

The division by T was only necessary to make the right-hand
member a difference of entropy.   By the aid of the characteristic equation and of equation (a), we can eliminate v and v,
and introduce the pressure p.   The equation then shows us
how the quantity σ of ice formed varies with the change of
pressure.   But the details of the process are of less interest
to us than the limits within which it takes place.   Hence we
let the index 0 refer to the state when the mixture just
reached the temperature 0°, in which therefore ice was not
present, and where $\sigma_0 = 0$.   The index 1 refers to the state
in which all the water is just frozen, in which therefore the

temperature just begins to fall below $0°$. Here clearly $\sigma = \mu - \nu$, since ice and vapour alone are present. If we insert these values, after introducing the pressure, we get

$$0 = \lambda \text{AR} \log \frac{p_0 - e}{p_1 - e} + \lambda \frac{\text{R}}{\text{R}_1} \frac{e}{p_1 - e} \frac{r + q}{\text{T}} - \lambda \frac{\text{R}}{\text{R}_1} \frac{e}{p_0 - e} \frac{r}{\text{T}}$$
$$- \mu \frac{q}{\text{T}}. \qquad \text{(III)}.$$

This equation connects the pressures p_0 and p_1, at which respectively the third stage is entered and quitted.

It is not necessary to furnish e and T with an index, for they have the same values at the beginning and end of the stage.

Stage 4. When the temperature falls still lower, we have only steam and ice. The investigation is the same as for Stage 2, and the final formula also is the same. But here the latent heat of vaporisation has a different value. Here it is $r + q$, for the heat necessary to evaporate the ice directly must clearly be the same as that required to first melt it, and then evaporate the water produced. If we wish to be quite rigorous, we must not take q to be constant, but must suppose it to vary slightly with the temperature; but the differences are so small that they may be neglected here. Thus in this fourth stage we shall reach those temperatures at which the air itself can no longer be regarded as a permanent gas.

The four stages which we have distinguished might very properly be called the dry, the rain, the hail, and the snow stages.

If now we are compelled to follow exactly the changes in a mixture containing a considerable percentage of water, there is no choice but to make use of these complicated formulæ. In that case we proceed as follows. We first substitute the values of λ and μ in all the equations. Then we substitute the values p_0 and T_0 for the initial state in equation I. The resulting equation and equation (b) we regard as two equations to determine the unknown quantities p and T. Solving for these we get the transition state between the first and the second stage. The values obtained are then substituted for p_0 and T_0 in equation II. By putting $\text{T} = 273$ in the resulting equation we get the p_0, which occurs in the equations of the third stage. If now we determine from equation III the final pressure p_1 of the third stage, this pressure and the temperature $273°$ constitute the p_0 and T_0 in the equations of the fourth stage. It will frequently happen that the temperature down to which the first stage holds, lies below the freezing-point; then we pass on at once to the fourth stage, the second and third disappearing. After we have in this way determined the coefficients and limits of validity of all the equations, we may employ them to determine for any desired p the corresponding T, and *vice versâ*. These calculations can only be performed by successive approximations, and it will be advisable to take the necessary approximate values from the table. When we have determined p and T for any state, its remaining properties are easily deduced. The density of the mixture follows from the corresponding characteristic equation. The equation (a) gives the quantity of vapour, and thus also that of the water condensed. We may often need to know the difference of height h, which corresponds to the different states p_0 and p_1, on the assumption that the whole atmosphere is in the so-called adiabatic state of equilibrium. The exact solution of the problem is given by the laborious evaluation of the integral

$$h = \int_{p_1}^{p_0} vdp,$$

but as in this particular respect an exact determination is never of any special use, we may always use the convenient diagram here given.

B. If we were here concerned with one mixture of one determinate composition, *i.e.* with only one value of the ratio $\mu\lambda$, we could exactly represent the formulæ deduced by a diagram showing directly the adiabatic changes of the mixture, starting from any state whatever. We could use pressure and temperature as coordinates of a point in a plane, and could cover the plane with a system of curves connecting all those states which can pass adiabatically into each other. Then it would only be necessary from a given initial state to follow the curve passing through the corresponding point, in order to trace the behaviour of the mixture through all its stages. But as meteorology has of necessity to deal with mixtures of very various proportions, it would for this method require a large number of diagrams. But we find it possible to manage with only *one* diagram, if in the first place we confine ourselves to cases in which the pressure and weight of the aqueous vapour are small compared with those of air; and if, secondly, we expect no greater accuracy from the results than corresponds to a neglect of the former quantities as compared with the latter. For if we neglect μ in comparison with λ, and e in comparison with p, the form of the curves to be drawn is the same for all the different absolute values of μ; so that the same curves may be used for all the various mixtures. The points where the various stages pass one into the other are situated very differently for different mixtures, and hence special means must be devised to determine these points. The diagram is constructed in accordance with these principles.

In the net of coordinates the pressures are introduced as abscissæ through a range from 300 to 800 mm. of mercury, and temperatures as ordinates from $-20°$ to $+30°$ C. As will be seen, a constant increase of the coordinate does not represent a constant increase of pressure or of temperature; but the diagram is so drawn that equal increases of length correspond to equal increases of the logarithms of the pressure and of the absolute temperature. The advantage of this arrangement is that the curves of special importance become straight lines, in part exactly, in part approximately; and this is of considerable importance for the accurate construction and employment of the diagram.

When μ is neglected in comparison with λ, the adiabatics of the first stage are given by the equation

$$\text{const} = c_p \log T - AR \log p.$$

The logarithms are natural ones throughout. With Clausius we must put

$$c_p = 0·2375 \frac{\text{calorie}}{\text{degree C.} \times \text{kilogr}},$$

$$A = \frac{1}{423·55} \frac{\text{calorie}}{\text{kilogràmme-metre}}.$$

$$R = 29 \cdot 27 \frac{\text{kilogramme-metre}}{\text{degree C.} \times \text{kilogr}} \cdot$$

These adiabatics are straight lines in our diagram. One of them is marked by the letter (a), and we may denote the system by this letter. The individual lines are so drawn that the value of the constant, the entropy, increases from one line to the next by

$$0 \cdot 0025 \frac{\text{calorie}}{\text{degree C.} \times \text{kilogr}} \cdot$$

Thus they are equidistant. One of them is drawn through the point $0°$ C. and 760 mm. pressure.

Now the curves of the second stage satisfy the equation [1]

$$\text{const} = c_p \log T - AR \log p + \frac{R}{R_1} \cdot \frac{r}{T} \cdot \frac{e}{p} \cdot$$

R/R_1 is the density of aqueous vapour referred to air, i.e. $0 \cdot 6219$. r, according to Clausius, is equal to $607 - 0 \cdot 708$ $(T - 273) \frac{\text{calorie}}{\text{kilogr}}$. The values of e for the various temperatures I have taken from the table calculated by Broch.[2] The curves run from the right-hand top corner to the left-hand bottom corner with a slight curvature. One of them is marked β. They also are drawn so that the entropy per kilogramme increases from one curve to the next by $0 \cdot 0025$ calorie/degree C., and so that one of them passes through the point $0°$ C., 760 mm.

The portions of the curves which correspond to the third stage coincide with the isothermal $0°$ C.

Lastly, the curves of the fourth stage are very similar to those of the second, but yet are not quite the same; for their equation is got from that of the former curves by putting $r + q$ for r, where $q = 80$ calorie/kilogr. They are marked γ

---

[1] Even though μ is neglected in comparison with λ, yet it is doubtful whether $c\mu$ should be neglected compared with $c_p\lambda$; for c is four times as great as c_p. Though in the diagram μ is no more than $\frac{1}{10}$ of λ, still the ratio $c\mu/c_p\lambda$ amounts to $\frac{1}{10}$. For meteorological applications we must, however, remember that in these extreme cases the liquid water will not all be carried about with the air. Frequently a large proportion will be deposited as rain, so that we may be nearer the truth in neglecting the specific heat of the liquid water altogether than in taking the whole quantity into account.

[2] *Traveaux du Bureau international des poids et mesures*, tome i.

and are drawn according to the same scale as a and β; but in general they are not continuations of the curves β.

Means must now be provided for finding the points of transition between the various stages. The dotted lines serve to determine the end of the first stage. They give in grammes the greatest amount of water which one kilogramme of the mixture can just retain as vapour in the various states, calculated by means of the formula $\nu = \mathrm{R}e/\mathrm{R_1 T}$. Thus the curve 25 connects together all those states in which 1 kilogramme of the mixture is just saturated by 25 grammes of steam. These curves are drawn for every gramme. If a mixture contain n grammes of steam in every kilogramme, we may follow the curve of the first stage up to the dotted line n; then we must change to the second, or the fourth stage, as the case may be.

The boundary of the second and third stages is given by the intersection of the corresponding adiabatic β with the isothermal 0° C. The pressure p_0, corresponding to this intersection, and μ, the amount of water present, determine p_1, the pressure at which we must pass from the third to the fourth stage. To determine p_1 we must use the small supplementary diagram, which is just below the larger one. It has for abscissae the pressures arranged as in the large diagram, and for ordinates the total quantity μ of water in all the stages, in grammes per kilogramme of the mixture. The inclined lines of the diagram are merely the curves which correspond to equation III of the third stage, when in this equation we regard p_0 as constant, but p_1 and μ as variable coordinates. These lines are not quite straight, though on the scale of the diagram they are not to be distinguished from straight lines. The highest point of each line corresponds to the case $p_1 = p_0$. The corresponding value of μ is not zero, but is equal to ν, the least value μ must have in order that the mixture may be saturated at 0° and that the supplementary diagram may be required at all. When for given values of p_0 and μ we require the corresponding value of p_1, we must look out the inclined line whose highest point has the abscissa p_0, and follow it down to the ordinate μ. The pressure at which this ordinate is reached is p_1, the pressure sought. With it the point of transition to the fourth stage is found.

M. P.   X

Now that in this way we have determined the whole of
the series of states which the mixture traverses, we may for
each individual state find as follows the remaining quantities
which interest us :——

1. The dotted line, on which we are, shows at once how
many grammes of water are present as vapour in the corresponding state. If we subtract this from the total amount μ
of water present originally, we get the amount of water
already condensed.

2. The density δ of the mixture with the approximations
introduced may for all states be calculated from the formula
$\delta = p/\mathrm{R}T$ or $\log \delta = \log p - \log T - \log \mathrm{R}$.   Graphically it
would be read off at once if the diagram were covered by a
system of lines of equal density. These lines are seen to be
a system of parallel straight lines. Only one of these lines,
δ, is actually drawn on the diagram, so as not to overload it.
But we may by the help of this line alone compare the
densities in two states 1 and 2 according to the following
rule. From the points 1 and 2 draw two straight lines
parallel to δ and cutting the isothermal for 0° C. ; and read
off the pressures p_1 and p_2 at these intersections. The densities at 1 and 2 are in the ratio $p_1 : p_2$. For the densities in
the states p_1, 0° and p_2, 0° are by Boyle's law in the ratio
$p_1 : p_2$, and they are equal to the densities in 1 and 2, as they
lie on lines of equal density.

3. The difference of height h, which corresponds to the
passage from the state p_0 to the state p, on the assumption of
an adiabatic equilibrium state, is given by the equation

$$h = \int_p^{p_0} v dp = \mathrm{R} \int_p^{p_0} T \cdot \frac{dp}{p}$$

Here we would now find T as a function of p from the
diagram and then evaluate the integral mechanically. In
actual practice the supposition of an adiabatic equilibrium
will never be satisfied so nearly as to make an exact development of its consequences of any importance. And again we
shall only commit a comparatively slight error for moderate
heights if we give to T a mean value and then regard it as

constant. For within the limits of the diagram it varie
only from 253 to 303; so that if we give it the constant
value $T_0 = 273$, the error in h will hardly ever exceed $\frac{1}{9}$ of
its total value. If we choose to neglect this error, we get h
$= \text{const} - RT_0 \log p$, and may at once introduce the heights
as well as the pressures as abscissæ. Everywhere indeed
equal increases of length of the abscissa will correspond to
equal increases of height. The scale of heights is marked at
the foot of the diagram; its zero is placed at the pressure
760 mm., because this is usually regarded as the normal
pressure at sea-level.

C. In order to explain the use of the diagram by an
example, let us consider the following concrete problem. We
are given at sea-level a quantity of air, whose pressure is
750 mm., temperature 27° C., and relative humidity 50 per
cent. Required to find what states this air passes through as
it is transferred without loss or gain of heat to higher strata
of the atmosphere and thus to lower pressures; and also at
what heights approximately above sea-level the various states
are reached.

First, we look out on the diagram the point which corresponds to the initial state. It is the intersection of the
horizontal isothermal 27 and the vertical isobar 750. We
observe that it lies almost exactly on the dotted line 22.
This means that each kilogramme of our air would contain
22·0 grammes of water-vapour when saturated. But as its
relative humidity is only 50 per cent it contains only 11·0
grammes per kilogramme. This we note for further use.
Again we follow the isobar 750 down to the scale of heights
at the foot of the diagram and read off 100 metres. Thus
the zero of the scale of heights lies 100 m. beneath the sea-
level chosen by us as our starting-point; and we must subtract
100 m. from all actual readings of the scale of heights in
order to get heights above sea-level. If now we raise up our
mass of air, the series of states traversed by it is first given by
the line of system a which passes through the initial state.[1]
There is no such line actually drawn, so we must interpolate

[1] The letters a, β, γ, which denote the systems, are given at the edge of the
diagram, enclosed by small circles. One line of the system which the letter
denotes is continued right up to it. The changes of state of our example are
marked by a special line of dots and dashes in the diagram.

one. If the number of lines crossing each other appear confusing, we may lay a strip of paper parallel to the system of lines considered, when all confusion will be avoided. In order to find out the state in the neighbourhood of the height 700 m., we seek out the point $700 + 100 = 800$ in the scale of heights, and go vertically upwards to meet our line a. The point of intersection gives the pressure 687 mm., and the temperature $19°·3$. But we must only use the line a down to the point at which it cuts the dotted line 11. For reaching this line means that we reach a state in which the air can only just retain 11 grammes of water per kilogramme in the form of vapour. And as we have 11 grammes per kilogramme, any further cooling produces condensation. The pressure for the point of incipient condensation is 640 mm., the temperature $13°·3$. This is not the temperature of the initial dew-point, but is lower. The dotted line 11 cuts the isobar 750 at $15°·8$, which is the initial dew-point. But since our air has increased in volume in addition to having cooled, the water has been able to keep itself in the state of vapour down to $13°·3$. The height at which we find ourselves corresponds to the lower limit of cloud formation; it is about 1270 m. To trace still further the changes of state we draw through the point of intersection a curve of the system β and follow its course. This curve is much less inclined to the axis of abscissæ than the line a previously used; so that now the change of temperature with height is much less than before, owing to the evolution of the latent heat of the steam. When we have risen 1000 m. above the point at which condensation commenced, the temperature has only fallen to $8°·2$, *i.e.* only $0°·51$ for every 100 m. We find ourselves on the dotted line 8·9, and thus see that 8·9 grammes of water still exist as vapour, so that 2·1 grammes of water per kilogramme of air have been condensed in this first thousand metres of the cloud-layer. We reach the temperature $0°$ at a pressure 472 mm. and at a height 3750 m., while we should have reached it at a height of 2600 m. if the air had been dry and we had not had to forsake the line a. 4·9 grammes of water, or 45 per cent of the whole contents, are now found to have condensed; and this portion on further expansion begins to freeze to form hail. But until the last trace of water has frozen, the temperature cannot fall any further, and thus we shall for a certain distance keep at a constant temperature of 0°. To ascertain how far, we use the small supplementary diagram between the larger one and the scale of heights. We follow the isobar 472 down to the dotted line of this diagram. Through the point of meeting we draw a line parallel to the sloping lines of the diagram, and follow this line to its intersection with the horizontal line characterised by the number 11, the total weight of water. This latter line is easily interpolated between the horizontal lines 10 and 15 drawn. As soon as we reach this line we read off the pressure $p = 463$ mm. and return to the large diagram. At the pressure thus found the process of freezing is completed; the layer within which it took place has a thickness of about 150 m. It will appear strange that, according to the dotted lines, the amount of water in form of vapour has increased a little during the freezing. But this is quite true, for the volume has increased, without any corresponding fall in temperature. At the pressure 463 mm. we leave the temperature 0°. The water which henceforth condenses passes directly into the solid state. As in a short time little water is left in the form of vapour, the temperature begins to fall more rapidly with increase of height. We find the various states by following that one of the lines γ which passes through the point 463 on the isothermal 0°. The temperature $-20°$, up to which the diagram is available, is reached at the height 7200 m., and at the pressure 305 mm.; only 2 grammes of water per kilogramme remain as vapour, the other 9 are condensed. If we wish to know how the density in this state compares with the initial density, we draw two lines through the corresponding points parallel to the line δ. These meet the isothermal 0° at the pressures 330 and 680. The densities are in the ratio of these pressures, i.e. as 33 : 68, and they are in the ratios 33 and 68 to 76 to the density of air in the normal state at a pressure 760 mm. and a temperature 0°.

All these results have been read off direct from the diagram. Errors which could cause inconvenience are probably only to be found in the heights given. For these in strictness relate to a rise through an atmosphere everywhere at the same temperature 0°. But in most cases it may be assumed that the temperature of the atmosphere is everywhere the same as that of the mass of air ascending through it. We may considerably reduce the error due to this cause with a very small amount of calculation. Thus we found the point of incipient condensation to occur at a pressure 640 mm. This corresponds to the height 1270 m. only when the temperature is 0°. In our case it lay between 27° and 13°, so that the mean was about 20°. At this temperature the height is greater by $\frac{20}{273}$ or $\frac{1}{14}$ than at 0°, since the density of the air is less by the same fraction; hence in reality the height lies between 1350 and 1400 m.

We must now complete the example by mentioning some special cases :—

1. We assumed that during the hail stage the whole of the original quantity of water, 11 grammes, was still contained in the air. Now this is only true when the ascent is very rapid; in other cases the greater part of the condensed water will probably have been deposited as rain, and thus only a fraction will become frozen. If we can form an estimate as to the size of this fraction, the diagram still permits of a determination of the correct amounts. If in our example we had reason to suppose that one-half of the water condensed down to 0° had been removed, then on reaching the isothermal 0° there would have been present only 8·5 grammes of water in each kilogramme of air. Then, in using the supplementary diagram we would have gone not as far as the horizontal line 11, but only down to the line 8·5; and would have left the temperature 0° at the pressure 466 mm. This would have been the only alteration.

2. If we had in our example assumed only 10 per cent relative humidity in place of 50 per cent, we could have used the line a down to the dotted line 2·2. This point of intersection occurs at 455 mm. and −13°·6, i.e. far below zero. We should never have had any liquid water formed at all; thus no hail stage would have occurred, but merely a sublimation of the water from the gaseous to the solid state. From the point of intersection with the line 2·2 we should at once have followed the line of the system γ passing through this point. It is of some interest to inquire how high the dew-point of our mixture may be in its initial state of pressure and

temperature, so that the condensation of liquid water, *i.e.* condensation above 0°, may just be avoided. To find the answer we follow the line *a* as far as the isothermal 0° and here meet with the dotted line 5·25. Thus we cannot have more than 5·25 grammes of water per kilogramme of air. To find at what temperature the air would then be saturated at the pressure 750 mm., we follow the line 5·25 up to the isobar 750 mm. and meet it at the temperature 4°·8. This is the required highest value of the dew-point.

[The following editorial note occurs at the end of the number of the *Meteorologische Zeitschrift* in which this paper appeared.]

We had already begun to print off this number when a letter from Dr. Hertz arrived, a part of which we take the liberty of printing. At the same time we are glad to have the opportunity of publishing in our journal the introductory part of his paper. It is all the more valuable because its results agree satisfactorily with those of Guldberg and Mohn, while the method by which they are obtained is to a certain extent different and follows more closely the papers of Clausius, etc. The papers by Guldberg and Mohn, to which we have drawn the attention of Dr. Hertz, are not easily accessible, and the subject is of so much importance in meteorology that an exposition of it in another journal is by no means out of place. Dr. Hertz writes us :—

"My best thanks for the paper by Guldberg and Mohn which you have so kindly sent me. Had I known of it before I should have omitted the whole of part A of my paper ; for, as a matter of fact, except in notation, it corresponds exactly with the calculation of Guldberg and Mohn. Yet in investigating with the· aid of my diagram the example calculated by Guldberg and Mohn I became rather alarmed. Down to 0° things went all right, but on proceeding further I found that, according to my diagram, the mixture reached the temperature −20° at 320 mm. pressure, whereas Guldberg and Mohn with their formulæ get 292·73 mm.

"An error of 28 mm. was too large, and I felt much afraid that I had made some mistake in the construction. But it appears that Guldberg and Mohn have made an error in working out the numerical example, for I have repeatedly made the calculation with their own formulæ and constants, and always find 313 mm. for the pressure in question. Thus there is at most a difference of 7 mm. between the exact formulæ and the readings of the diagram, and an error of this magnitude is accounted for by the approximations which of necessity have to be made. I believe that in ninety cases out of a hundred such an error would be of no importance in meteorology, and that it would be outweighed by the vastly greater convenience. In fact I estimate that at least three or four hours would be required for accurately calculating Guldberg and Mohn's example, whereas it can be worked out on the diagram in a few minutes. Besides, these 7 mm. are no greater than the uncertainty introduced into the whole calculation by the fact that only a part of the condensed water is carried along by the air.

" Is there still time for me to add a note of ten or fifteen lines acknowledging the priority of Guldberg and Mohn, and pointing out the cause of the above discrepancy? I am afraid others may compare the diagram with their example, regard it as inaccurate to the extent of 28 mm., and hence reject it. But to the priority you have yourselves referred. . . .

" H. HERTZ."

KIEL, 8th Dec. 1884.

ON THE RELATIONS BETWEEN LIGHT AND ELECTRICITY

A LECTURE DELIVERED AT THE SIXTY-SECOND MEETING OF THE GERMAN ASSOCIATION FOR THE ADVANCEMENT OF NATURAL SCIENCE AND MEDICINE IN HEIDELBERG ON SEPTEMBER 20TH, 1889. ·

(Published by Emil Strauss in Bonn.)

WHEN one speaks of the relations between light and electricity, the lay mind at once thinks of the electric light. With this the present lecture is not concerned. To the mind of the physicist there occur a series of delicate mutual reactions between the two agents, such as the rotation of the plane of polarisation by the current or the alteration of the resistance of a conductor by the action of light. In these, however, light and electricity do not directly meet; between the two there comes an intermediate agent—ponderable matter. With this group of phenomena again we shall not concern ourselves. Between the two agents there are yet other relations—relations in a closer and stricter sense than those already mentioned. I am here to support the assertion that light of every kind is itself an electrical phenomenon—the light of the sun, the light of a candle, the light of a glow-worm. Take away from the world electricity, and light disappears; remove from the world the luminiferous ether, and electric and magnetic actions can no longer traverse space. This is our assertion. It does not date from to-day or yesterday; already it has behind it a long history. In this history its foundations lie. Such researches as I have made upon this subject form but a link in a long chain. And it is of the chain, and not only of the single link, that I would speak to you. I must confess that it is not easy to speak of these matters in a way at once intelligible and accurate. It is in empty space, in the free ether, that the processes which we have to describe take place. They cannot be felt with the hand, heard by the ear, or seen by the eye. They appeal to our intuition and conception, scarcely to our senses. Hence we shall try to make use, as far as possible, of the intuitions and conceptions which we already possess. Let us, therefore, stop to inquire what we do with certainty know about light and electricity before we proceed to connect the one with the other.

What, then, is light? Since the time of Young and Fresnel we know that it is a wave-motion. We know the velocity of the waves, we know their length, we know that they are transversal waves; in short, we know completely the geometrical relations of the motion. To the physicist it is inconceivable that this view should be refuted; we can no longer entertain any doubt about the matter. It is morally certain that the wave theory of light is true, and the conclusions that necessarily follow from it are equally certain. It is therefore certain that all space known to us is not empty, but is filled with a substance, the ether, which can be thrown into vibration. But whereas our knowledge of the geometrical relations of the processes in this substance is clear and definite, our conceptions of the physical nature of these processes is vague, and the assumptions made as to the properties of the substance itself are not altogether consistent. At first, following the analogy of sound, waves of light were freely regarded as elastic waves, and treated as such. But elastic waves in fluids are only known in the form of longitudinal waves. Transversal elastic waves in fluids are unknown. They are not even possible; they contradict the nature of the fluid state. Hence men were forced to assert that the ether which fills space behaves like a solid body. But when they considered and tried to explain the unhindered course of the stars in the heavens, they found themselves forced to admit that the ether behaves like a perfect fluid. These two statements together land us in a painful and unintelligible contradiction, which disfigures the otherwise beautiful development of optics. Instead of trying to conceal this defect let us turn to electricity; in investigating it we may perhaps make some progress towards removing the difficulty.

What, then, is electricity? This is at once an important and a difficult question. It interests the lay as well as the scientific mind. Most people who ask it never doubt about the existence of electricity. They expect a description of it —an enumeration of the peculiarities and powers of this wonderful thing. To the scientific mind the question rather presents itself in the form—Is there such a thing as electricity? Cannot electrical phenomena be traced back, like all others, to the properties of the ether and of ponderable matter? We are far from being able to answer this question definitely in the affirmative. In our conceptions the thing conceived of as electricity plays a large part. The traditional conceptions of electricities which attract and repel each other, and which are endowed with actions-at-a-distance as with spiritual properties—we are all familiar with these, and in a way fond of them; they hold undisputed sway as common modes of expression at the present time. The period at which these conceptions were formed was the period in which Newton's law of gravitation won its most glorious successes, and in which the idea of direct action-at-a-distance was familiar. Electric and magnetic attractions followed the same law as gravitational attraction; no wonder men thought the simple assumption of action-at-a-distance sufficient to explain these phenomena, and to trace them back to their ultimate intelligible cause. The aspect of matters changed in the present century, when the reactions between electric currents and magnets became known; for these have an infinite manifoldness, and in them motion and time play an important part. It became necessary to increase the number of actions-at-a-distance, and to improve their form. Thus the conception gradually lost its simplicity and physical probability. Men tried to regain this by seeking for more comprehensive and simple laws—so-called elementary laws. Of these the celebrated Weber's law is the most important example. Whatever we may think of its correctness, it is an attempt which altogether formed a comprehensive system full of scientific charm ; those who were once attracted into its magic circle remained prisoners there. And if the path indicated was a false one, warning could only come from an intellect of great freshness—from a man who looked at phenomena with an open mind and without preconceived opinions, who started from what he saw, not from what he had heard, learned, or read. Such a man was Faraday. Faraday, doubtless, heard it said that when a body was electrified something was introduced into it ; but he saw that the changes which took place only made themselves felt outside and not inside. Faraday was taught that forces simply acted across space ; but he saw that an important part was played by the particular kind of matter filling the space across which the forces were supposed to act. Faraday read that electricities certainly existed, whereas there was much contention as to the forces exercised by them ; but he saw that the effects of these forces were clearly displayed, whereas he could perceive nothing of the electricities themselves. And so he formed a quite different, an opposite conception of the matter. To him the electric and magnetic forces became the actually present, tangible realities ; to him electricity and magnetism were the things whose existence might be disputable. The lines of force, as he called the forces independently considered, stood before his intellectual eye in space as conditions of space, as tensions, whirls, currents, whatever they might be— that he was himself unable to state—but there they were, acting upon each other, pushing and pulling bodies about, spreading themselves about and carrying the action from point to point. To the objection that complete rest is the only condition possible in empty space he could answer—Is space really empty ? Do not the phenomena of light compel us to regard it as being filled with something ? Might not the ether which transmits the waves of light also be capable of transmitting the changes which we call electric and magnetic force ? Might there not conceivably be some connection between these changes and the light-waves. Might not the latter be due to something like a quivering of the lines of force ?

Faraday had advanced as far as this in his ideas and conjectures. He could not prove them, although he eagerly sought for proof. He delighted in investigating the connection between light, electricity, and magnetism. The beautiful connection which he did discover was not the one which he sought. So he tried again and again, and his search only ended with his life. Among the questions which he raised there was one which continually presented itself to him—Do electric and magnetic forces require time for their propagation? When we suddenly excite an electromagnet by a current, is the effect perceived simultaneously at all distances? Or does it first affect magnets close at hand, then more distant ones, and lastly, those which are quite far away? When we electrify and discharge a body in rapid succession, does the force vary at all distances simultaneously? Or do the oscillations arrive later, the further we go from the body? In the latter case the oscillation would propagate itself as a wave through space. Are there such waves? To these questions Faraday could get no answer. And yet the answer is most closely connected with his own fundamental conceptions. If such waves of electric force exist, travelling freely from their origin through space, they exhibit plainly to us the independent existence of the forces which produce them. There can be no better way of proving that these forces do not act across space, but are propagated from point to point, than by actually following their progress from instant to instant. The questions asked are not unanswerable; indeed they can be attacked by very simple methods. If Faraday had had the good fortune to hit upon these methods, his views would forthwith have secured recognition. The connection between light and electricity would at once have become so clear that it could not have escaped notice even by eyes less sharp-sighted than his own.

But a path so short and straight as this was not vouchsafed to science. For a while experiments did not point to any solution, nor did the current theory tend in the direction of Faraday's conceptions. The assertion that electric forces could exist independently of their electricities was in direct opposition to the accepted electrical theories. Similarly the prevailing theory of optics refused to accept the idea that waves of light could be other than elastic waves. Any attempt at a thorough discussion of the one or the other of these assertions seemed almost to be idle speculation. All the more must we admire the happy genius of the man who could connect together these apparently remote conjectures in such a way that they mutually supported each other, and formed a theory of which every one was at once bound to admit that it was at least plausible. This was an Englishman—Maxwell. You know the paper which he published in 1865 upon the electromagnetic theory of light. It is impossible to study this wonderful theory without feeling as if the mathematical equations had an independent life and an intelligence of their own, as if they were wiser than ourselves, indeed wiser than their discoverer, as if they gave forth more than he had put into them. And this is not altogether impossible : it may happen when the equations prove to be more correct than their discoverer could with certainty have known. It is true that such comprehensive and accurate equations only reveal themselves to those who with keen insight pick out every indication of the truth which is faintly visible in nature. The clue which Maxwell followed is well known to the initiated. It had attracted the attention of other investigators : it had suggested to Riemann and Lorenz speculations of a similar nature, although not so fruitful in results. Electricity in motion produces magnetic force, and magnetism in motion produces electric force ; but both of these effects are only perceptible at high velocities. Thus velocities appear in the mutual relations between electricity and magnetism, and the constant which governs these relations and continually recurs in them is itself a velocity of exceeding magnitude. This constant was determined in various ways, first by Kohlrausch and Weber, by purely electrical experiments, and proved to be identical, allowing for the experimental errors incident to such a difficult measurement, with another important velocity—the velocity of light. This might be an accident, but a pupil of Faraday's could scarcely regard it as such. To him it appeared as an indication that the same ether must be the medium for the transmission of both electric force and light. The two velocities which were found to be nearly equal must really be identical. But in that case the most important optical constants must occur in the electrical equations. This was the bond which Maxwell set himself to strengthen. He developed the electrical equations to such an extent that they embraced all the known phenomena, and in addition to these a class of phenomena hitherto unknown—electric waves. These waves would be transversal waves, which might have any wave-length, but would always be propagated in the ether with the same velocity—that of light. And now Maxwell was able to point out that waves having just these geometrical properties do actually occur in nature, although we are accustomed to denote them, not as electrical phenomena, but by the special name of light. If Maxwell's electrical theory was regarded as false, there was no reason for accepting his views as to the nature of light. And if light waves were held to be purely elastic waves, his electrical theory lost its whole significance. But if one approached the structure without any prejudices arising from the views commonly held, one saw that its parts supported each other like the stones of an arch stretching across an abyss of the unknown, and connecting two tracts of the known. On account of the difficulty of the theory the number of its disciples at first was necessarily small. But every one who studied it thoroughly became an adherent, and forthwith sought diligently to test its original assumptions and its ultimate conclusions. Naturally the test of experiment could for a long time be applied only to separate statements, to the outworks of the theory. I have just compared Maxwell's theory to an arch stretching across an abyss of unknown things. If I may carry on the analogy further, I would say that for a long time the only additional support that was given to this arch was by way of strengthening its two abutments. The arch was thus enabled to carry its own weight safely; but still its span was so great that we could not venture to build up further upon it as upon a secure foundation. For this purpose it was necessary to have special pillars built up from the solid ground, and serving to support the centre of the arch. One such pillar would consist in proving that electrical or magnetic effects can be directly produced by light. This pillar would support the optical side of the structure directly and the electrical side indirectly. Another pillar would consist in proving the existence of waves of electric or magnetic force capable of being propagated after the manner of light waves. This pillar again would directly support the electrical side, and indirectly the optical side. In order to complete the structure symmetrically, both pillars would have to be built; but it would suffice to begin with one of them. With the former we have not as yet been able to make a start; but fortunately, after a protracted search, a safe point of support for the latter has been found. A sufficiently extensive foundation has been laid down: a part of the pillar has already been built up; with the help of many willing hands it will soon reach the height of the arch, and so enable this to bear the weight of the further structure which is to be erected upon it. At this stage I was so fortunate as to be able to take part in the work. To this I owe the honour of speaking to you to-day; and you will therefore pardon me if I now try to direct your attention solely to this part of the structure. Lack of time compels me, against my will, to pass by the researches made by many other investigators; so that I am not able to show you in how many ways the path was prepared for my experiments, and how near several investigators came to performing these experiments themselves.

Was it then so difficult to prove that electric and magnetic forces need time for their propagation? Would it not have been easy to charge a Leyden jar and to observe directly whether the corresponding disturbance in a distant electroscope took place somewhat later? Would it not have sufficed to watch the behaviour of a magnetic needle while some one at a distance suddenly excited an electromagnet? As a matter of fact these and similar experiments had already been performed without indicating that any interval of time elapsed between the cause and the effect. To an adherent of Maxwell's theory this is simply a necessary result of the enormous velocity of propagation. We can only perceive the effect of charging a Leyden jar or exciting a magnet at moderate distances, say up to ten metres. To traverse such a distance, light, and therefore according to the theory electric force likewise, takes only the thirty-millionth part of a second. Such a small fraction of time we cannot directly measure or even perceive. It is still more unfortunate that there are no

adequate means at our disposal for indicating with sufficient
sharpness the beginning and end of such a short interval.
If we wish to measure a length correctly to the tenth part
of a millimetre it would be absurd to indicate the beginning
of it with a broad chalk line. ' If we wish to measure a time
correctly to the thousandth part of a second it would be absurd
to denote its beginning by the stroke of a big clock. Now
the time of discharge of a Leyden jar is, according to our
ordinary ideas, inconceivably short. It would certainly be
that if it took about the thirty-thousandth part of a second.
And yet for our present purpose even that would be a thousand
times too long. Fortunately nature here provides us with a
more delicate method. It has long been known that the discharge of a Leyden jar is not a continuous process, but that,
like the striking of a clock, it consists of a large number of
oscillations, of discharges in opposite senses which follow
each other at exactly equal intervals. Electricity is able to
simulate the phenomena of elasticity. The period of a single
oscillation is much shorter than the total duration of the discharge, and this suggests that we might use a single oscillation
as an indicator. But, unfortunately, the shortest oscillation
yet observed takes fully a millionth of a second. While such
an oscillation is actually in progress its effects spread out
over a distance of three hundred metres; within the modest
dimensions of a room they would be perceived almost at the
instant the oscillation commenced. Thus no progress could
be made with the known methods; some fresh knowledge was
required. This came in the form of the discovery that not
only the discharge of Leyden jars, but, under suitable conditions, the discharge of every kind of conductor, gives rise to
oscillations. These oscillations may be much shorter than
those of the jars. When you discharge the conductor of an
electrical machine you excite oscillations whose period lies
between a hundred-millionth and a thousand-millionth of a
second. It is true that these oscillations do not follow each
other in a long continuous series; they are few in number
and rapidly die out. It would suit our experiments much
better if this were not the case. But there is still the possibility of success if we can only get two or three such sharply-
defined indications. So in the realm of acoustics, if we were

denied the continuous tones of pipes and strings, we could get a poor kind of music by striking strips of wood.

We now have indicators for which the thirty-thousandth part of a second is not too short. But these would be of little use to us if we were not in a position to actually perceive their action up to the distance under consideration, viz. about ten metres. This can be done by very simple means. Just at the spot where we wish to detect the force we place a conductor, say a straight wire, which is interrupted in the middle by a small spark-gap. The rapidly alternating force sets the electricity of the conductor in motion, and gives rise to a spark at the gap. The method had to be found by experience, for no amount of thought could well have enabled one to predict that it would work satisfactorily. For the sparks are microscopically short, scarcely a hundredth of a millimetre long; they only last about a millionth of a second. It almost seems absurd and impossible that they should be visible; but in a perfectly dark room they *are* visible to an eye which has been well rested in the dark. Upon this thin thread hangs the success of our undertaking. In beginning it we are met by a number of questions. Under what conditions can we get the most powerful oscillations? These conditions we must carefully investigate and make the best use of. What is the best form we can give to the receiver? We may choose straight wires or circular wires, or conductors of other forms; in each case the choice will have some effect upon the phenomena. When we have settled the form, what size shall we select? We soon find that this is a matter of some importance, that a given conductor is not suitable for the investigation of all kinds of oscillations, that there are relations between the two which remind us of the phenomena of resonance in acoustics. And lastly, are there not an endless number of positions in which we can expose a given conductor to the oscillations? In some of these the sparks are strong, in others weaker, and in others they entirely disappear. I might perhaps interest you in the peculiar phenomena which here arise, but I dare not take up your time with these, for they are details— details when we are surveying the general results of an investigation, but by no means unimportant details to the investigator when he is engaged upon work of this kind.

They are the peculiarities of the instruments with which he has to work; and the success of a workman depends upon whether he properly understands his tools. The thorough study of the implements, of the questions above referred to, formed a very important part of the task to be accomplished After this was done, the method of attacking the main problem became obvious. If you give a physicist a number of tuning-forks and resonators and ask him to demonstrate to you the propagation in time of sound-waves, he will find no difficulty in doing so even within the narrow limits of a room. He places a tuning-fork anywhere in the room, listens with the resonator at various points around and observes the intensity of the sound. He shows how at certain points this is very small, and how this arises from the fact that at these points every oscillation is annulled by another one which started subsequently but travelled to the point along a shorter path. When a shorter path requires less time than a longer one, the propagation is a propagation in time. Thus the problem is solved. But the physicist now further shows us that the positions of silence follow each other at regular and equal distances: from this he determines the wave-length, and, if he knows the time of vibration of the fork, he can deduce the velocity of the wave. In exactly the same way we proceed with our electric waves. In place of the tuning-fork we use an oscillating conductor. In place of the resonator we use our interrupted wire, which may also be called an electric resonator. We observe that in certain places there are sparks at the gap, in others none; we see that the dead points follow each other periodically in ordered succession. Thus the propagation in time is proved and the wave-length can be measured. Next comes the question whether the waves thus demonstrated are longitudinal or transverse. At a given place we hold our wire in two different positions with reference to the wave: in one position it answers, in the other not. This is enough—the question is settled: our waves are transversal. Their velocity has now to be found. We multiply the measured wave-length by the calculated period of oscillation and find a velocity which is about that of light. If doubts are raised as to whether the calculation is trustworthy, there is still another method open to us. In wires, as well as in air, the velocity of electric waves is enormously great, so that we can make a direct comparison between the two. Now the velocity of electric waves in wires has long since been directly measured. This was an easier problem to solve, because such waves can be followed for several kilometres. Thus we obtain another measurement, purely experimental, of our velocity, and if the result is only an approximate one it at any rate does not contradict the first.

All these experiments in themselves are very simple, but they lead to conclusions of the highest importance. They are fatal to any and every theory which assumes that electric force acts across space independently of time. They mark a brilliant victory for Maxwell's theory. No longer does this connect together natural phenomena far removed from each other. Even those who used to feel that this conception as to the nature of light had but a faint air of probability now find a difficulty in resisting it. In this sense we have reached our goal. But at this point we may perhaps be able to do without the theory altogether. The scene of our experiments was laid at the summit of the pass which, according to the theory, connects the domain of optics with that of electricity. It was natural to go a few steps further, and to attempt the descent into the known region of optics. There may be some advantage in putting theory aside. There are many lovers of science who are curious as to the nature of light and are interested in simple experiments, but to whom Maxwell's theory is nevertheless a seven-sealed book. The economy of science, too, requires of us that we should avoid roundabout ways when a straight path is possible. If with the aid of our electric waves we can directly exhibit the phenomena of light, we shall need no theory as interpreter; the experiments themselves will clearly demonstrate the relationship between the two things. As a matter of fact such experiments can be performed. We set up the conductor in which the oscillations are excited in the focal line of a very large concave mirror. The waves are thus kept together and proceed from the mirror as a powerful parallel beam. We cannot indeed see this beam directly, or feel it ; its effects are manifested in exciting sparks in the conductors upon which it impinges. It only becomes visible to our eyes when they are armed with our resonators.

But in other respects it is really a beam of light. By rotating the mirror we can send it in various directions, and by examining the path which it follows we can prove that it travels in a straight line. If we place a conducting body in its path, we find that the beam does not pass through—it throws shadows. In doing this we do not extinguish the beam but only throw it back: we can follow the reflected beam and convince ourselves that the laws of its reflection are the same as those of the reflection of light. We can also refract the beam in the same way as light. In order to refract a beam of light we send it through a prism, and it then suffers a deviation from its straight path. In the present case we proceed in the same way and obtain the same result; excepting that the dimensions of the waves and of the beam make it necessary for us to use a very large prism. For this reason we make our prism of a cheap material, such as pitch or asphalt. Lastly, we can with our beam observe those phenomena which hitherto have never been observed excepting with beams of light—the phenomena of polarisation. By interposing a suitable wire grating in the path of the beam we can extinguish or excite the sparks in our resonator in accordance with just the same laws as those which govern the brightening or darkening of the field of view in a polarising apparatus when we interpose a crystalline plate.

Thus far the experiments. In carrying them out we are decidedly working in the region of optics. In planning the experiments, in describing them, we no longer think electrically, but optically. We no longer see currents flowing in the conductors and electricities accumulating upon them: we only see the waves in the air, see how they intersect and die out and unite together, how they strengthen and weaken each other. Starting with purely electrical phenomena we have gone on step by step until we find ourselves in the region of purely optical phenomena. We have crossed the summit of the pass: our path is downwards and soon begins to get level again. The connection between light and electricity, of which there were hints and suspicions and even predictions in the theory, is now established: it is accessible to the senses and intelligible to the understanding. From the highest point to which we have climbed, from the very summit of the pass, we can better survey both regions. They are more extensive than we had ever before thought. Optics is no longer restricted to minute ether-waves a small fraction of a millimetre in length; its dominion is extended to waves which are measured in decimetres, metres, and kilometres. And in spite of this extension it merely appears, when examined from this point of view, as a small appendage to the great domain of electricity. We see that this latter has become a mighty kingdom. We perceive electricity in a thousand places where we had no proof of its existence before. In every flame, in every luminous particle we see an electrical process. Even if a body is not luminous, provided it radiates heat, it is a centre of electric disturbances. Thus the domain of electricity extends over the whole of nature. It even affects ourselves closely: we perceive that we actually possess an electrical organ—the eye. These are the things that we see when we look downwards from our high standpoint. Not less attractive is the view when we look upwards towards the lofty peaks, the highest pinnacles of science. We are at once confronted with the question of direct actions-at-a-distance. Are there such? Of the many in which we once believed there now remains but one—gravitation. Is this too a deception? The law according to which it acts makes us suspicious. In another direction looms the question of the nature of electricity. Viewed from this standpoint it is somewhat concealed behind the more definite question of the nature of electric and magnetic forces in space. Directly connected with these is the great problem of the nature and properties of the ether which fills space, of its structure, of its rest or motion, of its finite or infinite extent. More and more we feel that this is the all-important problem, and that the solution of it will not only reveal to us the nature of what used to be called imponderables, but also the nature of matter itself and of its most essential properties—weight and inertia. The quintessence of ancient systems of physical science is preserved for us in the assertion that all things have been fashioned out of fire and water. Just at present physics is more inclined to ask whether all things have not been fashioned out of the ether? These are the ultimate problems of physical science, the icy summits of its loftiest range. Shall we ever be per-

mitted to set foot upon one of these summits? Will it be
soon? Or have we long to wait? We know not: but we
have found a starting-point for further attempts which is a
stage higher than any used before. Here the path does not
end abruptly in a rocky wall; the first steps that we can see
form a gentle ascent, and amongst the rocks there are tracks
leading upwards. There is no lack of eager and practised
explorers: how can we feel otherwise than hopeful of the
success of future attempts?

ON THE PASSAGE OF CATHODE RAYS THROUGH THIN METALLIC LAYERS

(*Wiedemann's Annalen*, 45, pp. 28-32, 1892.)

ONE of the chief differences between light and cathode rays is in respect of their power of passing through solid bodies. The very substances which are most transparent to all kinds of light offer, even in the thinnest layers which can be prepared, an insuperable resistance to the passage of cathode rays. I have been all the more surprised to find that metals, which are opaque to light, are slightly transparent to cathode rays. Metallic layers of moderate thickness are of course as opaque to cathode rays as they are to light. But if a metallic layer is so thin as to allow a part of the incident light to pass through, it will also allow a part of the incident cathode rays to pass through; and the proportion transmitted appears to be larger in the latter than in the former case. This can be demonstrated by a very simple experiment. Take a plane glass plate capable of phosphorescing, best a piece of uranium glass: partially cover one side, which we shall call the front side, with pure gold leaf, and in front of this fasten a piece of mica. Expose this front side to cathode rays proceeding from a flat circular aluminium cathode of 1 cm. diameter, say at a distance of 20 cm. from the cathode. So long as the exhaustion is but moderate the cathode rays fill the whole of the discharge tube as a powerful cone of light, and the glass only phosphoresces outside the patch which is covered with gold. At this stage the phosphorescence is chiefly caused by the light of the discharge, and only a very small part of this penetrates through the gold.   But as the exhaustion increases there is less and less light inside the discharge tube, and the rays which impinge upon the glass are more purely cathode rays.   The glass now begins to phosphoresce behind the layer of gold leaf, and when the cathode rays have attained their most powerful development, the gold leaf, when observed from the back, simply looks like a faint veil upon the glass plate, chiefly recognisable at its edges and by the slight wrinkles in it.   It can scarcely be said to throw a real shadow.   On the other hand the thin mica plate, which we have superposed on the gold leaf, throws through this latter a marked black shadow upon the glass.   Thus the cathode rays seem to penetrate with but little loss through the layer of gold.   I have tested other metals in the same way with the same result— silver leaf, aluminium leaf, various kinds of impure silver and gold leaf (alloys of tin, zinc, and copper), silver chemically precipitated, and also layers of silver, platinum and copper precipitated by the discharge in vacuo.   These latter layers were much thinner than the beaten metallic leaves.   I have not observed any characteristic differences between the various metals.   Commercial aluminium leaf seems to work best.   It is almost completely opaque to light but very transparent to the cathode rays : it is easily handled, and is not attacked by the cathode rays, whereas a layer of silver leaf, for example, is soon corroded by them in a peculiar manner.

It might be urged, against the assumption that the cathode rays in these experiments penetrate right through the mass of the metal, that such thin metallic layers are full of small holes, and that the cathode rays might well reach the glass through these without going through the metal.   It is the behaviour of the beaten metallic leaves that is most surprising, and one is bound to admit that these contain many pores : but the aggregate area of the holes scarcely amounts to a few per cent of the area of the leaf, and is not sufficient to account for the brilliant luminescence of the covered glass. Furthermore, the covered part of the glass exhibits no luminescence when it is viewed from the front, i.e. from the side on which the cathode is.   Hence the cathode rays must have reached the glass by a way which the light excited by them cannot retrace ; so that they cannot have reached the glass through openings in the metallic leaf which lies close against it. Again, if we place two metallic leaves one on top of the other, the number of coincident holes must become vanishingly small. But the cathode rays are able to make glass luminesce brightly under a double layer of metallic leaf; even under a three or fourfold layer of gold or aluminium leaf we can perceive the phosphorescence of the glass and the shadows of objects in front of the leaf. I have been rather surprised by the extent to which the rays are weakened by passing through a double layer; it is much larger than one would expect from the slight weakening produced by a single layer. I think the following sufficiently explains this phenomenon. The metallic layer has a reflecting surface by which the phosphorescent light is reflected. This reflecting surface prevents the light from radiating towards the cathode, but it doubles the intensity of the light in the direction away from the cathode. If we assume that the metallic layer allows only $\frac{1}{3}$ of the cathode rays to pass, it will not reduce the luminescence to $\frac{1}{3}$ but only to $\frac{2}{3}$ of its previous value : whereas the second layer will reduce it to $\frac{2}{9}$, and further layers will soon cause the phosphorescence to vanish. If this conception is correct, metallic layers capable of transmitting more than half of the cathode rays should not weaken the luminescence at all : behind such metallic layers the glass ought actually to phosphoresce more strongly than in parts where it is not covered. I think I have been able to verify this expectation in the case of layers of silver chemically precipitated and of suitable thickness : but the observation is not quite trustworthy, because in the uncovered parts one cannot avoid seeing through the phosphorescing glass the greyish-blue luminescence of the gas, and it is not easy to separate with any certainty the brightness of this from that of the green phosphorescence light.

Lastly, if the cathode rays went right through the holes in the metal they would afterwards continue their rectilinear path. But this is just what they do not do; by their passage through the metal they become diffused, just as light does by passing through a turbid medium such as milk glass. Let part of a cylindrical discharge tube be shut off, say at a distance of 20 cm. from the cathode, by a metal plate extending right across it but containing a circular aperture a few

millimetres in diameter; let this aperture be closed by a piece
of aluminium leaf. If we now place a suitable glass plate
close behind the aperture we get, as might be expected, a
distinct and bright phosphorescent image of the aperture upon
the glass; but if we remove the glass plate even one or two
millimetres, the image becomes perceptibly larger and suffers
a corresponding loss of brilliancy, its edge at the same time
becoming indistinct. When the glass plate is moved back
several millimetres the image of the aperture becomes very
indistinct, large and faint; and when the plate is shifted still
further away, the tube behind the diaphragm appears quite
dark. That this is simply due to the feebleness of the cathode
rays which have been diffused from the small aperture can be
shown by introducing into the diaphragm several such
apertures closed by aluminium leaf. For this purpose the
diaphragm is best made of wire gauze hammered flat; upon
this is stretched a piece of aluminium leaf. Behind such a
diaphragm the whole of the discharge tube becomes filled
with a uniform, moderately bright light. The phosphorescence
is sufficiently strong to allow of our obtaining separate beams
by means of further diaphragms: with these we can convince
ourselves that even after passing through metallic leaf the
cathode rays retain their properties of rectilinear propagation,
of being deflected by a magnet, etc.

There must be some connection between the phenomenon
of the diffusion of cathode rays on passing through thin layers
of bright metal and another phenomenon, namely, that
when cathode rays impinge upon such a surface the portion
reflected back is diffused, as E. Goldstein has shown.[1]

---

[1] See *Wiedemann's Annalen*, 15, p. 246, 1882.

XXII

HERMANN VON HELMHOLTZ

(From the Supplement to the *Münchener Allgemeine Zeitung*, August 31, 1891.)

In Germany the men who now stand upon the threshold of old age have inaugurated and lived through a period of rare felicity and success. They have seen aims attained and desires realised, and this not only in matters political: they have seen mighty developments in the arts of peace; they have seen our Fatherland take its place in the front rank of nations, not only in our own estimation but in that of others. Even in the beginning of this century the natural sciences were far from being neglected in Germany: the labours of a Humboldt, the undying fame of a Gauss, were sufficient to keep alive respect for German research. But side by side with the wheat of true effort there sprang up the tares of a false philosophy which flourished so luxuriantly as to hinder the full growth of the crop. Up to the middle of the century sober progress along the path of experimental investigation lacked the glory which accompanies international success; and the successes of a fictitious natural philosophy were very properly not greeted with the same exultation abroad as in Germany. Germans followed eagerly and diligently the discoveries made in other lands; but they always expected the great discoveries and successes to come from Paris and London. Thither young investigators travelled to see famous scientific men and to learn how great investigations were carried on: thence they obtained the materials for their own researches; there alone could new discoveries be properly and authentically published. They found it hard to believe that things could ever be otherwise. But all this has long since been changed. In science Germany is no longer dependent upon her neighbours : in experimental investigation she is the peer of the foremost nations and keeps in the main well abreast of them, sometimes leading and sometimes following. This the country owes to the cooperation of many eager workers; but it naturally honours most the few whose names are most closely connected with the actual successes. Of these some have already left us for ever : others still remain, and we hope long to have them with us.

The greatest among all these, the acknowledged representative of this period of progress and well-earned fame, the scientific leader of Germany, is Hermann von Helmholtz, whose seventieth birthday we celebrate to-day after he has for nearly half a century astonished the scientific world by the number, the depth, and the importance of his investigations. To the countless tributes of admiration and gratitude which will this day be laid at his feet we would with all modesty add our own. As Germans we are glad and proud to claim as our countryman one whose name we deem worthy to be placed among the noblest names of all times and all nations, confident that subsequent generations will confirm our judgment. As men we cherish the same feelings of admiration and gratitude. Other nations, too, will join us in paying honour to him to-day, as indeed they have done in the past. For although nations may appear narrow-minded in political affairs, men have not wholly lost the sense of a common interest in matters scientific : a Helmholtz is regarded as one of the noblest ornaments of humanity.

Let us try to recall the achievements for which we to-day do him honour. Here we at once feel how impossible it is to make others share fully in our admiration if they are not themselves in a position to appreciate his work. It is a mistake to suppose that the importance of an investigator's work can be gauged by stating what problem he has solved. A man must see a picture, and must see it with the eyes of an artist, before he can fully appreciate its value. Even so scientific investigations have a beauty of their own which can be enjoyed as well as understood ; but in order to enjoy it a man must understand the investigation and steep himself in it. Take one of Helmholtz's minor researches, *e.g.* the theoretical paper in which he discusses the formation of liquid jets. The problem is not one that appeals to the lay mind: its solution is only attained by the aid of assumptions which correspond but indifferently to the actual conditions; the influence of the investigation upon science and life can scarcely be called other than slight. And yet the manner in which the problem is solved is such that in studying even a paper like this one feels the same elevation and wonder as in beholding a pure work of art. Upon our comprehension of the difficulties to be surmounted depends the depth of this feeling. We see a man of surpassing strength spring across a yawning chasm apparently without effort, but in reality straining every nerve. Only after the leap do we clearly see how wide the chasm is. Instinctively we break out into applause. But we cannot expect the same spontaneous enthusiasm of spectators from whose standpoint the chasm is not visible, and who can only learn from our descriptions how trying the feat was.

To give a brief but fitting sketch of Helmholtz's work is difficult on account of its many-sidedness as well as its profundity. His scientific life interests us like an Odyssey through the whole region of exact investigation. He began as a doctor: he had to study the laws of that life which he wished to succour, and this led him to the study of physiology, which is the scientific part of medicine. He found himself hampered by the gaps in our knowledge of inanimate nature: so he set about filling these and thus drifted more and more towards physics. For the sake of physics he became a mathematician, and in order to probe thoroughly the foundations of mathematical knowledge, and knowledge in general, he became a philosopher. When we look through the technical literature of any of these sciences we meet his name: upon all of them he has left his mark. Without attending to chronological order we shall here only describe briefly three of those great achievements which constitute his title to fame.

I consider that the most beautiful and charming amongst these, although not the highest, is the invention with which he has enriched practical medicine. I mean the ophthalmoscope. Before him no one was able to investigate the

living eye. Beyond the doubtful and unreliable feelings of
the patient there were no means of diagnosing the disease or
determining the defects in refraction. Before any cure was
possible it was absolutely necessary for the surgeon to acquire
an accurate knowledge of the disease; and this, in the
majority of cases, was only attainable after the invention of
this simple instrument. Ophthalmic surgery rapidly rose to
its present high level. Who can say how many thousands
who have recovered their sight owe it to our investigator—to
him personally, although they are unconscious of this and
think that their thanks are simply due to the surgeon who
has treated them! The invention of the ophthalmoscope is
like vaccination against smallpox, the antiseptic treatment of
wounds, or the sterilisation of children's food—one of those
great gifts which enrich all without impoverishing any, one of
those advances which are gratefully acknowledged everywhere
by all men, and which keep alive in us the belief that there is
such a thing as progress.

Equally powerful as a protection against blindness on the
intellectual side are the advances which physiology owes to
Helmholtz, although their value may not be so easily or
generally recognised. Here we may remind the reader in
passing that he was the first to measure the speed with
which sensation and volition travel along the nerves: this
would have sufficed to establish the fame of any other man,
but it is not this that we now have in mind. His chief
investigation in this science, the work of his mature years, is
the development of the physiology of the senses, especially of
sight and hearing. Within our consciousness we find an
inner intellectual world of conceptions and ideas: outside
our consciousness there lies the cold and alien world of
actual things. Between the two stretches the narrow borderland of the senses. No communication between the two
worlds is possible excepting across this narrow strip. No
change in the external world can make itself felt by us unless
it acts upon a sense-organ and borrows form and colour from
this organ. In the external world we can conceive no causes
for our changing feelings until we have, however reluctantly,
assigned to it sensible attributes. For a proper understanding of ourselves and of the world it is of the highest import-

ance that this borderland should be thoroughly explored, so
that we may not make the mistake of referring anything
which belongs to it to one or the other of the worlds which
it separates. When Helmholtz turned his attention to this
borderland it was not in a wholly uncultivated state; but he
found the richest fields in it lying fallow, and on either
side its limits were badly defined and hidden by a luxuriant
growth of error. He left it carefully defined and well
parcelled out, and much of it had been transformed into a
blooming garden.

His celebrated treatise *On the Sensations of Tone* is
known to a fairly wide circle of students. That which outside ourselves is a mere pulsing of the air becomes within our
minds a joyful harmony. What interests the physicist is the
air-pulsation, what interests the musician and the psychologist
is the harmony. The transition between the two is discovered
in the sensation which connects the definite physical process
with the definite mental process. What is there outside ourselves which corresponds to the quality of the tones of musical
instruments, of human song, of vowels and consonants? What
corresponds to consonance and dissonance? Upon what does
the æsthetic opposition between the two depend? By what
ideas of order within us were those codes of music, the musical
scales, developed? Not all the questions which are prompted
by a thirst for knowledge can be answered; but nearly all
the questions which Helmholtz had to leave open thirty years
ago remain unanswered to the present day. In his *Physiological
Optics* he discusses similar questions relating to sight. How
is it possible for vibrations of the ether to be transformed by
means of our eyes into purely mental processes which
apparently can have nothing in common with the former; and
whose relations nevertheless reflect with the greatest accuracy
the relations of external things? In the formation of mental
conceptions what part is played by the eye itself, by the form
of the images which it produces, by the nature of its colour-
sensations, accommodation, motion of the eyes, by the fact
that we possess two eyes? Is the manifold of these relations
sufficient to portray all conceivable manifolds of the external
world, to justify all manifolds of the internal world?

We see how closely these investigations are connected

with the possibility and the legitimacy of all natural knowledge.   The heavens and the earth doubtless exist apart from
ourselves, but for us they only exist in so far as we perceive
them.   Part of what we perceive therefore appertains to ourselves : part only has its origin in the properties of the heavens
and the earth.   How are we to separate the two ?   Helmholtz's physiological investigations have cleared the ground for
the answering of this question : they have supplied a firm
fulcrum to which a lever can be applied.   His own inclinations have led him to discuss these very questions in a series
of philosophical papers, and no more competent judge could
express an opinion upon them.   Will his philosophical views
continue to be esteemed as a possession for all time ?   We
should not forget that we have here passed beyond the
bounds of the exact sciences : no appeal to nature is possible,
and we have nothing but opinion against opinion and view
against view.

As on the one hand Helmholtz was led by the study of
the senses to the ultimate sources of knowledge, so on the
other hand the same study led him to the glories of art.
The rules which the painter and the musician instinctively
observe were for the first time recognised as necessary consequences of our organisation, and were thereby transformed
into conscious laws of artistic creation.

Great and manifold as are these discoveries, they are all
eclipsed by another with which the name of Helmholtz will
ever be connected.   This is a physical discovery of a more
abstract nature.   Here the human observer with his sensations
retires into the background : light and colour fade away and
sound becomes fainter; their place is taken by geometrical
intuitions and general ideas, time, space, matter, and motion.
Between these ideas relations have to be found, and these
relations must correspond to the relations between the things.
The value of these relations is measured by their generality.
As relations of the most general nature we may mention
the conservation of matter, the inertia of matter, the mutual
attraction of all matter.   Of new relations discovered in this
century the most general is that which was first clearly
recognised by Helmholtz.   It is the law which he called the
Principle of the Conservation of Force, but which is now

z

known to us as the Principle of the Conservation of Energy.
It had long before been suspected that in the unending
succession of phenomena there was something else besides
matter which persisted, which could neither be created nor
destroyed, something immaterial and scarcely tangible. At
one time it seemed to be quantity of motion measured in this
way or that, at another time force, or again an expression
compounded of both.

In place of these obscure guesses Helmholtz brought
forward distinct ideas and fixed relations which led immediately to a wealth of general and special connections. Magni-
ficent were the views which the principle opened up into the
past and future of our planetary system; in every separate
investigation, even the most restricted, its applications were
innumerable. For forty years it has been so much expounded
and extolled that no man of culture can be quite ignorant of
it. It is noteworthy that about this time other heads began
to think more clearly of these things; and it came about that
as far as the phenomena of heat were concerned other men
had anticipated Helmholtz by a few years without his knowing it. It would be far from his wish to detract from the
fame of these men; but it should not be forgotten that their
researches were almost entirely restricted to the nature of
heat, whereas the significance and value of the principle lie
precisely in the fact that it is not limited to this or that
natural force, but that it embraces all of them and can even
serve as our pole-star amongst unknown forces.

It is not generally known that in his mature years Helmholtz has returned to the work of his youth and has still
further developed it. The law of the conservation of energy,
general though it is, nevertheless appears to be only one half of
a still more comprehensive law. A stone projected into empty
space would persist in a state of uniform motion, and thus its
energy would remain constant: to this corresponds the conservation of energy in any system, however complicated that
system may be. But the stone would also tend to retain its
direction and to travel in a straight line: to this behaviour
there is a corresponding general behaviour on the part of
every moving system. In the case of purely mechanical
systems it has long been known that every system, according

to the conditions in which it is placed, arrives at its goal along the shortest path, in the shortest time, and with the least effort. This phenomenon has been regarded as the result of a designed wisdom : its general statement in the region of pure mechanics is known as the Principle of least Action. To trace the phenomenon in its application to all forces, through the whole of nature, is the problem to which Helmholtz has devoted a part of the last decade. As yet the significance of these researches is not thoroughly understood. An investigator of this stamp treads a lonely path : years pass before even a single disciple is able to follow in his steps.

It would be futile to try to enter into particulars of all Helmholtz's researches. Our omissions might be divided amongst several scientific men and would amply suffice to make all of them famous. If one of them had carried out Helmholtz's electrical researches and nothing else, we should regard him as our chief authority on electricity. If another had done nothing but discover the laws of vortex-motion in fluids, he could boast of having made one of the most beautiful discoveries in mechanics. If a third had only produced the speculations on the conceivable and the actual properties of space, no one would deny that he possessed a talent for profound mathematical thought. But we rejoice to find these discoveries united in one man instead of divided amongst several. The thought that one or other of them might be a mere lucky find is rendered impossible by this very union : we recognise them as proofs of an intellectual power far exceeding our own, and are lost in admiration.

And yet these actual performances give but an inadequate idea of his whole personality. How can we estimate the intellectual value of the inspiration which he imparted, at first to his contemporaries, and afterwards to the pupils who flocked to him from far and near ? It is true that Helmholtz never had the reputation of being a brilliant university teacher, as far as this depends upon communicating elementary facts to the beginners who usually fill the lecture-rooms. But it is quite another matter when we come to consider his influence upon trained students and his pre-eminent fitness for guiding them in original research. Such guidance can only be given by one who is himself a master in it, and its value is measured by his own

work.   Here example is of more value than precept; a few
occasional hints can point out the path better than formal and
well-arranged lectures.   The mere presence of the marvellous
investigator helps the pupil to form a just estimate of his own
efforts and of those of his fellow-students, and enables him to
see things *sub specie æterni* instead of from his own narrow
point of view.   Every one who has had the good fortune to work
even for a brief period under Helmholtz's guidance feels that
in this sense he is above all things his pupil, and remembers
with gratitude the consideration, the patience, and the good-
will shown to him.   Of the many pupils now scattered over
the earth there is not one who will not to-day think of his
master with love as well as admiration, and with the hope
that he may yet see many years of useful work and of happy
leisure.

Printed by R. & R. CLARK, LIMITED, *Edinburgh.*

ImTheStory.com

Personalized Classic Books in many genre's

Unique gift for kids, partners, friends, colleagues

Customize:

- Character Names
- Upload your own front/back cover images (optional)
- Inscribe a personal message/dedication on the
  inside page (optional)

Customize many titles Including
- Alice in Wonderland
- Romeo and Juliet
- The Wizard of Oz
- A Christmas Carol
- Dracula
- Dr. Jekyll & Mr. Hyde
- And more...

CPSIA information can be obtained at www.ICGtesting.com
Printed in the USA
LVOW100843080313

323225LV00025B/339/P